# FAMILY RELATIONAL HEALTH,

## A Biblical, Psycho-Social Priority

A Renewed Approach from the Biblical, Psychological, and Sociological Perspectives, for the Family at Home and Professionals at work, in Treating Relationships the Healthy Way!

ANTHONY L. GORDON Ph.D.

authorHOUSE

*AuthorHouse™*
*1663 Liberty Drive*
*Bloomington, IN 47403*
*www.authorhouse.com*
*Phone: 833-262-8899*

*Published by AuthorHouse   10/20/2022*

*ISBN: 978-1-6655-3205-1 (sc)*
*ISBN: 978-1-6655-3203-7 (hc)*
*ISBN: 978-1-6655-3204-4 (e)*

*Library of Congress Control Number: 2021914292*

*Print information available on the last page.*

*Any people depicted in stock imagery provided by Getty Images are models, and such images are being used for illustrative purposes only. Certain stock imagery © Getty Images.*

*All scriptures taken from the King James version of the Bible.*

*This book is printed on acid-free paper.*

# Dedication

This book is lovingly and caringly dedicated to the family relational health and well-being of the multitude of 'specimens' who made up my family relational health laboratory, upon which 'specimens' I practiced over the past thirty-five-plus years.

## My Immediate Family Lab

My dear wife, Deloris; children Delthony, Delthonette, Esther, and Andrew; grandchildren Jonathan, Nathan, and Hadassah; and niece and nephew Stacy and Delroy Dally.

## My Professional Family Lab

My thousands of clients (office, home, and online) in Jamaica, the wider Caribbean, North and South America, Canada, Europe, Asia, Africa, and Australia.

## The Loving Memories

My mother and 'father', Miss Inez V. Williams (Mom!), who single-handedly brought me up through life, setting the base for the construction of my family and professional labs; and my professional father and mentor, Mr W. R. Veitch, whose erudite and self-sacrificing professionalism rescued and inspired me on the path toward professional development and self-actualization.

# Diagrammatic Representation of the Conceptual Construct of Family Relational Health

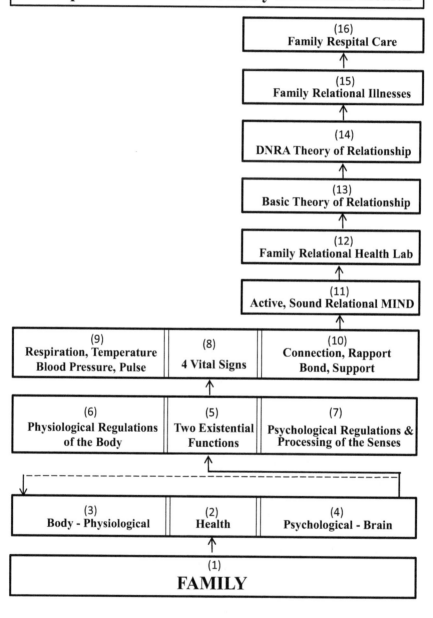

**(16)**
**Family Respital Care**

**(15)**
**Family Relational Illnesses**

**(14)**
**DNRA Theory of Relationship**

**(13)**
**Basic Theory of Relationship**

**(12)**
**Family Relational Health Lab**

**(11)**
**Active, Sound Relational MIND**

| **(9)**<br>**Respiration, Temperature**<br>**Blood Pressure, Pulse** | **(8)**<br>**4 Vital Signs** | **(10)**<br>**Connection, Rapport**<br>**Bond, Support** |
|---|---|---|
| **(6)**<br>**Physiological Regulations**<br>**of the Body** | **(5)**<br>**Two Existential**<br>**Functions** | **(7)**<br>**Psychological Regulations &**<br>**Processing of the Senses** |
| **(3)**<br>**Body - Physiological** | **(2)**<br>**Health** | **(4)**<br>**Psychological - Brain** |

**(1)**
# FAMILY

# FRH Flowchart
## – The Study and Practice at a Glance –

The concept of, advocacy for and practice of family relational healthcare (FRH) as coming out of nearly forty years of work: study, research, writing and practice, across thirty countries around the world, is presented in part in this volume from a Biblio-psycho-socio-clinical perspective. The total work on family relational health which will be presented in another six volumes (now in advanced stages of preparation—see list on the inside back), all from the psycho-socio-clinical perspective, can be a daunting, mental and intellectual exercise, given that the concept is one that is virtually unheard of. As a society, we know of physical health, mental health, emotional health, social health and spiritual health, but: family relational health!?

This diagrammatic representation is designed to provide an at-a-glance, graphic overview of sixteen of the major conceptual constructs of the teachings and practice of family relational health, beginning from its bedrock, foundational, substratum—the original biological family, compromising the husband-father, wife-mother and children, and the ever-expanding categories of family members (See Categories of Families, p. 466). The diagram is further intended to indicate the development of the said practice up to the ultimate delivery of professional treatment at an equally new concept—The Family Respital Healthcare facility—for family relational illnesses reverberating reciprocally between the family and the general society, as a result of the natural (and in so many cases, negative) impact of the one upon the other.

The sixteen ordinal components of this unique flowchart give a developmental portrayal of the wide spectrum of issues that the study and practice entail. Some of the components might be new to some readers, for example:

1. The definition and differentiation of the Active, Sound Mind;
2. The Two Theories of Relationship and the DNRA;
3. The Four Vital Signs of Family Relationship;
4. Relational Illness differentiated from Mental Illness;
5. The Family Relational Health Laboratory
6. A Respital Care facility

It might be helpful for the reader who is interested to grasp the concept and engage in the practice, to use a fast-track method toward accomplishing that goal. Firstly, review and consolidate the understanding of those components on the chart with which he or she has a working familiarity.

Secondly, preview the unfamiliar ones, using the Glossary and the Topical Index. In this way, this flowchart could be used as a head-start and an inspiration and motivation, not only to read the entire book thoroughly, but to begin the acquisition of the professional knowledge, skills, competence and proficiency towards the delivery of family relational healthcare.

# Preface

# What This Book Is Not, and What It Is

## To: Whomsoever May Read

This book is written for *All* persons generally, who might desire a higher perspective from the regular, ordinary teaching and concept about *family life* and who are genuinely interested to become knowledgeable of the psycho-social perspective on the renewed approach of *family relational health*. Primarily, it is written for the ardent, practicing, Genesis to Revelation—Bible-believing Christians, millions of whom are living around the world as family members in their homes in different categories (See p. 466), and who are serving at workplaces (institutions, organizations) in various capacities as: students, vocational workers, entrepreneurs, professors, administrators, parliamentarians and lawmakers, scientists, psychologists, different medical and allied practitioners, chaplains, social workers, guidance counsellors, educators among an array of other professionals.

The book is NOT written to contend with, condemn, oppose, or incite ill-will of any form conceivable to any individual, group, organization of any sex, gender-orientation, racial, religious, cultural, political, or any other identity. (See the expressed teaching of Jesus in this regard on page 41).

The Christian family lives in the same world as all others and must grapple with all the issues and challenges of the society, among which issues and challenges are some that are diametrically and vehemently openly opposed to the biblical foundation on which their faith is anchored. Leaders of the Bible-based Christian faith would have reneged in their God-given responsibility and failed in their flock-watchmanship duty, if they do not do their 'spiritual SWOT analysis' with emphasis on the *Threats*.

They are to identify the issues that endanger the flock, and educate them on how to know such threats and what they ought to teach and do in their homes, churches, schools and institutions to ward off the impact of such advancing forces. (See God's solemn warning to His under-shepherds in Ezekiel 33: 1-11. See also Song # 48 in <u>FRH Songs of Praise and Bible Verses Paraphrase</u>)

It is against that sense of God-inspired responsibility and accountability that some of the publicly known and potentially controversial issues are named or alluded to, for the purpose of sensitization and education of the faithful. The underpinning non-adversarial clarion call mirroring Paul's counsel in Ephesians 6:10-12 is: *The Family Is Under Attack, Let Us Fight Back*! The 'fight-back' is anchored in the uncompromising teachings of God's family book, the Holy Bible, to fortify the minds of the members and all who else will listen.

The book further acknowledges that sometimes there could be a thin or even blurred line between presenting the unadulterated, uncompromising biblical prophetic truth about some societal sensitive and controversial issues and at the same time, respecting, protecting and preserving the inalienable human rights of everyone. Every effort is made, under the inspiration of the indwelling Holy Spirit (to Whom the origin of this work is attributed), to deliver the unquenchable word of Bible truth, supported by scientific, psychological, medical, historical and current facts and developments with no calculated offence to anyone, and more so in the interest of love and good Bible-based family relational health (See p. xxxiv).

This book is not another academic treatise on perspectives of human relationships in general. It is not a work on traditional family-life mediation and counseling programs. Nor is it a clinical tool for treating mental illnesses or related issues.

This book is a work designed to raise the bar of the professional services provided for the growing dynamics of family relational challenges in homes as manifested in broken marriages, distraught parenting, feuding siblings, and a multiplicity of other relationships illnesses. It is designed to address the similar relational issues in the Church, at school, in the business place, and in society at large, all stemming essentially from the home. The goal is to raise the bar on the quality of such services from the traditional societal stigmatized and tabooed concept of family counseling.

By rebranding the service from *counseling* to *treatment*; retooling professionals with the concepts, principles, and practices of family relational health care; and correctly juxtaposing the practice beside physiological health care where it rightly belongs, the treatment and care for hurting family relationships will in time be lifted to the level of the accepted, respected, and, in most cases, eagerly sought-after physiological health care in hospitals and clinics.

It is understood why the medical team is so respected, because in the eyes of the general populace, they are clearly the bridge between life and death. Meanwhile, professional services for family relational challenges are held in low regard by most of the population. Such care is derided in some places and is the subject of ridicule, laughter, and even questions about people's sanity: "Anyone who wants counseling is mad or something is wrong with his (or her) head."

In one episode of the comedy *George Lopez*, the 11-year-old son, Max, was acting up at home in reaction to the pressures he was experiencing at school. He was not sleeping well, and in one instance, he was ripping up the pillows, among other unhealthy behaviors that clearly showed that he needed professional help. In response to the mother's suggestion that Max get an appointment to see a child psychologist, her husband vehemently objected, "Psychologist, no way. He is not going to a psychologist until the doctor tells him to. He is not crazy!"

That clip from the comedy is a good example of the general attitude in the community toward treatment of the mind. These are among some of the most disparaging remarks made about counseling, but when some of the same persons have a persistent headache or any other arresting physical discomfort, they are prepared to even empty their bank accounts to get to the medical doctor because they do not want to die.

As a result of these social misconceptions and attitudes toward traditional counseling services, most family relational issues go untreated. The unresolved issues are buried alive and remain alive in the subconscious mind. Eventually, negative residual effects surface and manifest themselves in unhealthy behaviors that are inimical to relational well-being and consequently wreak havoc on society. In the long run, they may become an undue burden for physiological health care in overcrowded hospitals and general medical care systems.

When such relational illnesses, as they should be clinically categorized, go untreated, they build up mayhem and social dislocation in society, showing up in broken homes and maladjusted youngsters who get caught up in crimes and violence of every magnitude, proportion, and intensity.

It is worth noting, however, that in the current (2020) international battle against the COVID-19 pandemic, among the frontline warriors of the medical team are the psychological team of psychiatrists, psychologists, counselors, chaplains, and social workers, augmenting and balancing the treatment program offered to the sick, the dying, and the surviving bereaved family members. The critical need for balancing these major aspects of health became the driving thrust behind the tagline of Family Relational Health Services International:

"Treating relationships the healthy way." (See the Epilogue for further explanation and application of this tagline pp. 391-394).

We emphasize the raising of the bar mentioned, and anchoring it in the foundation of the teachings of the Bible, God's family book. In so doing, treatment will be provided for improving the quality of life and relationships, beginning in the home, on the sound foundation of God's words supported, as we said earlier, by scientific, sociological, psychological, medical and other necessary knowledge and skills which, from a Christian's perspective, are attributable to God's endowment in His children (See p. xxxiv). The resultant positive ripple effects will be felt in schools, churches, workplaces, and society at large—all of whose members originally came from families in the homes (See p. 13).

Simply put, this work aims to attract and even arrest the attention of the leaders in every sphere of society to the need for bringing balance to the focus placed on physiological and medical healthcare compared with that placed on psychological healthcare, with a specific emphasis on family relational healthcare as defined herein.

This balanced approach to wholistic health (treating the total being) is God's original intent, as can be seen in Psalm 139:14 and 3 John 2. Both verses, correctly analyzed, make clear the need for balancing the two main aspects of health: the physiological and the psychological. By *psychological*, this work goes beyond the traditional focus on mental health and mental illness and brings to the fore the need to address family relational health and, in the case of its impairment, family relational illness.

Let us now take a further, deeper, historical look at where the idea of treatment for family relational illness originated.

"Elder, can you come *now*! We need you!"

It is about 11:30 p.m. Yes, bedtime. In fact, I was in bed. But such calls are not unusual; they are part of the ministry to families.

So I got up, and got dressed.

They called again: "Are you coming? It is *urgent.*"

"Yes, I am coming … I'm on the way."

Hazard lights! Honking horn! Flashing headlights! Emergency! Left, right! Up, down! Carefully through stop signs, through stoplights! It's an emergency! Life is at stake!

This is no figment of the imagination. This is not a script for a Lifetime Movie (LTM). It is real life. Scenes like this have been repeated numerous times with varying intensity over the thirty-plus years that I have been privileged to be working with families.

But on the Monday morning following the trauma and drama of the weekend before, I sat under my St Julian mango tree reflecting on what had happened at that home. How much did I succeed in helping them? How was the treatment?

Oh, did I say *treatment*? Yes, you got it right: treatment! Thanks be to God, they were stabilized. An emotional tourniquet was applied through professional challenge and confrontational techniques, securely tightened with a spiritual band of prayer. The oozing out of the marital blood was controlled, thus reducing the relational dizziness that was causing them to topple over each other when I reached their home. But all that was just first aid. The question still remained: How were they to be treated?

So, I sat in concerned concentration under the mango tree. I contemplated a marriage counseling program for them, with the main focus on managing marital conflicts (See No. 8, p. 454). But given the depth of the wounds that I saw, given the magnitude of the convulsions and shocks that were registered on the emotional Richter Scale, given the evidence that their relational vital signs were so arrestingly low, I was convinced that they needed more than some counselling sessions on managing marital conflicts.

## Family Relational Health Treatment: Two Perspectives

The Spirit of the God of families illuminated my mind as He promised, "But the Comforter, which is the Holy Ghost, whom the Father will send in my name, he shall teach you all things, and bring all things to your remembrance, whatsoever I have said unto you" (John 14:26). This helped me to reflect on what I had studied and seen before, so that I could clearly see this family's condition from two perspectives: professional and spiritual.

### The Professional Perspective

I saw that their state of marital and relational health required a personalized, custom-built, structured treatment program. Such a treatment plan would factor in their relational antecedents, family dynamics, issues diagnoses, relational assessments, prescribed action plans, monitoring, prognoses, and follow-ups. In the first phase of the treatment plan, undoubtedly, there would be the need for some surgeries and naturally some suturing. Who knew what the relational mind scans might reveal? Maybe some deep issues within the tissues of their relational minds might need radiation and oncological applications to reduce the risk of remission. Yes, treatment!

Let us be clear. None of the above medical analogies are tritely conceptualized and used here. There is a straight parallel that can be found in virtually all aspects of medical care of the body and psychological care of the mind. We will not be able to exhaust those parallels in this book, but several of them will be demonstrated through the pages ahead. In most instances, they will be introduced with a phrase like "to the same extent that the body … so it is that the mind ..." or "to the same extent that professional medical/physiological care ... so it is that professional psychological/counseling/therapy ..." Throughout the book, the phrase will be marked with (CPH²), denoting the double comparison point of physiological and psychological health.

## The Spiritual Perspective

At the heart of the marital case mentioned in the weekend story above, and in all other human conflicts before and after them, is the key issue of *relationship*. From Genesis to Revelation, the Holy Bible records the story of relationships initiated by God with His created beings. It paints the picture of relationship lost in the Garden of Eden (Gen. 3:22–24) to relationship regained in the New Jerusalem (Matt. 25:20–23; Rev. 22:14 See the Genesis Foundation). The relationship between heaven and earth was first affected when, out of selfishness, the first couple (our parents) decided to disobey God. (See Chapters 10 and 11 for a more detailed, analytical perspective on the family relationship issue that began in the Garden of Eden).

# The Original Relationship Impairment

The relationship impairment between God and man automatically impaired the relationship between the first two human beings, and the ripple effects have continued down through the ages to this day. It is versions of these relational debacles that have been cited—from the factual account in the weekend story to those that will be mentioned in the chapters ahead—that will lay the foundation for the thrust of this publication.

God in His omniscience looked down the corridors of time and saw the catastrophic effects that impaired relationships would have on His children. Thus, in response to the broken relationship issue, He declared the protoevangelium recorded in Genesis 3:15: "And I will put enmity between thee and the woman, and between thy seed and her seed; it shall bruise thy head, and thou shalt bruise his heel." It was then prophesied that although the forces of evil had succeeded in damaging the relationship that He, God, had put in place, He was still in charge, and those forces would not prevail. "And I say also unto thee, That thou art Peter, and upon this rock I will build my church; and the gates of hell shall not prevail against it" (Matt. 16:18).

God also offered assurance that He would eventually see to the full restoration and ultimate accomplishment of His eternal relationship plan: "So shall my word be that goeth forth out of my mouth: it shall not return unto me void, but it shall accomplish that which I please, and it shall prosper in the thing whereto I sent it" (Isa. 55:11) and "What do ye imagine against the LORD? He will make an utter end: affliction shall not rise up the second time" (Nahum 1:9).

The entire gospel story, therefore, from Genesis to Revelation, is about making healthy family relationships a priority. What we are hurting from now in the twenty-first century as we seek to grapple with the distorted, damaged, and broken relationships between husbands and wives, parents and children, family members, colleagues, and other forms of relationships in the human circle, all began from Eden and are provided for in the broad plan of salvation. Restoring healthy relationships is a priority for the God of families.

It is this truth about healthy family relationships and the plan of salvation, which the enemy of souls has succeeded in obscuring for so long, that we are hoping to highlight in the pages ahead. The Bible is replete with counsels and guidelines on the importance of family relational health for the well-being and quality of life of the individual and family group here on earth, and its potential influence on their readiness for the life to come when Jesus returns.

# The Genesis Foundation

A FRH 'Biblical Archaeological Excavation' Project
(In Search for Our Family Beginning)

How far back can, or do we need to go anthropologically, archaeologically, biologically, chronologically, and historically-speaking in order to find the truth about our beginning?

**Our Existential Questions:**

1. Where did we come from?

2. How did we get here?

3. Who is responsible for our being here?

4. What are we doing here?

5. Where are we going from here?

**Our Conviction:**

"In the beginning God." (Genesis 1: 1) – This is where, how and with Whom we all began. Full STOP!! According to James Weldon Johnson (1871 - 1938): "And God stepped out on space and looked around and said: I'm lonely, I'll make me a world..." (See p. 265) This is frail, fallible human being, exercising what is left of his dwarfed intelligence by the effects of sin, but nonetheless, enough to be impressed and empowered by the Holy Spirit, using feeble expressions to bring out the enthrallment of his mind of the majesty of God. This is very much like what Carl Boberg (1859 - 1940) experienced when he wrote: "O Lord my God, when I in awesome wonder, consider all the things Thy hands have made..."

**This We Believe:**

1. That the Bible and the Bible only ('sola scriptura') has the total and complete answers to our existential questions with no need for scholarly erudition, lower or higher criticisms, hermeneutical or other methods beyond the "Thus saith the Lord" for understanding; We do not make light of the tools of academia mentioned above, but given that correctly understood, they are part of the endowment of God in building human intelligence, they should be used towards His honour and glory. Such scholarly endeavours are to be used for enhancing and affirming His original words and teachings, and not to introduce speculations, conjectures, hypotheses and theorizings, aimed at projecting personal or other agenda that eventually will bring God's words into disrepute.

2. That the Book of Genesis has the total record of the beginning of the human family;

3. That the total and complete guidance for ideal, quality family relational health exists between Genesis 1 and 2 and that it requires 'spiritual archaeological excavation' to uncover, discover and mine-out the simple but profound truths for all families of all generations;

4. That we need a 'Tour Guide' with omniscience about Human Family Archaeology. The only One qualified to do this is the 'Divine Archaeologist', the Holy Spirit, Who, Himself was a Member of the Creation Team (Genesis 1:1), and correctly referred to as The God of Families;

5. That Genesis 3:1 unto Revelation 22: 21 holds the full record of what happened to the IDEAL family structure and relationship that God established, and the resultant REALITY that was set in by the advent of sin. Between those two points (Gen. 3: 1

and Rev 22: 21) are recorded the twists and turns (see p. 43), distortions and deviations, complexities and complications; and that therein also lies God's responsive projection and plan for the ultimate recovery and restoration of His original family blueprint.

**What to Look for in the Excavation Expedition Ahead:**

Throughout the up-coming extensive study 'excavation' be sure to look for these treasure troves:

1. The beginning of the family

2. The beginning of family work and worship

3. The ideal family structure

4. God-appointed family leadership – supporting roles and responsibilities

5. The ideal pattern of family relationship;

6. The Male-Female complementing/complimenting roles in portraying the image of God

By the grace of the God of Families, the Architect of time and Archeologist of our existence, we hope to unearth all the above in the pages ahead.

# Acknowledgments

Bringing an eight-year (2014–2022) project of this magnitude to fruition is by no means a one-man's effort. At best, it is the result of teamwork, with each member playing different but significant roles toward its accomplishment. From its conception under the St Julian mango tree at my home (See p. xiv)—which conception can only be attributed to inspiration from the Holy Spirit—the work has been supported by the following persons, to whom I owe a debt of gratitude:

- my dear wife of 46 precious years, Deloris, for her unswerving encouragement and assistance in researching, typing, editing, and consulting

- my loving children, Delthony, Delthonette, Esther, and Andrew, for their individual supportive ways of researching, reading, and encouraging

- Dr Roy Dennis, Dr Kemar Douglas, Dr Bathsheba Osoro, Ms Sandra Parker, Ms Millicent Pryce, Dr Denton Rhone, Dr Patric Ruttherford, Dr Orlean Brown-Earle, and Mr Yenoh Wheatle for sectional reading, observations, recommendations, and encouragements

- Dr Althea McMillan for editorial assistance in the early stage of writing.

- scores of professional colleagues, church members, friends, and clients from around the world who affirmed the project, continually checking on its progress, and encouraging its completion

# Contents

# Introduction

# Family Relational Health and
# a Good Christian Life

There is an inextricable link between family relational health and being a good Christian. Put frankly, one cannot be a good Christian if he or she is not practicing and experiencing good, healthy family relationships between himself or herself and those in his or her sphere of influence. "If a man says, I love God, and hateth his brother, he is a liar: for he that loveth not his brother whom he hath seen, how can he love God whom he hath not seen? And this commandment have we from him, That he who loveth God love his brother also" (1 John 4:20–21). One cannot be a good Christian if he or she refuses to be a good family member.

The operative word here is *refuse*. That is to say, if a family member does not make the necessary efforts—if such a person does not seek to equip him or herself with family relational skills in order to improve the quality of the relationship between himself or herself and the significant others in his or her life—then that neglect would be considered a refusal to improve his or her family relational health.

But what is a healthy relationship? Why this term *relational health*, and even more pointedly, *family relational health*? (See differentiations in Glossary pp. 403 & 412). And deepening the question and concern raised already is the suggestion that the concept of family relational health is a biblical, psycho-social priority! On what ground is that position and teaching based? Is there unequivocal scriptural support for such a proposition?

## Physiological Health Compared with Family Relational Health

These questions are among the large array that this book will seek to answer. In the accompanying book to this one, *Family Relational Health: A Missing Dimension in Comprehensive Health Care* (written for the medical and related communities), the point is made that there is an imbalance between the importance that mainstream society places on physiological health—the state and functions of the body—and psychological health—the state and functions of the mind.

Equally so, there is a bewildering amount of evidence that the Church, in general, does not place equal importance on quality family relational health and what some would call *straight gospel*. One needs only see the proliferation of radio and television religious programs with an emphasis on the preaching of the Word (prophecies, eschatology, grace, law, creationism, health, and various other doctrines) as straight gospel compared to the number of such programs that focus on biblical family life. The difference is alarming and does call for an explanation.

This fact is so glaring that in some quarters, the health message is referred to as the right arm of the gospel. It can be understood that health, especially in the physiological sense of the word, is critical to the quality of Christian life and teaching, given that it is based on God's original plan for the overall well-being of His children from the Garden of Eden (Gen. 2:9, 16; Gen. 3:22, 24; Rev. 2:7; Rev. 22:2, 14).

However, the focus on physiological health should ideally be juxtaposed with family relational health, given that sequentially speaking, the relationship impairment in the Garden of Eden preceded the consequential deterioration of physiological health in that the broken relationships in the mind took place before the degeneration of the body actually began. It stands to reason that while the health message (essentially focusing on the body temple) could correctly be seen as the right arm of the gospel, family relational health could be seen as the foundation of the gospel, given the correctly understood order of their announcement. There is no competition intended here, as when correctly viewed, the two main aspects of health, physiological and psychological, are complementary to each other so that the person can experience balanced, total health.

Today, health-focused programs in most churches are generally more structured and organized than those for family life, even with more appeal and support from some in the top leadership. One of the big promotional crowd-pullers for evangelistic campaigns or gospel outreach programs is health fairs, with many types of medical services being offered. These services range from blood pressure checks and urine analysis to mammography, pap smears, PSA blood tests, and prostate (DRE) exams, dental, optical, nutritional among others. Sometimes a family seminar/counseling component is added, but it is not always promoted with the same degree of urgency and importance to life as the health component, and the resulting attendance and participation is just as low-keyed.

Credit must be given to the many churches that pay balanced attention to family-life programs with the other aspects of church life, including health programs. Some churches host family-life crusades, retreats, conventions, and other features that focus on different aspects of the family. Some have very strong clubs and organized groups for married couples, singles, parents, seniors, and other subcategories of family life. It seems natural that the leadership of such churches not only believe in good, Bible-based family life but are themselves experiencing healthy family relationships.

## The Protoevangelium and the Marriage at Cana of Galilee: Common Message

However, in the broad picture, as implied above, there seems to be an assumption that embracing the gospel and accepting Christ automatically makes one a good family member. Worse yet, it appears that most leaders in Christianity have missed the main message of the protoevangelium announced in Genesis 3:15 and that of Christ's first miracle recorded in John 2:1–11: "This beginning of miracles did Jesus in Cana of Galilee, and manifested forth his glory; and his disciples believed on him." (See p. 102)

In the first case, the promised coming "seed" of Genesis 3:15 was to come and heal and restore the broken family relationship and consequently the impaired family relational health that sin had caused: "And I will put enmity between thee and the woman, and between thy seed and her seed; it shall bruise thy head, and thou shalt bruise his heel."

Secondly, Christ's presence at the marriage ceremony at Cana of Galilee was the Godhead's endorsement (2 Cor. 5:18–19) and reaffirmation of God's original family blueprint. beginning with marriage: "And all things are of God, who hath reconciled us to himself by Jesus Christ, and hath given to us the ministry of reconciliation; To wit, that God was in Christ, reconciling the world unto himself, not imputing their trespasses unto them; and hath committed unto us the word of reconciliation." (See pp. 34 & 35)

These two powerful stories carry the common message of God's vested interest in our human relationships. But it is not just relationships that are to be established and maintained in families, it is *healthy* relationships that count. Those have eternal implications, and the Bible is replete, from Genesis to Revelation, with consistent lessons on this fact.

The Bible is the supreme family book, and the principles of family relational health permeate its pages. But alas! Too many of those lessons are missed, even by some of the most zealous and professed preachers and practitioners of the Word.

Fourteen popularly quoted and well-known verses of the Word have been carefully selected and used to anchor the family relational health posture of this book. They have been paraphrased and interpreted in the context of the subject itself and will be used in each chapter to show the critical importance of our family relationship and, more specifically, family relational health, to our eternal salvation. In the companion to this book- <u>FRH Songs of Praise and Bible Verses Paraphrase</u>, 52 such paraphrased verses are published, one to be studied each week for the year.

## Potential Spiritual Disturbance

It would not be surprising if the material contained in this book could even cause some emotional and spiritual disturbances. A good case for such a possibility is the application to the family relational health of Jesus's combined, three-pronged teaching about anger management and interpersonal reconciliation, and making or bringing an offering (worship) to the Lord:

> But I say unto you, that whosoever is angry with his brother without a cause shall be in danger of the judgment: and whosoever shall say to his brother, Raca, shall be in danger of the council: but whosoever shall say, Thou fool, shall be in danger of hell fire. Therefore, if thou bring thy gift to the altar, and there rememberest that thy brother hath ought against thee; Leave there thy gift before the altar, and go thy way; first be reconciled to thy brother, and then come and offer thy gift. (Matt. 5:22–24)

His three-point counsel is stark and blunt:

1. Stop where you reach with your offering (worship) upon remembering that all is not well between you and your brother (family member, church member, fellow human being … whoever).

2. Go back and address the impaired relationship.

3. Then return and continue your offering (worship) to me.

The implied assurance is that the Lord will wait on you when points 1 and 2 take place, because that is the only time when your offering (worship) will be acceptable to Him. The message is profound: Good human relationship is an important part of divine worship. This straightforward, unambiguous approach to working on relationships, and the implication if it is not followed, could indeed be a new dimension to understanding this very arresting parable of the Lord.

The explanation above is not necessarily to be taken in the fullest, literal sense of application. That is to say, if while one is at worship in the temple, he or she remembers that all is not well between him or her and another person, he or she should stop, leave worship, find the person with whom there is a relational challenge, make it up, and then return to continue worshipping the Lord. Not at all! At the same time, he or she should consciously and conscientiously seek out every possible opportunity to find the other person and make it right after the worship service.

In fact, while there in worship, if the Holy Spirit reminds you of the strained relationship between you and the other person, you can stop or pause in your heart (mind), accept the impressions of the Spirit, and proceed to pray for the other party. You will also make a commitment that at the earliest opportunity, which you can make a deliberate effort to bring forward, you will address the matter with him or her.

# The Communion Service and Family Relational Health

Holy Communion (also called the Passover, the Eucharist, or the Lord's Supper), as one of the sacred rites of the Christian church, serves the following purposes, as clearly taught in the Bible:

1. A symbol of the cleansing of the soul by Jesus. This is especially so through the Ordinance of Humility or feet-washing (John 14: 4–10).

2. A lesson of humility and servanthood—not servitude. This is the second lesson from the Ordinance of Humility (John 14:12–17).

3. The prophecy and promise of the Great Marriage Supper of the Lamb to be celebrated in the New Jerusalem (Matt. 26:29; Mark 14:25; Luke 22:15–19; Rev. 19:7–9; 21 and 22).

Undoubtedly, there are other great extrapolations and deeper insights and lessons that can be drawn from the three purposes of this sacred rite of the New Testament church. Here is one such lesson that can be extrapolated, in the context of family relational health. The Communion service provides a much-needed opportunity for the strengthening and stabilization of strained relationships and for the healing and restoration of impaired relational health in biological and ecclesiastical (church) families.

It is for this very reason that the Communion service is to be announced ahead of time, thus providing the opportunity to make wrongs right with each other so that when all gather at the Lord's Table, none will partake unworthily (2 Cor. 11:27–33) because he or she is knowingly harboring an unhealthy relationship with a fellow worshipper:

> Wherefore whosoever shall eat this bread, and drink this
> cup of the Lord, unworthily, shall be guilty of the body

and blood of the Lord. But let a man examine himself, and so let him eat of that bread, and drink of that cup. For he that eateth and drinketh unworthily, eateth and drinketh damnation to himself, not discerning the Lord's body. For this cause many are weak and sickly among you, and many sleep.

May the Holy Spirit of the God of families illuminate our minds and help us to see that the quality of our human relationships is a sound, clear indicator of the quality of our relationship with Christ, and ultimately our eternal relationship with the saints of all the ages. Family relational health is a biblical, psycho-social priority of life in the here and now and in the hereafter.

## Special Notes

### Gender Sensitivity

This book has been written with a balanced view of the male-female relationship and is in no way intended to convey any bias for either of the biological sexes or sociocultural genders. However, to avoid the cumbersome and repetitious usage of his/her or "him/her" or he/she, we have interchangeably used one of the pronouns to refer to both sexes/genders, with the understanding that *him* or *her*; *she* or *he*; *his* or *hers* could be used in the generic sense, making reference to one or both. This is *not* alluding in any way to unisexism.

### (CPH²)

One fervent effort of this work is to make a balanced comparison between physiological health care and psychological health care, with an emphasis on family relational health care. This abbreviation is used to indicate the points in the book where such comparisons are made. See the Glossary for a more detailed explanation of (CPH²).

## Paraphrased Anchor Texts

The Bible is repeatedly referred to as God's family book, but not every text in the Bible seems to speak directly and immediately to a specific family issue. Throughout this book, the Anchor Text are paraphrased for the purpose of achieving immediate, direct, applicable use of the verse in the context of the family case or issue under discussion, thus affirming the position that the Bible is indeed God's family book.

## Chapter Closing

Each chapter closes with a basic aspect of the treatment plan for family relational health and is presented under the caption "Suggestions for Action." These five suggestions form a type of summary of the chapter from an application perspective. Here, the reader is encouraged to make a commitment to either reaffirming what he is already doing or challenging himself to apply any new skill, principle, or effort learned so as to leave the chapter better than when he began reading it.

## General Disclaimer

As stated in (CPH[2]) above, and as an expansion thereof, there are several comparisons, parallels, and analogies cited in this book in an effort to promote balanced social acclaim, respect, and support between the combined professional practices of medical and psychiatric health care and that of psychological and, more definitively, family relational health care, the subject of this work.

At the same time, in addition to the sectional disclaimers made in different chapters herein, it is here further understood that at no time, and in no way, shape, or form, does any aspect of this work claim to give any guidance, advice, counsel, or offering of a medical, psychiatric, or related nature. It is therefore understood that any part of this publication cited or referenced outside of the context of family relational health anchored in the teachings of the Holy Bible as presented herein shall be at the reader's own choice or risk, with no responsibility whatsoever on the part of the author.

## Affirmation/Claim and Declaration

Throughout this work, there is a sustained effort to establish the differences, comparisons, and commonalities between mainstream medical, psychiatric and psychological healthcare and the proposition of the book, Family Relational Healthcare.

Whereas, Family Relational Healthcare as presented in this volume, is primarily anchored in the Holy Bible (God's main family manual) and there are times when a contrast is made between mainstream scientific, medical/clinical perspectives and what is proffered as the biblical/family relational health perspective, it is to be clear that the latter is not devoid of scientific and clinical under-girding. In fact, science, correctly understood, as originating from God, is a major influence behind this work, as will be seen repeatedly throughout the pages (See DNRA, Preamble 1, p. 173).

Whereas many practitioners in mainstream, modern science, (the driver of medical, psychiatric and psychological healthcare) make no attribution of their researches, findings, declarations and practices to the God of Creation, this work, making full use of many such scientific data, information, knowledge and education, gives total credit (praise, glory and adoration) to God as the original and ultimate Source of all that man, His masterpiece of creation, knows and will ever come to know. (Proverbs 2: 6; 9: 10; Isaiah 11: 2)

Family Relational Health affirms the incalculable and invaluable work of the scientific community—medical, psychiatric, psychological, pharmaceutical, sociological, anthropological and the many sub-divisions and fields in equally a diverse chain of interdisciplinary institutions and practices, all of whom contribute to the body of knowledge and practice for the advancement of the quality of life in so many spheres of society. (See Limited Human Effort, p. 294)

## Family Relational Health Foundational Pillars

For many readers, the concept, idea, or knowledge of family relational health might be simply unheard-of, and at the same time intriguing. In order to whet the appetite for understanding this new combined perspective on psychotherapy, counseling, and physiological health care, seven foundational anchors of family relational health are presented below.

These seven pillars are the bedrock on which the family relational health laboratory has been constructed over the years, as referred to in Chapter 1. As you read through the twelve chapters, you should discover the expansion and development of each pillar, so that by the end, you can embrace the title of the book: that family relational health is indeed a biblical, psycho-social priority.

### Pillar 1: Relational Health

This is the dichotomized functionality of the mind, separate from but existing in tandem with or complementarily to mental health—and, to the same extent that there is mental illness, which is the impairment of mental health, there is relational illness, which is the impairment of relational health (CPH² See Glossary pp. 412 & 413 for detailed explanation).

### Pillar 2: Balanced Health

In mainstream society, reference to health tends to be limited to the state and function of the body (physiological health); but, to the same extent that the absence of war does not mean that there is peace, so it is that the absence or apparent absence of disease or infirmity does not necessarily mean that there is total health, where the psychological health (the state and function of the mind, and more specifically the relational aspect thereof) is not taken into account (CPH²).

## Pillar 3: The Four Vital Signs

Whereas there are four basic vital signs of the health of the body—temperature, respiratory rate, heartbeat (pulse), and blood pressure—that give the medical doctor an indication of the state of physiological health, equally there are four basic vital signs of psychological health, with specific reference to family relational health: connection, rapport, bond, and support. Correctly evaluated, these give the family relational health therapist an indication of the quality of any particular relationship in the mind of the person being assessed (CPH²).

## Pillar 4: Relationship Begins in the Mind

All human relationships begin and continue to exist in the active, sound mind. A mind can be active but not sound and therefore cannot forge and keep a healthy relationship. (See the Glossary p. 395 for a more detailed difference between the two descriptions).

## Pillar 5: The Active, Sound Mind

An active, sound mind is the engine of our being. Being = body + mind. That was the sum total of David's proclamation in Psalm 139:14 that he was fearfully and wonderfully made (physiologically) and that his soul (mind) knows well what is right (psychologically). This concept of wholistic health is also affirmed in 3 John 2.

## Pillar 6: Developmental Notifiers of Relational Aptitude (DNRA)

The skills, competences, proficiencies, and knacks formed in part by the impact of one's family of origin on the frontal lobe of the brain or prefrontal cortex, is a major antecedent (subject to sociological/environmental factors) to the kind of relationship that one can forge and keep through one's lifespan. Altogether, the signs, signals, patterns, and trends (called *notifiers*) of those impressions and behaviors provide a further indication, clue, or intimation of the likely quality of family relationship that an individual will be able to forge and keep if the developmental trajectory does not change (See Chapter 8).

**Pillar 7: The Protoevangelium and Family Relational Health**

When God made the first announcement of the gospel (Genesis 3:15), it was His planned response to heal and restore the broken relationship between the families of heaven and earth,(Gen. 3: 8-10) and the human family members of earth, beginning with the first married couple, Adam and Eve (v.12), and by extension, all subsequent families after them (Rom.3:23). Quality family relational health here on earth is a prerequisite for living with the families of all the ages when Jesus comes for the second time and the earth is made new.

**Reader-friendly Study/Cross-referencing**

*Cross-text referencing* is a reader-friendly feature used in this book to assist the Reader to make easy correlations, comparisons and co-ordinations between supportive or different subjects and topics. It demonstrates how the same concept, idea or perspective on a topic is used elsewhere in the book for validation, expansion or for more examples or other usages.

Examples: On Page ix Para 1: Line 8 ...*family members in different categories*, the Reader is directed to (p. 466). On that page there is elaboration on the categories of family members. The Reader can get a quick understanding of the *categories of the family* and then return to the main subject that is being read.

On Page 19 reference is made to *chemical imbalance*. The Reader might be intrigued with that statement and want to know where else it is mentioned and probably in another context, so he is directed to (See pp. 211, 327). Using this method, the book is not merely being read, it is being studied.

This principle of **cross-referencing** is in keeping with the teaching/learning method advocated in Isaiah 28: 9 & 10 and the expressed goal of Ephesians 4: 12-15: "Whom shall he teach knowledge? and whom shall he make to understand doctrine? ....For precept must be upon precept, precept upon precept; line upon line, line upon line; here a little, and there a little." ... Till we all come in the unity of the faith, and of the knowledge of the Son of God, unto a perfect man, unto the measure of the stature of the fullness of Christ: (Eph. 4:13).

# Chapter 1

# The Family Relational Health Laboratory: Background and Development

**Anchor Text: Galatians 5:22–23**

"But the fruit of the Spirit is love, joy, peace, longsuffering, gentleness, goodness, faith, meekness, temperance: against such there is no law."

**Paraphrased for Families**

*Characteristic of a Maturing, Relationally Healthy Christian*

For the characteristic of a maturing, relationally healthy person (family or church member) is genuineness, graciousness, honesty, humility, simplicity, sincerity, sweetness, thoughtfulness and thoroughness; against such and similar characteristics, no one can truly judge you as being immature, unfriendly and unkind.

*Characteristics of a Failing, Relationally Unhealthy Christian*

For the characteristics of a failing, relationally unhealthy person (family or church member) is harshness, strictness, insensitivity, rigidity, abrasiveness, mean-spiritedness, hypersensitivity, tactlessness, and spitefulness; with these and similar characteristics of unhealthy relationship, you should not be found (named among you - Eph. 5: 13).

*Anthony L. Gordon Ph.D.*

# General Laboratory Defined (Scientific)

Maybe the first time we met the word *laboratory* or lab was in high school (or some advanced primary schools) when we began to pursue studies in biology and integrated or other aspects of general science, chemistry, or physics. Then, as the education continued to develop with an expanding curriculum, many schools became equipped with other labs, such as reading, computer, language, and home economics, to the point now that there is nearly a lab for every subject area in most high or secondary schools in the developed and developing world.

As we moved out into the broader society, we found more expansive, developed, and sophisticated facilities that provide controlled conditions in which scientific, medical, or technological and other types of researches, experiments, and measurements are performed. They are in all sectors of science, business, manufacturing, entertainment, engineering, performing arts, sports, and other industries and trading enterprises of the world.

Every so often, there are some breaking news or big, celebrated announcements about discoveries, new developments, designs, innovations, and improvements that are made in different labs. Society is always waiting, as it were, for the next declaration or proclamation of the findings.

Some of these announcements either come from leading hospitals and clinics in the developed world as well as from research laboratories, medical schools and teaching hospitals connected to major and renowned universities. Independent, private research entities, many associated with the giants in the pharmaceutical industries, bio-engineering and other scientific bodies are among the medical and healthcare luminaries who are on the frontline of the breaking news. The BBC's "Health Check" presented by British renowned award-winning broadcaster and psychologist, Claudia Hammond, is about

2

one of the most must-listen-to and current international broadcasts that follow and carry such breaking news.

Maybe the most current case in point were the expectations from the various laboratories between China, Europe, America, and others for the creation of the vaccine to treat the coronavirus— COVID 19 (2020). Hot on the heels of the Covid 19 vaccine was the announcement by the WHO of the successful creation of the anti-malaria vaccine (2021).

Medical laboratories, with which the populace is more acquainted, provide a variety of services for physicians' offices, clinics, hospitals, drug manufacturing companies, and the list is virtually endless.

## Family Relational Health Laboratory Defined (Technical)

Applied to the subject of this book, the family relational health laboratory is a testing and research facility, called *home*, in which family members hone their intra- and interpersonal skills in the dynamics of family relationships. This honing of family relational skills is in preparation for family members to make a meaningful contribution to the quality of life, firstly there in the home and next in the society outside of the home.

From there, with the support of the team members—that is, fellow researchers and practitioners, in the person of husband, wife, father, mother, brother, sister, etc.—a family member can make an experiential proclamation of the discoveries made and affirmed as to what works and does not work in a family relationship. Sometimes, consent has to be sought from team members before some discoveries are made public, depending on the sensitivity of a proverbial skeleton in the family cupboard. From the family lab, individuals can even come out with some specific knowledge with reference to the possible whats, whens, hows, whys and wheres of family relationships. (See the Glossary for the general definition, p. 406.)

**Study Family Members in Your Home Lab**

When asked how she came to know so much about her uncle, whom she sometimes imitate and whose responses and comments she can at times predict, Mrs Stacy Gordon-Dally responded with confidence: "When you love someone, that's what you do—study them!" She did not take any time to search for the answer. It was, as it were, on the tip of her tongue, and that sent a profound message as to the foundational state of mind of the members in the family lab: they love each other.

That is the basic and sustained factor in relationships love. It motivates each family member in a positive, healthy way to spend quality time to study, learn, and know each other. When you love someone in the family lab, you healthily observe and take note of his or her taste, likes, dislikes, concerns, fears, strengths, and areas for growth. In the process, we practice the skills of affirmation, appreciation, commendation, encouragement, and challenge. It is in this lab that we work to improve the quality of the relational vital signs of connection, rapport, bond and support.

When we say that "from the family lab, individuals can even come out with some specific knowledge with reference to the possible whats, whens, hows, whys, and wheres of family relationships," this does not mean that family members will impose their family practice on others. Instead, they can offer suggestions, guidelines, or ideas based on the quality research in the family lab in which they practice. These they can share based on their healthy developmental experiences in their home labs.

**Structures and Operations in the Family Laboratory**

In order to better understand the concept of the family laboratory, let us take an analytical look at its twenty-five structural and operational components.

1.  **Name of Facility**:
    Family Relational Health Laboratory

2.  **Location**:
    Home

3.  **Purpose**:
    *   Continuing the Family Creation Project which God started from the Garden of Eden
    *   Producing quality families and people for society

4.  **Output/Quantity Target**:
    Fill up and replenish the earth

5.  **Architects/Designers**:
    The Godhead: Father, Son, and Holy Spirit (See Letusism in Glossary p. 407)

6.  **Chief Overseeing Engineers**:
    Son and the Holy Spirit

7.  **Contractors and Builders**:
    Husband and wife; father and mother

8.  **Site Overseers**:
    The Church

9.  **Site Managers**:
    Pastors, elders, and leaders

**10. Lab Blueprint and Construction Manual**:
The Holy Bible

**11. Lab Foundation**:
Marriage (holy wedlock)

**12. Lab Development**:
Parenting (biological, adoptive …)

**13. Lab Expansion**:
Siblings, in-laws, all other categories (see "Categories of Family Members" in Appendix 2, p. 466)

**14. Lab Researchers**:
Each family member/group in order as they are named (see "Categories of Family Members" in Appendix 2, p. 466)

**15. Lab Specimens**:
Each family member, working on and studying each other (see "Categories of Family Members" in Appendix 2, p. 466)

**16. Main Product/Output**:
Quality, healthy family relationships

**17. Lab Quality Control**:
Contractors and builders in consultation and coordination with Chief Overseeing Engineers

**18. Lab Main Operations**:
Worshiping and working, loving, caring, sharing, respecting, affirming, commending, appraising, encouraging, and challenging

**19. Lab Process**:
Interacting and interrelating with the Fruit of the Spirit as base ingredient

**20. Lab Procedures**:
Engaging minds with conscious, conscientious, consistent, serving, and blending of the ingredients (See The 3 C's, p.157)

**21. Project Duration**:
Work of a lifetime

**22. Project Financing**:
Bank of Heaven: "Jesus Paid It All"

**23. Lab Testing**:
The natural, healthy relationships between lab specimens initiated by the contractors and builders; testified to by specimens on their own volition; and manifested by the sustained quality of the four vital signs—connection, rapport, bond, and support for each other, and the ultimate impact that they have on the relationships with others (conditions applied) when they get into the consuming marketplace, that is, the broad society

**24. Lab Product Approval and Stamp Officer**
God the Father

**25. Product Final Destination**:
Eternity for the New Earth

## The Fruit of the Spirit Applied in the Family Lab

Each family unit is here compared to a laboratory that is in constant production of samples and supplies for the consuming market: the broad society. Those who are to be in charge of quality control—that is, husbands and wives, fathers and mothers, and designated caregivers—need to be knowledgeable of the material or ingredients being put into the manufacturing process.

From the two versions of our paraphrased Anchor Text, we see two different, distinct, and opposing packages of qualities (ingredients) that are put into the working specimens and will in turn determine the potential products from every family relational health laboratory. It is important to take note that in the original text, the fruit is referred to in the singular number: "the *fruit* of the Spirit *is*" and not "the *fruits* of the Spirit *are*." The message to be learned here is that a person cannot possess one aspect of the character of the Spirit and not possess the others. All the parts work in sync to make the whole fruit. So one cannot be truly loving or joyful and at the same time being cantankerous and impatient with others. There is no such thing as having a part of the Spirit, as in having a slice of a fruit. A slice of the fruit is simply not the whole fruit (See p. 78).

When the Holy Spirit infuses the mind, that infusion permeates the entire being, and the lifestyle and behavior harmonize with the total character of the Spirit Himself. Understandably, there will be the occasional evidence of human frailty, but such evidence is to be the exception and not the rule in the lifestyle. God does understand that, having assured us in Psalm 103:13–14 that "Like as a father pitieth his children, so the LORD pitieth them that fear him. For he knoweth our frame; he remembereth that we are dust, that He knows that we are flesh." (See further Assurance in 1 John 2: 11).

This same principle of what we could call *all-in-one—one-in-all* applies to observing God's Royal Law: the Ten Commandments (James 2:8). According to James, one of Jesus's biological brothers and a faithful follower of His teachings, "Whosoever shall keep the whole law, and yet offend in one point, he is guilty of all" (2:10). In chapter 3:8–12, he maintained his passionate appeal against relational duplicity by using analogies of the stream giving bitter and sweet water, and the vine bearing two contrary types of fruits.

It is understood that there is room for growth and that this requires symmetrical development of character in the *many-parts-one-fruit* or the *all-in-one—one-in-all* teaching. There is provision and room for our timely development. We do not all develop at the same rate, biologically and physically. To the same extent that our metabolism, our nutritional assimilation, and the resultant growth and development rates of our bodies differ, so do our personal qualities, strengths, personalities, and integrity take time to result in the desirable character we want to admire and cherish. They do not all take place simultaneously (CPH$^2$).

At the same time, the *many-parts-one-fruit* and *all-in-one—one-in-all* teaching of James 2:8 discourages and abhors any attitude of mind that consciously seeks to highlight and even go on to live one quality or aspect of the character of the Spirit over the other. We should strive by His grace to grow and develop symmetrically, demonstrating all the qualities of the fruit of the Spirit.

In the same breath, the practicing relationally unhealthy person can hardly display one feature of the undesirable characteristics without evidence or trace of the others. Harshness and spitefulness, for example, can be seen in those who are insensitive, rigid, or unkind. Notwithstanding, there are hypocrites who are adept at showing selected characteristics and behaving the opposite at other times and places. Such persons cannot last for long without being found out. "But if ye will not do so, behold, ye have sinned against the LORD: and be sure your sin will find you out" (Num. 32:23)

## Family Microcosm Reflecting the Societal Macrocosm

In each family lab, the main activity is relationship-building, which is a process of engaging one mind ideally *with* the other mind. To engage one mind with another mind suggests that they two are together. There is agreement and conversation with commonality of purpose. There is no negative competition. The engagement is positively healthy. The reality is, however, that this ideal is not always attained or maintained, and sometimes the engagement process can be *against* instead of *with*. There are no relationships in which human beings are always *with* each other.

We differ, we agree, we contend, we support, and we withdraw, among other forms of relating. The variation of our reactions and responses (see definitions of these in the Glossary pp. 411 & 414) can be very wide and polarized at times, simply because our relational minds are different. No two minds think alike in every situation.

This complex reality in the relationship-building process in the lab at home could be cited as a microcosm of the macrocosm in society at large. To a large extent, the quality of life in the home is an index of the quality of life in society. As researchers and practitioners in these home labs make their findings, experiences, patterns, and types of relational behaviors, they in turn interact with other members who they meet coming from different and varied home labs in the same society.

## Home Labs Extend to Society Labs

These interactions are also intended to forge and build new relationships, also of different categories. In home labs, the relationships are essentially marital, parental, sibling, and general familial: cousins, aunts, uncles, grands, in-laws, etc. In the new labs outside the home, the relationships are going to begin generally as acquaintances: class/school/study mates, professional/working colleagues, friends, and church and/or club and association members. Some might go on to become closer-knit and move into being marital, stronger collegial, transactional/business, or social bonds. It is the same process of building relationships at home that will be used in these new relationships—that is, the engaging of mind with mind.

The differences in these new processes are more likely to be stark and outstanding than when they were in the comfort and safety of their private labs at home, assuming that the processes they went through were healthy and good. In this new relational lab, there could be much more uncertainty, questioning, wondering, and concerns about what is going on in the mind of the other person.

In the home labs from which we come, there was established familiarity and camaraderie and commonality of togetherness. Now, in this new relational lab setting, sometimes the processes are fraught with elements of suspicion, lack of trust, or search for trust, among other unsettling of the minds. It should be remembered that some of these negative states of relational minds could have been experienced in the relationship process at home, in the individual's family of origin. If such negative brought-forwards were never healed, the natural residual effects could influence how that individual relates in the new relationship-building process outside of the home.

Regrettably, there are times when interactions between new minds do not yield the desired results, and the parties become severely confrontational in different ways and at different intensities. Sometimes they require the intervention of another party to help them in managing the relational challenges. The multiplier effect of the differences can result in mayhem and upheavals—in the new home, at school, at the workplace, and even at church.

The aftereffects of these newly attempted relationships can wear heavily on the relational minds of all the persons involved. In many instances, they require a more equipped lab with more experienced and competent practitioners than those less-experienced ones in the home. In these new, out-of-the home labs, relational cases are studied and analyzed, and a professional treatment plan is designed to address the challenges. The development and operations of the family relational health laboratory detailed below is one such example.

By understanding and appreciating the concept of families at home as laboratories in society, we can further agree that as these home labs multiply, they will eventually need the work of a larger, more equipped lab to address their combined challenges. With that comprehensive overview, one can further appreciate the details of the background and development of the established family relational health laboratory.

**Two Objectives of the Family Lab Concept**

It is hoped that by reading the development account, the reader will be better able to understand and appreciate that which is shared in chapters 2 through 12 on the various aspects of the theory, principles, lessons, and practices of family relational health. It is important to uphold the healthy, sentimental, and emotional perspective of the family as a loving, caring group of individuals living together harmoniously at home. In addition, by looking positively at this fundamental, cellular unit of the human society as a lab, we can accomplish two important objectives:

1. *For the family at home*—The goal is to reduce or even remove a take-it-for-granted attitude toward each other and to better manage the differences we encounter as we interact in the process of building relationships. This goal will be accomplished when we learn and accept these differences, even to affirming and encouraging the healthy, positive ones and tolerating and managing those that have room for growth and improvement. It is by carefully and even painstakingly studying each family member (specimen) of the home lab that we can learn how best to blend and integrate and harmonize our personalities, temperaments, likes, dislikes, idiosyncrasies, and peculiarities.

2. *For the Family in Society*—The same family members who are produced in the home labs go on to establish the industrial, scientific, and technological ones in the broader society. We are awed and astonished sometimes by their mind-boggling

accomplishments and feats. Some of the modern inventions and innovations are seen as mind-blowing and belying logic. The pronouncements, probabilities, audacious assumptions and attempts, research, trials, and relentless efforts backed by billions of dollars invested into the various laboratories explain why we are captivated and even awestruck by the work of the geniuses of our times.

**Invest in Studying Home Labs** (See pp. 394 & 474)

Unfortunately, the efforts to research and understand and improve family relationships pale in comparison to those that we barely scratched the surface to mention above. The family as a lab? Preposterous! Not when there are so many more arresting matters, such as disease control and prevention, space exploration, environmental and greenhouse gas management, robotic surgery, and engineering, among others, to commandeer our attention, research, and investment.

A family lab? Is this proposal suggesting that we are to invest corporate funding in studying how families are to operate? We should leave fathers and mothers (more so the mothers) to figure out how to grow, discipline, and bring up the children, while the big brains—the scholars, scientists, technologist, experts (who do not seem to be products of those homes! (See p. xiii))—address the larger issues of the developments and advances of society.

What more human and family relational catastrophe than the global destabilization of family life and the consequential breakdown in law and order do we need to be jolted into remembering that society is made up of people, and people are products of homes, and homes are where families are made, grown, and dispatched into society? In too many cases, the products of the homes seem to be merely hatched, patched, and dispatched into society, only to rehash the process through which they were produced, and the vicious cycle continues.

Since long before the 2020 outbreak of the global pandemic of COVID-19, and even before the 1918 Spanish flu pandemic (and others of the kind), the pandemic of bad human and family relational health has been known and growing exponentially. Maybe, much to our international failure, there has been no WHO, or preferably, no FWHO (Family World Health Organization), to galvanize world family consensus and arrest the matter of the decadence of human relationship and behavior. We know for sure that this viral human relationship plague did not begin in Wuhan, Hubei Province, China, but in virtually every hamlet, village, community, town, city, and indeed in every country in the world.

By raising the bar and seeing the family as the basic, fundamental lab unit of society, we will better understand the complex dynamics of its inner working and of family relational health. We will be better able to produce the quality of life about which we can only dream amidst the thundering triumphs of the scientific, industrial, technological, and other laboratories of this twenty-first century.

Who knows? Family relational health, as detailed in the pages ahead, could be the miracle vaccine that brings the healing for which the world stands in dire need. This new panacea could be safely administered in the equally new family relational health treatment facilities, *respitals*, mentioned in the Epilogue of this book, and which will be fully detailed in book two: *Family Relational Health: A Missing Dimension in Comprehensive Health Care.*

## Family Relational Health Laboratory: Early Beginnings and Development

This book is the product of Family the relational health laboratory work that began over thirty years ago. It was then that I started working and relating in a general way with families in various capacities, such as school teacher, principal, and college department director. In those capacities, I had numerous opportunities to observe relational issues between fathers and mothers, parents and children, students and students, teachers and students, parents and parents, parents and teachers, and teachers and teachers. Sometimes the combination was tripled and more.

More or less, this is the life and experience of those in the teaching profession, and more so those who ascend to the leadership level. However, in hindsight, after listening to others at that level over the years, I can say that there was a clear difference in the impact, the impressions, and the effects that the combined experiences mentioned above produced.

## Laboratory Issues and Challenges

Involvement in the family relational challenges of those being served transcended the obvious and expected academic leadership and directives of teacher, chaplain, principal, and director. There was a need to rise to the call to provide families with mediation and guidance, advice, counsel, and support as they, in more ways than one, sought to grapple with their expressed and implied relational challenges. Those challenges were mostly manifested in their liking or dislike for conflicting personal attributes among themselves, such as temperaments, personalities, dispositions, and behaviors in various situations as they interfaced and interacted with each other.

Although the areas of their complaints or concerns about the other person(s) were, in many cases personal and not academic in nature, these did have a negative impact on the desired academic and scholastic performance of the children at home who became the students at school. It was further seen that those complaints, concerns, and conflicts affected the supportive roles and input from the adults, (teachers and parents and guardians) in the programs of the institution. The results (some lasting up to this day!) of what was cited by many as the caring interventions and interest offered to them in their personal and family welfare, made it clear that there were the hidden but deeply felt needs to address the issues and challenges from a humane and relational, and not just from an academic, standpoint.

From time to time, many academic administrators and staff (with the exception of guidance counselors, chaplains, and deans of disciplines) are heard to say, "I am here to teach the lessons, to ensure that the syllabus is completed and examinations are passed, not to deal with relationships and personal issues." No one can justifiably argue against such positions, because they are technically and in most cases advisedly correct. Ethically, it is understood that any extension of oneself beyond one's boundary of preparation and competence has to be carefully thought out and addressed, with the understanding of the potential implications and even complications that such extension and involvement can cause.

**Period and Development**

Against such mounting and sustained validations from those being served, and from the positive and arresting effects on me, the challenge was taken on to dovetail the academic leadership with the appreciated and accepted family relational care that was successfully being delivered. Therefore, with additionally acquired professional and clinical training, qualifications, experiences, and developing competencies, for the last twenty-five-plus years, I have gradually transitioned out of the academic and educational setting into counseling and psychological practice.

The nature of the laboratory work also changed and became exclusively locked in as that of a family-life educator, counselor, psychologist, and human resources manager. The outreach scope widened into the national and international community with the assumption of capacities such as associate chaplain (volunteer) of the police force; family counselor on television and radio; and featured family counselor and contributing writer to newspapers and magazines, locally and overseas.

**Working Laboratory Specimen**

In these advanced and evolving capacities, the wider and more intense gamut of behind-closed-door family relational issues and challenges were met. From the single, repeated, and multiple face-to-face sessions for individuals, couples, and groups, the exposure began to expand. Hundreds of active, sound relational minds—in the persons of fiancés and fiancées, husbands and wives, parents and children, grands, steps, in-laws, uncles and aunts, cousins, and all the other categories of family members—have been seen annually growing into thousands over the decades, as all opened up for relational treatment.

As these persons felt safe and confident in the professional and nonjudgmental setting and atmosphere that was created for them, and as they shared their innermost issues, one could not help but be arrested by the fact that access was now being granted to the most private part of the client's being—the family relational mind! It is in the family relational mind that individuals become positively connected or negatively entangled, sometimes in relentless efforts with mixed intentions, ignorantly or calculatedly, desiring one of the following:

1. To identify with and live healthily together
2. To separate from and even hurt and destroy the other

In the process, clients were seen displaying every manifestation from calm, composed, controlled, and reconciliatory emotions and behaviors to raw, unbridled, convulsive, and confrontational ones. What was heard and seen ranged from loving, affirming, assuring, consoling, and supportive expressions and embraces to demeaning, aggressive verbal abuses and physical altercations.

During these interventions, clients permitted, consented to, and cooperated with a deepening of the assessment into the folds and crevices of their family relational mind (See p. 477). Those surgical interventions sometimes had to be performed with a heavy dose of emotional anesthetic, such as comfort and care; assurance and reassurance; and prayer (for faith-based clients only and others if requested). What was seen as a result of these interventions was the individual's inner thoughts, perspectives, and concepts of love, hatred, concerns, pride, shame, anger, guilt, desires, intentions, fears, hopes, despair, sensitivity, affection, bitterness, jealousy, trust, anxiety, and all the other relational emotions that were alive and active in both the conscious and subconscious chambers of the mind.

Each of the laboratory specimens—these thousands of active, sound relational minds, whether they came for a personal, premarital, marital, parental, social, collegial, or professional operation and treatment—was unique and different. They had much human commonality, but as each one opened up and divulged the depth within, what became even clearer were the intricacies and complexities and the different colors and shades of the family relational mind.

**Laboratory Cases**

In this family relational health laboratory, whether it was set up in the office or went mobile to a home or a church vestry, school or business/company office, street side, the shade of a tree, or an open field (all of these are real), what was encountered was the comingling of sweat, tears, and blood; freshly inflicted wounds and mutilated, decomposing bodies; manifestations of domestic abuse and violence, drug and substance abuse, mayhem and trauma, suicide, grief, divorce, abandonment, sexual molestation and rape; rage, resentment, and uncontrolled anger; trampled self-esteem; and mental illnesses, including schizophrenia, phobias, paranoia, hysteria, psychosis, and dementia.

It must be noted that some of these mental illness cases were the outgrowth of impaired and damaged, destroyed, unmanaged, and untreated family relationships over short and long periods. Of equal note is the unfortunate fact that many mental illnesses which are a direct result of impaired relationships go on to get a clinical diagnosis of chemical imbalance (See pp. 211, 327) and malfunctionality of aspects of the brain and the glandular system, with no antecedent reference to the impaired traumatic relationship that the persons experienced in the first place. (All cases of mental illnesses are professionally referred for psychiatric treatment.)

**Laboratory Geographic and Economic Scopes**

These family relational health laboratory cases have been seen in various instances across a wide international spectrum, with clients representing different nationalities, cultures, tribes, and languages, covering over sixty countries in the Caribbean, North and South America, Canada, Europe, Asia, Africa, the Middle East, and Australia, and from islands not directly connected to the major mainlands. Clients have come from every academic, professional, economic, and social stratum, age group, culture, race, faith, and language (some necessitating translation/interpretation).

# Family Relational Health Laboratory: Concerns, Theory, and Position

The overall goal in the practice laboratory has been "treating relationships the healthy way," with emphasis on bringing balance to the natural, understood, and acceptable, yet incorrect, bias that society places on our physiological/medical health care compared to the scant measure given to psychological, not to mention relational, health care. The focus and care given to the body far outweighs that given to the mind in general and relationships in particular; thus the birth of the concept to treat family relationships "the healthy way".

In this way, the bar will be raised to an appropriate level of awareness. Contrary to the thinking of many in the mainstream health care sector that the state of a relationship is not a straight health issue (a position also supported by the DSM-5), it will be seen and accepted that treating relationships the healthy way is the answer to a healthier, more balanced society. This will also be seen as a way to manage and reduce the exponentially expanding global annual health/medical care bills.

The driving, unique theory of family relational health is that all human relationships begin and continue to exist in the active, sound mind (see differentiations and analyses of these two descriptions of the mind in the Glossary), with over 80 percent of human life being influenced negatively or positively by the various relationships (marital, parental, collegial, social, etc.) in which we get engaged, via the mind. The remaining 20 percent of relationship in the human mind is mostly of a one-way connection, and to a less degree, mutually and beneficially interactive, with animals and plant life and inanimate, material things.

This is the mind that is described as "sound" in 2 Timothy 1:7, and in which the four vital signs of healthy human relationship— connection, rapport, bond, and support—exist. There are about eighty other similar and different descriptions (negative and positive) of the mind in the Bible. The four vital signs are direct formulation in the family relational health laboratory, developed over the years under review.

We further observed that the virtual, lopsided conventional focus on health as the care of the body (physiological health) at the expense of equal focus on the care of the mind (psychological health, and more pointedly, the relational aspect thereof) has resulted in a preponderance of hitherto unknown psychosomatic illnesses of mind-boggling proportion. Raise the bar of the quality of the professional care that is offered to families with relational challenges, thereby improving the quality of life in the homes, and see the positive ripple effects in schools, churches, workplaces, and society at large.

## Laboratory Practices

### *Theories and Therapies*

For the *caring* and *treatment* process of family relational challenges and illnesses, a combination of various international standard professional theories and therapies has been employed, including psychoanalysis/psychodynamic theory, cognitive behavior therapy (CBT), behavior modification therapy (BMT), affective behavior therapy (ABT), elements of the humanistic approach, and holistic/integrative therapy. Various professional skills, strategies, methods, and techniques (see sample instruments designed for such in Appendix 2) have been added to the entire treatment program.

### *Consultation Procedures and Objectives*

In preparation for the consultation or first session, the client completes the following:

1. A *pretherapy exercise* indicating what he or she desires or hopes to experience at the end of the treatment program. That exercise is compared to a road map and is intended to be followed and therefore checked periodically to see if the client is reaching where he or she desired to reach upon entering the program.

2. A *consent and declaration of intent*. In addition to the pretherapy exercise, the client also signs the consent and the declaration of intent forms (see Appendix 2).

3. A *treatment plan*. The overarching aim and guiding principle of treating relationships the healthy way is to ensure, as much as professionally and humanly possible, that clients leave each therapy session better than they came in. The following fundamental objectives are therefore the expected outcome

of the treatment program in tandem with the pre-therapy exercise:

- Raise and deepen the client's awareness of where he or she is, where he or she desires to be, and possible ways and means to get there.
- Straighten and align the client's focus and attitude toward the desired goal.
- Modify and adjust the client's behavior as is necessary along the way toward the goal.
- Enhance and enrich the client's relationship(s).
- Arm and equip the client with relational and management skills.
- Guide and monitor the client's decision-making and actions toward a better quality of life

As a standard practice, continuous research, training, case conferencing, professional collaborations, peer reviews, and consultations (while maintaining the professional ethics of clients' case confidentiality) are used to assess, interpret, modify and confirm various clinical issues from time to time and to keep abreast of development in the professional field.

**Laboratory Resources**

A number of resources have emerged out of the multiplicity and diversity of family relational health laboratory experiences over the years, including the following:

- hundreds of PowerPoint seminars for personal, premarital, marital, parental, singles, and other presentations (see the twenty-five sample topics in Appendix 1)

- books, newspapers, and magazine articles on family relational health

- education and counseling

- DVDs and CDs in some of the same areas as those covered in the books

- evaluation and assessment instruments for use in diagnosing, testing, and treating various family relational health illnesses. (see sample instruments in Appendix 2).

- professional training material for pastors, family ministry leaders, educators, mental and social health practitioners, and others in the helping professions

## Laboratory Usage

Given the genesis of this book, coming from a family relational health laboratory perspective, it is presented as hybrid in nature, such that it can be used by the professional and the layperson who desires to understand and apply the concept and perspectives on family relational health. It is intended to be seen as a well-packed first aid kit that can be utilized by family members in the home; by professionals in seminar presentations at churches, schools, workplaces, and other groups; and by academicians in lecture halls, at which level it can inspire the thrust for higher critical and analytical research and thinking. Referring to this work as a first aid kit actually reflects the title of one of the laboratory resources mentioned above. That resource material is the six-manual publication titled *The First-Aid Kit for Successful Family Life* (1995).

The title of the book you are reading now is specifically *Family Relational Health* and not generally *Relational Health*. The emphasis on *family* is intended to set the work apart from the generalization approach to relationships. The focus is on the biblical, foundational concept of family in the home. In admiration and appreciation for the sentiments of family-ness, the title (family) has been adopted from its original source (the home) and brought over into all the other institutions that emanate from it: school, church, corporate business, and society in general.

So all-pervading is the adoption of the name *family* and the infusion of its sentiments in society that it is not only husbands and wives and fathers and mothers (or household leaders) who are heard reminding and challenging the group that "We are a family here and we ought to live and relate with each other in that spirit." We hear the exact sentimental appeal going out from pastors and priests to their congregants, and from school principals to their staff and students. Even in the boardroom, corporate presidents, supervisors, managers and leaders are heard galvanizing support and team spirit and togetherness by making the appeal, "We are a family here." We have even heard of the *family islands*, a term used to describe the islands in the Caribbean, and no doubt other closely knit groups of islands elsewhere with many commonalities and shared identities.

It is with this knowledge of the all-pervasive, pervading, and penetrative nature of *family* that *relational health* is presented, and not from an academic treatise perspective of human relationship in general. This book acknowledges that there are other theological, anthropological, sociological, and psychological analytical definitions, concepts, and perspectives on the composition, functions, and operations of the family.

However, until the word *family* in its Biblical, original, and foundational meaning, understanding, and application is declared globally obsolete (which seems to be the subtle goal of many at all levels of the society), *relational health*, from the home to corporations, cannot be fully discussed and appreciated without incorporating the underpinning sentiments of relationships for which *family* has come to be known and accepted worldwide.

**Suggestions for Action**

1.  Look again at the construction of the family laboratory. Ask yourself, "How much is my family lab constructed off that order? Is there anywhere that we need to do some corrective construction so that we can be blessed as God wants us to be?"

2.  See your family as your active laboratory. How healthily are you studying each individual in your lab? How much do you affirm each one for the positive qualities you see in them?

3.  Make yourself open and vulnerable so that your family members can feel free and safe to study and know you better. Be healthily responsive to their observations and comments about you.

4.  Study the fruit of the Spirit and pray that God will help you give evidence of the full fruit in your life.

5.  What effects flow from your home laboratory into society? Pray to God and work with the members of your home to ensure that good influence flows out and blesses those who come in contact with your family lab specimens.

# Chapter 2

# The Family Under Attack

**Anchor Text: Ephesians 6:12**

"For we wrestle not against flesh and blood, but against principalities, against powers, against the rulers of the darkness of this world, against spiritual wickedness in high places."

**Paraphrased for Families**

For we wrestle not against ordinary marital, parental, and general family relational challenges, but against the continuous deteriorating standards of this world; against the subtle forces set at destroying God's original family ideals; and against the corrupt, immoral practices of this age, operating from high academic, religious, social, and other influential stages in society.

In the Introduction, reference was made to the desire to understand the nature, and to identify the cause of the condition of a family that was encountered over the weekend. In answer to my prayer, the God of families illuminated my mind via the Holy Spirit (John 16:33), and I was able to see their condition from two perspectives: professional and spiritual.

- **Perspective 1:** The use of the term *professional* points to the clinical treatment aspect of care that the individual or family group needs. As was already stated in the Introduction, the professional perspective addresses the treatment plan, which is carefully woven into each chapter of this book and is succinctly summarized at the end under the caption "Suggestions for Action."

- **Perspective 2:** Let us consider this second perspective through the lens of our Anchor Text above. Ephesians 6:12 is one of the Bible passages that church evangelism leaders use to inspire and motivate members into an evangelistic, militant mode. They emphasize that the warfare which the church is engaged in is not primarily with visible, flesh-and-blood forces. The archenemy of souls is hell-bent on taking as many as he can to his final and destructive destination (Matt. 25:41). The members are therefore urged to get enlisted in the battle, hence they are to "sound the battle cry" because they are "Christian soldiers, marching on to war."

What a great experience it would have been in that church if the leaders with responsibility for family life could have captured the same urgency and seen that the enemy of souls is succeeding in his mission by attacking the very foundation of the church: the family.

## Natural Disaster Analogy with Satan's Efforts

The devil is undoubtedly a master strategist, crafty and cunning at his art of deception and destruction. In his demolition strategy for the church and society at large, he takes the approach of an earthquake rather than a hurricane. A hurricane does its destructive work mainly from the top. Its primary target is the roof of the house. Invariably, even when it succeeds in decapitating the house, the walls, columns, and floor remain intact, depending on the nature of the material and the quality of the construction.

An earthquake, on the other hand, strikes at the foundation of the structure. Once the bedrock, the anchor, or the substratum shakes, cracks, and breaks up, the superstructure naturally comes crumbling down. If the family is still considered as the nucleus, the core, and the anchor of society, it goes without saying that the way to destroy society and all its superstructures is to destroy the families that comprise that society. This does not require the proverbial rocket scientist to make the discovery.

It seems that another of the devil's strategies is to pull a veil over the eyes of church leadership in general, shifting their focus from the critical importance of good quality, Bible-based family life in the salvation plan, so that he can do his work of destruction, eating away at the family. Subtle is a perfect description of the devil's work, beginning from Eden. (Gen. 3:1)

Let us analyze the paraphrased version of our Anchor Text, examining every key word or phrase to look at the magnitude of its message. Then we will discuss our findings in the context of our encounter with that weekend family. We will regard each pullout as an extrapolation and italicize the section or word for analysis.

## Extrapolation 1

*Original:* "For we wrestle not against flesh and blood"

*Paraphrased for Families:* "For we *wrestle* not against *ordinary* marital, parental, and general family relational *challenges*"

Most people through experience would agree that success in almost every good endeavor in life is only achieved with some amount of struggle. That seems to be a fact of life. In fact, that is what the Lord actually told Adam after he sinned: "And unto Adam he said, because thou hast hearkened unto the voice of thy wife, and hast eaten of the tree, of which I commanded thee, saying, Thou shalt not eat of it: cursed is the ground for thy sake; in sorrow shalt thou eat of it all the days of thy life; Thorns also and thistles shall it bring forth to thee; and thou shalt eat the herb of the field; In the sweat of thy face shalt thou eat bread, till thou return unto the ground;

for out of it wast thou taken: for dust thou art, and unto dust shalt thou return" (Gen. 3:17-19).

## Life Struggles and Conflicts

We can conclude, therefore, that struggle is concomitant with the pursuit of life's goals. However, there is struggle and there is struggle. The magnitude and intensity is determined by the source from which it comes and what might be motivating that source. When struggling becomes *wrestling*, it implies confrontation with opposing forces with the intent to destroy the opposing party.

The struggle within families, beginning with husbands and wives and spreading to parents and children and all the other categories, begins first of all because there are two active, sound minds that are forging a relationship. The one does not necessarily think like the other. They have, and are entitled to, differing views by virtue of their different thought processes.

Conflict in a healthy, genuine relationship is not necessarily bad. Correctly managed, conflict can redound to the benefit of all the parties concerned, in that better understanding can be achieved. As each party respectfully listens to the view of the other (not necessarily opposing), he or she will exercise openness of mind, tolerance, and acceptance of another viewpoint. When it is his or her turn to express an opinion on the issue, it will be done genuinely, honestly, and truthfully. This contribution to the discussion is not to counteract or oppose, as is the nature of government and opposition in parliamentary debates. It seems sometimes that they just oppose for the mere sake of opposing!

With the two views, positions, or opinions now fully expressed, differing though they may appear, the pace is set for negotiation, compromise, and a genuine effort to come together for the common good. This is summarizing healthy conflict at its best, which should be the experience in all families, and more so in the Christian family.

However, the struggle, and indeed the *wrestling*, that our Anchor Text addresses is not healthy in nature. It is correctly described as not being *ordinary*. That is to say, it does not resemble the above description. It is not regular. This kind of struggle is not borne out of an intent to understand and achieve consensus. It is not normal! In other words, the *wrestling* that is experienced in very troubled relationships that threatens to drive the family members asunder is abnormal.

We need to look deeper and more intently to discover what is motivating them. They are not ordinary! A force outside of the parties involved with destructive intention is motivating the wrestling. In the case of marital conflicts, the husband and wife are being pitted against each other without being aware that they are pawns in the hands of a power greater than themselves, and so it is for all other types of family conflicts that are wrestling in nature.

**Family Problems Versus Challenges: A Mind-set**

The next key word in the phrase is *challenges*. Relational issues, relational conflicts, and relational disagreements are not necessarily bad. The emotional label we place on them can determine to a large degree how they are managed. In so many instances, the conflicts, struggles, and disagreements in relationships are labeled *problems*. We hear "I can't take problems!" or "I don't like problems!" or "We have too many problems!" These are common complaints made in marital or general family counseling sessions.

Except in mathematics, where *problem* is not considered to be negative or potentially destructive, the word stirs up negative emotions between two parties when their differing positions on an issue are so labeled. In human relationships of any kind, *problem* is perceived as bad, undesirable, and that which is to be avoided. Who really wants to live with problems?

It is therefore healthier to see the differing states of mind in a relationship as *challenges*. The emotional response is less negative and therefore less combative. When the issue is seen as a challenge, it summons less adrenaline and cortisol in the bloodstream, which in turn summons the negative fight-or-flight approach. Instead, it elicits more cordial and mutual resolve to find solutions, resulting in more endorphin and even oxytocin being produced and built up in the bloodstream. (See Relational Problems in Chapter 9, page 236).

## Extrapolation 2

*Original:* "but against principalities"

*Paraphrased for Families:* "but against the *continuous deteriorating standards* of this world"

We have been correctly taught that the family is the nucleus of society, and consequently, society is made up of families. It is also true that the dynamics of society do have reverberating effects, both positive and negative, on those very families. This is so because of the different mixtures and identities, the varying norms and mores, the differing values and world views, among other factors, that each family carries from its home into society's melting pot.

It is from this diverse, complex, and complicated mixture that each family draws and returns to its individual home. Upon returning from school, from work, from church, or from a social event, each may have picked up an idea, an attitude, or even a skill regarding a certain relational matter and deliberately or inadvertently introduced it into the family.

## External Influences on the Internal Family

At home, family members need to determine how much of outside knowledge, attitudes, and behaviors will be adopted and kept, and how much will be discarded. Some type of home and family filtering system needs to be in place which at best is the objective, active, sound relational minds. It is easier writing this counsel than experiencing and practicing it. Sometimes the novelty of the new idea can be so commandeering and alluring that it threatens the continuation of that which was a cherished family practice and principle.

There are times when the unique characteristic and identity of the family becomes vulnerable and endangered with the infusion of some new idea, concept, or attitude that was brought in from the outside. Today, when so many bedrocks of traditional, Biblical family life are being weathered away, it is safe to conclude that ideals, standards, values, and morals are waning in a continuously deteriorating world.

The family is not naturally immune from all this deterioration. That immunization has to be desired, needed, and sought after by family members who are aware of the predicament in which they find themselves. They need to connect with an opposite force or power of Biblical family stabilization in order to avoid the effects of deterioration.

# Extrapolation 3

*Original:* "against powers"

*Paraphrased for Families:* "against the subtle forces set at destroying God's original family ideals"

Many of the deteriorating standards that affect quality, Bible-based family life today cannot be seen by the ordinary eye, simply because we are not wrestling against *ordinary* marital, parental, and other general family challenges. These challenges are *covidic* in nature. The present COVID-19 pandemic has the world in bewilderment, and one of the crying comments of just about everyone is: "and you can't even see it!"

That is very characteristic of the many issues and challenges eating away at quality family life. They are simply not seen until their devastating presence is felt and their work of destruction is well underway. Families need their relational eyes to be washed with "eye salve" (Rev. 3:18) that only the spiritual lachrymal glands can produce under the inspiration of the Holy Spirit.

Why is this so? It is so because the forces are subtle (inasmuch as they are becoming more overt as the deterioration descends deeper and deeper) and are not easily seen. The subtlety of the forces of evil against quality family life is not new. The first account that the Bible offers for the breakdown of the family was that "the serpent was more subtle than any beast of the field which the LORD God had made ..." (Gen. 3:1). The poor unsuspecting snake, as an animal, was only used as a ventriloquist's dummy by a master in the art of deception: Satan himself.

The word *subtle* means "operating from under; away from the view of the general eye; in a disguised, concealed way with an intent to deceive." That was how sin entered into the world, and that subtle, camouflaging characteristic has not changed today. The devil is still as cunning now as he was then, and he has invested all his allies, angelic and human, with the same craftiness, cunningness, and deviousness in their art of deception.

The purpose of their shrewdness and deceitfulness is to undermine and ultimately destroy everything that is called by God's name. The creation of man, and by extension the family, was God's masterpiece of creation. God established the original family ideal right there and then by beginning the family with one mature adult male and one mature adult female. That is as original as any anthropologist can get.

That original family ideal is now under vicious attack by the extended arm of the opposing forces to biblical godliness. There are various versions and explanations of what and who constitutes a married couple and consequently a family (Read again p. ix).

The original, Bible-based marriage and family structure is under attack! Let us be honest: this attack is not a twenty-first-century phenomenon. The attack began as far back as "Bible days," as modern-day Christians express it. Indeed, nothing is new under the sun (Eccles. 1:9). What we are experiencing now, in this modern day, is the frightening and potentially multiplying effect of what began centuries and millennia ago.

## Extrapolation 4

*Original:* "against the rulers of the darkness of this world"

*Paraphrased for Families:* "against the corrupt, immoral practices of this age"

Given the nature of the following sections the reader is advised to read again the explanation of, **To Whomsoever May Read** at the beginning of the Preface

So how do the subtle and at times overt forces of deception manifest themselves? The answer is clear: If God sets clear, simple guidelines for human inter-relational behavior, as contained in the last six principles of the Ten Commandments, then those foundational, bedrock principles would be the obvious point from which the opposing forces of God's creation plan would seek to attack the family.

God's established version of good, stable family life begins with the marriage of one husband to one wife. And even though the original sin affected the quality of the marriage relationship, God still upheld the pre-sin ideal in the post-sin reality: "until death do them part" (Matt. 19:3–6). And Jesus reaffirmed that ideal when He began His public ministry by performing His first miracle on behalf of the catering husband at the marriage at Cana of Galilee (John 2:1–11). Any possible embarrassment in a marriage must be avoided at all cost, and God has a miracle waiting for every asking couple.

In this age, adultery, fornication, and every other form of sexual practice except for the God-designed healthy version between the male husband and his female wife (Heb. 13:4) is on the increase. To no less extent is the alarming exponential growth of the violation of the codes of parental honor, the sanctity of life, honesty, truthfulness, and altruism. There is so much confusion regarding what is moral and right in family life particularly, and in society generally, that certain words and terms that were the hallmarks of propriety, good behavior, and decent living are either being modified or declared obsolete.

According to Joseph Fletcher, one of the propounders of situational ethics, nothing is intrinsically right or wrong; the situation determines that. In the same breath, whereas codes of ethical behavior were once either moral or immoral, today none of the two might serve the correct declaration. Therefore, the behavior is now preferably described as being amoral—a middle ground which has no place in God's original blueprint for healthy interpersonal behavior in the home, community, and broader society. These practices, teachings and philosophies, are inordinately calculated to confuse and attack ordinary, simple, well-thinking family members who believe in God's original family blueprint in which behaviours are either simply right or wrong.

## Extrapolation 5

*Original:* "against spiritual wickedness in high places"

*Paraphrased for Families:* "operating from *high academic, religious, social, and other influential stages*"

The final question that we need to ask as we look at the attacks on God's original family blueprint is, "Where are these corrupt, immoral practices of this age coming from? What are the sources, and through what channels does Satan unleash them?"

Let us go back to the Garden of Eden. Satan did not appear himself. He used what he could manipulate, a dumb, unsuspecting animal—the serpent. Since then, he has doubled, trebled, and further multiplied his strategies, and he has successfully woven his subtleties into every fabric and strata of society. He has his agencies and mouthpieces at every level and in every corner of the world.

Some of the greatest insanities and insidiousness expressed against God's moral codes of conduct come from some of the high halls of academia and the intelligentsia. Many philosophers, researchers, scientists, anthropologists, and others of their kind are heard making some of the most astounding pronouncements that virtually belie logic. And all the major national and international news agencies— printed and electronic—herald them as having news-breaking status.

Some examples of these are the grandiose announcements of those well-to-do celebrities who have established that are diametrically opposed to God's original design. They are held up to the world as living perfectly happy lives, much to the shame of those who claim to be following God's ideal plan but have failed to hold it up because so many of their efforts without God crumble in demise. Satan exults at these successful outcomes of his devious design, in both instances (See pp. 112 & 113).

Maybe one of the crowning cases of his crafty acts of interference in God's design for healthy family life—and for which he has secured international media coverage—is the case of the "woman who became a man," and subsequently "he" became a mother. "He" then wanted the court to declare "him" as the first man to give birth, and land a place in the Guinness Book of Records. In the end, good sense prevailed, and the judge denied "his" petition by reminding "him" that only mothers—meaning females—can give birth, so "he" needs to decide which "he" really is. There are many versions of this case especially in the liberal west.

## Protecting the Inalienable Rights of the Majority and Minority

It is understood that in this pluralistic and, as some describe it, fluid society, the rights of the minority are to be respected, and each one has the inalienable right to practice what he or she believes. It is unfortunate, however, that the vast majority is being made to feel constrained and muzzled to equally express their position, not to mention objection to what is being forced upon them. They cannot "come out" as the others are always heralded and cheered for doing. This appears to be the new norm of society where freedom of choice is concerned.

To the same extent that most countries have moved to protect the nonsmoking majority of the population from second-hand smoke, not by infringing on the right of the minority who are smokers, but providing them with designated places for their practice (except in small, restricted areas shared by both, such as on an airplane), would it be too much for the same society to protect the right of the majority to speak of their moral ideals without the threat of prosecution for what is labeled as the opposite of love speech? Will the majority get a fair hearing and justice in the courts if it cries out that such diametrically opposite proclamations to the values it holds is a speech other than that which is love, and that they feel threatened by the pounding and virtual overpowering of the minority over them? Will someone now argue that this is the way that the minority was feeling before they could "come out"?

The rational questions could then be: Is justice being served by swinging the pendulum from one extreme to the other? Will there be equity when one successfully political party forms the government and secures the spoils for its supporters at the expense of the equal distribution of the welfare of the state for all its citizens? Zooming in closer on issues of the morality of family life, shouldn't the various sides be left to coexist without one side being kept under, or threatened with state surveillance as to what is taught and proclaimed to those who come within the private places of their practice, that is their homes, churches, schools, and other institutions all of which fall under their charter of rights?

No one can successfully argue against the restrictions or parameters placed on public proselytizing so as not to infringe on another who has a right to share such open public spaces—parks, plazas, community centers, halls, and all such common spaces. But isn't it equally true that each one or group of those who embrace common beliefs and practices is entitled to their rights of space, of mutual assembly, and of what they do in such spaces once they are no threat to life and property?

Are not adult nightclubs and blue-movie producers and others of their kind free to advertise, promote, and practice their kind of entertainment, against which strict Bible-believing Christians are vehemently opposed? The former does not cry about speech that is not loving coming from the latter. They are aware that Christians in general disagree with their practices and ways of life and speak out against such practices, but they do not seek the courts to protect them. Both groups coexist!

Are not Hollywood and others in the film and entertainment industry free to produce and sell to the consuming public their movies and films, many of which are loaded with immorality, adultery, fornication, debauchery, and wantonness, including violence, against which the same Christian community preaches and teaches, without being charged by the state for 'anti-love' speech against those institutions? They coexist, and the entertainment media is not complaining and crying victims or seeking state protection from the teaching that the church relentlessly makes against the productions.

Hospitals, shopping plazas, educational institutions, and all places that provide service to the public post a disclaimer for any loss or damage to the vehicles parked in the designated parking lots, however such might have occurred. They post these disclaimers although they make passionate and emotional advertisements and promotions inviting and appealing to the public to come in and patronize their goods and services. Shouldn't places of worship and private educational institutions be able to practice and proclaim what they believe, with the understanding that all who come within their precincts and thereby expose themselves to what is being taught, cannot go out and claim damage to their delicate sensitivities and that they were subject to speech other than that which they interpreted as love?

If Christians visit places like brothels or the red-light districts, who would entertain or listen to their cry and any case they would seek to make that their moral values and sensitivities were offended by the practices that they saw? Would the state be careful and protective and defend them and mandate that those places modify the programs to protect the sensitivity of the Christians?

If the above comparisons and probabilities are correct, they evoke a number of questions:

1.  Why are some states, especially in the west, so adamant about restraining, constraining, and even threatening with prosecution those who exercise their inalienable right to publicly disagree with those who "come out" against traditional and more specifically Bible-based family life, beginning with marriage?

2.  What is driving the obvious, injustice against the Christian church in its bid to uphold the Bible-based teachings, values, and principles that have formed the millennia-old acceptable bedrock and social fabric of the home and society at large?

3. Is there any plot or plan that is to be executed by some unseen forces which are merely using the strong arms of the innocent, human legislative and judiciary and even the executive arms of the state to work under the guise of civil rights and liberty?

4. Why doesn't the state protect the rights of the opposing party in parliament, however diametrically diverse their views and policies are, when they come under venomous and sometimes malevolent verbal attacks from the other side? What is the category of those speeches that are made over taxpayers' money?

5. What kind of restraint and constraint can the United Nations in New York, the International Court of Justice in the Hague, and other world bodies exercise over rogue states or countries—or, and more so, the big and powerful ones—who threaten to destroy and annihilate others who do not share their policies? What is the category of such speeches?

When one considers the number of controversies over the two sexes, the genders, and marriage raging out of control like the wild catastrophic fires of Australia and California, and takes specific note that the debates all impinge on Bible foundational family life, one cannot help but raise the alarm level and reiterate questions two and three above with greater intensity.

Why is the original time-and-nature-tested form, structure, and proven pattern of family life coming under such relentless attack by those who, themselves, came into being by the very basic God-designed means for propagating the human species: the male-female sexual relationship? The societal ideal (Christian and non-Christian) still remains that this act is best engaged in through marriage for the establishment of a healthy family. Now opponents of this ideal seem to be turning their backs and questioning its validity, implying that there are other possible means which they seem to know to achieve the same purpose. Again, is there some plot or plan somewhere?

## God Does Not Require State-enforced Worship

Let us remind ourselves that God does not require state-enforced obedience to His commandments or requirements. He gives His created children the power of choice to obey Him through loving obedience. Jesus strongly counseled His followers not to hurt those who order their lives contrary to His divine will (Matt. 13:24–30 and Luke 9:53–56). That is why there is no record of Nebuchadnezzar's expressed hasty, state-enforced obedience to Daniel's God as having been carried out (Dan. 3: 28 & 29). His spiritual shock and high enthrallment upon witnessing God's power to save His faithful servants from the effects of the fiery furnace were short-lived.

The message to present-day followers of Christ is: With the aid of the indwelling Holy Spirit, order your lives in accordance with your knowledge and understanding of God's requirements for your life. Preach and teach and encourage others to do likewise, but leave them to their choices as Joshua did (Josh. 24:15). Respect them as part of your obligation to all men, and "If it be possible, as much as lieth in you, live peaceably with all men" (Rom. 12:18).

This means that the child of God will not support those countries where legislation is passed to prosecute, imprison, or, worse yet, execute those who choose to order their lifestyles contrary to the Biblical standards of marital relationship as fundamentally established in the Garden of Eden, and which we believe still stands with no natural alternative today. "Let them alone" (Matt. 15:12–14) is the divine counsel, but ensure that you are faithfully adhering to what you profess to believe, because the same fate that awaits those who openly violate God's will also awaits those who do so in any form secretly.

From time to time, there have been cases of persons being arraigned in court for cursing, insulting, or blaspheming the name of God. God has no blessing in store for such ardent and even hard-line supporters and prosecutors in His name. The case of Saul, the vicious persecutor, who became Paul the valiant preacher, is a sound Bible example here. (Acts 7:58-9:1-31 & 2Tim. 4:1-8) God does not condone violence from His followers against those who wish to disobey His will. It is ultimately His prerogative to relate with even this group of His children.

That is why Jesus rebuked His ardent but impetuous disciples for conceiving evil against those who did not receive Him. (Luke 9:54-56) Jesus gave another sound warning to His faithful followers then and now in the parable of the wheat and tares recorded in Matthew 13: 24-36. In essence, He cautioned that it is not our responsibility to condemn and separate because in our human limitation, we are only able to see outward (1 Sam. 16: 7), while in His divine discernment, He sees the heart/mind and knows who and what will be eventually.

We are to preach and teach Bible truth publicly in common and permissible places with hatred to no one. We are to teach and live fervently, sincerely and faithfully in our homes, churches, and institutions and He will come and reward everyone accordingly. (Rev. 22: 12)

In the same breath, the state should not use its power to circumscribe how much God's people can do or not do in professing their faith, especially in their designated places of worship, as long as they do not incite violence against nonbelievers. Where God's words talk about His blessing plan for the obedient and whatever opposite it says for those who live and behave contrary to His will, His followers should not be monitored, restrained and circumscribed in their delivery of His message. They are mandated by God to preach and teach about the bounties of His blessings for the loving, obedient children, and the opposite result to the others for their disobedience.

Such monitoring and restraining is what the police of the state does in protecting and upholding the laws. Those who operate in accordance with the laws of the land will get a "Thank you, have a good day!" when stopped for spot checks. Those who violate might get a warning depending on the offence, or they may have to face the proverbial long arm of the law: "It's the law of the land … follow me, please!"

The great difference between the police officer and God's mouthpiece in the person of His faithful followers is that the police officer protects and prosecutes, while the child of God lives exemplarily, teaches and warns unequivocally, but leaves the prosecution and any possible penalty to God. "Dearly beloved, avenge not yourselves, but rather give place unto wrath: for it is written, Vengeance is mine; I will repay, saith the Lord" (Rom. 12:19).

Many religious and theological lecture halls and the dogmas they present are no less guilty of the spread of moral degradation, as they also succumb to the deceptions of the devil. The Holy Scriptures are twisted and turned, even by some of those of the cloth, resulting in God's words becoming points of debate and vain babbling. It was against these religious and theological sophistries that Paul repeatedly cautioned young Timothy in 1 Timothy 1:6 and 6:20; 2 Timothy 2:16; and Titus 1:10 and 2:9. Satan is the mastermind behind them all.

The social powers and influential voices—whether in politics, show business, or industry and commerce—add their bits and pieces of treachery and sinister jabs at the principles of good quality family life the Bible way. The combined effects of these forces are so overpowering that the Bible cautions they could even deceive those who are elected to do God's will (Matt. 24:24).

With such an ominous threat hanging like the sword of Damocles over the head of Bible-believing families—husbands and wives, fathers and mothers, parents and children, siblings, married and singles, and all the categories of relatives—what shall we do? What can we do? The rallying, militant call is simple but very profound: "Let Us Fight Back! Let us build up the pressure!" Put the two statements together, and with the power and force and conviction of Joshua's army (Josh. 6: 20, Heb. 11:30), make a spiritually confrontational shout so that the forces of evil will tremble and their academic, social, and philosophical walls against God's original family ideals will come down. "The Family Is Under Attack. Let Us Fight Back!"

## The Family at the Proverbial Crossroads

Ah! We wish victory could be accomplished in a militant and spiritual confrontational shout! It takes much more than that. Some of the families that Satan has succeeded in destroying have been heard to be leading such shouts and singing, "We are marching to Zion!" and "Onward Christian Soldiers, marching unto war." What might have happened to them? Somewhere along the line, they lost focus. Their vigilance, awareness, and watchfulness were compromised, and they became reduced to mere presenters and hearers of the Word and not doers (Rom. 2:13; Jas. 1:22).

The ultimate effect of these combined forces is that they have pushed the family to the proverbial crossroads. When one is said to be at a crossroads in life, such a person is in a mental state of confusion, uncertainty, bewilderment, and dilemma. Those are apt descriptions of the family in general today. All the pillars, all the ancient landmarks of good healthy family relationship are removed or are being removed.

Relativity and conditionality are the new norms of measurement of behavior in every aspect of relationship. The advocacy of the age seems to be saying that there are no expectations or standards that anyone needs to strive toward anymore. Each man (husband, wife, father, mother, child, relative) sets his or her own standards and moves out to achieve them in this free society without boundaries

(See p. 441 & 442). Little wonder, therefore, that the family is in an utter state of confusion, uncertainty, bewilderment, and dilemma at the crossroad, not knowing where to turn.

## Suggestions for Action

1. Be always mindful that your family is not immune to the attacks of Satan, so be always vigilant and sober (1 Pet. 5:8).

2. Have a positive, healthy state of mind toward family conflicts; see them as challenges instead of problems. Your mind will be better able to grapple together on the confronting issues and find results, aided by inspiration from the God of families.

3. Be conscious and know if you are or your family member is at the crossroads of confusion, uncertainty, dilemma, or bewilderment. Pray to the God of families and seek professional help if the situation continues into or beyond three months and is getting worse.

4. Pray to God for discernment. Allow the Holy Spirit to anoint your eyes with family "eye salve" (Rev. 3:18) so that you can see clearly when a family matter of a potentially destructive nature is arising and take necessary, positive, healthy steps to ward it off and save your family.

5. Practice unprejudicial listening to your family member. Remember, you are not supposed to relate to each other as the opposing political parties do in the parliaments. They listen with the sole intent of opposing and cutting down the other side. Listen to your family member with a healthy, open mind so that together you both or you all can achieve mutual success.

# Chapter 3

# Family Relational Health: A Biblical, Psycho-Social Perspective

**Anchor Text: 3 John 2**

"Beloved, I wish above all things that thou mayest prosper and be in health, even as thy soul prospereth."

**Paraphrased and Applied to Families**

Dear members of the household or family of faith, my greatest wish for you is that you succeed, get ahead in life, do well, enjoy living good, and be healthy physically, mentally, emotionally, socially, and relationally; equally or to (CPH³) the same extent that you are prospering spirituality in a healthy relationship and connection with God and your fellow believers, and in your witnessing and evangelistic life.

## *Priority* Explained

For any matter to be considered a *priority*, it must be seen and evaluated as of prime concern; most important; critical importance; of a pressing nature; of a primary issue. A priority matter has preeminence over all others; it has to be attended to first above, before, and beyond all others. Two immediate and current examples of priority attention are:

1.  **Triage principle**—In the medical prehospital care principle, cases are categorized for attention on the basis of urgency. Priority causalities are those that have life-threatening

conditions and are therefore tagged red for immediate attention. The principle here is that even if other cases arrived earlier, the triage nurse will understandably have them wait and attend to the vitals and other matters of those cases considered a priority.

2. **Aeroplane boarding principle**—There are passengers who fall into the priority class for various reasons, and at the time of boarding, they are identified and invited to board first before all the other passengers.

Against these explanations and examples, let us consider this title chapter: *Family Relational Health: A Biblical, Psycho-Social Priority.* That in itself is a very strong and even powerful statement that could evoke surprising and questioning responses from Bible scholars and general religious thinkers. Comments such as "Really! Where in the Bible is that subject?" or "This topic of family relational health, where in the Bible is it mentioned as psycho-social priority!? I have never seen it in all my reading, studying, and teaching of the Bible!"

As a matter of priority, therefore, let us firstly establish two simple disclaimers where the Bible is concerned, as well as the topic itself. The term *relational health* is not in the King James version of the Bible, from which all verses in this book are quoted except as otherwise stated. Interestingly, the words *relate*, *relational*, and *relationship* are not there either. Of the eighteen times the word *health* is used in the KJV, twelve made direct reference or allusion to physiological health (the state and function of the body), and the other six made inference or allusion to psychological health (the state and function of the mind), as well as to psychosomatic health (the impact of the mind on the body).

So indeed, there is no book or chapter in the Bible that addresses the subject of family relational health, yet the title before us suggests that it is a priority in, or for, the Bible. It therefore makes more relevant and demanding the two questions that were raised earlier.

# Family Relational Health Defined

To set the stage for opening the subject and analyzing the paraphrase of the Anchor Text, let us revisit the working definition of *relational health* as set forth in the Glossary, p. 412. "The quality of the intra- and interpersonal relationship that exists in the active, sound mind of an individual, indicated by the strength, intensity, trend, and patterns of the four psychological vital signs of connection, rapport, bond, and support that influence the individual's daily overall existence as manifested in thoughts, words, perceptions, actions, and general world view."

In summary, what we see here is that family relational health has to do with the quality of the intra- and interpersonal relationships between the individual and him or herself first, then between that individual and other individuals and groups. Those groups could be combinations of persons from the biological family members at home, church members in the temple, study mates or colleagues at school or in the workplace, or in any social setting. If we reduce the definition to a single word, it would be *relationship*.

So the question gets more intense: How does the issue of *family relational health* or simply *relationship* become a biblical, psycho-social priority as laid out above? Let us bring back our paraphrased Anchor Text to help us unpack the issue before us. As we did in Chapter 2, we will pull out each key phrase and analyze it.

## Extrapolation 1

*Original:* "Beloved"

*Paraphrased for Families:* "*Dear* members of the *household or family* of *faith*"

Expressions of endearment like *beloved* are sentiments representing a healthy relational mind. When the apostle Paul made that salutation, his focus was on the members of the household of faith (Gal. 6:10)—fellow Christians, believers, and members of the church. While the church is a religious body of believers (the Body of Christ—1 Cor. 12:27; Eph. 4:12), it is also a social gathering. For a gathering of diverse family members to bond and hold together, their relationship has to be healthy, and who knows that better than God Himself!

**The Early Breaking of Bread**

Consider, for example, the early fellowship gathering from house to house as recorded in Acts 2:42: "And they continued steadfastly in the apostles' doctrine and fellowship, and in breaking of bread, and in prayers." That "breaking of bread" was not the Communion Service only; it was also fellowship meals—potlucks, if we want to contemporize them. Those sittings between brothers and sisters could only be experienced by persons who had a healthy relationship that was common to all. The concept of being in such a relationship was repeated for emphasis in the same chapter, verse 46: "And they, continuing daily with one accord in the temple, and breaking bread from house to house, did eat their meat with gladness and singleness of heart."

God knows that for His church to survive the natural human failure at staying together healthily, He could not leave it to them. That is why, in His divine wisdom, He inspires so many of His appointed leaders to emphasize the critical importance of healthy relationship among the brethren and balance it with the teachings and doctrines that need to set them apart from other social gatherings, hence their being called the Church—the *ecclesia* (Greek), the called-out ones.

In just about all the books of the New Testament era, the clarion call on the members of the church is to relate with each other in a loving, healthy way. Family relational health was a core message of the early, founding leaders of the church. The members were kept together, not firstly by the doctrines, but by the quality of their relational bond; hence, they were comfortable with such terms of endearment as *beloved* and *brothers and sisters.*

## Extrapolation 2

*Original:* "I wish above all things"

*Paraphrased for Families:* "my greatest wish for you is"

Other renditions of the family paraphrase, could be "As a matter of priority, when all my teachings, admonitions, and exhortations are over, this is what I ultimately desire for you … I hope that your experience as a good, practicing Christian will be this" or "When all is said and done, this is what I wish that you will experience as a Christian, as a member of the household of faith."

### Eternal Life Begins in This Life

It is a fact that eternal life begins here in this mortal life, right here on earth amidst the drudgery of sin that the Christian must experience. "Fight the good fight of faith, lay hold on eternal life, whereunto thou art also called, and hast professed a good profession before many witnesses" (1 Tim. 6:12). Our relationship with God should result in our having a foretaste of living the good life here and now. This, in itself, will be a testimony of God's keeping power. This is confirmed in the book of Jude verse 24: "Now unto him that is able to keep you from falling and to present you faultless before the presence of his glory with exceeding joy …"

The keeping power does not mean that the Christian is going to live in isolation or quarantine from the real day-to-day life of the world in which he lives. He is going to live and exist, for all that means, in the same world, same society, and same community as the non-Christian, but there must be palpable, evident difference. God's keeping power will constrain and preserve him from participating in and doing just about everything that everyone else does when such things are not in harmony with what he professes as a practicing Christian. (Read again paragraph 3 of the Preface, p. ix).

He is not going to be a prude or a killjoy. He is not going to be necessarily queer and odd and go out of his way to be a misfit. He is going to be different and distinguishable while being a part of what is happening around him as a good citizen. Paul's statement of wish has an immediate application fervor that is driving it. He wanted his "beloved" to start the joys of their Christian experience in the here and now, and not to wait until the hereafter.

## Extrapolation 3

*Original:* "that thou mayest *prosper*"

*Paraphrased for Families:* "that you succeed, get ahead in life, do well, enjoy living good"

What was the tenor of Paul's pregnant exhortation? What is included in this "above all" that he wanted his "beloved" to experience? What was of such great "priority" that he took time to single it out and present it to them as a virtual stand-alone? The answer is simply profound: that you *prosper.* That is to say, "that you succeed, get ahead in life, do well, enjoy living good."

To a large extent, the churches in Christendom are somewhat divided over the issue of prosperity. There are some who seem to thrive on, but are criticized by others for, preaching a prosperity gospel. Wikipedia defines the prosperity gospel thus:

> Prosperity theology (sometimes referred to as the **prosperity gospel**, the **health and wealth gospel**, or

the gospel of success) is a religious belief among some Christians, who hold that financial blessing and physical well-being are always the will of God for them, and that faith, positive speech, and donations to religious causes will increase one's material wealth. Prosperity theology views the Bible as a contract between God and humans: if humans have faith in God, he will deliver security and prosperity.

Prosperity theology has been criticized by leaders from various Christian denominations, including within the Pentecostal and Charismatic movements, who maintain that it is irresponsible, promotes idolatry, and is contrary to scripture. Secular observers have also criticized prosperity theology as exploitative of the poor.

## Two Extreme Understandings of Prosperity

There are two possible extremes that Christians in general seem to embrace on the issue of prosperity.

### *Prosperity Extreme 1:*
### *Material Prosperity as Manifestation of God's Blessings*

Sometimes there are questions and finger-pointing at the owners and operators of some of the megachurches, and smaller ones too, who teach their members that the test, the evidence, and the manifestation of their relationship with God is their material prosperity. This might be the reason that some of their ministers and leaders have to give clear evidence of that by owning and ever increasing their mansions and airplanes (not just for church or mission but personal, private jets). Some cars are custom-built. They have heralds, as it were, running—that really means driving or flying—before them, announcing their triumphant arrival to conduct some services.

There are those who even run into fraudulent situations with the government, especially on the matter of personal tax obligations.

Some are dragged before the courts to account for their use (misuse/abuse, misappropriation) of the church's money.

***Prosperity Extreme 2:***
***Leanness and Piety are God's Requirements of His People***

The other extreme Christian position on prosperity is that where there is evidence of material success, it is a sign that the person is materialistic and is "building mansions down here and does not want to leave this earth." Some 'saints' even go to the very extreme and pronounce such materially successful persons as going to hell. The spiritual soothsayers declare and decree upon such persons: "Let them go on and enjoy their material now, because they are not going to heaven." They are quick to cite the story of the rich young ruler (Matt. 19:16–29) to substantiate their position.

They conclude that being a good Christian means that you live on your bread and water, which will always be sure (Isa. 33:13–16), and that surviving on the bare minimum is a life of sacrifice, piety, and the hallmark of the true follower of Christ. Some of these persons, however, secretly envy the Christians and others in society with accumulated material gains. Sometimes they express suspicion and cast doubt as to how such success might have been accrued. They brand these persons as Dives and see themselves as Lazarus (Luke 16:19–31). They cite many biblical accounts, some out of context or with convenient (mis)interpretation, to support their position that a Christian who acquires reasonable, visible material possessions is temporal, but they see themselves as spiritual.

Truth be told, neither of the two extremes is correct, nor is it biblical. It was never God's intention for His people to live in abject poverty, but He did caution against material aggrandizement at the expense of seeking one's soul salvation. Jesus addressed such a sordid spiritual case in the parable of a rich man. He closed the story with the counsel: "And I will say to my soul, Soul, thou hast much goods laid up for many years; take thine ease, eat, drink, and be merry. But God said unto him, Thou fool, this night thy soul shall be required of thee: then whose shall those things be, which thou hast provided? So is he that layeth up treasure for himself, and is not rich toward God" (Luke 12:19–21).

## Extrapolation 4

*Original:* "and be in health"

*Paraphrased for Families:* "and be healthy physically, mentally, emotionally, socially and relationally"

This text is one of the most quoted from the Bible during presentations on health. Next to it would be: "If my people, which are called by my name, shall humble themselves, and pray, and seek my face, and turn from their wicked ways; then will I hear from heaven, and will forgive their sin, and will heal their land" (2 Chr. 7:14) and "Is there no balm in Gilead; is there no physician there? why then is not the health of the daughter of my people recovered?" (Jer. 8:22)

The challenge with Paul's use of the word *health* is that, as is the tendency in mainstream society, the church also mainly focuses on the physiological aspect of health. Sometimes it includes a limited reference to mental health, but it certainly does not mention family relational health.

But if Paul were speaking under inspiration, as we know he was, it is safe to believe that his use of *health* would have covered the whole man and gone beyond physiological health - the state and function of the body. God declared man "perfect" at creation. Man was whole and complete and conditionally immortal, subject to his sustained obedience. The man whom God made in His likeness, in His image, and the same man who continued down the centuries to this day, despite the wear and tear of sin, was, and continues to be, a composite being—primarily a twin combination of body and mind (Psalm 139:14).

The body is the visible (external and internal) part, including the brain, and the mind is the active, sound, invisible part. Both aspects functioning with equal treatment and calibration represent God. God would therefore not have us paying keener interest or attention to any aspect of our being, but that we would live with the balanced understanding of our being as "The Temple of the Holy Ghost which is in you, which ye have of God, and ye are not your own? For ye are bought with a price: therefore glorify God in your body, and in your spirit, which are God's" (1 Cor. 6:19–20).

**Health of the Total Person**

We affirm, therefore, that God's servant Paul would not be following his mainstream society then, as ours now, and limit his wish of prosperity in health to the physiological. The Christian life is to be modeled after Christ, and the medical doctor, Luke, gave Him a sound, clean bill of health, as no other of the writers did. "And Jesus increased in wisdom and stature, and in favour with God and man" (Luke 2:52). The pattern of Jesus's earthly human life was one of total balance—intellectually (wisdom), physically (stature), spiritually (favor with God), and socially (favor with man).

To be socially in favor with man—family members; coworkers; church members, affectionately referred to by Paul as "beloved"; and all other combinations—would suggest that there is healthy relationship. And healthy relationship is the mathematical commutative property of relational health. That is to say, healthy relationship = relational health = healthy relationship. We can safely conclude that Paul's inspired wish that his "beloved" be in health, covered the physical, mental, and social/relational aspects of their being.

Paul's wish for his "beloved" did not end with a focus on health. He continued with a significant four-letter word: *even.* In English language class, we are taught that words are dynamic and can have different meanings depending mainly on the context in which they are used and, as well as other factors. The word *even* in the context of Paul's exhortation is categorized in English as a figure of speech. A figure of speech is explained as a word or phrase used in a nonliteral sense for rhetorical or vivid effort. In the case of *even* in our study, it is clear that it falls into the figure of speech called Simile or Comparison. Translated, even means "same as, just like; to the same extent; in the same way."

With what was Paul making a comparison when he wished his "beloved" prosperity and health? Let us remember that he was addressing members of the household of faith—fellow believers and fellow Christians. Look again at the completion of his wish: "that you prosper and be in health, *even* as thy soul prospereth." There is an implied assumption and expectation in that statement. Firstly, consider the assumption/expectation and then the application.

**The Assumption: Spiritual Prosperity—An Expectation**

Earlier, when we spoke about the various aspects of health, we mentioned the physical, mental, and social/relational, but we did not mention the *spiritual.* That omission was deliberate based on the analysis of this particular verse. Paul evidently made reference to the "beloved's" *spiritual prosperity* after he wished for material and health prosperity. Was Paul being materialistic? Was he relegating the spiritual prosperity of his beloved to the back or the last of his wish list for them? Nothing of the kind!

What we see here is what could be called an implied assumption. Paul said to his beloved then, and to those of us upon whom the end of the world has come, "By virtue of the fact that you are a member of the household of faith, a fellow Christian, one who loves the Lord, it can be clearly assumed and expected that you are already experiencing spiritual prosperity." That is tightly packed in the expression as your "soul prospereth."

Paul would continue his reasoning and counsel: "That being so, my beloved, let me remind you to keep and maintain balance to your Christian life in the here and now. God expects you to give good evidence of His blessings, not only that you have a sound, good spiritual connection with Him, but that He is blessing you totally and holistically—physically, materially, socially and mentally."

**Trophies of God's Prosperity**

God does not want His Christian witnesses to be imbalanced in testifying about His care and goodness. We should not go about flaunting our wealth and health, in the same way that we should not go about parading our spirituality (the Pharisees in the marketplace, Luke 7:32; the Pharisees and the Publican, Luke 18:10–13) or imposing how much we are in connection with God more than others. We ought to be trophies that God can refer to as evidence of His well-balanced, well-rounded children.

Paul did not begin with wishing his beloved spiritual prosperity, because it is assumed, expected, and understood that since their first calling was as Christians, their qualifier to be called *beloved*, they would already be on the trajectory to spiritual prosperity. But if they were to be focused on only that aspect of prosperity, they would be unbalanced. They would not do the all-encompassing blessing nature of the gospel much good. They should be able to say to the world: "Look on us, see how balanced we are!" That is one evidence of fulfilling the ambassadorial call of Christ to His followers as recorded by Peter, saying that we are called to show forth the marvelous light (1 Pet. 2:9).

## Extrapolation 5

*Original:* "as thy soul prospereth"

*Paraphrased for Families:* "to the same extent that you are prospering spiritually"

We have been using the term *spiritual prosperity*, pulling that out of the final part of Paul's wishing admonition. However, the word *spiritual* is not in the text. He used the word *soul*, so let us do our regular analysis in order to substantiate our conclusion of spiritual prosperity.

### Biblical Understanding of the Soul (See "soul" on page 285)

The apostle says "as thy soul prospereth." Let us establish first of all that there is not an entity or component of the human being that is called the *soul*. At the Creation, God declared that when He blew His breath of life into the clay/earth body He had formed, His breath made the body into a living soul. He did not say that He placed a soul into the man. He said that His breath of life made the man a living soul—implying that before His breath, man was a dead (or preferably a *pre-sin unalive*), not-living soul. (*Dead* was only applicable after sin). God's life-giving breath electrified the not-living soul. It stimulated all the parts—cells, nerves, tissues, glands, organs—and brought them into a functional, living, operational state.

Prior to the creation of man, God did make some living, moving, functional bodies. He simply called them into being, and He did not declare them souls. One stark difference between those living creatures—animals and birds—and the man whom He created is that there was immediate interaction between God and the man. A *connection* was made and a *rapport* began; they (God and man) began to *bond* as Adam experienced *support* from God. All these have at least one common element: they influence relationships, and therefore our relational heath began with God, hence it is a biblical priority (See 4 Vital Signs of Relational Health, p. 417).

When we speak of our spirituality, the root or origin of the concept is from the Bible account of who God is. It says: "God is a Spirit and they that worship Him, must worship Him in Spirit and in truth" (John 4:24). Our spirituality then is the quality and means of our connection and relationship with God (See pp. 291 & 292).

Going back to the Creation account, when God made man, He built in him a unique capacity to communicate and relate with him, whether they were face to face (Gen. 2: 19) or He, God, was in heaven (Gen. 28:17, Deut. 26:25) and man remained on earth. That means was through the diverse, multifunctional brain–mind combination. Let us not be confused over the twin word *brain–mind* combination with which God made man. We can pause and go to the working definition of the terms *brain* and *mind* in the Glossary (pp. 399 & 408).

As we compare Paul's wish for our prosperity in health to our soul prosperity, the poignant question is: How does the Christian measure or give evidence that his soul is prospering or that he is prospering spiritually?

**Measuring the Prospering Soul**

Firstly, he measures his spirituality by the pattern of his deep, inner conviction of the living presence of God. He measures the same trend by the fervency of his prayer life and study of God's words. He measures his soul prosperity by the depth, simplicity, sweetness, sincerity, and genuineness of his relationship with those "beloved" of the household of faith, beginning with those in his own family and household.

The Christian knows if his soul is prospering by the consistency of his witnessing through his lifestyle, words, and works. He knows the level of soul prosperity based on the level of the rapport that takes place between his mind, conscience, heart, and the Holy Spirit. When we summarize all those tests and assessments of determining the quality of our soul or spiritual prosperity, it boils down again to one word: relationship. Are we prospering? Are we doing well in our relationship with God? Are we getting ahead in our relationship with those of the household or family of faith? How are we doing with our relationship in the community by living and witnessing?

Earlier in this chapter, we agreed that there is a mathematical commutative property between relationship and relational health. Let us take it one step further. The quality of the relationship influences the quality of the relational health and the relational health influences the quality of the relationship.

We could not close this chapter if we did not speak to the issue of psychosomatic health and its implication in Paul's admonition. A quick reminder: Psychosomatic health in essence is the result of the impact of the mind (psychological health) on the body (physiological health). The mind is the engine of the human system. It masterminds (indeed) and commandeers who we are and who we are not. If the state of the mind is healthy, it naturally engenders healthy relationships, and the converse is true. The fulfillment of Paul's wish for us to prosper—to succeed materially, physically, socially, mentally, and spiritually—will be realized primarily by the health of the mind.

Our relational health is critical to our survival at all levels. We have also established that the quality of the connection, rapport, bond, and support between us "beloved" members of the family or household of faith is vitally important. It follows then that this title chapter and the posture of the entire book are true and Bible-based. Relational health is indeed a biblical, psycho-social priority.

## Suggestions for Action

1.  Understand what family relational health really means. Study and repeat it so that you can give your own simple explanation to others.

2.  Check the quality of the relationship that you have with your close family members, church members, and others with whom you relate. Address your mind and determine what you can do to improve. Remember that the largest room in the house is the room for improvement!

3.  Remember that the quality of your life now is an indication of your readiness to live eternally when Jesus returns. Live simply, honestly, and lovingly with all those in your sphere of influence. Run a checklist in your mind and see how you stand with those in your world.

4.  Live humbly within your means. If you are blessed with wealth, be sure to use it wisely to honor and glorify God and bless those around you, especially those who are in need. If you are not wealthy, remember that "godliness with contentment is great gain" (1 Tim. 6:6–12).

5.  How is your spiritual health? That means your relationship with God. Read again the full explanation and pray that the Holy Spirit will inspire you to improve daily through the process of sanctification.

# Chapter 4

# Family Knowledge vs Ignorance

**Anchor Text: Hosea 4:6**

"My people are destroyed for lack of knowledge …"

**Paraphrased for Families**

Many family relationships have been, are being, and will be destroyed due to the lack of knowledge about the vital signs of their God-given family relational health and the necessary skills to improve it.

In considering the impact of ignorance on family relational health, two well-known quotations on ignorance come to mind. One is from God's words, and the other is from man's laws. One of man's core principles of jurisprudence is "Ignorance of the law is no excuse." That means a person who is unaware of a law may not escape liability for violating that law merely because he was unaware of its requirements or expectations.

Under inspiration, Paul counsels on God's behalf, "And the times of this ignorance God winked at; but now commandeth all men everywhere to repent" (Acts 17:30). The understanding here is that God "knows our frame" (Ps. 103:8–14) that we are prone to sin because of ignorance. Unlike man's rigid, unyielding, unmerciful position, He winks. That is to say, He passes it over and offers forgiveness on the basis of the violator's unawareness of the expectations of His law. He does this on the individual level and even the national (See p. 443 in reference to Nineveh).

However, God did not stop there at forgiveness. He went on to issue a warning: "but now," seeing you were offered forgiveness and made aware of the wrong committed, "repent!" Change your course; do not continue on the same path. If you commit the violation again, you will be held responsible and accountable at that time (See p. 248).

In nearly four decades of ministering to families around the world, I have found that ignorance is rife. It is all-pervasive. It is surprising, even alarming, to discover that that which appears as common sense for some is capital ignorance for others. That state of mind is expressed in so many ways:

- "Counselor, the truth is I did not know that would cause such a problem!"

- "I honestly did not know better; I thought it would be okay with him."

- "I was shocked when I saw how he reacted. I did not know that a simple comment that I made could be seen that way."

The bemoaning, the regret, the remorse, the pleas, and the apologies go on and on, but ignorance had already played its woeful part. Alas!

## God Bemoans His People's Ignorance

God had His "Alas!" moment over His people because of their ignorance. Our Anchor Text captures the Creator-Redeemer's parental sadness and pain: "My people are destroyed for lack of knowledge." There is one single word that captures the intensity of the phrase "lack of knowledge". It is *ignorance*. On the basis of previous and future comments on the subject, it is safe to declare that the greatest threat to quality family relational health around the world is ignorance.

It is this discovery coming out of the family relational health lab that led to the paraphrase of God's lament over His people, applied directly to families. Let us continue now to do our analytical work, as we have done with previous paraphrased verses.

## Extrapolation 1

*Original:* "My people are destroyed for lack of knowledge"

*Paraphrased for Families:* "Many families *have been* ... destroyed for lack of knowledge."

Most adults have seen family breakups in their lifetime. Marriages have broken up after one month, one year, ten years, twenty years, thirty years, and more. Parent–child relationships have been destroyed, as evidenced by many coming before the courts for resolution and ruling.

The same is true of sibling relationships, in-laws, and all the other categories of family relationships. Tune in to Judge Judy, Dr Phil, Montel Williams, Lauren Lake (on Paternity Court) among others on US television and in other countries. Open a newspaper, magazine, or tabloid—there they are. There is always a hefty serving of family feuds and sensational stories of sordid family life. Commendations to those programs that offer off-stage professional care for those who will access the service.

Family breakups are now so normalized that some stories have become serialized into staple entertainment. Washing one's proverbial dirty linen in the public domain has seemingly become one way to stardom and celebrity status (See p. 243).

But let us not fool ourselves. Many of those in the audience who are cheering and laughing are evidently being entertained, but in deeper, quiet, reflective moments, they grimace at the sights and sounds they experienced on the show. Those among the "bold" and some who are really "beautiful" who come forward on those programs also have their moments of painful reflection, introspection, and recrimination.

So, after the slew of lurid entertainment—lambasting and counter-lambasting, denunciating and disparaging, and overexposures (not just verbally, but in extreme cases literally too)—one can't help but ask: Why do members of hurting families go through such pain, regret, and remorse, resulting in personal and even subsequent family dysfunction?

The reality is that God did not wire the human relational mind to experience grief, loss, and pain. All these are the result of sin. God made the mind, the highest faculty of man, to be in a healthy relationship with Him, and subsequently with his fellow human beings, beginning with the marriage partner, children, other relatives, and friends.

## The Eye and Mind Sensitivity Analogy

Like the eye, which cannot accommodate foreign matter, the relational mind cannot accommodate foreign relational matters as described above. The mind was originally wired to accommodate joy, happiness, peace, togetherness, love, harmony, and the like. But there is yet another reason for the painful residual effects of relational tirading. God Himself has given the answer in Hosea 4:6, following immediately after His lament: they reject knowledge, quite simple and straightforward!

## Rejection of Family Knowledge

Rejection of knowledge is the acceptance or embrace of ignorance. We just cannot have both. It is a matter of choice. One either chooses to be armed with the knowledge of quality, healthy family relationship or to live with the consequences of the natural opposite: destructive ignorance. Rejection of knowledge can be done in one of the following ways or a combination of the two:

## 1. Utter defiance

This is the case of dismissal or denial by the individual of what is presented. There are countless instances when persons have been exposed to the biblical sound teachings and admonitions on how they should order their lives morally and in accordance with God's ideals for family life. Many of those—especially among the young, vibrant, and vivacious—say outrightly that such teachings are not for them. They consider many biblical, moral boundaries to be restrictive and even antiquated, especially marriage, the original ideal for beginning a family. They say things like:

- "This tie-down business is not for me!"
- "I have to live some life first before I tie myself down to family life."
- "Getting married and settling down is for older people; I am not ready for that!"

Unfortunately, some of them eventually never got the opportunity to return from their chosen wayward pattern of life. They get stuck, and unlike the prodigal son (Luke 15:11–32), they are destroyed therein. Then there are those who, after expending quite an amount of their substance in riotous living, do get back on the right path of family life, but with limited time and quality to offer. Sometimes they are a burden, in more ways than one, to those with whom they join themselves.

Some of these persons look back over the foolish, sometimes wanton, lifestyles from which they narrowly escaped. Then they become so rigid, demanding, and overbearing with their children and spouses that they run the risk of destroying their family in an effort to prevent others from following their own previously mistaken path.

## 2. Deliberate, conscious avoidance

This is manifested when one is aware that knowledge and sound teaching are available but chooses not to access them. Here is a touching example. Everything was set for a two-week family-life series to be conducted in a major city in Jamaica. Upon hearing of the upcoming meetings, a prominent member of the host church told another, "I will not be attending, because I know that it is Elder Gordon who will be making the presentations. I know what he is going to say, and at this time, I am not ready for that kind of straight talk. I prefer not to hear." She did not attend, and her failing marriage and family did crumble.

At worst, that was a case of relational and familial suicide. But that is the result of rejecting knowledge using the deliberate avoidance method.

At the end of the day, whether the rejection is by defiance, denial, or avoidance, the result is the same: damaged or ultimately destroyed family life.

Before God made that lamenting pronouncement about the imminent destruction of His people in Hosea 4, He had presented a litany of family relational grievous ills of which they were guilty (verses 1–5): lying, swearing, murders, adultery, and similar immoralities. Sounds like He was talking about our present, twenty-first century societal ills. Prophetically, He was!

In so many cases, the records of the Bible are as prophetic as they are historical. That is what Paul in Romans 15:4 and 1 Corinthians 10:11 was teaching. It is not enough to read about the errors, mistakes, and failures of previous generations. The records were preserved in the interest of posterity, with the hope that those who came after would not mount the same horse and gallop down the same road. But alas! We never seem to learn.

## Extrapolation 2

*Original:* "My people are destroyed for lack of knowledge"

*Paraphrased for Families:* "Many families ... *are being* ... destroyed for lack of knowledge"

The late televangelist Pastor Charles D. Brooks, in his sermon "Sodom-Bound" (1980), gave a very powerful, contemporary, imaginative account of the beginning of sodomy as recorded in Genesis 13:13 and Genesis 19. He described the society then as "being pleasure mad." He said they were so obsessed with pleasure-seeking that they seemed to have run out of pleasure. One day, some fellow put money into a pot for anyone who could come up with some new and rare kind of pleasure that had not been tried before.

Pastor Brooks, in his characteristic dramatic style, hit a crescendo to his mental, inspirational ingenuity. He said: "And your mind cannot imagine what they came up with!" He said it so gruelingly slow and pathetic that the congregation shuddered as he portrayed, with disgusting imagery, the new low to which sin made the society descend.

It sounded like our state of moral decadence today as a pleasure-mad society. In the process of relentless pleasure-seeking, many families are being destroyed. Amidst the monumental scientific, and technological advances of the times, family relational health is on the decline. The old landmarks of good, stable family life are being removed at the extreme expense of freedom to be oneself. This is reminiscent of the days in ancient Israel when everyone did what was pleasing in his own sight and was therefore a law to himself (Judg. 17:5 and 21:24-25).

## Being Lost with Light in Hand

It is pathetic that in this age of enlightenment, when the prophecy that "knowledge shall increase" (Dan. 12:4) is being continuously fulfilled (not only theologically but psychologically and relationally), we are witnessing the continuous decline and disintegration of quality human and family life. The application of this section of our paraphrased verse, "many families *are being destroyed* for lack of knowledge," is a perfect example of a man being lost with the light in his hand.

Why is he lost? The first and most obvious reason is that he never turned on the light. The second is a remote likelihood, but not improbable: he did not know how to turn on or how to use the light. Let us apply these two possible reasons to the families upon whom this agonizing fulfillment is taking place.

1.  **They have not turned on the light.**

    This means that many families who are being hurt, frustrated, not finding quality relationships, or opting out have more than survival knowledge at their fingertips. This is literally so: at their fingertips! Twenty, thirty, or more years ago, information and knowledge about good family life was only available in books. Today, these books run the risk of being described as boring.

    In the past, there were volumes of heavy books, various compendiums of encyclopedias, and others. Today, we have the same and even more information and knowledge in soft copies. There are audio versions. Downloadable apps are proliferating everywhere. There is do-it-yourself material for just about every imaginable question, concern, instruction, or counsel. And of course, we can simply ask Google, say, "How should a husband treat his wife?"

    Actually, I just tried it. I am sitting and writing under my famous St Julian mango tree (from which one ripe mango just fell!), and I picked up my Samsung smartphone, went onto Google, and asked that very question! The pages of answers and related questions and links that popped up were overwhelming.

So there is light, and light, and more light! Why then are so many families today lost and ultimately destroyed for lack of knowledge? One clear reason is negligence. They have the light; they have the instructions, counsels, and guidelines to improve, stabilize, and enrich family life but are negligent in applying them.

One extended reason for this negligence is that family members, beginning with husbands and wives and fathers and mothers, are too distracted. Their focus is diffused, and in the process of time, they become victims of the forces of evil (identified in Chapter 2) who have the family under attack.

The glitz and glamour of the age have dazzled the eyes of many, even well-intentioned families. They become deceived by the charms of life—"For all that is in the world, the lust of the flesh, and the lust of the eyes, and the pride of life, is not of the Father, but is of the world" (1 John 2:16). They are left only to realize that their vision of a good family life has become impaired. They have been attracted to, and become distracted by, lights other than those which they set out to embrace, own, and follow. They fail to turn on their own light and instead follow others that appear to be brighter, but which pull them down the path of destruction. They are lost with the light in their hands.

## 2. They don't know how to use the light.

The second reason for the man being lost with the light in his hand is that he might not know how to use it. He might not have the simple, basic skill necessary to turn it on. In applying this possibility to families being destroyed for lack of knowledge, the operative word in the explanation is *skill*. That is the how-to. Many relationships have been damaged because the average person simply does not know how to avoid it.

Some acts of life and relationship are instinctive, ingrained, or some would say we were born knowing how. It is equally true that some are learned and acquired along the path of growth and development. We do not just get up and automatically experience good family relational health. Some aspects of it have to be taught and learned. Not everything happens or is learned merely by nature. Some have to be nurtured.

With direct reference to the growth in the Christian's life, the apostle Paul posed these questions: "How then shall they call on him in whom they have not believed? And how shall they believe in him of whom they have not heard? And how shall they hear without a preacher?" (Rom. 10:14). The answer is simply that all those ideals and expectations are not possible if the one who is supposed to preach, teach, and impart the necessary knowledge and skills to those who need them in order to grow, has not done his or her job.

This same principle is applicable to family life. There are husbands and wives, fathers and mothers, children and family members who genuinely do not know how to meander through some mazes of life. They just do not know how. Ignorance is not just rife, it is real. And, as strange as it might sound to some, ignorance is natural.

Someone has suggested that marriage is a gift from God with a do-it-yourself label. Maybe one of the greatest evidences of this fact is that, unlike equipment and appliances that come with operational manuals, babies come with none! This may explain why many young parents experience some amount of anxiety, confusion, uncertainty, frustration, and even depression as they grapple with the challenges of parenting through all the stages of the child's development.

Many crying babies have become victims of shaken baby syndrome due to the ignorance of parents or caregivers. This is just one case of lack of skill in family life.

Lack of knowledge takes on multiple forms throughout the life cycle of the family, from obstetrics through pediatrics on to geriatrics. Ignorance in the form of lack of relational and management skills, kills!

I remember one day in my office when I had to exercise my clinical skills of emotional restraint to avoid breaking down and crying with a client. His marriage was breaking apart, and he and his wife had come for marriage counseling on the insistence of their adult child. But the wife had laid out her cards up-front: "Anything that can help him and me as individuals is fine with me. But as for the marriage, I have had enough. I am not prepared to continue in it any longer, not being sure what will happen."

And so it was for that marriage. All the vital signs were not merely low, they were nonexistent. It became terminal, and it died. So what was the clinical restraint that I had to exercise on myself with reference to the husband? In one of his private, individual sessions, he unashamedly admitted to errors he had made in the marital relationship. Of course, he had gone through it in the couple's session as well, but his wife heaped skepticism and scorn on his acceptance of guilt and responsibility by saying, "Counselor, I heard that and saw him like that before." For her, his contrition meant nothing.

As the husband recounted his litany of failures, which was therapeutic and even cathartic for him, he pulled his chair closer to my desk. He bowed his head on the desk for support, and in a deep, resonant voice, summed it up: "Counselor, I did not know better. I did not know that those things could cause this" (meaning the break-up of the marriage). His cry mimicked those of the lost souls on the Day of Judgment: "The harvest is past, the summer is ended, and we are not saved" (Jer. 8:20). These persons are pining, "Too late."

I sorrowed deeply for this middle-aged husband and father. Based on the consistency of his account during the sessions, I had no reason to question his honesty and truthfulness in that summative statement: "I did not know better." I have heard similar comments many times, before and after that case. Fortunately, some explained their lack of knowledge after their ignorance was expunged, and they had the opportunity to make amends, improve, and continue their relationships. Unfortunately, others sought help too late.

**The Do-It-Yourself (DIY) Principle of Family Relational Health**

Marriage and family life operate to a large extent as DIY, simply because each couple and each family is different. Each is unique. Each has its own endemic identity and culture. No two couples or families are the same, even if they were formed by identical twins.

Behind closed doors, each family develops its own brand of general practices and relationships. This remains true even if family members observe, admire, and copy something from their family of origin or from others with whom they interact. When they bring the copy to their own home, they intuitively apply their DIY, rebrand it, and it becomes their unique version. This is DIY at its best (Review The Family Relational Health Lab, pp. 9-11).

At the same time, with all the diversions and differences that set each individual, each couple, and each family apart, there are equally commonalities that we naturally share. Therefore, like everything else in life, DIY has its limitations. We all need common knowledge and skills in several aspects of life. "No man (no couple and no family) is an island; no one stands alone." We do need each other. Complete knowledge of good family life and relational health is not resident with any one couple or family.

Churches and schools need to understand how important it is to plan and provide marriage, parenting, family life, and relational health seminars and training programs for families that are a part of their communities. Companies and business enterprises need to similarly invest in these aspects of their human resource development programs. A healthy family relationship at home will be carried over into the workplace and positively affect productivity and overall performance.

Shared knowledge and shared skills in family relational health, done in an unimposing way and added to the natural DIY understanding, can only help to dispel relational ignorance and save many families from being destroyed for lack of knowledge.

## Extrapolation 3

*Original:* "My people are destroyed for the lack of knowledge"

*Paraphrased for Families:* "Many families … *will be* destroyed for lack of knowledge"

Despite the intensity and gripping imagery of the appeal and caution regarding ignorance about relationships, some are still going to fall prey. Why would any couple or any family, with limitless and available diverse resources on family relational knowledge and skills, suffer destruction for lack of knowledge? Why would they not heed God's passionate appeal: "Say unto them, As I live, saith the Lord GOD, I have no pleasure in the death of the wicked; but that the wicked turn from his way and live: turn ye, turn ye from your evil ways; for why will ye die, O house of Israel?" (Ezek. 33:11).

There are two possible answers: the mystery of iniquity and the I Did It My Way (IDIMW) approach, which is the extreme version of DIY.

**The Mystery of Iniquity**

The Bible gives two accounts in Isaiah for the separation between God and man. They are sin and iniquity: "But your iniquities have separated between you and your God, and your sins have hid his face from you, that he will not hear" (Isa. 59:2). In the original Greek, *sin* means "to miss the mark." As a result of the impairment that sin has caused in man's mind (the avenue that God created for communication), he has not regained total control over it and therefore cannot naturally hit the mark of righteousness or right-doing in accordance with God's standards of holiness.

With all his good intentions, man sometimes misses the mark. This is the struggle that Paul captures in Romans 7:19–20: "For the good that I would I do not: but the evil which I would not, that I do. Now if I do that I would not, it is no more I that do it, but sin that dwelleth in me." We can conclude therefore that sin is a disease affecting the mind and its relational functions.

The good news is that victory is possible through God's grace. Even if this victory is intermittent, God makes provision, remembering that we are human. That is why He counsels, consoles, and encourages the struggling sinner: "My little children, these things write I unto you, that ye sin not. And if any man sin, we have an advocate with the Father, Jesus Christ the righteous" (1 John 2:1).

The negative effects of sin naturally affect the human family. Each individual in the group makes his 'contribution' to the sin effect on them all. "As it is written, there is none righteous, no, not one: There is none that understandeth, there is none that seeketh after God. They are all gone out of the way, they are together become unprofitable; there is none that doeth good, no, not one" (Rom. 3:10–12).

### The Power of Choice: Man's Only Real Possession

A brief review reminds us that at Creation, God made a perfect man with conditional immortality subject to His loving obedience to his Creator. Man's mind was perfect and had the power of choice, which up to this day is the only personal possession any human being has. Even his thoughts are not truly his own! They are either inspired by the indwelling Holy Spirit or motivated by the impressions on the mind by the warring, opposing evil forces around us. The power of choice is all that we have to determine which side we prefer: the side of God and His righteousness, or the side of Satan and his unrighteousness.

God started off Adam and Eve with a perfect mind through which He was to maintain communion between them. They chose the route of disobedience and unrighteousness, and their minds consequently became tainted and damaged by sin. But as we have already noted above through John, God never gave up on them.

Following God's pattern, family members ought to cultivate and practice the spirit of forgiveness and reconciliation. "And forgive us our debts, as we forgive our debtors" (Matt. 6:12). No one has the right to hold a hard end against the other, bearing in mind that the forgiver today might need to be the forgiven tomorrow.

### Sin Vs Iniquity

Sin, correctly labeled, is a mental disease. It distorts the aim and projection of the mind toward good, resulting in our missing the mark, firstly in our own relationship with God and consequently in our relationship with our fellow human beings, beginning with our family members.

When sin goes unheeded and unchecked, and ingrains itself in the mental psyche of the individual, the Bible raises the danger bar from yellow or amber to red and calls it *iniquity*. This advanced stage of sin is not a mere missing the mark of righteousness. It is a conscious, consistent, calculated choice to defy righteousness and embrace evil. Sin is a mental disease. Iniquity is psychic!

Sin is the transgression of the law—God's moral standards of behavior. "Whosoever committeth sin transgresseth also the law: for sin is the transgression of the law" (1 John 3:4). These laws or commandments or precepts are what God, in His divine wisdom, established to guide man in his relationship with his Creator (the first four of the Ten Commandments) and with his fellow human beings (the last six of the ten) in Exodus 20.

### Relational Ingression, Transgression, Digression, and Regression

To transgress is to aim right but end up going away from the target. The prefix *trans* means "away from," "beyond," and "across." The last one, *across*, is even more significant when taken against James's statement that "For whosoever shall keep the whole law, and yet offend in one point, he is guilty of all. For he that said, Do not commit adultery, said also, Do not kill. Now if thou commit no adultery, yet if thou kill, thou art become a transgressor of the law." Applied, that means: When you transgress in one point, the effect goes across and affects the others. It metastasizes in spirit and damages the quality and validity of all the other nine, because all ten are inextricably bound together. One is not and cannot be observed or kept without or while violating the other.

The same principle applies to the fruit of the Spirit (Gal. 5:22–23). Note carefully that it is not plural *fruits* but singular *fruit*. "But the fruit of the Spirit is love, joy, peace, longsuffering, gentleness, goodness, faith, meekness, temperance: against such there is no law." The principle applied means that one cannot have a part of the fruit and claim to have the whole fruit. One cannot display one or two of the characteristics of the Spirit (i.e. the Spirit of Christ; Romans 8:9) and behave contrary in other respects and aspects of life (Review p. 8).

The struggling sinner, the struggling family member, most times has his or her eyes on the target—the ideal quality family relationship. Unfortunately, between aiming and throwing, between deciding and acting, between intention and decision, his or her vision gets blurred, and upon throwing or acting, the ideal or the mark is missed. That is the effect of sin on the relational mind.

When the target is achieved, when the mark is hit, we can borrow the verb *ingress* from the biological term *ingression* and make it into the opposite of transgression. To *ingress* means to go or grow or enter within. Applied as the opposing action of *transgress* in human behavior, it means to grow within or enter into harmony via the mind with the law or established principles or expectations.

It is experiencing the fulfillment of the Lord's promise: "I will put my law in their inward parts, and write it in their hearts; and will be their God, and they shall be my people" (Jer. 31:33). In the context of family relational health, it means that the trying husband or wife, father or mother, or any family member is succeeding in harmony with the standards, expectations, and desires of healthy relationships, as he or she is growing inwardly in relationship with God and his family.

### Keeping Growth through Affirmation and Encouragement

Much caution needs to be exercised here. Without affirmation, encouragement, and challenge to keep progressing, we run the risk of *digressing* and ultimately *regressing*. It is still true that encouragement sweetens labor. One sure way to help family members remain on the right path of healthy relationship is to affirm, encourage, and, where necessary, challenge them to keep on keeping on.

Too many well-intentioned efforts fail because affirmation and encouragement were not given to help stabilize and sustain the correct action and behavior. Validation plays an important role in the continuation of that which is good and right. When positive support is not given, regression can set in. If the regression is not corrected in the right way, and if remorse gives way to indulgence, then a sweet taste (characteristic of sin) begins to develop in the mind. Thus, a trajectory toward iniquity can become established. Sin without remorse and a desire for repentance, restoration, and reconciliation becomes iniquitous.

### Last Day Signs

In this deteriorating state of mind, the degree of the wrong committed is not only sinful, it is iniquitous. It becomes reprehensible. It is done glaringly and spitefully. The prophecy is that in the last days, iniquity shall abound. "And because iniquity shall abound, the love of many shall wax cold" (Matt. 24:12). Before that last-day pronouncement, the Bible records the preflood state of society: "For as in the days that were before the flood they were eating and drinking, marrying and giving in marriage, until the day that Noe entered into the ark, and knew not until the flood came, and took them all away; so shall also the coming of the Son of man be" (Matt. 24:38–39). And "Which sometime were disobedient, when once the longsuffering of God waited in the days of Noah, while the ark was a preparing, wherein few, that is, eight souls were saved by water" (1 Pet. 3:20).

It is interesting to note how God summarized the combination of the three (sin, transgression, and iniquity) through the Prophet Ezekiel with reference to the deeds of one king of Babylon, and which summary is quite timely and appropriate for the sinful despots of our day: "Therefore thus saith the Lord GOD; Because ye have made your iniquity to be remembered, in that your transgressions are discovered, so that in all your doings your sins do appear; because, *I say*, that ye are come to remembrance, ye shall be taken with the hand. And thou, profane wicked prince of Israel, whose day is come, when iniquity *shall have* an end" (Ezek. 21:24–25). God's guarantee is that they (sin, transgression, and iniquity), regardless of their might and main, shall end.

Our conclusion then is that as a result of the abounding degree of recalcitrance, stubbornness, and obstinacy, all compounded into iniquity, many families will be destroyed because they would have trampled on knowledge and willingly become and remain ignorant.

## The IDIMW and Cherished Ignorance

The second reason some families will be destroyed for lack of knowledge is their practice of the extreme version of DIY, which we will call *IDIMW—I Did It My Way*. Earlier, we affirmed the positive, necessary, and understood practice of DIY. We considered its limitations and potential dangers. When a family member decides to push his DIY with a narcissistic attitude and portrays himself as knowing it all, he is on a path to self-destruction.

This commentary is not criticizing Frank Sinatra and his song "I Did It My Way." The sentiments of his song were essentially an affirmation of the positive, uplifting sense of self-esteem, self-actualization, and accountability—a positive sense of satisfaction on one's life journey. The IDIMW state of mind that leads to individual and family destruction begins on the path of *cherished ignorance*. This means that the IDIMWist knows that he does not know but fools himself by trying to impress others that his not knowing does not matter because he will get by just like the others who know.

### *Impulsive Corrective Disorder (ICD)*

One little-known characteristic of this narcissistic personality is what we will call in this analysis, impulsive corrective disorder (ICD). Such a person is always seeing and pointing out the faults, errors, and weaknesses in others. It is an inordinately pedantic attitude that makes the person always show off his knowledge at the expense of the comfort of others. As such, he thrives in the attitude of correcting, modifying, and offering his own spin on what was already clearly stated before he spoke. The intent is not to give credit to the first speaker but to show his "better" way of putting it forward.

ICD is a kind of self-importance that comes with comparing oneself to others, using one's own standards of achievement and behavior as the means of judgment, and then showing oneself to be the victor in this self-devised competition. It involves an inordinate sense of self-importance and exaltation. It is completely pharisaical in nature. (Luke 18:9–14). This attitude is more than self-sufficiency; it is self-conceit. It means not knowing but not wanting to know; pretending to know but not knowing; and being proud of and even seeming to enjoy one's ignorance.

Cherished ignorance that goes by unchecked does not end there; it leads to *practiced arrogance.* This descending stage is known by the person's regard for virtually no one. He respects no one or gives respect in a patronizing way. The arrogant person is full of himself and cares about, or for, no one except for his chosen few, who in most cases are his lackeys who benefit from his spoils.

The downward path of the IDIMWist continues on its way to destruction, gathering momentum and becoming *persistent annoyance.* Who can be more irritating and annoying and revolting than an arrogant character who is always hurting and upsetting others? The persistent annoyance makes the possessor always disagreeable and naturally unfriendly except to people of his or her kind.

### Terminal Relational Incorrigibility (TRI) and Hypnotism

With little or no feelings for others, this person, who is relationally terminal, drops to a new and final low and demonstrates *overbearing intolerance.* The first victim is himself. He is very impatient with and tends to be hard on himself. This is not a case of setting high performance standards. It is the feeling that "I should never be outdone and certainly not corrected." This is a case of terminal incorrigibility and is the final stage of relational illness. This intolerant person is easily upset and almost unforgiving—unless the forgiveness will be to his advantage.

Eventually, the IDIMY person hits rock bottom, and *devastating grievance* pervades his mind, the home atmosphere, and the entire relationship circle to which he belongs. This is manifested in psychological abuse in all forms: emotional, social, and spiritual. Physical abuse is also employed if he believes that is necessary to achieve his goal to stay on top. He is really at the bottom of the human relationship scale but is mesmerized into thinking the very opposite.

This is self-applied relational hypnotism. He is seeing relationships in a false light and genuinely believes that this is the way to be, because things are going the way that he steers them to go. This person has reached the point of no return and will carry all within his power headlong to destruction. At this final and terminal level, he or she might be aptly described as satanic, which is the total and complete opposite of being godly.

Family relational health can either strive toward the peak of quality and goodness or plunge into the abyss of degradation. This is influenced by the values that families place on arming themselves with education, thereby warding off ignorance. Their individual and corporate decisions will determine whether or not this prophecy will be fulfilled upon them. Ignorance needs not consume any individual or family group. There is enough family relational knowledge and skill available to keep everyone relationally healthy. It all comes down to the power of choice.

# Suggestions for Action

1.  Make every effort to arm yourself with knowledge and family relational skills. Look out for and attend good family-life seminars and other activities. Get on a good reading program and strengthen your knowledge about good family relationships.

2.  Exercise your power of choice always to do good. Be always conscious of what you are doing. Do good conscientiously, and enjoy doing so consistently (See the 3 C's p. 157).

3.  Practice affirmation and encouragement to help your family members to do what is right. Do not selfishly withhold commendation for the good efforts of others.

4.  Be always aware of the effects that your behavior and attitude can have upon others. Avoid being arrogant, annoying, and intolerant, and do not cause others to be grieving due to your wrong attitude toward them. This is dangerously unhealthy.

5.  If you know or discover that you have narcissistic traits or behaviors, you need professional help. Do not pretend it away; you will only grow deeper in that state of mind until you can no longer be helped. Get help now.

# Chapter 5

# The Restoration Plan

**Anchor Text: Luke 4:18–19**

"The Spirit of the Lord is upon me, because he hath anointed me to preach the gospel to the poor; he hath sent me to heal the brokenhearted, to preach deliverance to the captives, and recovering of sight to the blind, to set at liberty them that are bruised; to preach the acceptable year of the Lord."

**Paraphrased for Families**

The Spirit of the Lord is within the Church, which He has appointed to preach the gospel of good family relationship to the poor and wounded family members. He has sent the church to heal the brokenhearted spouses, parents, children, and singles; to preach deliverance to the captives of unholy deadlock instead of holy wedlock and recovery of the sight of loving admiration for spouses and others in the family; to set at liberty those family members who are spiritually, emotionally, socially, and relationally oppressed; to preach the acceptable time for family reunion, in preparation for the Lord's return.

## The Church–Hospital Analogy

"The Church is not a rest bed for saints; it is a hospital for sinners." This very powerful church–hospital analogy is often used as church leaders challenge their members to remember the mission of the Church. That mission is to offer hope and healing to the sin-sick souls in the sphere of influence of the Church. One way that the sickness of sin is manifested is in the poor relational health that is experienced between so many husbands and wives, parents and children, siblings, and all other family members.

Relational illness is not endemic to the homes in which it begins. On the contrary, it is very contagious and contaminates other families in the Church whose relational-health immune system is already weak or is compromised because they themselves are not experiencing anything close to healthy relationships.

**Contagious Family Relational Illness**

There are times when it seems that family relational illness is seasonal with serious breakouts. In most cases, the virulence depends on which family becomes infected first. If it is in the leadership core of the Church, for example—the pastor's or elder's or some other prominent family—it appears to spread faster, and if it is not quickly contained, the whole church comes down with various manifestations of relational illness (See p. 244).

There is no immunization program that the Church can implement to make its members immune to relational illness. Therefore, it will always need to have an emergency ward, equipped and ready to respond to any case of illness. Unfortunately, there are times when it appears that the Church has lost its focus or forgotten its core mission. In general, Church leaders are heard to say that the mission of the Church is to prepare souls for the return of Christ. And they are correct. However, there seems to be a reason for the Church's loss of focus, and that is the preparation method that it uses.

It seems that the leadership is not sufficiently aware of the magnitude of relational illness that plagues the Church. If they were, they would be treating the member-patients with the right balance and measurement of spiritual and psychosocial medication. It is disheartening to hear caregivers in the church–hospital negatively lamenting over and even lambasting those who are not relationally well.

Too many times, relational illness between husbands and wives, parents and children, and other family members becomes the topic of the sermon and is presented in scathing attacks and sometimes even ridicule. It is not unusual to hear fun and mimicry being made of challenges that some families have gone through and are even going through, although such comments are usually made with some amount of attempted disguise. But relationally ill members are very sensitive and can pick up innuendoes and even sweeping generalizations. We also know that such persons can be hypervigilant and hypersensitive.

**Incompetent Sermonizing/Care Protocol**

On the next extreme of the ridicule is the lament that is expressed when it becomes known that a particular member is relationally affected: "What is happening in this Church? This is the Lord's house, and this should not be happening to members! Those of you who can't live good faithful lives together better shape up or get ready to ship out!" Certainly there is room for challenges to be expressed, and strong exhortation and upbraiding can be made. But such strong sermonizing medication in this hospital for sinners, ought to be carefully dispensed. If it is not administered in a spiritually clinical way, it runs the risk of driving away the very member-patient it is intended to treat.

Sometimes, spiritual exuberance in pastors and preachers—generally, those without the prerequisite competence and skill to treat certain relational illness—causes more harm than good. Such incompetent care protocol causes many church members to be hesitant in seeking help from their pastor. They do not feel safe and confident, fearing that their personal business might be fodder for the next sermon.

What is the answer to the existing and potential dilemma of relational illness that seems to be ever-present in the Church? The answer has many parts. The first is that the practitioners and caregivers of relational health in the Church ought to be constantly reminded of the environment in which they are operating. It is one of unrelenting and continuously increasing aggressive attacks on the family. It could be described as ebolic in nature, in that it spreads in a rapid and deadly way, like an outbreak of the dreaded Ebola disease.

Let us revisit the paraphrased Anchor Text from Chapter 2: "For we wrestle not against ordinary marital, parental, and general family relational challenges, but against the continuous deteriorating standards of this world; against the subtle forces set at destroying God's original family ideals; and against the corrupt, immoral practices of this age, operating from high academic, religious, social, and other influential stages of society."

**Terrestrial and Cosmic Relational Toxicity**

The relational environment in which families live today, inside and outside of the Church, is negatively charged with relational toxicity from a combination of terrestrial and cosmic forces. It is not in any way ordinary, and therefore it requires more than ordinary treatment, as is customary of many Church clinicians. It would fall into the category of "this kind ..." that Jesus spoke about in Matthew 17:21 and Mark 9:29. Church leaders will therefore need to heed the counsel to "anoint thine eyes with eye salve" (Rev. 3:18) so that they can discern the true source and nature of family relational illnesses and equip themselves to treat it accordingly.

When there is an outbreak of certain diseases, the medical team has to know the environmental conditions under which they are going to work. They know that they need to be armed, equipped, and prepared. They have to get proper briefing on the existing conditions and what they will be up against.

In the case of an outbreak of Ebola, for example, and more currently, that of the 2020 Covid19 Coronavirus Pandemic, responding members of the medical and support teams inclusive of *Doctors Without Borders* or <u>*Médecins Sans Frontières (MSF)*</u> among other first responders, have to go through the preparation protocol before they can arrive on the scene to offer professional help. Doctors wanting to help cannot just get up and go. They have to be properly prepared with their necessary PPEs – PFP3 Masks, Visors, Goggles, Long-sleeve Gowns.

Similarly, those who treat relational illnesses in the homes, the Church and in the community must be properly prepared to offer the necessary assistance, or they, along with those they went to help, will all be victims. Mere willingness and spiritual exuberance will not be able to minister to the on-going outbreak of relational illness in the Church today (See pp. 473 & 476).

**Symptoms and Some Types of Relational Illnesses**

Since we have been talking repeatedly about relational illnesses, let us take a very quick look at some of the major ones. First, let us consider some major symptoms (See p. 107). When family members find themselves displaying any of the following symptoms in a consistent or increasing intensity for three weeks or more, they should not take it lightly. This should be even more arresting to them if there used to be regular, healthy relationships between them and none of the following were present:

- suspicion
- tension
- persistent quarreling
- unresolved conflicts
- poor communication or breakdown in communication
- lack of sensitivity or feeling
- lack of intimacy

- temper tantrums
- lack of family devotion
- bouts of rage and anger
- staying away/out late from home
- lack or reduction of home-based fun and social life

These and similar symptoms result from serious relational illnesses that might have been present or dormant, or are developing due to causes known or unknown. These include the following:

- abuse
- hatred
- uncontrolled anger
- sexual perversion
- unfaithfulness
- betrayal
- divorce
- depression
- grief
- loss
- abandonment

While we are cautioned against being overly reactive and panicky about symptoms of physiological illnesses, we are equally warned to be careful not to take them too lightly. Any onset of debilitating lethargy, dizziness, chest pains, and other arresting conditions like these are among the cautions expressed here. It is to the same extent that family members are to address their relational minds to the onset of the symptoms listed above (CPH[2]).

Church leaders should be aware of such manifestations and prepare members to identify and relate to them properly. In fact, pastors, elders, and family ministry leaders ought to prepare the congregation to be able to detect any possible onset of relational illness and equip them with the necessary first-aid first-responder treatment plan. This can be done through family relational health seminars, training, and awareness programs (See Appendix 1, p. 448).

Against this understanding, it is time to identify the major components of our paraphrased Anchor Text and apply them from the perspective of the Church–hospital analogy.

## Extrapolation 1

*Original:* "The Spirit of the Lord is upon me"

*Paraphrased for Families:* "The Spirit of the Lord is within the church"

The Church is God's called-out agency on earth to carry out His will. There are several Bible references that capture the assurance of the presence of the Spirit in the Church, and equally the assurance that the will of the Lord will be accomplished therein. Here are a few of them:

- **Matthew 10:7–8:** "And as ye go, preach, saying, The kingdom of heaven is at hand. Heal the sick, cleanse the lepers, raise the dead, cast out devils: freely ye have received, freely give."

- **Matthew 28:19–20:** "And Jesus came and spake unto them, saying, All power is given unto me in heaven and in earth. Go ye therefore, and teach all nations, baptizing them in the name of the Father, and of the Son, and of the Holy Ghost: Teaching them to observe all things whatsoever I have commanded you: and, lo, I am with you alway, even unto the end of the world. Amen."

- **John 14:12-14:** "Verily, verily, I say unto you, He that believeth on me, the works that I do shall he do also; and greater works than these shall he do; because I go unto my Father. And whatsoever ye shall ask in my name, that will I do, that the Father may be glorified in the Son. If ye shall ask any thing in my name, I will do it."

- **John 16:13:** "Howbeit when he, the Spirit of truth, is come, he will guide you into all truth: for he shall not speak of himself; but whatsoever he shall hear, that shall he speak: and he will shew you things to come."

When this mandate from the Lord is correctly understood, and especially being aware of the forces against which the Church operates, it can seem daunting. But God's biddings are His enablings. Having called the Church to perform His will, God would already have put in place provision for its success. He will equip and empower her to perform the mandate and accomplish the mission. Therefore, she has no excuse for failure except her failure to rely on His enabling power.

Church leadership and members alike should always be conscious of the spirituality of the membership. They should always be aware of the abiding presence of the Holy Spirit in and among them as individuals and as a congregation. They should always evaluate themselves against the standards to which God holds His Church: "Thus speaketh the LORD of hosts, saying, Execute true judgment, and shew mercy and compassions every man to his brother: And oppress not the widow, nor the fatherless, the stranger, nor the poor; and let none of you imagine evil against his brother in your heart" (Zech. 7:9–10).

Pastors and Church leaders need to constantly check the spiritual pulse to see how well the heart of the Church is beating in harmony with the will of God. Let them delineate the four standards of individual and congregational relational health mentioned in the above counsel from the Lord through Zechariah. That is one sure way to tell how much the Spirit of the Lord is present among them.

## Unspiritual and Unbiblical Acts of Benevolence

Church leaders ought not to fool themselves into believing that the Spirit of the Lord is there when it might not be manifestly so. If they do, they run the risk of having to adopt the name of "Ichabod" (1 Sam. 4:21–22). The Spirit departs when we fail to do His bidding and are not aware of our failure and, ultimately, His consequential departure.

The Church, like any good social group, humanitarian society, organization, or club, might be engaged in acts of kindness and welfare to the community at large, but if the works are not done in the Spirit of the Lord, they would still not be regarded by God as fulfilling His will. They would be seen as unspiritual benevolence. God's counsel through the prophet Micah bears this out:

> Wherewith shall I come before the LORD, *and* bow myself before the high God? shall I come before him with burnt offerings, with calves of a year old? Will the LORD be pleased with thousands of rams, or with ten thousands of rivers of oil? Shall I give my firstborn *for* my transgression, the fruit of my body *for* the sin of my soul? He hath shewed thee, O man, what is good; and what doth the LORD require of thee, but to do justly, and to love mercy, and to walk humbly with thy God? (Mic. 6:6–8)

The hallmarks of the maturing child of God and the servants in His church are Christlike humility, genuineness, simplicity, sincerity, and sweetness. These are anchored in each individual's conscious, conscientious, and consistent personal study of God's Word (the Holy Bible), other inspired books, and a private, personal prayer life following the example of our Lord as recorded in Matthew 14:23; Mark 1:35, and Luke 6:12. The latter is the most critical, as it should keep us humble, always seeking the inspiration and approval of God for every act performed in His name.

Let us also be careful not to interpret this to be advocating religious piety that might not be inspired by the total indwelling of the Holy Spirit. That indwelling also leads the individual to order his or her life in harmony with the total pattern of the life of Christ inclusive of adherence to all of God's commandments (1 John 2:4).

## Extrapolation 2

*Original:* "because he hath anointed me to preach the gospel"

*Paraphrased for Families:* "which He has appointed to preach the gospel of good family relationship"

### The Original Purpose of the Gospel

It appears that present-day Church leadership, to a large extent, has forgotten the original purpose of the gospel. The good news (gospel) was first recorded in Genesis 3:15 in response to a broken relationship issue. Too many in the Church have lost this fundamental, critical fact about the gospel.

The relationship between heaven and earth was damaged at the moment that man sinned in his mind. The immediate effect was the estrangement between man (Adam) and his Creator (Gen. 3:10). Naturally and consequently, the relationship between the first two human beings, the first couple, and the first family was impaired (Gen. 3:12). The impairment began with the blame game, thus the beginning of family relational illness.

We reiterate with strong emphasis that the protoevangelium of Genesis 3:15 was announced in response to a broken relationship in gradual proportion. *Gradual proportion* means that the efficacy of the intervention of Christ was not all revealed at one time. From the time that Adam and Eve sinned, the redemptive grace of God through

Christ toward the sinner was gradually taught, understood, and implemented, and will be culminated at the second return of Christ.

Satan has a vested interest in seeing our relational illness go undetected, untreated, uncured, and ultimately unhealed. In this way, his plan, which is the total destruction of the human family and his hopeful usurpation and overtaking of the throne of God, will be realized (Isa. 14:13–14). God does not want our relational hurts and wounds to be merely cured and therefore noticeably absent. Instead, He wants us to experience total healing (body and mind) so that we are complete in Him.

## Healing of the Family Equals Healing of the Church

Correctly understood, salvation is about healing the broken relationship between God and man, and the evidence of that healing here on earth is the healthy relationship between human beings, beginning with the various family categories and groupings as we continue to list them, always beginning with the foundation relationship of husbands and wives (See them on pp. 466-468).

The Church is that corporate gathering of all the families, and that corporate gathering is referred to as the body of Christ (1 Cor. 12:12–27). Whatever the historical, theological, doctrinal, or any other teachings of the Church, it must redound to "the perfecting of the saints, for the work of the ministry, for the edifying of the body of Christ: Till we all come in the unity of the faith, and of the knowledge of the Son of God, unto a perfect man, unto the measure of the stature of the fullness of Christ" (Eph. 4:12). The sum total of this book is a healthy relationship between human beings (husband-wife, father-mother, parents-children, and other family members) and between human beings and God. This is the gospel of good family relationship that all Church leaders and members need to embrace, live, and teach.

# Extrapolation 3

*Original:* "to the poor"

*Paraphrased for Families:* "to the poor and wounded family members"

Among the functions that God expects the Church to carry out is the healing of the sick. Contrary to the apparent interpretation of most present-day Christians, healing is not limited to the miraculous, and even instantaneous, visible recovery from physical infirmities and maladies.

There are TV and radio evangelists who thrive on the promotions for their meetings: "Come for your miracle, come experience your healing from ..." hypertension, cancer, skeletal malfunctions, disabilities, and the list goes on. Some reportedly tag a financial "seed of faith" as a sure condition for such healing. In some cases, the amount of money, still called an offering, is determined by the size of the needed miracle. A larger life-threatening need requires a larger seed of faith. There is no biblical evidence for bartering of faith on financial grounds (See Acts 8: 14 – 24).

## Jesus's Model of Healing

We believe that the safest understanding of healing is the model established by Jesus Himself. He had a mind-body-restoration combo approach, and in that order. Consider the case of the man sick of the palsy (modern paralysis) recorded in Mark 2:1–12 and elsewhere. The condition for the man's healing was his faith, but that faith had to be established in the mind and work its way into the body. So Jesus went to that source to begin the healing process, much to the awe and controversy of His detractors, the Jews.

The healing of the body is dependent largely, and in many instances firstly, on the healing of the mind. Psychosomatic illnesses, which in many cases go undiagnosed, is on the rise because the mind is the engine of the body. When the mind is not well, primarily from relational conditions, it triggers an incalculable round of physiological illnesses that manifest themselves in mind-boggling proportions. It is the mind that propels the body into so many of its functions, no-functions, and malfunctions. (See the definition of *mind* in the Glossary (p. 408)).

Poor and wounded family members need healing in their sin-sick relational minds, thus paving the way for the natural healing of the body, and where necessary, for further miraculous interventions as God sees fit. Relational wounds (see *relational illness* in the Glossary (pp. 412-413)) make relationships impoverished. Therefore, wounded family members need the kind of healing that will replenish their emotional strength and stabilize their relationships.

## Extrapolation 4

*Original:* "he hath sent me to heal the brokenhearted"

*Paraphrased for Families:* "He has sent the Church to heal the brokenhearted"

Let us be reminded that the description of *poor* mentioned in Extrapolation 3 is not limited to the lack of material possessions—money, land, facilities, and amenities. Poor, as used here, refers to the lack or deprivation of relational knowledge and skills to forge and keep a healthy relationship.

This is by no means downplaying the importance of having an ample supply of the material things of life. The unfortunate fact is that the cemetery is filled with some of the materially richest bodies (including the caskets and trappings) that need not have gone there so early. They died as paupers of the relational quality of life. Had they some of the simple free luxuries of relational health—love, care, affirmation, kindness—they would have lived so much longer. Alas!

**Broken Heart vs Heart Attack**

Clinical broken-heartedness due to impaired relationships is a secret killer and could be taking away so many more than some of the medically known silent killers, such as hypertension, diabetes, and heart disease. Clinical studies have demonstrated the difference between dying from a heart attack (myocardial infarction) and a broken heart (Takotsubo cardiomyopathy, also known as stress cardiomyopathy). The website hopkinsmedicine.org gives this definition:

> Stress Cardiomyopathy Symptoms and Diagnosis Stress cardiomyopathy, also referred to as "broken heart syndrome," takotsubo cardiomyopathy, and apical ballooning syndrome, is a condition in which intense emotional or physical stress can cause rapid and severe heart muscle weakness (cardiomyopathy).

On the subject of how to fix a broken heart, Dr Guy Winch wrote the following:

> By far, the most pronounced aspects of heartbreak is the paralyzing emotional pain it causes. Indeed, our very understanding of what it means to have a broken heart is so tightly bond to the incredible anguish it causes, the two are practically synonymous. In many ways they should be, as the story of heart-beak is a tale of emotional pain, our responses to that pain, and our efforts to recover from it. (Winch and Kim 2018)

Out of ignorance, family members often break each other's heart. When words or silence, deeds or inaction, have such an intense emotional impact on the mind, it triggers glandular, muscular, or organic malfunctions. This is so because we are "fearfully and wonderfully made" (Psalm 139:14), part of which makeup is our mysteriously well-coordinated sympathetic nervous system. Three of the major organs of the body - brain, heart, and lungs - can have an adverse reactions to relational stressors and in turn throw the intricately complex physiological system off course. This is psychosomatic illness simplified.

**Classic Case of Psychosomatic Illness: Near Broken-heartedness**

I sat at the bedside of one of my clients after he returned home from several weeks in hospital, having undergone a plethora of -oscopies', scans, X-rays, and -ologies. These were felt necessary after he reported experiencing intense chest pains and the accompanying shortness of breath and weakening of some vital signs. The cost of general hospital care and facilities, inclusive of consultants' fees, were astronomical and even questionable. But a life was at stake, so even if it meant emptying all bank accounts, it would have been worth it.

He invited me to pull my chair closer to him and to close the door, because he wanted to share privately with me. "Counselor," he began, "we had a very heated argument that morning, much like we have had many times in the past. I was sitting on the bed, and she stormed toward the door, looked back at me, and with vengeance steaming out of her eyes, told me, 'I don't love you anymore!' In the same rage, she bolted through the door. The weight of the five words struck me so hard, I felt something gave way in my chest, and I could not breathe."

The wife had already stormed away in a fit of rage and left the house. Other family members later found him in a state of virtual breathlessness and lethargy of body and rushed him to the ER. His wife was more than supportive when she returned and heard that he had been taken to the hospital, because in her mind, his life was apparently at stake, and after all, she was his wife. Of course, she was totally oblivious to any possible connection between her outburst and denunciation of him earlier and his state of sudden illness.

As relates to the other family members, they all simply had to accept and believe the GP's and cardiologist's diagnosis that he'd had an inexplicable case of heart attack. Inexplicable because, based on his age, family history, and lifestyle, supported by the negative results of his blood work and other tests, nothing added up to a clinical heart attack (myocardial infarction).

When the cardiologist suggested that he might have to insert a stent as part of the treatment regimen, the patient asked the attending physician if there was a family counselor with whom he could speak. A stent is a tube-like device that cardiologists insert in a blood vessel as a procedure to aid or relieve any obstruction of blood flow, especially in narrowing coronary arteries in order to keep them open. The patient was promised that they would get him a family counselor, as he requested, but that promise was not fulfilled. He told the doctor everything that had transpired on that fateful morning, but apparently it was not taken seriously or factored into consideration as a cause for his condition. Fortunately for him, his signs of improvement were good enough to ward off the application of the stent.

He lamented the amount of money that his wife gladly spent in covering the astronomically high hospital bills. He expressed appreciation for the tender care his parents and other family and church members lavished on him. But he alone knew the truth, the fact of his illness. It weighed so heavily on him. At the risk of having a flashback and even worse, a recurrence of the emotional trauma, he had to get it out. Hence his sharing with me, his therapist.

After treatment through various psychotherapy sessions, assurance, reaffirmation, hope, and relational survival skills, this under-40-year-old strong man resumed his normal life. That was a classic case of (takotsubo cardiomyopathy) broken heart to which so many family members have fallen victim unaware. And worse yet, to which many medical practitioners appear to be oblivious or do not have the clinical preparation to treat.

# Extrapolation 5

*Original:* "to heal the brokenhearted"

*Paraphrased for Families:* "spouses, parents, children, and singles"

Husbands and wives are not the only ones to suffer from broken hearts. Other family members are equally subject to such conditions. This probability of being simplistic is made deliberately in order to bring out the point that too often, family-life presentations at Church tend to be focused primarily on husbands and wives and parents and children. The other categories of family members are referred to in some places rather patronizingly: "Oh, we will have to do something for the singles too." Then, sometimes, a bold person might ask remonstratively: "What about those of us who are …?" (See p. 357)

The family today is more complex and diverse than it was two or three decades ago. Family dynamics continue to evolve, and the leadership of the church needs to keep abreast of the changing times and structure its ministry to the family based on needs assessment of its various combinations. Each group, each category, has its different needs, and one treatment plan cannot fit all (See p. 462).

## Categories and Subcategories of Family Demographics

For the important case of delineation, let us look at the categories of the family and their subgroupings:

- **Spouses**
  Husbands and wives

- **Singles**
  Once-married and Never/Not-yet married (the fastest-growing category in the Church and community)

- **Parents**
  Fathers and mothers, grandparents, step-parents, in-laws, foster-parents, adoptive parents, single parents, and families with special needs. Depending on the part of the world where the family is from, there are local and cultural family structures with versions of categories.

- **Sons and daughters**
  Same subgroups as parents

- **Siblings**
  Brothers and sisters, with the same subgroups as parents

- **Extended Family**
  Uncles, aunts, and cousins, with the same subgroups as parents. (For a more detailed description of the three tiers, sixteen groups, and thirty subcategories of the family system, see Appendix 2 pp. 466–468.)

The categorization and subsequent provision for the education and relational-skills acquisition of the family must also factor into the different age ranges and other family demographics, such as gender, education, economic status, and cultural and social orientation, among others.

Members in some groups and subgroups suffer silently, and it is the responsibility of the Church to give them the voice, hearing, and attention they deserve. It is only by taking such a clinical and analytical approach that the leadership of the Church can help to prevent and, where it has happened, heal brokenheartedness in the diverse structure of the family.

## Extrapolation 6

*Original:* "to preach deliverance to the captives"

*Paraphrased for families:* "to preach deliverance to the captives of unholy deadlock instead of holy wedlock"

### Family Complexity and Diversity

We hear that "Marriage is under attack!" and the rallying call is for us to "fight back". *Us* here means the entire Church community, married and unmarried, men and women, young and elderly, and everyone in-between. Understandably, those who are married are to be in the forefront of the battle, because each couple (husband and wife) has their own marriage to save. But the entire Church ought to have a vested interest in the well-being of the marriages that are in it, because marriage, correctly understood according to Genesis 2:24, is the foundation of the family, and according to Ephesians 5 is an extension of the teaching of the gospel.

God uses the marriage relationship as a symbol of His relationship with His people (Jer. 3:14). Marriage was the first human institution that God created in the Garden of Eden (Gen. 2:21–25). It was in response to the first marital issue that the protoevangelium (the first proclamation of the gospel) was made (Gen. 3:15). And it was at a marriage ceremony that Jesus performed His first miracle (John 2:1–11). (Review p. xxviii)

What more assurance could the Church need that the marital relationship is of top priority of all human relationships to God? Little wonder that it is Satan's primary target. Remember the hurricane-earthquake analogy in Chapter 2: destroy the foundation and the superstructure will crumble to the ground (Review p. 27).

The first relationship that the forces of evil attack is marriage. What should be a holy wedlock has become for many couples an unholy deadlock. Marriage in so many people's experience is a prison, and the wedding ring is the padlock. Unfortunately, it is clear that for these couples, it was not the hearts and minds that were engaged and bonded together in the marriage. Instead, it was the bodies that were motivated by the populist social acclaim, "They are now married!"

There are so many societal ills, stigmas and taboos that assail all the categories of the human family, and the marriage relationship heads the list of those which suffer. Satan and his cohorts are having a field day as he sees this divine institution being trampled under the feet of society, including some segments of the very Church that God has appointed to uphold its dignity and sanctity.

How far-fetched would one consider it to suggest that the innumerable cases of failure of the biblical, fundamental marriage of male to female have given rise (in part) to the various versions of what is considered conjugal love springing up in these days? Some might even reason that if the original form of marriage is failing so miserably, its claim to absoluteness is questionable; therefore, any other model that works should be quite as good and deserves the same respect and status rights. Again we lament: Alas! Satan is having a field day! The Church must rally a godly response.

**God Owns the Copyright for Marriage**

Deliverance for married couples comes firstly from their understanding that there can be no successful marriage without God being a part of the husband's personal life as equally as He is of the wife's personal life. When He made the man who later became the husband, He, God, established a relationship with him before he (Adam) met his wife. Equally so, when God made Eve, before He brought her to Adam and she became a wife, He established a relationship with her. Adam and Eve knew their Creator, God, before they knew each other.

In premarital counseling, the couple ought to be reminded that an active personal, private premarriage prayer life should not be merged into one active married couple's prayer life. It is critical that each one maintains his and her individual prayer life connection with the Lord, and that itself will strengthen their prayer life as a couple when they meet to light the family altar.

God is the designer of marriage, and He owns the copyright. It is not an institution designed by man. Therefore, its success will be influenced, to a large degree, by the couple's total dependence upon Him for inspiration and guidance. The remainder of the success possibility depends on the combined individual choice of each spouse and their access and use of knowledge and marital relational skills.

Running parallel with the couple's dependence upon God for His inspiration and guidance, and their combined power of choice, is the Church's responsibility to provide adequate, competent, professional strategies for developing marital relational skills. The last bastion of hope for the survival of the family in this age of corruption and moral decadence is the Church. The leadership needs to rise to the occasion and raise the bar of quality relationship by precept and example, so that those within its sphere of influence can receive and give clear and unequivocal evidence that God is still in charge.

For this ideal to be realized, Church leaders need to first live and set the solid, clear example of simply, good Christian married life. In this regard, they should be able to borrow from the apostles and proclaim: "Be ye followers ... as I am of Christ" (1 Corinthians 11:1) and "Look on us" (Acts 3:4).

# Extrapolation 7

*Original:* "and recovering of sight to the blind"

*Paraphrased for families:* "and recovery of the sight of loving admiration for spouses and others in the family"

## The Take-for-Granted Attitude

One of the worse spirits and signs of degeneration to affect family relational health is a take-for-granted attitude. This devastating state of the relational mind begins with husbands and wives. After the couple returns from their honeymoon and lands back on terra firma, that is where their true life journey begins. When the novelty of the new is past and the reality of the routine of life sets in, they run the risk of descending into a take-for-granted attitude. The high esteem, friendship, chivalry, and endearment are short-lived for too many.

With the pressures and challenges of work; the desire for self-actualization (especially for the younger and academically and/or professionally-minded couples); the paying of the bills; other demands, expectations, and the vicissitudes of daily living, life begins to get real. The first aspects of the relationship on which this reality takes a toll are the little entreaties and courtesies that were demonstrated in the courtship period. Personal tiredness, impatience, and stress slowly make their way into the experience, and the couple could begin to lose the common touch and feelings for each other. Loving admiration begins to wane as tension and even suspicion raise their ugly heads.

If the couple does not get help to correct that onset of poor quality of relational health, and they go on to become parents, the additional demands and responsibilities will more likely make their situation worse. Thus, the child(ren) will be born and raised in an unhealthy atmosphere as the decline takes deeper root.

Sometimes there is a little resurgence of the good, first feelings with the novelty of the new child. Both parents can be ecstatic about the new addition, and for a while, the child dominates their attention. But without the proper nurturing of the marital relationship and the acquisition of parental management knowledge and skills, frustration can again set in as the routine of the regular raises its head for a second time and the decline begins again.

Recovering and maintaining the sight of loving admiration for each other in the family is an important factor in keeping the family bond strong. In the case of the husband and wife, it means that each one continues to see the other as the dream lover of yester-times. There remains a secret admiration and healthy desire to get and remain close, even airtight.

Sustained admiration means that there is a positive impression in the mind for each other. It means that the admired one fills the eyes of the admirer, and there is no space left to accommodate anyone who does not belong to that family. This kind of admiration is not general, as for friends and associates. There is a positive, familial affinity that naturally grows from the mutual family identity, and all the members are instinctively committed to cherish and keep it.

Regardless of the number of persons in the family, each member has the God-given capacity and capability to healthily love and admire all the others. Each needs 100 percent from the other (See p. 295). Positive admiration leads to affirmation, appreciation, and attention. We will always be healthily and positively attracted to each other and help the other to be the best that he or she can be.

God expects the Church to teach family members how to affirm each other; dream with and for each other; and bring out the best in each other. Admiration, approbation, and approval coming from each member of the family will help to stabilize and strengthen the unity within the group. It is in such a family that each one can embrace the sentiments in Charles Dicken's novel Nicholas Nickleby (1839): "When I speak of home, I speak of the place where—in default or of a better—those I love are gathered together, and if that place were a gypsy's tent or a barn, I should call it by the same good name, notwithstanding."

## Extrapolation 8

*Original:* "to set at liberty them that are bruised"

*Paraphrased for families:* "to set at liberty those family members who are spiritually, emotionally, socially, and relationally oppressed"

Ideally, one's family home should be a citadel of peace. That is the very sentiment to which our last quotation above alludes. On the contrary, the worst place on earth where a person can feel oppressed and not belonging is that very place called home.

Unfortunately for so many family members, that is their painful experience. Maybe the most recent and current evidence of this painful home experience is what is reportedly happening in many homes across the world in the wake of the COVID-19 pandemic. Families are now being forced to stay in their homes in order to control the spread of the deadly virus.

For many, home (better referred to as the house in which they live) was merely a domicile to which they returned after the activities of the day at work or school or wherever they happened to be. By the dawn of the new day, some not even seen by the others the day before, are out again. There is very little or, in some cases, no commonality at all. Each man for his own! COVID-19 has drastically disturbed that "peace." (Revisit symptoms on pp. 88 & 89)

By virtue of the directive from the health authorities to stay home, many find themselves forced, as it were, to interact, much to their discomfort. They detest the enforced familiarity which even has its negative impact on some husbands and wives who, prior to Covid-19, had already been practicing not only physical and social distancing but emotional and spiritual distancing as well. For such family members, familiarity now breeds contempt indeed! Ideally, it should be that this extended familiarity breeds contentment in the home, with all family members present and together.

In a normal state of mind, one could be hard-pressed to come to terms with the idea of the home as a place of oppression. One expects that the home is a place of love and care and beauty, where each member of the family looks out for the well-being of the other. Home ought to be a place where family members feel uninhibited and free to be themselves, and are cheered on by the others to do just that. As intricate as it might sound, the freedom to be oneself is not grasped selfishly, without thought and consideration of what is best for the unit as a whole. Each one has a vested interest in the happiness and success of the other, and each one's success is shared by all (See FRH Songs of Praise Number 15).

Christopher Phillips, in *A Fresh Taste of Philosophy: Socrates Café*, agreed with Mark Twain and expressed their mutual feeling about home thus:

> Is where I am, for all intents and purposes, who I am? Is my home one I carry with me, my way of being in the world? Are my world and my worldview one and the same? What if I said where I am is who I am? Would that seem outlandish? Is the where consistent with the who? At times I feel about my home the way Mark Twain did about his house in Hartford, Connecticut, where he wrote: "Our house … had a heart, and a soul, and eyes to see with us; and approvals and solitudes and deep sympathies; it was of us and we were in its confidence, and lived in its grace and in the peace of it benediction.

It must have been this high ideal to which the apostle was referring in his speech to the Philippians recorded in chapter 4:2–4:

> Fulfill ye my joy, that ye be likeminded, having the same love, being of one accord, of one mind. Let nothing be done through strife or vainglory; but in lowliness of mind let each esteem other better than themselves. Look not every man on his own things, but every man also on the things of others.

This very emotionally charged and familially sentimental counsel was evidently addressed to the congregation, but it could only be experientially actualized in the homes that made up the congregation. Indeed, the home is the church away from the temple. (See Chapter 11 Items 2 - 4, pages 314).

**Spiritual Oppression**

Against this high ideal of the Christian family life and against our paraphrase, we must curiously ask: How can one family member oppress another? Let us consider some examples of calculated and inadvertent or unintentional oppression in the family at home:

- one family member making unjust demands of another
- setting unrealistic expectations and goals for another person
- making mean and unnecessary comparisons, and demeaning one who is perceived to be less or a loser
- deprivation of one's rights and privileges, position, and possessions
- dissociation and ostracism—cutting one out of the social life of the family

In our paraphrase, we suggested that some family members are oppressed "spiritually, emotionally, socially, and relationally." Maybe the one most challenging to understand in a Christian home is *spiritual oppression.* Let us take a quick look at it. When a family member lauds and flaunts his or her feeling or sense of knowledge of godliness and righteousness over another, that is an act of spiritual oppression.

This 'righteous' attitude is aimed at putting down the one who is perceived to be weaker or less spiritually mature. When such a 'holy' person speaks questionably and sometimes disparagingly of another's weak understanding of biblical matters, or maybe his or her inability or lack of confidence to pray or testify or any such expected activities in the Christian circle, such demeaning attitude is oppressive and leads to the lowering of the spiritual self-esteem of the one so treated. Sometimes this oppressive feeling can also incite rebellion and break-away from the family bond and faith.

That is the pharisaical attitude against which Jesus spoke in the parable of the two men who went into the temple to pray:

> And he spake this parable unto certain which trusted in themselves that they were righteous, and despised others: Two men went up into the temple to pray; the one a Pharisee, and the other a publican. The Pharisee stood and prayed thus with himself, God, I thank thee, that I am not as other men are, extortioners, unjust, adulterers, or even as this publican. I fast twice in the week, I give tithes of all that I possess.
> And the publican, standing afar off, would not lift up so much as his eyes unto heaven, but smote upon his breast, saying, God be merciful to me a sinner. I tell you, this man went down to his house justified rather than the other: for every one that exalteth himself shall be abased; and he that humbleth himself shall be exalted. (Luke 18:9–14)

The crushing application of this parable to family life is when the temple is the very home they share together.

## Oppressive, Enmeshed Family Relationship

One of the subtle means of oppression in the family at home is the matter of enmeshed relationships. In this form of unhealthy bonding, family members are psyched into surrendering their individual rights to identify and connect with others outside the family unit. They are expected to make a vow, as it were, to protect what might be seen as the proverbial family skeleton in the closet. (Review the reference to this in Chapter 1 p. 3, on the family relational health laboratory.) This is not merely a case of protecting sensitive issues which the family would prefer to manage by themselves.

Most families do have some keep-safe matters which outsiders do not necessarily need to know. With the exception of such situations—which only require healthy, positive family pride to protect—stifling a family member's right to relate with colleagues, friends, and associates is relationally oppressive and turns the family unit into a cult.

The most emotionally crippling of such experiences is that of a wife or husband who is banned or prohibited from connecting with his or her family of origin, or any other persons. This is not what God intended. The home should be a place where one can grow to one's fullest God-given potential and connect healthily with others outside of the immediate nuclear family circle.

The Church needs to provide education and professional therapy sessions for members who are oppressed in any of the forms identified here. Family members grow best in a home atmosphere where each one feels free to breathe his or her own God-given breath and not to live under the pall of fear and trepidation due to the hard and heavy hand of oppression. Home is intended to be the safest place, a little heaven on earth.

# Extrapolation 9

**Original:** "preach the acceptable year"

**Paraphrased for families:** "preach the acceptable time for family reunion"

Given that both the original Bible-based family structure and God's ideal for family life are fiercely and relentlessly being attacked, now is the time for healthy family reunion. In sheep-rearing countries like Australia, one of greatest predators of the sheep is the dingo or the fox. Some of these predators set the field for an attack by going on a high rock within jumping proximity to the sheep and give out a bloodcurdling roar. The strategy is that the roar will immobilize the timid, faint-hearted flock and make it easy to attack.

Indeed, the strategy does work, but only in part. The weak, terrified sheep, in panic and shock, huddle so tightly together that when the enemy makes the victory jump and dashes upon them, it ends up with a mouthful of wool instead of flesh, all because of the tight closeness into which the sheep bond themselves.

This is quite a fitting analogy to juxtapose with Solomon's counsel in Proverbs 6:6: "Go to the ant, thou sluggard; consider her ways, and be wise." We could use a paraphrase at this juncture: "Go to the sheep under attack, thou vulnerable family members; observe how they bond together in times of adversity and attack, and in unity help to save each other. Do likewise, and you shall defeat the onslaught of the enemies of healthy family life."

## Dysfunctional Families: Fodder for the Enemy

A dysfunctional, broken family relationship is fodder in the hands of the forces united to destroy God's original family blueprint. When families, especially those in the Church, are disjointed and fractured, they give ample evidence to the adversaries to prove their point that traditional family ideals have failed. Therefore, they argue that any form, structure, type, or combination that works is just as good, as long as the parties have a meaningful relationship (Revisit p.36, Para. 4).

This is a sad case of the Christian family that cannot apply Peter's admonition of being able to give an answer for the faith (paraphrased: "the family love, the family bond, and keeping power") that is within you (1 Pet. 3:15).

It is unfortunate and even regrettable that in today's society, the practice of family reunion is observed only on holidays. We cannot make light of the beauty and great purpose of such occasions. As a result of migration for different purposes and sound reasons, family members do look forward to such times of reunion, and they need to be encouraged. However, the well-being and healthy family bonding should not be left only to such times, especially when efforts can be made to do better.

Family events of togetherness need not be seasonal only. Nor should the family reunion be limited for the purpose of social gatherings—food, fun, and frolic. Family reunions should also be spiritual and developmental in nature.

**Two New Types of Family Reunion**

Every day ought to be a family reunion experience. There are at least two major reunion experiences that each family can have daily. Let us consider them:

*Daily Family Reunion 1: Waking Up in the Morning*

The first stanza of a well-loved morning hymn by John Keble (1792–1866) reads:

New every morning is thy love, Our waking and uprising prove, Through sleep and darkness safely brought, Restored to life and power and thought. (From his poem "Hues of the Rich Unfolding Morn," Hymntime.com)

During the hours of sleep, although some might be sleeping in the same bed, they are technically separated. The sleep experience is as individual as death, such that Jesus made a close comparison between the two, using Lazarus as the point of reference (John 11:11–14).

There are countless times when two family members go to sleep and only one awakens the next morning. The other failed to reunite, as he or she goes off into the permanent sleep, awaiting the resurrection. All who pass through the darkness of night and reappear in the light of the new day together should see that reunion as a cause for praise to God and a recommitment to the well-being of each other. That is the purpose of family morning devotion. It serves the purpose of relinking us together and with God. (See Song Number 51 – FRH Songs of Praise and Bible Verses Paraphrase).

### *Daily Family Reunion 2: Returning Home*

When family members have to leave home for work or school, or any other place, especially for an extended period, the time of separation from home can be filled with anxiety, hope, and even concern for each other's safety and well-being. They look forward to their reunion. Sometimes they text and call each other, enquire about their mutual welfare, and express longing for the one who is away to return home. They look forward to sharing experiences of what happened in and outside of the home. In a healthy relationship, these reunions have esteemed value, and in a definite way, they strengthen the bond that keeps the family strong.

# Extrapolation 10

*Original:* "to preach the acceptable year of the Lord."

*Paraphrased for Families:* "in preparation for the Lord's return."

All the forms of healthy family reunion mentioned above should influence more than just the strong family bond here on earth. They could verily fit into the futuristic implication that the apostle Paul's explanation makes for the purpose of the various gifts that the Lord has placed in the Church. He said that those gifts are to be used "for the perfecting of the saints, for the work of the ministry, for the edifying of the body of Christ: Till we all come in the unity of the faith, and of the knowledge of the Son of God, unto a perfect man, unto the measure of the stature of the fullness of Christ" (Eph. 4:12–13).

The quality of our family reunions here on earth could influence our readiness for the Second Coming of the Lord and the reunion with the saints of all the ages. They could be interpreted with a kind of parallel to the counsel on the importance of the Communion Service recorded in 1 Corinthians 11:26: "For as often as ye eat this bread, and drink this cup, ye do shew the Lord's death till he come."

Our regular paraphrasing of the text could read: "As often as you have healthy family reunions that positively strengthen your earthly family ties, you do show your anticipation and preparedness for the grand family reunion of all the ages, when the Lord returns."

This ought to be the ultimate purpose of all the ministries in the Church—that is to prepare the members to be "Looking for that blessed hope, and the glorious appearing of the great God and our Saviour Jesus Christ" (Titus 2:13). This is the epitome of the ministry and mission of family relational health, which is a psycho-social priority for good, quality family life here on earth, and certainly a biblical priority for the life to come.

## Suggestions for Action

1. Where a relational illness persists over three weeks and gets more intense, while praying earnestly about it, seek professional help. Remember: Early detection and professional treatment of relational illness not only save relationships but lives, too!

2. Be responsible with your relational illnesses and keep them from spreading and infecting others who should not be affected at all. Do not wash your dirty linen abroad! Get help to heal the family relational challenges at home.

3. Be careful about the words used in heated relational conflicts. Harsh, intense, fiery words and expressions can cause heartbreak, and family members do die from broken hearts.

4. Remember to practice healthy family separation (when leaving the home) and reunion (when you return home). Let your family members know each time that they share a memorable place in your heart and that you always look forward to being with them.

5. Always bear in mind that your healthy family life here is in preparation for the healthy family life when Jesus returns, but you must begin to practice and experience it here in order to be ready to go there when Jesus comes back.

# Chapter 6

# A Needed Spiritual
# Mind Scan/X-Ray

**Anchor Text: Hebrews 4:12**

"For the word of God is quick, and powerful, and sharper than any two-edged sword, piercing even to the dividing asunder of soul and spirit, and of the joints and marrow, and is a discerner of the thoughts and intents of the heart."

**Paraphrased for Families**

For the family relational counsels and guidance that come from the Word of God can, at times, be challenging and forceful, and more specific than any multipronged human psychotherapy approach; moving directly against, and even separating between ambivalence of thought and action, showing up undesirable behaviors and the true nature and intents of the mind. To the same extent that we x-ray or scan the tissues of the body so does the Holy Spirit scans/xrays the issues of the mind. (See Glossary, p. 414)

## The Bible: the Comprehensive Family Book

The Holy Bible is truly the supreme family book. In its divisions there are entire books, entire chapters, sections of chapters, and numerous verses that speak about the beauty and ideals, the issues, challenges, and problems of the human family. Its records are totally comprehensive historically and prophetically, as it portrays the beginning of the family from God's creation in the Garden of Eden to these present times. It is equally balanced as it shows the successes and failures, the joys and sorrows, the exemplary and detestable patterns of marriage, parenting, and all other aspects of family life.

Some of its references are directly about the family, while others are indirect. In some cases, the family is used as an analogy or object lesson that the Lord wants His people to know. The Bible also cites the family of earth as a symbol of the redeemed when God, the Eternal Father, will be reunited with His children in the earth made new, and the original plan from Creation is restored (Rev, 21:3–4; Isa. 65:21–25).

Until that grand and eternal redemption and restoration is realized, the mystery of iniquity will continue to affect every family of earth. Maybe the most palpable, most visible, and most harmful way that sin and iniquity will show up in the human experience is in the quality of relational health between family members. Sometimes the manifestations are overt and blatant; at other times, they are subtle and shrewd.

**The Conundrum of the Mind**

This evil combination of sin and iniquity can come from different fronts, different bases or origins. Regardless of their source or target, they land ultimately on the family, with the mind being their safe and favorite hiding place. That same mind is the residence and anchorage of all human relationships. Against this fact, note the basic theory of family relational health, the driving force behind this work: "All human relationships begin and continue to exist in the mind." (See Pillar 5, p. xxxvi)

If ever there were conundrums, if ever there were mysteries, they would be the differing states and functions of the *relational mind*. It simply cannot be understood. The mind is the core of our human existence, the very engine of our being, where our loving, our endearing marriage, parenting, and all other relationships are based and from which they operate. At the same time, it is equally the seat from which treachery, deception, and destruction arise and destroy relationships in the home and the entire society (Revisit pp. 17 & 18).

This enigmatic state of the human mind raises the following questions: Who can understand it? Who can explain the quandary and predicament of human relationships? In this state of bewilderment, confusion, and perplexity, humanity continues to struggle. Is there more to family life than problems, uncertainties, and ambiguities?

The inspiration from the God of Families shines through with hope and answers. God understands the human relational mind and has provided direct responses and solutions to the dilemma of human relationships in the family manual, the Holy Bible. Let us spend the remainder of this chapter analyzing our paraphrased Anchor Text with the support of other Bible passages to obtain more proof that family relational health is really a biblical, psycho-social priority— God's priority.

## Extrapolation 1

*Original:* "For the word of God is"

*Paraphrased for families:* "For the family relational counsels and guidance that come from the Word of God can, at times, be"

### God Made the Human Mind

Our first bewildering question about the human relational mind is, "Who can understand it?" The Bible clearly states that God can. First of all, He made man after His own image and into His own likeness (Gen. 1:26–27). The image and likeness were not in the form and structure of the created being but more so in his mind.

God made the mind as the channel through which communication and relationship between Him and His children would be established, maintained, and developed ad-infinitum. God also gave them (male and female) the power of choice and the opportunity to align their minds individually with His through loving obedience (Gen. 2:15–17).

In His divine wisdom, God knew what was and would always be best for His people, because He made them (Jer. 29:11–13). The record of the impaired relationships began with the chosen path of disobedience by the first family, when they yielded their minds to the corrupt, rationalizing process of questioning God's instructions to them:

> And when the woman saw that the tree was good for food, and that it was pleasant to the eyes, and a tree to be desired to make one wise, she took of the fruit thereof, and did eat, and gave also unto her husband with her; and he did eat. And the eyes of them both were opened, and they knew that they were naked; and they sewed fig leaves together, and made themselves aprons. (Gen. 3:6–7)

**The Botanical and Oncological Imagery and Treatment for Sin**

From that first fatal incident of disobedience, the mind of man began to deteriorate and drift slowly away from God. Indeed, he began to die by gradually disconnecting himself from the very Source of his life and existence. Jesus spoke to His disciples then and now in very graphic botanical imagery:

> I am the vine, ye are the branches: He that abideth in me, and I in him, the same bringeth forth much fruit: for without me ye can do nothing. If a man abideth not in me, he is cast forth as a branch, and is withered; and men gather them, and cast them into the fire, and they are burned. If ye abide in me, and my words abide in you,

ye shall ask what ye will, and it shall be done unto you.
(John 15:5–7)

God, the Creator, painfully saw the catastrophe of man's chosen path, hence His first lament over His masterpiece of creation as recorded in Genesis 6:3–6:

> And GOD saw that the wickedness of man was great in the earth, and that every imagination of the thoughts of his heart was only evil continually. And it repented the LORD that he had made man on the earth, and it grieved him at his heart.

God decided that the temporary intervention to the pandemic of viral audacity of the degenerate minds of His children at that time was the Great Flood. Only eight persons were saved, specifically one family, who were obedient to the Lord's will. But alas! It did not take long after their miraculous preservation and salvation for their minds to go into sinful remission, and the vicious cycle and reenactment of sin was underway.

We can question or conjecture that the spiritual oncological hydrotherapy treatment that God used did not burn or wash out every single sinful cell from their minds. Evidently, based on the MRI result of His omniscience on the mind of man, God decided that the final treatment will be radiation (by fire) next time. "But the fearful, and unbelieving, and the abominable, and murderers, and whoremongers, and sorcerers, and idolaters, and all liars, shall have their part in the lake which burneth with fire and brimstone: which is the second death" (Rev. 21:8), after which "affliction shall not rise up the second time" (Nahum 1:9).

We find therefore that centuries after the flood, there remained continued evidence of the distorted and warped mind of man. God spoke about it through the prophet Jeremiah in chapter 17, verse 10: "The heart is deceitful above all things, and desperately wicked:

who can know it?" That searching question was not an expression of bewilderment on God's part as it is on our part, when we ask it in the same way today. God's question was rhetorical and directed to man, whose dwarfed intelligence by sin could not reveal his own lack of self-knowledge.

## God Reveals the True State of Man's Mind

God did not give man any time to frustrate himself further in searching for an answer to the question that He posed. Instead, He continued very authoritatively: "I the Lord search the heart, I try the reins, even to give every man according to his ways, and according to the fruit of his doings" (Jer. 17:10)

Here God asserts His claim, His creatorship, and His absolute knowledge (omniscience) of the state and function of the sin-riddled mind of man. He does it with authority as only the Creator can, with no comparison to any psychoanalyst, psychologist, psychiatrist, behaviorist, or therapist, because all of them, being human, have the same heart-mind need for His spirituo-psycho-clinical analysis.

This awesome awareness of the state of the mind captivated the consciousness of Paul in Romans 7:14–24:

> For we know that the law is spiritual: but I am carnal, sold under sin. For that which I do I allow not: for what I would, that do I not; but what I hate, that do I. If then I do that which I would not, I consent unto the law that it is good. Now then it is no more I that do it, but sin that dwelleth in me. For I know that in me (that is, in my flesh,) dwelleth no good thing: for to will is present with me; but how to perform that which is good I find not.
>
> For the good that I would I do not: but the evil which I would not, that I do. Now if I do that I would not, it is no more I that do it, but sin that dwelleth in me. I find then a

law, that, when I would do good, evil is present with me. For I delight in the law of God after the inward man: But I see another law in my members, warring against the law of my mind, and bringing me into captivity to the law of sin which is in my members. O wretched man that I am! who shall deliver me from the body of this death?

Paul, in full, positive self-recrimination, accepts the utter helplessness of his mind to will and do according to God's pleasure (Phil. 2:13). The apostle was under inspiration, speaking for all honest human beings who face the limitation of their natural mind to do good. Having completed His full scan of the mind and having revealed the result to Paul, the Holy Spirit led the humble sinner to confess the need for Christ to dwell in his mind. Here is Paul's conclusion of hope, faith, and confidence: "I thank God through Jesus Christ our Lord. So then with the mind I myself serve the law of God; but with the flesh the law of sin" (verse 25). Mind here = Soul in Psalm 139: 14

**The Tongue: Visible Symbol of the Mind**

The Lord used another apostle, James, to speak for Him regarding the mind and its influence on relationships. This time, James uses the tongue, that visible section of the speech mechanism. Here are his detailed findings, loaded with several apt analogies with which we can fully identify:

My brethren, be not many masters, knowing that we shall receive the greater condemnation. For in many things we offend all. If any man offend not in word, the same is a perfect man, and able also to bridle the whole body. Behold, we put bits in the horses' mouths, that they may obey us; and we turn about their whole body. Behold also the ships, which though they be so great, and are driven of fierce winds, yet are they turned about with a very small helm, whithersoever the governor listeth.

Even so the tongue is a little member, and boasteth great things. Behold, how great a matter a little fire kindleth! And the tongue is a fire, a world of iniquity: so is the tongue among our members, that it defileth the whole body, and setteth on fire the course of nature; and it is set on fire of hell.

For every kind of beasts, and of birds, and of serpents, and of things in the sea, is tamed, and hath been tamed of mankind: But the tongue can no man tame; it is an unruly evil, full of deadly poison. Therewith bless we God, even the Father; and therewith curse we men, which are made after the similitude of God.

Out of the same mouth proceedeth blessing and cursing. My brethren, these things ought not so to be. Doth a fountain send forth at the same place sweet water and bitter? Can the fig tree, my brethren, bear olive berries? either a vine, figs? So can no fountain both yield salt water and fresh?

Who is a wise man and endued with knowledge among you? let him shew out of a good conversation his works with meekness of wisdom. But if ye have bitter envying and strife in your hearts, glory not, and lie not against the truth. This wisdom descendeth not from above, but is earthly, sensual, devilish. For where envying and strife is, there is confusion and every evil work. But the wisdom that is from above is first pure, then peaceable, gentle, and easy to be intreated, full of mercy and good fruits, without partiality, and without hypocrisy. And the fruit of righteousness is sown in peace of them that make peace. (James 3:1–18)

God has total knowledge of how the mind affects the relational health of His people. The tongue, which symbolizes speech, which comes from our thoughts, which are produced in the mind, must be brought under the full and complete control of the Lord. "The tongue of the just is as choice silver: the heart of the wicked is little worth" (Prov. 10:20). "But those things which proceed out of the mouth come forth from the heart; and they defile the man. For out of the heart proceed evil thoughts, murders, adulteries, fornications, thefts, false witness, blasphemies" (Matt. 15:18 & 19 – See p. 138).

The Bible shows that throughout human history, man can only experience a successful relationship with his God and his fellow men if he brings his thoughts into captivity to the will of God (2 Cor. 10:5). He will then learn to take heed to the counsels of the Lord, his Maker, as chronicled in God's Word.

## Extrapolation 2

**Original:** "quick, and powerful, and sharper than any two-edged sword"

**Paraphrased for Families:** "challenging and forceful, and more specific than any multipronged human psychotherapy approach"

We have agreed in Extrapolation 1 of this chapter that the Bible is replete with counsels from God regarding the relational challenges in the family. Unfortunately, the world in general does not see it that way. Those in the non-Christian philosophical arena, who do not embrace the biblical teaching of godliness and right living, still find that there is a need for counsels and guidelines beyond the regular, average personal knowledge and endeavor.

### Theories of Human Attitudes and Behaviors

As a result, there are endless volumes of research, studies, theories, philosophies, models, modalities, and viewpoints that seek to address the challenges of human behavior and relationships purely from humanistic and other philosophical perspectives. Wikipedia gives the main point of the humanistic, and to a large degree, other perspectives:

It is a psychological perspective that rose to prominence in the mid-20th century in answer to the limitations of Sigmund Freud's psychoanalytic theory and B. F. Skinner's behaviorism. With its roots running from Socrates through the Renaissance, this approach emphasizes the individuals' inherent drive towards self-actualization, the process of realizing and expressing one's own capabilities and creativity.

It helps the client gain the belief that all people are inherently good. It adopts a holistic approach to human existence and pays special attention to such phenomena as creativity, free will, and positive human potential. It encourages viewing ourselves as a "whole person" greater than the sum of our parts and encourages self-exploration rather than the study of behavior in other people. Humanistic psychology acknowledges spiritual aspiration as an integral part of the psyche. It is linked to the emerging field of transpersonal psychology.

Primarily, this type of therapy encourages a self-awareness and mindfulness that helps the client change their state of mind and behavior from one set of reactions to a healthier one with more productive self-awareness and thoughtful actions. Essentially, this approach allows the merging of mindfulness and behavioral therapy, with positive social support.

There is no question that there are aspects of this and many other theories that have made, and are continuing to make, remarkable impacts on the quality of life in society. The importance of self-awareness and self-esteem are critical for one's positive development. Discovering one's full potential through self-exploration and learning the arts of positive social behavior and support are skills and practices that everyone needs to focus on in order to become a good, rounded citizen.

**Limitations of Human Theories**

In fact, there are scriptural counsels that resonate with all these. For example, Paul's counsel to young Timothy: "Wherefore I put thee in remembrance that thou stir up the gift of God, which is in thee by the putting on of my hands" (2 Tim. 1:6). This seasoned, fatherly advice was clearly challenging the young man to explore his gift, his inner abilities and talents. But Paul went on to acknowledge the source from which they came to the young man. They were given to Timothy by the indwelling power of the Holy Spirit.

Amidst the ongoing preponderance of hypotheses, postulations, propositions, therapies, rehabilitations, analyses, modifications, and treatment programs aimed at improving behaviors and relationships in particular, the world continues to reel and writhe from the ongoing onslaught of man's injustice to man. Crime and violence are not decreasing. Thuggery, barbarism, ferociousness, bloodthirstiness, terrorism, insurrection, and all their synonyms are the order of the day at varying degrees and intensity around the world.

What we are being forced to accept is that the multipronged psychotherapy approaches from man's relentless efforts are not producing the desired results. The limitation in man's endeavors is stark, but God's words will come to the rescue. Here again, with emphasis on the paraphrased verse, "the family relational counsels and guidance that come from the Word of God can, at times, be challenging and forceful, and more specific than any multipronged human psychotherapy approach."

## Solomon Acknowledged God

Among the intellectual giants of history, the one who is credited with the rare combination of wisdom, knowledge and understanding, was the great king of Israel, Solomon. Firstly, he attributed that phenomenal intellectual prowess and aptitude to the God he had grown to love and serve. In earnest, deep consciousness of the magnitude and gravity of the responsibilities he faced as the newly crowned king, he humbled himself before God and prayed: "Give therefore thy servant an understanding heart to judge thy people, that I may discern between good and bad: for who is able to judge this thy so great a people?" (1 Kgs. 3:9). Characteristic of the loving God, He answered Solomon's prayer and even gave him extras:

> And God said unto him, Because thou hast asked this thing, and hast not asked for thyself long life; neither hast asked riches for thyself, nor hast asked the life of thine enemies; but hast asked for thyself understanding to discern judgment; Behold, I have done according to thy words: lo, I have given thee a wise and an understanding heart; so that there was none like thee before thee, neither after thee shall any arise like unto thee. And I have also given thee that which thou hast not asked, both riches, and honour: so that there shall not be any among the kings like unto thee all thy days. And if thou wilt walk in my ways, to keep my statutes and my commandments, as thy father David did walk, then I will lengthen thy days. (1 Kgs. 3:11–14)

It is noteworthy that in many of the philosophical and erudite circles of our times, references and allusions are made to Solomon's teachings, counsels, and guidelines for good behavior and quality relationships. Unfortunately, in most cases, they have not attributed these to God and given Him the glory and honour due to Him.

Being the frail, fallible human that he still was, Solomon failed repeatedly. His moral and spiritual lifestyle was more than questionable. In fact, there were many times when it was reproachable and detestable, but he never was unrepentant. Firstly, he admitted his gross errors and abhorred them. He then offered warnings, counsels, and instructions against the evils that he had committed. In his over three thousand proverbs and wise sayings, he relied completely upon God, and attributed them to the inspiration of the Lord.

## The Mind Is Off-limits to Fellow Human Beings

When all the correct human counsels and guidelines are given, and the therapies are administered, no human has direct access to a fellow human's mind. Not even the hypnotist has the ultimate privilege of total mind control of another, because the person being hypnotized will eventually come out of the stupor and regain some amount of control, except as he or she chooses to continue and surrender the will totally.

The mind is off-limits to another human. That is the way God designed it, and that is the way it will remain. The mind is His exclusive access to His created beings, but He does not set it to operate as a robot to do as He wills without the consent of the human. He respects the individual's choices and does come to the point when He proverbially backs off, as stated in Romans 1:28: "And even as they did not like to retain God in their knowledge, God gave them over to a reprobate mind, to do those things which are not convenient."

As long as the human does not continuously reject the impressions of the Holy Spirit, even though he appears to resist or reject the intervention of professional counselors, therapists, and behaviorists, the Spirit of the Lord can still make a breakthrough to the inner man—the deep recesses of the mind. Here is wise Solomon's testimony to that fact: "The spirit of man is the candle of the Lord, searching all the inward parts of the belly" (Prov. 20:27).

And Hanani, the seer in confronting the wayward King Asa, spoke pointedly: "For the eyes of the LORD run to and from throughout the whole earth, to shew himself strong in the behalf of them whose heart is perfect toward him. Herein thou hast done foolishly: therefore, from henceforth thou shalt have war" (2 Chr. 16:9). David had no less conviction about the penetrative power of the Spirit of the Lord to reach the inner soul: "Shall not God search this out? for he knoweth the secrets of the heart" (Psalm 44:21).

The most authoritative and absolute voice we can use to confirm that the counsels in God's word supersede the most authentic, well-intentioned human psychotherapy and treatment of the mind is that of Jesus Christ. He demonstrated that fact many times, as in the case of His encounter with the Scribes and Pharisees, recorded in Matthew 9:4: "And Jesus knowing their thoughts said, Wherefore think ye evil in your hearts?"

Another record of the same disciple, Matthew, in chapter 12:25 states: "And Jesus knew their thoughts, and said unto them, Every kingdom divided against itself is brought to desolation; and every city or house divided against itself shall not stand."

Dr Luke, with his scientific and medical background, also recorded that Jesus, being divine, had access to the human heart as no regular human has. He wrote to Theophilus in chapter 6:8, "But he knew their thoughts, and said to the man which had the withered hand, Rise up, and stand forth in the midst. And he arose and stood forth."

**The Holy Spirit Knows the Mind**

Upon getting ready to leave the earth, Jesus assured His current and future disciples that the Holy Spirit, the Comforter, would come after Him and do even greater, more intimate work of heart-searching, heart-impacting, and heart-changing:

> Nevertheless, I tell you the truth; It is expedient for you that I go away: for if I go not away, the Comforter will not come unto you; but if I depart, I will send him unto you. And when he is come, he will reprove the world of sin, and of righteousness, and of judgment: Of sin, because they believe not on me; Of righteousness, because I go to my Father, and ye see me no more; Of judgment, because the prince of this world is judged. I have yet many things to say unto you, but ye cannot bear them now. Howbeit when

he, the Spirit of truth, is come, he will guide you into all truth: for he shall not speak of himself; but whatsoever he shall hear, that shall he speak: and he will shew you things to come. (John 16:7–13)

We have established that only the power of God can effect any desired change in the heart of man. However, we will not discount or disregard the potential positive, and even life-changing effects of professional psychotherapy, especially as practiced by sincere Bible-believing Christian professionals. At the end of those sessions, we attribute the responses from, and changes in, the client to the working of the Holy Spirit, using human agents as conduits of His life-changing word, to which He gives life and power.

## Extrapolation 3

*Original:* "piercing even to the dividing asunder of soul and spirit"

*Paraphrased for Families:* "moving directly against, and even separating between ambivalence of thought and action"

### Natural Instability and Ambivalence of the Mind

Many family relationships are fraught with uncertainties, doubts, ambiguities, and indecision. If these undesirable attitudes of the relational mind persist for too long, they further produce discomfort, tension, suspicion, and even instability in the relationship.

Often, we hear husbands and wives challenging each other:

- "Make up your mind; you either want the relationship or you don't."

- "Listen, I am tired of the wavering. I want to move on with my life, so tell me what you really want."

- "I have never seen a person who can be swayed so easily! He does not know what he wants in life because he is influenced by everything that everybody says!"

- "My wife is a good woman, but she listens to everything her sisters and her mother tell her; even things she hears from ladies at her workplace. She allows them to influence her thinking. She is not always stable in her own decisions, not to mention much of what we decide on sometimes."

In the political arena, this is called *flip-flopping*. Opponents take advantage of the situation when they hear the other one change his mind on a promise or policy that was offered to the electorate. "He cannot be trusted to lead because he cannot make up his mind on the direction to take the country."

Unfortunately, these weaknesses of the relational mind are characteristic of humans in general. Every one of us at some point in life experiences some amount of ambivalence, incongruity, vacillation, fluctuation, and contradiction (See p. 231). Only God's words, assurances, and promises never change: "It is of the Lord's mercies that we are not consumed, because his compassions fail not. They are new every morning: great is thy faithfulness" (Lam. 3:22–23). And Malachi confirms it: "For I am the Lord, I change not ..." (Mal. 3:6).

**Psychotherapies and Analyses**

God's word is certain and immutable. He alone has the ability to offer total dependability to us. God alone can truly identify and label the deep instances of ambivalence that plague the human mind. He also has the remedies, cures, and total healing for debilitating relational health conditions.

Let us take the major sections of our paraphrased Anchor Text, cite the biblical records to support its relevance, and look at some heavenly psychotherapy for the specific conditions. Here it is again: "moving directly against, and even separating between ambivalence of thought and action."

To "move directly against" someone personally, or to be "separating from or between" oneself and another person's attitude, behavior, or plan, means to counter, oppose, resist, or remove the person or his plan out of the way. When such actions are taken, they can be seen as drastic, controversial, even confrontational, depending on a number of variables.

In the context of our paraphrased text, there are three questions to be answered:

***Question 1:*** Who will do the "moving against" or "separating between"?

***Answer:*** God Himself. Sometimes He gives directives to His servants. He may use His word to do the necessary "moving against" or "separating between", but He gets it accomplished. Here is evidence of this certainty from the Messianic prophet Isaiah:

> For as the heavens are higher than the earth, so are my ways higher than your ways, and my thoughts than your thoughts. For as the rain cometh down, and the snow from heaven, and returneth not thither, but watereth the earth, and maketh it bring forth and bud, that it may give seed to the sower, and bread to the eater: So shall my word be that goeth forth out of my mouth: it shall not return unto me void, but it shall accomplish that which I please, and it shall prosper in the thing whereto I sent it. (Isa. 55:9–11)

It is God's ultimate plan to move against, and cut away sin from His children (Prov. 35:1, Isa. 49:25; & 59:1; 1 Cor. 10:13; 2 Thes. 1: 6).

**Question 2:** What is the important issue that God's focus could be on, that could make Him feel the need to act so decisively and if needs be, drastically?

**Answer:** God's focus is on *relationship-building,* a cause for which He has even given His Son to die (John 3:16). Ever since the Garden of Eden, when the relationship between Himself and His first created beings was damaged, God has a permanently designed plan for its restoration. God has expressed a fervent and zealous appeal very often toward the restoration of healthy relationship between Himself and His people. For example, listen to Him in Isaiah 59:1–2 and Ezekiel 18: 30–32 respectively:

> Behold, the Lord's hand is not shortened, that it cannot save; neither his ear heavy, that it cannot hear: But your iniquities have separated between you and your God, and your sins have hid his face from you, that he will not hear.

> Therefore I will judge you, O house of Israel, every one according to his ways, saith the Lord GOD. Repent, and turn yourselves from all your transgressions; so iniquity shall not be your ruin. Cast away from you all your transgressions, whereby ye have transgressed; and make you a new heart and a new spirit: for why will ye die, O house of Israel? For I have no pleasure in the death of him that dieth, saith the Lord GOD: wherefore turn yourselves, and live ye.

**Question 3:** Against whom or what will God "move" or do the "separating"?

**Answer:** God will move against or do the work of separating any destructive force or attitude (whichever be their sources) that will block, retard, and destroy the good efforts of His people in building healthy relationships. God stands guard over the efforts of His people who set out to accomplish His will in their lives, and He will not permit others of an opposing spirit to thwart their good plans or bring about defeat. Even if they appear to succeed sometimes, He has the final word.

Among the evil attitudes, behaviors, and practices that are inimical to a good relationship, and which can defeat the efforts of the well-intentioned person toward healthy relationships, and for which we should have an insatiated sense of hatred, are the following:

- unhealthy or false pride,
- lying
- murders
- evil surmising
- gossiping
- mischief-making
- disharmony and conflict

**Healthy Hate in the Relational Mind**

As family members, we are to hate every thought and act of evil, whether we are doers or observers. This must have been God's mindset when He inspired eighty-seven references to *hate* as recorded in the King James Version of the Bible. He expressed protest against those relational evils.

Here He speaks through Solomon:

> These six things doth the Lord hate: yea, seven are an abomination unto him: A proud look, a lying tongue, and hands that shed innocent blood, An heart that deviseth wicked imaginations, feet that be swift in running to mischief, A false witness that speaketh lies, and he that soweth discord among brethren." (Prov. 6:12–19, emphasis on verse 16–19)

Then, through Zechariah, He offers heavenly psychotherapy to heal those malevolent, immoral, malicious and criminal acts:

> These are the things that ye shall do; Speak ye every man the truth to his neighbor; execute the judgment of truth and peace in your gates: And let none of you imagine evil in your hearts against his neighbor; and love no false oath: for all these are things that I hate, saith the Lord. (Zech. 8:16–17)

In looking at marriage, His foundation plan for human relationship, He healthily used the same word *hate* to express His indignation against those who distort it or make light of it, resulting in a divorce:

> Yet ye say, Wherefore? Because the Lord hath been witness between thee and the wife of thy youth, against whom thou hast dealt treacherously: yet is she thy companion, and the wife of thy covenant. And did not he make one? Yet had he the residue of the spirit. And wherefore one? That he might seek a godly seed. Therefore, take heed to your spirit, and let none deal treacherously against the wife of his youth. For the Lord, the God of Israel, saith that he hateth putting away: for one covereth violence with his garment, saith the Lord of hosts: therefore, take heed to your spirit, that ye deal not treacherously. (Mal. 2:14–16)

In an effort to destroy those forces that will incite, instigate, or engage in unhealthy relationships among His people, God provides a replacement therapy in order to stabilize and strengthen those relational minds. Through His inspired word, He shows the positive state of mind that will influence quality, steadfast relationships to be experienced firstly in the home, the Church, and then in society. He speaks through James:

> If any of you lack wisdom, let him ask of God, that giveth to all men liberally, and upbraideth not; and it shall be given him. But let him ask in faith, nothing wavering. For

he that wavereth is like a wave of the sea driven with the wind and tossed. For let not that man think that he shall receive any thing of the Lord. A double minded man is unstable in all his ways. (James 1:5-8)

Here we see God alluding to the issue of ignorance which can have untold negative effects on family relationships (Chap. 3).

In this treatment plan, God expresses an invitation to all family members to ask Him for wisdom as Solomon did. He assures them that He will supply it liberally. In Isaiah 1:18–19, He sought to arrest the mind and invites us to reason with Him in an effort to heal a broken relationship: "Come now, and let us reason together, saith the Lord: though your sins be as scarlet, they shall be as white as snow; though they be red like crimson, they shall be as wool. If ye be willing and obedient, ye shall eat the good of the land."

Once the relationship between us and God is healthy, and we allow Him to separate us from the forces of evil that impair our relationships, we will succeed. That is the goal, and it is fully achievable though Him who gives us the victory. (Romans 7: 25)

## Extrapolation 4

*Original:* "is a discerner of the thoughts and intents of the heart"

*Paraphrased for Families:* "showing up undesirable behaviors and the true nature and intents of the mind"

The sin-affected relational mind has a natural propensity to evil. Being good is not natural or normal for the individual family member or the family unit. The biblical diagnosis is: "God looked down from heaven upon the children of men, to see if there were any that did understand, that did seek God. Every one of them is gone back: they are altogether become filthy; there is none that doeth good, no, not one" (Ps. 53:2–3). God is all good, and the natural human heart/mind does not seek after God, and consequently cannot be good.

## Unhealthy Mind Directs Unhealthy Body Functions

Paul picks up the lamenting strain from David:

> As it is written, there is none righteous, no, not one: There is none that understandeth, there is none that seeketh after God. They are all gone out of the way, they are together become unprofitable; there is none that doeth good, no, not one. Their *throat* is an open sepulchre; with their *tongues* they have used deceit; the poison of asps is under their *lips*: Whose *mouth* is full of cursing and bitterness: Their *feet* are swift to shed blood: Destruction and misery are in their ways." (Rom. 3:10–16)

The five body parts identified here are all symbols of the mind and are used to show how various relationships are affected by the mind— employing, as it were, these organs as its agents to demonstrate its true state. The throat, the tongue, the lips, and the mouth are part of the speech mechanism, and the utterance which comes from them is powered by the mind (See pp. 124 & 197).

The feet represent the mobility aspect of the mind. One means of spreading the natural evil imaginations of the mind is for the body to move from house to house as stated in 1 Timothy 5:13: "And withal they learn to be idle, wandering about from house to house; and not only idle, but tattlers also and busybodies, speaking things which they ought not."

These and other challenges that come from God are not condemnatory; they are not belittling or disparaging. They are intended to create an awareness of the true state of the mind, seeing that we were all born in sin and shapen in iniquity (Ps. 51:5). It is not natural for us to do good from the corrupt and remorseless mind.

## Potentially Destructive Humanistic Theories

Our first brother, Cain, was the first painful example. This description of the true nature of man cuts against the grain of theories referred to earlier. The essence of the humanistic theory is that in each of us lies the natural potential to be good. We can do anything, and become the best, as long as we set our minds toward that goal. This reasoning is germane, but left by itself, it is deceptive (Jas. 1:22), because He who made the human mind and has the absolute facts about its degenerate state correctly counsels: "…for without me ye can do nothing" (John 15:5).

The good news here is that while God's word keeps "showing up undesirable behaviors and the true nature and intents of the mind," it balances them by showing the opposite desirable attitudes that we can adopt. In Psalm 37:4, David counsels: "Delight thyself also in the LORD; and he shall give thee the desires of thine heart." When we delight in God's word, our desires will be in harmony with His will for our lives.

## Mind Transplant Needed

It follows also that our behaviors will be changed, not merely modified as in behavior modification theory (See: Thought Canal Surgery – p. 436). Comparatively, while the leopard will not be able to change its spots nor the Ethiopian his skin, we who are accustomed to do evil can change (Jeremiah 13:23) because of the life-transforming power of God's word in our heart. This happens when we have a mind transplant by the spiritual surgery of the Holy Spirit. "Let this mind be in you, which was also in Christ Jesus" (Phil. 2:5).

Can we experience better, improved, and sustained family relational health? Yes, we can, but not of our own volition. The word of God must do its multipronged therapeutic work of "moving directly against, and even separating between ambivalence of thought and action, showing up undesirable behaviors and the true nature and intents of the mind." When antirelational diseases are expelled, the clean mind will be a sound receptacle for the living words of God to breathe life and health into dying relationships. Good-quality family relational health is still possible today. Thanks be to God!

## Suggestions for Action

1. Pray continuously that the Holy Spirit will inspire the right thoughts in your mind so that what you speak (by your tongue) will improve the relational health of those around you.

2. Know yourself and what gifts and abilities God has given you, then do what is necessary to improve on them.

3. "To thine own self be true." Be honest with yourself about any relational weaknesses that you know you have. Confess them to the Lord and seek His strength to overcome.

4. Do not practice or support any of the six attitudes which God hates. If you know anyone who practices these, pray for them and use gentle persuasion to help relieve them from the deadly clutches.

5. When you must make important decisions, spend adequate time to study the matter and make informed decisions. Do not allow ambivalence to dominate your state of mind. This is not healthy for good relationships.

# Chapter 7

# The Need for Transformation

**Anchor Text: Romans 12:2**

"And be not conformed to this world: but be ye transformed by the renewing of your mind, that ye may prove what *is* that good, and acceptable, and perfect, will of God."

**Paraphrased for Families**

And do not continue practicing the old, insensitive, or hypersensitive patterns of relationships of this world, but improve on them with a renewed, healthy state of mind, that you may experience that good, sensitive family relationship which God intends for you, and which will prepare you and others for the soon return of Christ.

This chapter is designed to address two major issues:

1. *The need for transformation* as taught in the Bible, in order to experience optimum family relational health amidst the downward trending of human relationship in society.

2. *The importance of sensitivity* in family relational health and the negative impact of its two extremes: insensitivity and hypersensitivity.

## Perspectives on Transformation

Transformation is one of the most expressed desires or goals across the wide spectrum of human life. The basic characteristic of transformation is a marked change in form, nature, or appearance. However, the perspective and outcome of transformation varies depending on the field or discipline in which it is defined and carried out. We will consider transformation from three perspectives:

**Transformation Perspective 1: Mathematics**

Mathematics is the abstract science of numbers, quantity, and space. In that aspect of science, transformation is defined as a process by which one figure, expression, or function is converted into another of similar value. Webster's Dictionary offers this summative, technical definition of *transformation*: "The operation of changing (as by rotation or mapping) one configuration or expression into another in accordance with a mathematical rule; especially a change of variables or coordinates in which a function of new variables or coordinates is substituted for each original variable or coordinate the formula that effects a transformation." The operative terms are *changing, configuration, substituted,* and *converted.*

**Transformation Perspective 2: Molecular**

Wikipedia defines *molecular transformation* as: "the genetic alteration of a cell resulting from the direct uptake and incorporation of exogenous genetic material from its surroundings through the cell membrane. For transformation to take place, the recipient bacteria must be in a state of competence, which might occur in nature as a time-limited response to environmental conditions such as starvation and cell density, and may also be induced." Key words are *uptake, incorporation, alteration,* and *competence.*

**Transformation Perspective 3: Types**

Study.com lists four main types of transformations: *translation, rotation, reflection,* and *dilation.* "These transformations fall into two categories: rigid transformations that do not change the shape or size of the preimage and nonrigid transformations that change the size but not the shape of the preimage." The term to note is *change*. And the study on scientific transformation could continue on endlessly!

It is clear that the common element in the concept of transformation is *change*. Applied to family relationships, it is equally a clear consensus that the most desirable, positive, upward expectation to improve the quality of family life is change. Christ, our Exemplar of relationships, challenges us to experience change and to aim toward perfection (Matt. 5:48).

To keep that same focus on *change* and apply the bigger word in which it is embedded—that is, *transformation*—to our world today in the context of relationship, it remains the most desirable when it comes to our behavior, deportment, comportment, and attitude toward each other. Change!

## Change Needed in All Relationships

In most hurting relationships, there is the languishing desire for healthy change. In relationships that are experiencing average quality, there is the desire for change upward. And in relationships that are above average and are abounding, family members are making sustained efforts to change even for the better. This good desire for better takes us back to early school days, when this memory gem was taught: "Good, better, best; never let it rest, until your good is better and your better best." It seems ingrained in the human psyche that there is always room for improvement, hence the suggestion that the largest room in the house is the room for improvement!

A constant reality and need that is facing society daily has to do with transformation. Science is so advanced that we can produce virtually any desired transformation in just about any*thing*—technological, physical, chemical, electronic, or in any combination we desire. But it is not as easy to produce that transformation in people generally.

The attitude and behavior of human beings, in whom such change is obviously needed, appear to be well-nigh impossible. Sometimes the need for the desired change is known by the person, and by others, but it is just not forthcoming. Sometimes it is even difficult or uncomfortable to mention to some persons that there is the evident need for change. To initiate change in human beings is a task that almost appears insurmountable. We can transform any*thing* but not any*one*.

## Relational Sensitivity: Nerves and Emotions

The next major issue that this chapter sets out to address is *sensitivity*. Let us employ a physiological analogy to offer an explanation. Nerves are to the body as emotions are to the mind (CPH²). According to Quora, the brain and the spinal cord process signals from over 60,000 miles of nerves in the network of the body, making us aware of nearly every impact that the body experiences.

The nervous system uses electrical and chemical means to help all parts of the body communicate with each other. One cannot help but remember David's expressed marvel at the complexity of the human body: "I will praise thee; for I am fearfully and wonderfully made: marvellous are thy works; and that my soul knoweth right well" (Ps. 139:14).

Relational sensitivity is far more complex for analytical and statistical recording than physiological and neurological sensitivity via the nerves. Given that the subject of relational sensitivity can be quite broad, we are working in the narrow context of the processing in the mind of the dynamics and vicissitudes of family relationships. We are keeping focus on the four vital signs of relationship arriving out of the family relational health laboratory that drives this work—*connection, rapport, bond,* and *support*—and the emotions these produce that affect the relational mind.

Emotions are so complex that they are more difficult to quantify and measure than nerves, inasmuch as they are real to the quality of behavior and relationships in the mind as nerves are real to the functions of conductivity of the body.

## Definition of Emotion

To do justice to the subject of the impact of emotions on relational sensitivity, let us consider a working definition of emotion, limited to this book. An emotion is the instinctive, automatic ingrained experience primarily in the form of a multiplicity of thoughts and feelings produced in the brain after it has processed the social and environmental messages that it receives from the senses. In the processing of these messages, there is a complex interaction of chemicals and electrical charges in the various lobes of the brain that produces an even more complex output of responses and reactions in the person.

*Output* is a key term here, as it takes us back to the very etymology (origin) of the word *emotion*. From its Latin origin, the prefix *e* means "out". A simple example of its usage is the second book of the Bible, *Exodus*, meaning *e* = "out" and *odus* = "away". Hence, Exodus means *out and away* from Egypt for the children of Israel. Another good example is *extract*. Here, *e/ex* = "out" and *trahere* = "to draw" or "pull". Hence, when extracting a tooth, the dentist simply *draws* or *pulls* it out!

Applied: *Emotion* means *e* = "out" and *movere* = "to move". The *output* of the physiological complexity of chemical and electrical charges in the billions of different cells of the brain is a result of the stimulus produced in it by the complex messages from the eyes, the ears, the nose, the tongue, and the skin. This output indicates motion or movement, and that is the sum total of the word *emotion*.

It is this *out-motions* or *movements-out* from the chemical and electrical interactions, produced from the stimuli of the messages from the senses, that are called *emotions*. Psychiatric and neurological researchers give the comprehensive study about the names and calibration of the chemicals, and the functional relationships between factors such as the spinal cord, synapses, receptors, neurons, axons, dendrites, impulses, and neurotransmitters, among others, all being a part of the study of emotions in the human experience.

For a clearer understanding of emotions in the context of family relational health, it is important that we revisit our definition of the mind. The mind is the composite working and functioning of the brain in coordination with its avenues or connections to the outside (of the cranium/skull) world—those are the senses—resulting in a complexity of emotions manifested in thoughts, perceptions, imaginations, and actions, affecting the quality of one's total life existence and that of those in his or her sphere of influence in an equally complex variety of ways. (See Active, Sound Mind in the Glossary pp. 395–397).

We conclude then that an emotion is the psychological product of the physiological (chemical and electrical) functionality of the brain as a result of the messages it receives from the senses. Theoretically, if the senses were to be totally cut off from the brain—that is to say, with disconnection of the optical, auditory, glossopharyngeal, and olfactory nerves and the spinal cord—its processing of social and environmental data would be grossly reduced if not ceased, thus compromising its full functionality, saving the internal regulatory, organic, and glandular functions (including the vagus nerve and other afferent and efferent nerve receptors), which no doubt themselves would be affected.

For the purpose of dichotomizing the physiological and psychological functions of the body, in the interest of highlighting family relational health, we suggest that emotional functions are therefore attributed more to the mind—the software from a psychological and, more specifically, relational perspective—than to the brain, the hardware from a biological, neurological, and physiological perspective.

## Simplified Summary of Emotion

An emotion is the psychological out-working motion or movement of the mind in response or reaction to the brain processing of the social and environmental messages that it receives from the senses.

## Types of Emotions

There are several schools of thought regarding the number of emotions in our human experience. First, there are what is referred to as the universal category of six human emotions: happiness, sadness, anger, surprise, fear, and disgust. However, the *Proceedings of the National Academy of Sciences* of the United States of America, in Berkley, California, reported in its September 2017 edition that their research has identified twenty-seven distinct emotional dimensions.

In 2014, on the other side of the Atlantic, researchers at the Institute of Neuroscience and Psychology at the University of Glasgow argued that there are only four such basic emotions, not six. They used computer imaging technique to measure facial expressions produced by the activation of the forty-two muscles in the face. The lead researcher, Dr. Rachael Jack concluded that *fear* and *surprise* are one and the same, as are *anger* and *disgust*, leaving us with the other two distinct emotions, *happiness* and *sadness*.

While we laud and applaud these and other groundbreaking scientific researches and exposés on these two issues of transformation and sensitivity, and their explanations on emotions and emotional behaviors, we are still going to be left lamenting and bewailing the gloomy fact that all evidences continue to point to the continuous deterioration of family relational health worldwide.

The masters and professors in our psychological, sociological, and anthropological communities have yet to come up with the winning formula to guarantee the positive change in behavior that will result in a stable, sustained quality of life in society. We are therefore forced to look for the answers from another source, and that source remains the Bible and its account of the origin of the species, not from Darwin's perspective but from the Creator, Himself, and His proffered answer to the human relational dilemma.

## Timely International Promotion of Emotions

### "United by Emotions" - Olympics 2020 Motto

Undoubtedly the most international and elevated reference to the relational importance of our emotional sensitivity is the Motto of the Tokyo 2020 Olympics and Paralympics: "United by Emotions". The Motto was ably narrated by Japanese born Naomi Osaka: "We are each different, and all so much the same. And in these moments we experience and these emotions we share, we change what we can imagine together." Naomi was appropriately chosen given her diverse background – born in Japan; father Haitian; mother Japanese; raised in the USA.

The motto resonates with this work on family relational health on the premise that when God made the human family at Creation, one of the binding ties of relational health that He placed in our minds was the ability to develop and use our powerful emotions.

Unfortunately, so many forces have tried over the centuries to stultify this essential quality of our being and make us robots instead of human. Relational emotions have been trampled upon so badly that it seems to be a badge of honour to proudly proclaim: "I am not the emotional type!" Some go as far as to denounce and repudiate its expression: "There is no room for emotion in this matter." "You are too emotional!" "It is a weak man who shows emotions."

At the Olympics Victory Ceremony however, emotions were not shown with any calculated poise and control. Instead, there were so many scenes when various emotions shown unbridledly by both men and women olympian victors as they proudly displayed their medals of triumph and achievement.

It can be assumed that the Tokyo 2020 planning team did not have the biblical, foundational healthy perspective of emotions when they chose the motto. Most likely, they were motivated by the sociological and cultural perspective. Here we see that God does work in mysterious ways and providentially uses this international gathering of over 10,000 athletes and representatives from more than 200 countries to awaken the world community to revisit the healthy use of His gift of emotions to help and bring people together. We hope the message might live long after the euphoria of the games is passed.

This reference to God's providential use of the Tokyo 2020 Olympics could be paralleled in a small way to His providential use of what happened at the cosmopolitan city of Antioch as recorded in Acts chapter 2. The Day of Pentecost was well timed as representatives from several nations were there and witnessed the outpouring of the Holy Ghost on the disciples, and heard and participated in the launching of the international spread of the Gospel of Jesus Christ.

Inasmuch as there will be no Pentecostal manifestation of the lessons about the positive, healthy power of human emotions at the Tokyo Olympics, yet the stage was set for psychologists, sociologists and all professionals in the behavioural disciplines to go beyond the transient emotions of the games as they joined in and enjoyed as all other human beings. They should capitalize on what happened there and through interviews, anecdotal stories, qualitative and quantitative researches among other means, get a new study and even create lasting papers and even books on the uniting force of emotions beyond mere Olympic Games. Posterity could be the beneficiary of the 2020 IOC's potentially iconic motto selection.

Commendations are due to Tokyo 2020 CEO Toshiro Muto and the organizing team for its visionary decision in selecting a most appropriate, timely and relevant motto when the world is cracking and breaking up at so many seams created by local, regional and international disunity, psychological effects of the pandemic, divergent and discordant views and attitudes to each other. This book further congratulates and at the same time, encourages and challenges all the athletes in the various sports for the discipline they showed.

Very special commendations to the many medallists who demonstrated in the eyes of the world the epitome of the motto as they bonded and cheered each other, regardless of their national, ethnic, and racial or any other personal identity. Writing on the Independence Day of the island of Jamaica, the national pride was palpable everywhere as the 4x4 Women's Relay Team of Briana Williams, Elaine Thompson-Herah, Shelly-ann Fraser-Pryce, and Shericka Jackson gave the nation another in its tally of Gold and other Medals. Of no less value is the Gold Medal brought to the Author's parish of St. Thomas by Hansel Parchment.

They, along with all the winners on that day and throughout the games should be ambassadors of Tokyo 2020 and carry the Olympic torch flaming with the message of healthy, positive human emotions, back to their homes, communities and nations, thereby helping the world to become a more emotionally sensitive place where unity and bond can be fully experienced (See Addendum to Glossary – 1 Mental Health on Tokyo 2020 Olympic Stage, p. 420).

# Extrapolation 1

*Original:* "And be not conformed to this world"

*Paraphrased for Families:* "And do not continue practicing the old, insensitive, or hypersensitive patterns of relationships of this world"

## Hypersensitivity versus High Sensitivity

With all of us human beings sharing the common ancestry of being: "born in sin and shapen in iniquity" (Ps. 51:5)—the Bible tells us up front that we automatically end up with the undesirable traits and relational patterns of our ancestors. "What mean ye, that ye use this proverb concerning the land of Israel, saying, The fathers have eaten sour grapes, and the children's teeth are set on edge" (Ezek. 18:2). Our first big brother, Cain, gave full evidence of the double-edged relational sword of insensitivity and hypersensitivity.

Cain was first hypersensitive to the exemplary ability of his brother, Abel, to be obedient to God's expressed requirements. He undoubtedly felt that Abel was imposing on him and would eventually show him up to be not as good and obedient. Compared with the psychological explanation of hypersensitivity, Cain's behavior would have to be labeled extreme, negative hypersensitivity with destructive propensity. His was not a case of high sensitivity as in a biological or chemical reaction or intolerance, or that of a weak relational coping skill. High sensitivity and hypersensitivity are not one and the same.

Abel's lifestyle was a rebuke to Cain, and it must have jarred the latter's emotions. In the end, he mysteriously flipped to the other extreme, became insensitive to the overtures of his brother, and slowly descended into disgust, anger, and hatred. Cain eventually lost all relational connection, rapport, bond, and support; he no longer saw his brother as his own flesh and blood. Those family relational health vital signs disappeared from his relational mind.

All scruples, conscience, and morality vanished, and it was as easy for Cain to maim and destroy his brother as it was for him to breathe. This is human insensitivity at subzero degree level. Cain's mysterious, violent act was the first full manifestation on earth of the ultimate mystery of iniquity, and Satan's plot was well sown in the human family.

**Partial Contextualization of the Russian-Ukraine War (2022) with Family Relational Health**

The most current international macrocosmic evidence of the continuation of Cain's insensitivity towards his brother is that of the leadership sovereignty violation of older Russian brother, Vladmir Putin (69) towards that of his younger, neighbouring Ukranian brother, Volodmyr Zelenskyy (44) in what is now known as the Russian-Ukraine War (February 2022).

Here, Putin in an apparent quest for establishing his political prowess and ambition on the world stage (somewhat reminiscent of Lucifer's ambition for the universal stage Ezekiel 28:12-19; Isaiah 14:14) and in continuation of the conflict which began in 2014 which has earlier historical backgrounds, has stultified and benumbed his God-implanted human emotional sensitivity to the horror, dislocation and death that his action would wreak upon the Ukranian nation.

Every act of violence and murder today—regardless of who the perpetrator might be; how gruesome, grisly, and horrific the method might be; and who the victims might be—all are an outgrowth of this first act by Cain. He seemed to have been able to induce an inexplicable sense of chemical imbalance in his brain, such that all his human relational vital signs of connection, rapport, bond and support, have dropped to sub-zero degree on the sensitivity scale.

At that level of politically self-induced insanity, Putin became embolden, and like our first brother, Cain, invade, attack, violate and destroy his brothers and sisters of whose welfare and lives he will probably answer: "Am I their keeper?" (Gen. 4:9), Putin claimed that his goal was to: "demilitarize and de-Nazify Ukraine" and to protect the people from what he referred to as eight years of the Ukrainian government bullying and acts of genocide. Protection—resulting in the loss of thousands of innocent lives?

The bad news is that this kind of local, national and international mayhem of man's inhumanity to man will continue until God, in His divine wisdom, sees that sin and iniquity must cease and the entire universe sees the fullness of His patience and long-suffering. (See Practicing deception page 225).

Then He will put an end to the mayhem that Satan began in heaven (Rev. 12:7–8), thus fulfilling the prophecy He made through Nahum: "What do ye imagine against the Lord? He will make an utter end: affliction shall not rise up the second time" (Nahum 1:9).

**Insensitivity and Hypersensitivity Explained**

Having established the biblical account for the origin of these relational traits, let us give the working definitions of both terms—*hypersensitivity* and *insensitivity*—by considering their root word: *sensitivity*. Wherever a healthy marriage, parent-child, or any other family relationship exists, one can expect to find a good mix of compassion, understanding, warmth, feeling, and thoughtfulness among family members. This would be considered a family with healthy sensitivity. It suggests that they care for, and are in touch with, each other's well-being. It further suggests that all four relational health vital signs are in the upper range of the relational health scale of one to ten.

On the other hand, when the family exists in a relationship characterized by indifference, apathy, lack of sympathy, lack of mutual interest, coldness, and lack of concern, that family relational health is impaired. There is no healthy connection, rapport, bond, or support among them. It would further suggest that each might be focused only on his own well-being, even at the expense of the other(s). Such is the branded sign of relational insensitivity.

In some instances, family members walk on the proverbial chalk line, constantly watching their Ps and Qs. This becomes necessary when individuals are easily offended. Suspicion and defensiveness are experienced often in these relationships, resulting in the need to rehearse a comment or anything that is considered serious or important to be said to another. This is done so as to avoid confrontation, altercation, and unwarranted disagreements.

When this is a pattern in their relationship, they might be considered to be living in a hypersensitive condition. One or more of the group members is clearly not comfortable, and the atmosphere is charged with mistrust, apprehension, and an undue sense of cautiousness and restraint. How much more unhealthy can a family relational living condition get!?

**Body and Mind Transformation—Not the Same**

Transforming *things*? Oh yes, definitely, we can! And we should point out that we have also mastered the skill of transforming sections of the human body. Cosmetic and plastic surgeries are heralded for making remarkable changes for good medical reasons as well as for persons who believe they need to be different for other reasons and motivations.

Transforming human beings from an undesirable social, behavioral, attitudinal, or mindset status is definitely not as easy, if at all possible. But such transformation is not only desirable; in many cases, it is a dire and urgent need. It is undoubtedly one of the most far-reaching and influential endeavors that could be embarked upon in building a healthy, stable society.

What is it that makes this all-important work of transformation in human beings so daunting and apparently well-nigh impossible? It is the complexity and the mysterious nature of that aspect of human beings called the mind. Let us remind ourselves that one aspect of the foundation theory of family relational health is that all human relationships begin and continue to exist in the active, sound mind.

If the mind is so complex, mysterious, and well-nigh impossible to transform, then it goes without saying that the relationships that begin and continue to exist in it would understandably share the same state of complexity, mysteriousness, and difficulty to be transformed toward the desirable end.

We have also suggested that the mind is the avenue through which the Holy Spirit communicates with man. Only God, who knows the mind, can bring about any real lasting change to it. Our proposed solution to the family relational health dilemma includes transformation and getting rid of insensitivity and hypersensitivity in the mind. All of this can only be accomplished by the indwelling power of the Holy Spirit.

**Transformation: A Divine and Human Effort**

Even though the work of transformation is primarily that of the Holy Spirit, it will not be realized without the full, active participation of the individual. The individual must be involved in his eternal welfare, doing his part as the Spirit motivates him into action for his own good. He must resolve in his mind to discontinue the undesirable attitude or behavior of insensitivity or hypersensitivity. He must detest them and settle in his mind that such behavior is inexcusable, and one that he abhors and eschews, as it was said of Job (Job 1:8).

The person who responds to the impressions of the Holy Spirit and applies for change through earnest and even agonizing prayer needs to add self-talk therapy to his action plan. This is also inspired by the Holy Spirit:

> In the same way the Spirit helps us in our weakness. We do not know what to pray for but the Spirit, Himself, intercedes for us through wordless groans. And He Who searches our hearts knows the mind of the Spirit, because the Spirit intercedes for God's people in accordance with the will of God. (Rom. 8:26–27, NIV)

David also, under the inspiration of the Holy Spirit, practiced self-talk therapy as recorded in Psalm 42:5: "Why art thou cast down, O my soul? and why art thou disquieted in me? hope thou in God: for I shall yet praise him for the help of his countenance." (See paraphrase in Chapter 9.)

The human therapist will advise and set up the behavior modification program, but the reality is that no human can reach the inner soul, the deep recesses of the mind. The Holy Spirit carries out the change with the cooperation of the individual. "For it is God which worketh in you, both to will and to do of his good pleasure" (Phil. 2:13).

Self-talk therapy means the same as "speak it into being". Correctly understood, we can only speak something into being when fully surrendering our hearts to the continued work of the Spirit. That must be accompanied by the practice of self-affirmation. Look for the evidence that you are bearing fruit. Look for the evidence of the changes you are making, and affirm yourself by developing that feeling of satisfaction that God is accomplishing His will in you. Challenge yourself to continue. If family members or friends observe the change and mention it to you, accept it humbly, tell them thanks, then continue to give God thanks.

## The 3 Cs: Consciousness, Conscientiousness, Consistency

In order for one to experience a sustained change, one needs to practice what is learned consciously, conscientiously, and consistently. *Consciously* means that you keep being aware that there is a change that you wanted to have made and that it actually took place and you want it to remain so. This process is said to take place in the cognitive domain of the mind. This is the intelligent aspect of our being, and we must always keep that awareness at the forefront of our thinking.

Now you want your intelligent consciousness to get into the deep aspect of your mind and set it beyond mere acceptance. In your quiet moments, you savor the new experience; your conscience is deeply awakened, and you resolve repeatedly that this is the best decision you could have made. At this stage, the decision you made and the change you experienced make you feel *new* and *refreshed*, and you even wonder how you took so long to get to this new point. This is the Holy Spirit inspiring your mind with a holy sense of satisfaction and accomplishment.

## The Replacement Stage in the Transformation Process

This is the stage of the *affective domain*, when the change begins to be experienced in the emotions—positive thoughts and feelings. This is considered as the change taking place in the psyche, which is further considered to be the deepest aspect of the mind, where change really becomes embedded. Your therapy or treatment is now in the *replacement stage*.

In order for this replacement therapy to fully become the new you, another important *C* must be brought into the final mix. Your practice of the change must be *consistent*. You must have the will to do what needs to be done without coercion, condition, or excuse. This is the stage referred to as the *psychomotor domain*, in which the behavioral effect is registered.

One school principal, Mrs Beryl McKenzie, said many decades ago: "Inconsistency is a curse." When one does not practice change consistently, one runs the risk of relapsing and going into remission. We are always exposed to temptations, challenges, and even luring situations that can put our best intentions and efforts to very strenuous tests.

Consistent prayer, consistent awareness, consistent working on that which is good, and an abiding faith in the Lord will help us to remain transformed. The benediction of Jude 24–25 will be the experience of the family member who wants to remain sensitive to the feelings and needs of others and avoid slipping to the two extremes of insensitivity and hypersensitivity.

The promise from the God of Families says it is possible: "Now unto him that is able to keep you from falling, and to present you faultless before the presence of his glory with exceeding joy, to the only wise God our Savior, be glory and majesty, dominion and power, both now and ever, Amen."

## Extrapolation 2

*Original:* "by the renewing of your mind"

*Paraphrased for Families:* "with a renewed, healthy state of mind"

Change without consistent practice is a transitory exercise, the impact of which will be short-lived. It will last only for a brief moment and will eventually be ineffective. To avert this sense of failure and disappointment, especially when the decision was taken earnestly at the beginning, there has to be daily renewal of the healthy state of mind. This daily renewal is a part of the consistency effort and can be achieved in several ways.

Every day, we are exposed to temptations, discouragements, and sometimes a sense of failure. There is nothing we can do to totally avoid these experiences, which themselves are part of what we call the vicissitudes and vagaries of life, or simply the ups and downs of daily living. They are, for the most part, inescapable, and at times can even be for our good. James puts it this way: "My brethren, count it all joy when ye fall into divers temptations; Knowing this, that the trying of your faith worketh patience" (Jas. 1:2–3).

**Persistence and Perseverance**

Patience, in the context of our discourse, could be interpreted to mean exercising endurance when things do not always go how we hoped they would. Practicing persistence and perseverance as we strive for the mastery in making the needed change is a mark of maturity. One of the best armors for these realities is to be fully aware of what is possible, any day, anywhere, anyhow, from anyone or in any manner. This positive level of alertness is not to be mistaken for the mental illnesses of *paranoia* and *hypervigilance*. Where those exist, professional and clinical care is required (See pp. 18, 232, 245).

Being transformed by the Holy Spirit and rejoicing in the healthy change does not mean that we are equally granted immunity from the forces that are hell-bent upon destroying our family relational health. Such forces become more vigilant and strategic in their attack, hence our need not only to keep abreast of them but to be as Peter advised: "Be sober, be vigilant; because your adversary the devil, as a roaring lion, walketh about, seeking whom he may devour" (1 Pet. 5:8).

The Anchor Text of Chapter 2 reminds us: "For we wrestle not against flesh and blood, but against principalities, against powers, against the rulers of the darkness of this world, against spiritual wickedness in high places" (Eph. 6:12). And the paraphrased version for families says:

> For we wrestle not against ordinary marital, parental, and general family relational challenges, but against the continuous deteriorating standards of this world; against the subtle forces set at destroying God's original family ideals; against the corrupt, immoral practices of this age, operating from high academic, religious, social, and other influential stage of the society.

The mind is a battlefield in which the fierce war between good and evil, right and wrong, and sin and righteousness are always being fought. The stage is set by the forces all around us, but depending on our daily renewal of the healthy state of mind, we can join in the defeat of those evil influences and powers, and come out the victor by the indwelling power of Christ.

He has already assured us that we can win, because He already won and will help us accordingly. His assurance is in John 16:33: "These things I have spoken unto you, that in me ye might have peace. In the world ye shall have tribulation: but be of good cheer; I have overcome the world." Paul in Phil. 4:13 expressed that level of confidence for himself and for all who come after him and rely upon Christ: "I can do all things through Christ which strengtheneth me."

## Closet Self-Affirmation and Daily Renewal

Each day, one needs to make a conscious expression of the good that "I will do …" It actually helps to verbalize this to oneself. Do not just think it, but speak it out in your quiet moments by yourself, so you hear it being said by yourself, in your own ears. And a good place to practice this very personal exercise of daily renewal is where Jesus recommends: in your closet. Here are His own words: "But thou, when thou prayest, enter into thy closet, and when thou hast shut thy door, pray to thy Father which is in secret; and thy Father which seeth in secret shall reward thee openly" (Matt. 6:6).

Your closet can be that secret space where you go for special prayer, especially in the early morning, following the Jesus model: "And in the morning, rising up a great while before day, he went out, and departed into a solitary place, and there prayed" (Mark 1:35). Those who follow this model can testify that it is an inspiring, refreshing way to start the day.

The closet could be under that tree; at that spot in the garden; in the bathroom, in the study or library, indeed in the clothes closet—wherever. Just make it a consistent practice until it becomes established between you and God that it is here you meet with Him privately. It works!

In the case where one has a known special area of weakness—"the sin which doth so easily beset us" (Heb. 12:1), and each one ought to know his or hers—a more deliberate, decisive commitment has to be silently and resolutely made. Sometimes, in addition to the one-and-one relationship with Christ through sincere, penitential, contrite prayer and fasting, it can help to share that commitment with a confidante who will help to keep you accountable. From a therapist's perspective, it must be mentioned that there is room for professional help in situations like these, so that the confidante referred to could be a family relational health caregiver.

Another very important reason for the daily renewal of the mind is the testimony that is offered to those in one's sphere of influence. The Christian's good, healthy lifestyle is not for himself alone. We ought to live and let others see us living. That in itself is a testimony to the power of the grace of the indwelling Christ.

Decades ago, the late Dr Paul Freed, president and founder of Transworld Radio, Bonaire, in preaching about the importance of one's life testimony, said, "Even if I don't believe what he says, I like a man who believes what he says." A more succinct rendition of that statement is the more popular, "I prefer to see a sermon than to hear one!" A renewed state of mind therefore maintains its responsibility to, and its potential influence on, others. It remains true in many instances that we are our neighbor's Bible.

## Spiritual Retooling

In the manufacturing and industrial aspects of business, a part of the annual or periodic budgetary provision is for retooling. It is understood that with the normal, regular wear and tear of operation, the machinery, in whole or in part, requires reconditioning, modernizing, and updating in order to maintain productivity and keep the business market share. To no less degree does the growing Christian need retooling. Every day is a new day, and the output from the Christian's life has to be in sync with the demands of that day.

In this context, renewal or retooling could mean acquiring new relational skills, aptitudes, and competencies to do more than coping, but to move to the higher level of managing what comes. To *manage* oneself means to be in charge, to possess, to lay hold of who you are. Paul said it this way to the Thessalonians: "That every one of you should know how to possess his vessel in sanctification and honor" (1Thess. 4:4). *Manage* comes from the Latin root *manus*, meaning "hand", from which comes other words such as *manipulate* and *manuscript*.

One has to mentally, emotionally, socially, and spiritually take charge of oneself on a daily basis. This is the epitome of daily renewal of the relational mind, rejuvenating and regenerating new thoughts and judgments, new contemplations and deliberations. It also means avoiding unnecessary hurry so as to reduce the likelihood of offending or violating principles when operating continuously in the proverbial fast lane of life. In the doctrine of Christian growth and maturity, this is called the process of *sanctification*, which is the daily setting aside of oneself to be inspired, directed, and used by the Holy Spirit.

This daily renewal, this daily retooling, of the relational mind of the husband, wife, children, and others in the family is only truly and completely possible through the working of the Spirit of Christ. The plausible scientific theories on transformation in mathematics, biology, chemistry, and technology, with keywords and operative concepts such as *converted, uptake, incorporate, alteration, competence, configuration,* and *substitute,* are all part of the process of Christian life. They all take place through the inspired working of the divine and human, as God originally intended it to be.

Therefore, we can safely conclude that the renewed relational mind does not merely conform with expectations. It does not experience a mere reformation or cosmetic makeover to please onlookers. Transformation is a work from the inside out, and in the life of Christian family members, this work can only be accomplished by the Creator of the human relational mind, God Himself.

## Extrapolation 3

*Original:* "that ye may prove"

*Paraphrased for Families:* "that you may experience that good, sensitive family relationship which God intends for you"

### Complaint About Boring Christian Life

It is most unfortunate that a number of persons who embrace the Christian faith and lifestyle report that they find it boring and restrictive. This is a common issue in some pastoral households or other church leadership families, especially among growing children. So, too, it is for some persons who enter the Church family through such mass movements as crusades and some other forms of media evangelism, where there might not have been sufficient teaching on what to be expected in the new life.

This complaint is also heard from those who merely followed relatives and friends without a personal, deep conviction. These are those about whom Jesus spoke in Mark 4:15–17:

> And these are they likewise which are sown on stony ground; who, when they have heard the word, immediately receive it with gladness; And have no root in themselves, and so endure but for a time: afterward, when affliction or persecution ariseth for the word's sake, immediately they are offended.

Such persons reportedly do not experience the inner joy of being a Christian, because, for more reasons than one, they do not own or hone their faith. For some, the Christian mode of family life seems to deprive them of the freedom that non-Christian families seem to be enjoying. These complaints and expressions of discontent, dissatisfaction, and displeasure suggest that they are not experiencing "that good and sensitive family relationship which God intends for you."

Clearly, something is wrong somewhere. To the same extent that pain in the body suggests that there is some malfunctioning taking place, these laments and fault-findings suggest that there is family relational malfunctioning taking place, maybe in the home and Church (CPH[2]). There is a missing dimension to their experience, and it needs to be found and addressed in the interest of their spiritual well-being and to prevent them from adversely influencing others.

**Assurances of Good Christian Living**

By the process of elimination, such chronic relational experiences cannot be attributed to God. Here is His assurance to those who commit themselves to follow His plan: "For I know the thoughts that I think toward you, saith the Lord, thoughts of peace, and not of evil, to give you an expected end. Then shall ye call upon me, and ye shall go and pray unto me, and I will hearken unto you. And ye shall seek me, and find me, when ye shall search for me with all your heart" (Jer. 29:11–13). We could not want it better and more reassuring.

As a result of the impairment that sin has caused on the mind, we do not even know what is best for us. God, who created us and knows us inside out, makes it clear that He already is not just mindful of what we need but has all the answers to meet our needs. He confirms it with a comparison between our thoughts and His thoughts, and then He issues a challenge and an invitation to us: "Seek ye the Lord while he may be found, call ye upon him while he is near: Let the wicked forsake his way, and the unrighteous man his thoughts: and let him return unto the Lord, and he will have mercy upon him; and to our God, for he will abundantly pardon. For my thoughts are not your thoughts, neither are your ways my ways, saith the Lord" (Isa. 55:6–8).

After enduring excruciating hardship, adversity, persecution, and suffering for the cause of Christ, Paul still maintained his faith: "Being confident of this very thing, that he which hath begun a good work in you will perform it until the day of Jesus Christ" (Phil. 1:6). He was not daunted or fearful or second-guessing the decision that he made to commit his life to Christ, because he knew that what Christ assured him of will be fulfilled.

Such was the experience and testimony of those referred to in Hebrews 12:1 as a cloud of witnesses: "Wherefore seeing we also are compassed about with so great a cloud of witnesses, let us lay aside every weight, and the sin which doth so easily beset us, and let us run with patience the race that is set before us."

We can conclude, therefore, that someone might not be experiencing that good and sensitive relationship which God intends because the retarding influence must be coming from the individual himself, or maybe from the whole family unit. It is often said that we are our greatest enemy. We are the ones who stymie or retard our own growth and progress, most times unknowingly.

**Three Conditions Applied for Experiencing God's Mercy**

For us to have this rich and fulfilling experience which God promises us, we must firstly give ourselves wholly and completely to Him. God's promises are sure, and although His gifts of grace and mercy, of joy and peace, are offered to everyone, conditions do apply on the part of the would-be recipients.

*Condition 1* Surrender the Total You

"Only fear the LORD, and serve him in truth with all your heart: for consider how great things he hath done for you" (1 Sam. 12:24). This was as true for the Children of Israel then as it is for us today. Jesus Himself said it, and we often repeat it as one of the favorite memory passages from the Bible: "And he answering said, Thou shalt love the Lord thy God with all thy heart, and with all thy soul, and with all thy strength, and with all thy mind; and thy neighbor as thyself" (Luke 10:27).

The condition or requirement is the total you or none at all. "No man can serve two masters: for either he will hate the one, and love the other; or else he will hold to the one, and despise the other. Ye cannot serve God and mammon" (Matt. 6:24). "And ye shall seek me, and find me, when ye shall search for me with all your heart" (Jer. 29:13).

*Condition 2* Believe God's Promises Without Wavering

"If any of you lack wisdom, let him ask of God, that giveth to all men liberally, and upbraideth not; and it shall be given him. But let him ask in faith, nothing wavering. For he that wavereth is like a wave of the sea driven with the wind and tossed. For let not that man think that he shall receive any thing of the Lord. A double minded man is unstable in all his ways" (Jas. 1: 5–8). "Let us hold fast the profession of our faith without wavering; (for he is faithful that promised;)" (Heb. 10:23).

To the same extent that inconsistency is a curse to achieving mastery and competence in any practice, so is wavering a setback and blight to spiritual growth and development. To the same extent that the prescribed course of medication is to be taken as directed by the physician, in the interest of the condition being treated, so it is that the believer ought to follow the counsels and impressions of the Holy Spirit without wavering in order to experience the desired spiritual growth (CPH[2]). It is a case of having the proverbial "one foot in and one foot out" so that one is never seen as fully on board. The condition or requirement is: No wavering or second-guessing!

"I know thy works, that thou art neither cold nor hot: I would thou wert cold or hot. So then because thou art lukewarm, and neither cold nor hot, I will spew thee out of my mouth" (Rev. 3:15–16). Disconnection and separation occur when we waver and second-guess in our relationship with Christ.

***Condition 3*** Be Actively Involved

"For as the body without the spirit is dead, so faith without works is dead also" (Jas. 2:26). Inasmuch as the Bible is so clear on the issue, the controversy over works vs grace in the salvation plan still rages on. Here is the summary: "But sanctify the Lord God in your hearts: and be ready always to give an answer to every man that asketh you a reason of the hope that is in you with meekness and fear." There is no part in the salvation plan to accommodate a passive spirit or attitude on the part of the practicing Christian.

The Christian who wants to experience that good and sensitive relationship which God intends for you must be actively involved.

You are a part of the answer to your prayer. And if that sounds too much like the human taking it onto himself, let us say it in a more appropriate way to show that it is still God who does the work: God uses us as a part of the answer to our prayers. We will only experience what God has in store for us when we make ourselves available for Him to use us, even to answer the prayers we send to Him.

## Faith Is More Than Mental Ascent or Believing

Jesus asked the blind man: "What wilt thou that I should do unto thee?" (Mark 10:51). Jesus knew what the man needed, but He asked the question to propel the man's faith into readiness for action. We can deduce the following from Jesus's faith-inspired, action-provoking question:

- "Have you settled in your mind what you want?"
- "Are you prepared to play your part by exercising your faith?"
- "Are you aware that faith is more than believing but also a readiness to act upon my bidding or instruction?"

The Holy Spirit inspired in the man's mind the answer to all those questions at a speed which only He can produce (See p. 436). He made the mind and knows best how to motivate it into action. The man had to yield his mind and be prepared to act on the impressions that it received from the Lord. Notice that through it all, the human is actively involved. He exercised the power of choice, which God created in us but which we must activate. This is faith in action.

The condition or requirement is this: Do your honest part! "And I say unto you, Ask, and it shall be given you; seek, and ye shall find; knock, and it shall be opened unto you" (Luke 11:9). How will you be able to experience that good and sensitive relationship which God intends for you?

- Be prepared to dedicate the total you or none at all. It must be the "full hundred".
- There can be no wavering or second-guessing. "This one thing I do" (Phil. 3:13).
- Do your honest part. "Take up thy bed and walk" (Mark 2:9).

God will crown your sincerity with success.

## Extrapolation 4

*Original:* "will of God"

*Paraphrased for Families:* "which will prepare you and others for the soon return of Christ"

In essay writing, we are taught that the theme of the piece is the golden thread that runs through the article and binds all thoughts and ideas together. As the article develops and nears its conclusion, the theme is to be felt reaching a crescendo. As one reads through, elements of the theme must be constantly felt and never get lost.

### Fixation of Purpose

In the same way, the coming of Christ is to pervade every effort, activity, and endeavor in which the Christian gets involved. The soon return of Christ is the driving theme and motivation in the Christian life at home, church, school, and work. The work of transformation, the practice of sensitivity, and the abhorrence of the opposite extremes—insensitivity and hypersensitivity—have the one ultimate goal: "Till we all come in the unity of the faith, and of the knowledge of the Son of God, unto a perfect man, unto the measure of the stature of the fullness of Christ" (Eph. 4:13).

"For the grace of God that bringeth salvation hath appeared to all men, teaching us that, denying ungodliness and worldly lusts, we should live soberly, righteously, and godly, in this present world; looking for that blessed hope, and the glorious appearing of the great God and our Savior Jesus Christ" (Titus 2:11-13). Impelled and propelled by the Holy Spirit, each family member will keep his or her focus on this great anticipated, climactic event of the ages.

Amidst the drudgery and struggles of daily living, we can keep that focus by borrowing from David and having a fixation of purpose on the Blessed Hope. "My heart is fixed, O God, my heart is fixed: I will sing and give praise" (Ps. 57:7). This suggests that there is resolution and finality in his relationship with the Lord. And then God chimes in and crowns that resolution with His assurance through Isaiah: "Thou wilt keep him in perfect peace, whose mind is stayed on thee: because he trusteth in thee. Trust ye in the Lord forever: for in the Lord Jehovah is everlasting strength" (Isa. 26:3–4).

The end result, the final work of transformation for the individual family member, is also Paul's advice to the Colossians: "As ye have therefore received Christ Jesus the Lord, so walk ye in him: Rooted and built up in him, and established in the faith, as ye have been taught, abounding therein with thanksgiving" (Col. 2:6–7). We are to be rooted, grounded, built-up, and established in a healthy relationship with each other and with God. Paul seals it this way to the Corinthians: "Therefore, my beloved brethren, be ye steadfast, unmovable, always abounding in the work of the Lord, forasmuch as ye know that your labor is not in vain in the Lord" (1 Cor. 15:58).

**Familial and Relational Accountability**

But the individual's responsibilities are not over. Let us revisit that scene of the first murder in the human family, which resulted from Cain's mysterious flipping from hypersensitivity to insensitivity. His response to the question that God asked him has a great lesson for each individual as he or she prepares for the Lord's return: "And the Lord said unto Cain, Where is Abel thy brother? And he said, I know not: Am I my brother's keeper?" (Gen. 4:9). The issue here is familial and relational accountability.

Even though we all are incensed by Cain's horrifying act and loathe his callous question, we still need to pay careful attention to any possible weak trace of that estrangement and disaffection between us and those we care about. Too often, there are family members who profess to be fervently preparing for the Lord's return but pay scant regard to the spiritual well-being of their relatives.

Our paraphrase did not stop at "prepare you … for the soon return of Christ." The "and others" is significant and should not be glossed over. Family relational health encompasses all aspects of our accountability for each other, and the greatest joy we can anticipate is to see each other in the kingdom. We are challenged: "And let us consider one another to provoke unto love and to good works: Not forsaking the assembling of ourselves together, as the manner of some is; but exhorting one another: and so much the more, as ye see the day approaching" (Heb. 10:24–25).

To *provoke* means to encourage, challenge, influence, and persuade. Heed the counsel: "Owe no man anything, but to love one another: for he that loveth another hath fulfilled the law" (Rom. 13:8). In the context of family accountability, it means do not deny each other the sincere, persuasive effort necessary to be ready for the Blessed Hope. The continuous, never-ending, even revolving debt that the apostle says we are to have for each other is the loving, sustained appeal in word and deed: "O taste and see that the Lord is good: blessed is the man that trusteth in him" (Ps. 34:8).

Family relational health is certainly a biblical, psycho-social priority when considered against the background of the transforming impact it can have in the lives of the family members. This will only be experienced when the transformation is carried out in the willing, yielding mind by the Holy Spirit. Only He can affirm and retain our positive relational sensitivity and remove the double-edged destructive satanic sword of relational insensitivity and hypersensitivity.

## Suggestions for Action

1. Cultivate and practice a good mix of genuine compassion, understanding, warmth, feeling, and thoughtfulness with your family members.

2. Avoid living a life of suspiciousness and defensiveness and tension with your family members. This is not healthy for anyone in a relationship.

3. Practice the three Cs of consciousness, conscientiousness, and consistency, and watch your relationships improve with the Lord's blessings.

4. Practice you daily private, personal prayer plan and improve your relationship with the Lord.

5. Review the three conditions for receiving God's mercy:

   - God wants the total you or none at all.
   - Serve the Lord without wavering or second-guessing.
   - Do your honest part; be active in doing your part in the plan of salvation.

# Chapter 8

# The DNRA Theory of Family Relational Health

**Anchor Text: Exodus 20:5 & 6 and 34:7**

"Thou shalt not bow down thyself to them, nor serve them: for I the Lord thy God am a jealous God, visiting the iniquity of the fathers upon the children unto the third and fourth generation of them that hate me; And shewing mercy unto thousands of them that love me, and keep my commandments. Keeping mercy for thousands, forgiving iniquity and transgression and sin, and that will by no means clear the guilty; visiting the iniquity of the fathers upon the children, and upon the children's children, unto the third and to the fourth generation."

**Partial Paraphrase for Families**

Be aware that the quality of the relationship that you have with Me, your God, whether it be a loving one through obedience, or a hateful one through disobedience, and consequently, the relationship that you have with your family members, has far-reaching effects, which does not end with your present family or generation; it has the potential to affect many more families and their offspring after you, and could even go on to influence your third and fourth generations, long after you are gone.

## Preamble 1: Language Tone

Unlike the previous chapters, most of the expressions and phraseologies of this one, addressing this new concept of the DNRA Theory (developmental notifiers of relational aptitude), especially in the first part, could come across more scientifically technical and probably making assimilation and understanding more challenging for any reader who might not be exposed to such literature. This is so because the subject employs more scientific terminologies and concept as against some subjects of the other chapters. (See Declaration, p. xxxiv) As the application of the concept is developed, the chapter will taper off to the regular language tone of all the other chapters.

## Preamble 2: Two Studies

The DNRA as a scholarly, psychosocially based study on family relationship is the result of decades of continuous studying, testing, researching, counselling, observing, analysing, writing, and editing. As mentioned on page xv, it is presented from two perspectives: biblical and scientific. The comprehensive work covers the major components of the development of an academic and scientific concept: *the issue/ problem, the hypothesis, the theory, the description, methods and procedures, instruments of assessment, interpretations and applications,* inter-alia and set to be published in a separate book - The DNRA Theory of Family Relational Health: A Psychosocial Perspective.

That which is presented in this chapter is the Bible-based, introductory version of the DNRA, anchoring the fact that all scientific discoveries and knowledge used in offering explanations to the complexities of nature, and aimed at improving the quality of life, have one true Source: God, the Creator. The material in this chapter is introductory, thus the expression *basic* will be used in many cases when a new idea or segment of the DNRA is introduced, with the understanding that the comprehensive details would be available in the other book mentioned above.

## The DNRA Theory: An Introduction

The DNRA (developmental notifiers of relational aptitude) is the study of the dynamic impact of the psychosocial impressions of human relationships which are continuously and imperceptively gathered and accumulated in a person's mind, beginning from conception in one's family of origin, and progressively incorporating all other environmental exposures and experiences throughout the developmental years to young adulthood (approximately 25–30). Those impressions are manifested in various combinations of the nuances between actions, conduct, demeanors, bearings, and deportments.

The quality of the manifestations and demonstrations of these impressions in the home and other social circles can be observed, studied, evaluated, monitored, and modified through clinical analysis of the intra- and interpersonal relational signs, signals, patterns, and trends, shown at different frequencies, regularities, and intensities in the person's life. Altogether, these signs, signals, patterns, and trends (called *notifiers*) of those impressions and behaviors provide a further indication, clue, or intimation of the likely quality of human relationship that an individual will be able to forge and keep if the developmental trajectory does not change.

**Simplified Summary**

If a child is carefully and progressively observed from birth, various behavioral and relational signs referred to as *notifiers* are displayed in different situations and circumstances and in different ways. If the variations in these signs are noted along with their different responses and reactions (See difference in Glossary, pp. 411 & 414), they can give an indication of how the child could possibly relate with those in his or her sphere of influence as he grows and develops. With such notations, the healthy *notifiers* can be affirmed and cherished and the unhealthy ones modified, corrected, and changed (See p. 204, para 2).

**Fifteen DNRA Theory Key Vocabularies**

Among the key terms and expressions in the study of the DNRA with which one needs to be familiar are the following fifteen. As recommended for the study of the Flowchart (p. viii) it is advisable that they be studied now and where indicated, checked in the Glossary, so that early familiarity will help in understanding them as they are referred to in the study.

1. **Developmental** (See Glossary p. 400)

2. **Conception**—the fertilization of the mother's egg by the father's sperm in the mother's fallopian tubes after sexual intercourse, or via invitro-fertilization

3. **Notifiers** (See Glossary p. 409) For a 'jump-start' go to p. 197 & 198)

4. **Impressions**—different sensations, feelings, ideas, and imageries created in the mind as a result of what the senses pick up in one's environment

5. **Aptitude** (See Glossary p. 398)

6. **Imperceptively**—happening and recording (in the subconscious) without one's awareness that that which is happening is actually taking place

7. **Relational and Relationship** (See Glossary pp. 412 & 413)

8. **Forge** and **keep**—to initiate, start-up, establish and then sustain and maintain; no giving up; staying the course

9. **Demonstrations and Manifestations**—evidences, clear indications of existences, showing, and actions

10. **Reactions and Responses** (See Glossary pp. 412 & 413)

11. **Emotions** (See Glossary p. 402, Review p. 145)

12. **Perception**—Generally these are unprocessed information or concepts or ideas formed in the mind as a result of what the senses initially pick up. Perceptions can be void of rational and analytical processing and can therefore change when such processing takes place.

13. **Brain** (See Glossary p. 399)

14. **Mind** (See Glossary p. 408)

15. **Trajectory**—an established path or pattern of movement or development

## Ten Basic, Primary Facts about DNRA Theory

In further preparation for study on this important, new perspective on family relational health, we consider ten facts which are basic to the understanding of the DNRA - **BFDNRA**: Some might seem repetitive but they are really emphatic.

**BFDNRA 1:** Human existence in its totality is all about relationships.

**BFDNRA 2:** Relationship is the major experience to be recorded as the senses become exposed and emotions begin to be produced in the brain. (Preview Glossary for definition of *emotions* p. 402).

**BFDNRA 3:** Imperceptive interpretation of emotions begins to lay the foundation for the perceptions of relationships in the tender growing years of the child.

**BFDNRA 4:** From as early as conception, the relational atmosphere in which the expectant parents, especially the mother live, can begin to influence the kind of relationship the child could forge and keep as he or she grows into adulthood.

**BFDNRA 5:** From a normal, healthy conception, a child's brain-mind, in its developmental stages is totally impressionable and is imperceptively recording impressions from his or her mother and the father (if he is present) as well as from other significant persons in whose sphere of influence the mother exists. All this gets to the child via the umbilical connection with the mother.

**BFDNRA 6:** From birth, the child's *active* and hopefully *sound* relational mind becomes activated as his or her senses begin their lifelong process of collecting and transmitting stimuli and messages to the brain. (See p. 146).

**BFDNRA 7:** From the time that the child makes that first sound, at birth signaling his or her presence here, she begins the relationship with the new out-of-the-womb environment: "I am here, I am now connected. Henceforth, I will be an integral part of what happens, and I will also influence what happens!"

**BFDNRA 8:** From birth, the child's mind begins to record impressions of relationship to which he or she is exposed. These impression are developmental and, if properly and carefully observed, *notifiers* of them will be seen in reactions and responses that the growing baby gives off.

**BFDNRA 9:** If these *notifiers* are also carefully and properly observed, monitored, and treated, they can give a good indication of the quality of the relationships that the child could grow up to forge and keep.

**BFDNRA 10:** All relationship vibes (aura) or connections are coded and loaded into the baby's brain-mind, and the decoding of each takes place gradually by associating them with meanings of actions and inactions during the course of development.

Ever since the development of the concept and theory of DNRA in the family relational health laboratory detailed in Chapter 1, announcements of seminars on the subject have always been met with questions or observations such as: "Do you mean *DNA?*" Or, "Is there an error with that *R?*" Or, "Is it *RNA* that is meant to be written, but the *R* is wrongly placed?"

The response, of course, is "No! It is not an error at all!" This initial reaction to the subject is understandable because in the scientific, genetic, biological, medical, or physiological world, we either hear of DNA or RNA, but not DNRA.

Is this suggesting that we could be off to a new frontier? Such is the dynamic nature of knowledge. In God's family book, the Holy Bible, it is recorded in Daniel 12:4 that "knowledge shall be increased." This prophecy was making direct reference to the fact that in the future, more knowledge would be had about the prophecies to which Daniel had just been exposed. It can also be applied in the paraphrased context of the dynamic and ever-changing nature of human relationship (which begins and continues to exist in the active, sound, dynamic mind) and the study and advancing knowledge of its complexity, of which this *DNRA* perspective could be an added dimension.

## DNRA Is Not New

These *developmental notifiers of relational aptitude* (DNRA) have always been with the human family, from the conception and birth of the first child, Cain (Gen. 4:1). "There is no new thing under the sun" (Eccles. 1:9). However, they might simply have not been identified, documented, and circulated. Like so many other "discoveries", they have always existed but have not been given notice and prominence in studies that address human relationship in general and family relational health in particular.

Another reason that the *notifiers* might have been 'unknown' could be that the time for their unearthing and study had not yet come, hence their being studied now in the "fullness of time" (Gal. 4:4), inspired by the Holy Spirit. It could also be simply the case that the developmental notifiers might not have been formally encoded as is being attempted here, to show the sustained and perpetual influence that they have on one's total relational life.

In carefully reading some articles and listening to some presentations in psychology, the behavioral and social sciences, and related fields, one can sense the concept of the DNRA. In some, they are alluded to while not being so named. In others, there is an indication or implication about them, but they might not be placed into the perspective of relationship development, as will be presented here. DNRA is not a mere relabeling of preexisting concepts of the study of relationships. Instead, it is a calculated and developed thrust on the recording and study of these *notifiers* in the context of their impact and influence on family relational health.

Given the far-reaching effects of these developmental notifiers of relational aptitude, as will be detailed later, when all are combined, they could constitute the proverbial "damaged nerve" that keeps eluding studies and research about the relational ills that affect the home and society in such continuously adverse, detrimental, and even destructive ways. At the same time, the positive opposite of the proverbial damaged nerve is the possibility that if these notifiers were to be correctly appraised, understood, and related to, they could very well be the means by which people could "live happily ever after," not only in marriage but in all aspects of family life.

# DNA: A Brief Review

To set the pace for a careful understanding of the DNRA theory, let us do a review of what we could call its forerunner, DNA, about which nearly everyone has some awareness or knowledge. In *Biology for Dummies, 3rd Edition*, Fester Kratz, PhD, gives this summary:

> The genes of the 46 chromosomes determine your characteristics, from your physical appearance to much of your behaviour. The science of genetics tracks the inheritance of the genes and studies how they determine traits. Through genetics you can understand why your skin is a certain colour and why some traits seem to run in your family ... So what exactly does all that mean?
>
> Here it is, plain and simple: DNA determines your traits because it contains the instructions for the worker molecules (proteins) that make your traits happen. Scientists are discovering more and more about DNA; they are also discovering tools to read and alter the DNA in cells ... Scientists use recombinant DNA technology to alter organisms used in food and medicine.

We find a similar basic explanation in Wikipedia: "The deoxyribonucleic acid (DNA) is what makes you uniquely you. It's that double helix that your genes are made of. Your DNA accounts for why you resemble your parents and it distinguishes you from your pet frog and from everybody else."

DNA is sometimes called "the molecule of life", as almost all organisms have their genetic material codified as DNA. Since each person's DNA is unique, *DNA typing* is a valuable tool in connecting suspects to crime scenes. You can also use the word less scientifically, as in, "It's not in my DNA to sit through six hours of meeting."

In addition to being used in connecting suspects to crime scenes, another commonly known use of DNA typing is for paternal identity. Unfortunately, there are many cases when a mother has to resort to a DNA test in order to identify the biological father to support the child(ren). Equally so are the cases of men who are alleged to be the biological fathers of children but question that assumed paternity and resort to the same test to verify the mothers' claim or to vindicate themselves. In too many of these cases, the children are the ones who bear most of the social stigma, especially with the colloquial interpretation of DNA as "Daddy Not Available!"

Consider these pointed, basic examples of parents' DNA manifestations in their children. It is established that one's temperamental traits are a good example, in part, of parent-child genetic connection, psychologically. Therefore, they demonstrate some of their parents' behavioral and social traits and attributes.

Further, as children grow, they exhibit some of the physiological characteristics of their parents, such as shape, height, body mass, skin tone and texture, eye and hair color, and more. The son may look, smile, or even stare like Mommy or Daddy. The daughter may have the same voice tone and sound like one or both of them. There could be similarities in walking, standing, and other aspects of posture. Parental likes and dislikes of foods, objects, and situations may also be reflected in their children. These and many others are examples of heredity, which we could facetiously call the hand-me-downs via one's DNA.

Coming out of this brief review of DNA, which we called the base study or forerunner for the DNRA, let us make a bridge to carefully cross over onto the deeper understanding of the latter. The key comparative and connecting terms of the two studies are *genes* and *notifiers*, respectively. Consider their definitions:

- ***Genes***

    These are the substructures in the chromosome of the human cell, part of which forms the DNA. According to Ginny Smith and Nicola Temple in their book *How the Body Works* (page 20), "If our DNA is the body's recipe book, then a gene within that DNA is equivalent to a single recipe in the book; it is the instructions for building a single chemical of protein. It's estimated that humans have around 20,000 genes that code for different proteins." The nontechnical definition of genes could simply be the units in the cell which are responsible for the transferring of the hereditary characteristics of parents to their offspring.

- *Notifiers*

  These are simple yet complex combinations of verbal and nonverbal responses or reactions produced in the relational mind from the impressions of relationships gathered by the senses from one's social circle or environment. Where properly monitored, observed, and evaluated, notifers can provide a cue or indication of the quality of relationship that a person will be able to forge and keep.

From these definitions, we can summarize the following:

1. *Genes* are to DNA as *notifiers* are to DNRA.
2. *Genes* are biological while *notifiers* are psychological.
3. *Genes* are fixed hereditarily while *notifiers* are psychosocially developmental.
4. Genes are fixed in numbers while *notifiers* are dynamic and ever-changing.
5. *Genes* transfer biological data from parents to children at conception, while *notifiers* indicate psychosocial, nonhereditary transmission of impressions from the minds of parents and others to children's minds, developmentally.

With the focus primarily on children, the study of DNRA is intended to raise the bar in helping parents and professionals with a vested interest in childcare and development to balance their alertness and vigilance and protection of the child's psychosocial welfare in the same way they carefully guard and protect the physiological health of that child. (CPH²).

## Parental DNRA Study of Samuel and Jesus

"And the child Samuel (son of Elkanah and Hannah) grew on, and was in favor both with the Lord and also with men." (1 Sam. 2:26)

"And Jesus (son of Mary 'and Joseph') increased in wisdom and stature, and in favor with God and man." (Luke 2:52)

Both sets of parents monitored these boys' growth and development, ensuring that each aspect received equal attention. Note the relationship that 12-year-old Jesus had with his mother as evidenced during their census registration trip to Jerusalem. The record is that "he went down with them, and came to Nazareth, and was subject unto them: but his mother kept all these sayings in her heart" (Luke 2:51). This suggests that Mary kept those expressed notifiers from her Son, Jesus, in her mind, and no doubt shared them with Joseph, then studied and monitored them as He grew.

It was the result of her keeping them in her heart, and watching Him grow, observing the consistency in his behaviour and pattern of development, and no doubt affirming them as a good mother, that Mary could confidently say to the ushers at the wedding at Cana of Galilee about 18 years later, "Whatsoever he saith unto you, do it" (John 2:5).

To no less extent, we are safe in believing that Hannah and Elkanah studied the growing Samuel, carefully observing, affirming, and monitoring those notifiers of his development, so that they could confidently take him to the temple and offer him to Priest Eli as a helper, knowing how he would deport himself. Of course, Hannah was honoring the commitment she had made to the Lord when she prayed earnestly to become pregnant (1 Samuel 1:10–18).

## Caution and Challenge to Parents

There is an important principle of making comparison and balancing reality that needs to be emphasized regarding the issue of children growing up and staying the course of family expectations. To the same extent that no amount of vigilance by parents can immunize a child from becoming infected by some childhood illness or endemic disease, so it is that no perfect relational home atmosphere can quarantine a child's mind from unhealthy psychosocial influences (CPH²). The fact is that visibly healthy children become ill or experience strange health conditions. Similarly, well trained and behaved children may deviate from the established social norms of their family of origin, some even earning the antisocial label "black sheep."

Upholding the above principle of comparison and balancing of reality, the study of DNRA challenges and encourages parents to aim for the ideal in the character development and behavior of their children, with the understanding that the unpredicted and surprising harsh reality of the child swaying away from cherished family values does happen. It is not in every instance of a child breaking out from the established, acceptable family pattern that the parents are to be judged as having failed in their parental stewardship.

The DNRA study does not advocate the position of expectation with absolute and total parental responsibility and accountability for a child who adopts a lifestyle contrary to the acceptable pattern of the family. Nor does it credit irresponsible parents who did not foster a healthy home atmosphere for children who eventually become successful, productive citizens because of their own effort and with help from others.

## Two Possible Accounts for Mysterious Childhood Behaviors

Children's surprising, disturbing, or even mysterious unacceptable behaviour can be frustrating and even embarrassing at times. The Bible presents at least two different possibilities as guidelines to address such probabilities, especially the first one above regarding children breaking out from the established, acceptable life patterns of their parents:

### *The Mystery of Iniquity (2 Thessalonians 2:7)*

The basis, reason, and accountability for sin, trespasses, and iniquities cannot always be found, hence their mysterious nature, at least to us mortals. Heading the Bible references to this is the record of the origin of sin, found in Isaiah 14:12–14 and Ezekiel 28:12–19.

These passages do not give full developmental details but pinpoint pride as the fundamental problem of Lucifer, the once "anointed cherub, son of the morning" who became the diametric opposites as Satan and the Devil: His "heart was lifted up."

How did that happen? For how long were pride and jealousy festering in his mind? What might have been happening around him that he did not correctly understand? Did a situation, perception, or misunderstanding on his part push him over the edge? This seems to be calling for a psychoanalysis to be done on Lucifer's mind. That, too, will remain a mystery!

There are times when the behavior of children from good, healthy homes just goes totally contrary to all the principles and practices of the family. Onlookers give their opinions and some make negative, judgmental comments. Some will even suggest that the child might have been reacting to some hypocritical, double-standard practices in the family closet. Unfortunately, there are many cases where these situations are true and children rebel against the hypocrisy that they see, and walk away in protest from the expectations of the family.

However, where there are no known, proven bases for these conjectures, they should be stopped, bearing in mind that the child does have a mind of his own, and the power of choice is as mysterious as sin itself. It is difficult at times for us to give a clear explanation for some of the choices that we make in life. Many times we exclaim, "I can't explain how I made that choice" or "What was I thinking when I did that!?" Paul called himself "O wretched man that I am!" (Rom. 7:24).

In our search for answers in these cases, room should be left for the possible out-working of the mystery of iniquity. Sin is originally a mental disease; its origin and its far-reaching effects elude us all the time. We should continue to exercise faith in the omniscient God, Who will, in His good time, reveal as much as He sees we can manage regarding these mysteries.

### For the Manifestation of God's Healing and Redemptive Power (John 9:1–41)

The main point of the story is: "And as Jesus passed by, he saw a man which was blind from his birth. And his disciples asked him, saying, Master, who did sin, this man, or his parents, that he was born blind? Jesus answered, Neither hath this man sinned, nor his parents: but that the works of God should be made manifest in him" (verse 1–3).

Clinically speaking, the case recorded here is one of apparent congenital birth defect, presented as blindness. It did not have to be as a result of some unhealthy practice or negative psychosocial behavior on the part of the mother that the child was born blind. Family and friends of the parents were evidently suggesting that the man was born blind because of something that his mother did or did not do.

Jesus countered them by exonerating the parents and saying that the case was necessary for the healing, saving power of God to be demonstrated, thus giving them (the disciples and others) another opportunity to believe that He was sent by the Father: "That they all may be one; as thou, Father, art in me, and I in thee, that they also may be one in us: that the world may believe that thou hast sent me" (John 17:21, See more. p. 273).

Interestingly, this second case (the child being born blind) was permitted by God with a "lifting-up" in mind, contrary to the first one (of Lucifer), whose intent was personal glory as his heart was "lifted up" (Ezek. 28:17 and Isa. 14:13–14). The second was for a good purpose, as God's created and redeemed children could lift up their hearts to Him and glorify Him for the clear evidence of His mercy and grace being available. Regardless of the origin and circumstance of their challenges in life, He had "healing in His wings" (Mal. 4:2) for them through Jesus Christ, His Son and our Savior.

Now, the comparative application of the healing of the blind man and the redemption of the wayward child might be seen as a stretch of the mind, but it is worth it. Whereas the blind man's condition was congenital and he had nothing to do with it, the wayward "black sheep," like the Prodigal Son (Luke 15), made a personal choice. Redemption, healing, and restoration were available for both of them. Both sets of parents could praise God for the miracle of His power to save both children, one from physical blindness of the eyes, the other from psychosocial blindness of the mind (CPH²).

## DNRA Theory Anchor Statement

Successful human relationships *do not just happen*! The fairy-tale, magic wand-waving dream of "and they lived happily ever after!" with reference to marriage stops just where it began: that is, at it being a fairy tale! Neither does good parenting just happen. No human relationship becomes good by happenstance. Whether it is marriage, parenting, sibling, collegial, social, or any other human relationship, they are all influenced by more factors than those which meet the eyes.

It takes more than good will, good intention, and being a good Christian. One major factor that influences the quality of family relational health is a person's developmental notifiers of relational aptitude (DNRA). Consider again the simplified summary in the introduction to this chapter.

## Six DNRA Theory Objectives

The six objectives for the study of DNRA are as follows:

1.  To provide a simple, clear understanding of the background of the theory from its earliest possible starting point.

2.  To identify some major potentially positive and potentially negative notifiers and consider the dynamics of each on human relationships in general and family relational health in particular.

3.  To help parents, teachers, caregivers, and all family members to see notifiers in the growth and developmental process of children and to know how to relate to them.

4.  To give professional guidelines, based on God's words, on how each one can acquire knowledge and skills for experiencing successful relationships based on the knowledge of one's DNRA.

5.  To help people understand their DNRA and praise God for who they really are and can become by His grace, thereby building their self-esteem and acceptance.

6.  As a result of number 5, each person can experience healthy growth and development, and be of benefit to those in their sphere of influence.

## DNRA Theory Background

Having established the objectives, let us look deeper at the basic concept of the DNRA. As each human being develops from conception into early adulthood (25–30 years of age), there are many signals that indicate the quality of the relationships that he or she will be able to forge and keep as he or she grows and matures. These signals, called *notifiers,* are based on the accumulated learning of the individual in the immediate family group, as well as from all others who influence his or her life directly and indirectly.

Let us consider five basic family relational health questions that will further stimulate interest in the study of the DNRA Theory:

1. Do you want to know how much your parents might have influenced or are presently influencing your state of mind and behavior and even your relationships?

2. Do you want to know the quality of the marital relationship that you might have if you are contemplating marriage?

3. Do you want to know the kind of parent you might become if you choose to have children?

4. Do you want to know why you behave the way you do at different times?

5. Do you want to know how your brothers, sisters, or other relatives might have influenced or are presently influencing you?

Most likely, the answers to the above questions are *yes.* We all want to know those facts. Unfortunately, the answers are not always as forthcoming as would be desired. In many cases, the questions are not even asked, or they might be pondered but not openly expressed.

To the same extent that we enquire into our family health ancestry and our personal health care history when we need a comprehensive medical assessment and treatment in order to establish where we are and how to proceed in our best interest, so it is equally important for our relational health that we address the ancestral and developmental issues raised in the above questions (CPH[2]).

If you have responded yes to the five questions above, or you want to consolidate what you already know, you could benefit from the identification of the developmental *notifiers* by carefully analysing the following ten basic facts about human relationships.

**Relationship Fact 1:**
**Human life is about relationships.**

Sixteenth-century English author John Donne wrote: "No man is an island, no man stands alone; Each man's joy is joy to me, each man's grief is my own …" For us to share those sentiments of joy and grief, there has to be some healthy relationship between the parties involved. There has to be a healthy *connection*, *rapport*, *bond*, and *support* for the emotional sharing of joy and grief. Once interaction and interrelation are initiated between two persons, their minds become engaged and a relationship is underway.

The length, quality, and impact of the interaction will influence the nature and type of the relationship. During the time of their interaction, the gap between them was progressively or gradually closed and became bridged by a mental state called *relationship*. This is a fact of life for human beings with active, sound minds.

As the gap between them gets narrower, so will be the thickening, or preferably the strengthening, of the relationship. Human life begins and continues on the basis of relationships. People need people! That's the way God designed it to be. We are indispensable to each other. We cannot live without each other. It is a fact that loneliness kills.

## Relationship Fact 2:
## Human Relationships have far-reaching influence.

About 80 percent of our lives are influenced by our relationships, whether marital, parental, sibling, sororal/fraternal, social, or business/transactional. In professional premarital counseling, emphasis is placed on the importance of carefully choosing one's life partner, because he or she will have a virtual lifelong influence on the quality of the other's life.

The proverbial statement "Show me your company (relationships) and I will tell you who you are" is a fact of life affirmed by the wise man Solomon: "He that walketh with wise men shall be wise: but a companion of fools shall be destroyed" (Prov. 13:20). Late US Air Chaplain Ronnie Melancon (1942–2021) renders it this way: "Show me your friends and I'll show you your future."

The apostle Paul adds his counsel regarding the impact associates can have on us: "Be not deceived: evil communications corrupt good manners" (1Cor. 15:33). Paraphrased with direct application to family relational health, the text might read, "Do not be fooled: if you become involved in a relationship with a questionable or evil person, your good qualities can be compromised and you become like that person. Be aware!"

## Relationship Fact 3:
## Human relationships begin from conception.

A relationship actually precedes and leads to conception. Except in the unfortunate, criminal case of a nonconsensual sexual relationship (rape, abuse, molestation), sexual intercourse, the precursor to most conceptions (other than in vitro fertilization), is the result of a relationship. (Review the working definition of *relationship* in the Glossary p. 413). In accounting for some pregnancies, it is not uncommon to hear either the man or the woman or both to say: "No, we were not in a relationship …"

Some will even account for the unwanted pregnancy to be the result of a one-night stand and not a relationship. This is one of the reasons for the questionable cases of abortion. - No reference to Roe Vs Wade!

However unplanned or unintentional the pregnancy was, other than in the criminal cases mentioned above, the sexual act that resulted in that pregnancy was entered into because two minds became engaged, and some form of consensual commonality was arrived at. A relationship, transitory or temporal as it might be, was entered into, by virtue of the engaged minds via the senses.

In the case of conception in marriage, ideally, the marital relationship between the husband and wife should be healthy; one evidence being their mutually fulfilling, satisfying, and bonding sexual intercourse. With that preparental relational health in place, the relational atmosphere of the conception is healthily, positively charged, and sets the pace for the expectant mother to be physiologically and psychologically composed and comfortable.

With a relational mind that is happy, relaxed, affirmed, fulfilled, safe, and secure, healthy hormones such as oxytocin and endorphin will flow naturally, and even the fertilized egg in the fallopian tube will make its way down to the uterus with peace and assurance of a future home. From there, the developed child will exit to the wider outside world nine months later. All this is influenced in part by the healthy psyche (state of mind) of the mother-to-be.

### Critical Role of the Expectant Father

The expectant father plays a pivotal function in this prebirth atmosphere of conception. His supportive role is indispensable. He is to be there for his expectant coparent mentally, emotionally, socially, and spiritually. His healthy state of mind should be that "While she alone can be pregnant, both of us are expectant!" He keeps himself abreast of every change and does his own monitoring of the developmental process taking place in her body. There is no inhibition or reservation between them. As the mother bonds with the zygote, fetus, and baby at the various stages of development, ideally, the expectant father is to be the guardian of the relational atmosphere in which the child is to be born.

The preconception and conception DNRA are established by the parents and transmitted to the child by the mother. It is established that while the biological DNA is passed on physiologically by the fusion of the sperm and the egg, the psychological DNRA is being developed primarily from the interaction of the two expectant parents, and again the mother is the carrier. This sets the pace for the DNRA version that the child will adopt, based on how sustained and consistent the parents are in the relational atmosphere that they have established. They must do this consciously, conscientiously, and consistently. They owe it to the developmental well-being of the child.

### Biblical Evidence of Prebirth Relationship

The principle of relationship beginning at conception is anchored in the Bible. In Jeremiah 1:5, God says He established His relationship with His people from conception: "Then the word of the Lord came unto me, saying, before I formed thee in the belly I knew thee; and before thou camest forth out of the womb I sanctified thee, and I ordained thee a prophet unto the nations." While this proclamation was made directly about the prophet, it is understood that God has the same prebirth relationship with all His people.

It is understood that parents would be actively involved in this relationship-building process. They are God's stewards for the children they produce by His procreational power in them. He lays His claim in no uncertain way through David, His mouthpiece: "Lo, children are an heritage of the Lord: and the fruit of the womb is his reward" (Ps. 127:3).

He further makes a comparison with the mother, establishing an assurance with a question and answer: "Can a woman forget her sucking child, that she should not have compassion on the son of her womb? yea, they may forget, yet will I not forget thee" (Isa. 49:15). Indeed, the relationship between God and human, and between human (the parents) and human (the child), begins at conception.

**Relationship Fact 4:**
**Human relationships are developmental.** (See also p. 238)

After God *created* the first adult man, Adam, and the first adult woman, Eve, all other human beings since then have been *born* and developed age by age, step by step, stage by stage. God planned that their development and growth would proceed in a progressive, orderly manner.

Of all life that comes through the birthing process from a pregnant mother, human beings have the longest journey between birth and adulthood—one to twenty years, as determined by national and cultural laws. The United Nations Convention on the Rights of the Child (1989) defines a *child* as "a human being below the age of 18 years unless under the law applicable to the child, majority is attained earlier." This is ratified by 192 of 194 member countries. In US Immigration Law, *child* refers to anyone who is under the age of 21. Any animal offspring born at the same time with a human baby over that same period would have either died by that age or would be considered a sage of the pack to which it belongs.

This slow, progressive process has been designed by God to allow for the development of the complex mind—indeed, the *relational mind*—which is only possessed by human beings. Ideally, this progressive development of the personhood of the child towards adulthood is intended to take place in an orderly manner, and the parents would do best to know how to relate with the various and varying *notifiers* of that developmental process. Animals do not do that.

## Relationship Fact 5:
## Human relationships are observational.

One of the first and surest ways we can tell how healthy a relationship is developing or can be developed is by observing the behavioral cues, hints, signals, and indicators that the persons show or do not show. While it is true that we cannot judge a book by its cover, it is also true that a first impression is indicative and can even be lasting. From the initial contact through the intervening times and occasions, the trends and patterns of the potentially fledgling relationship ought to be observed.

There has to be a careful calibration between these two statements of fact mentioned above, ensuring that neither of them dominates our perspectives about meeting and building relationships. From the time an acquaintance is established between any two persons, each one begins, intentionally or unintentionally, consciously or subconsciously, to observe and even study the other.

This is so at all levels of human relationship, including in the political and diplomatic setting. Journalists and political pundits take keen note of "how they greeted each other" or "how the handshake or embrace was initiated and taken" or "the position of the clasping hands," among other relational observations. There are even protocols—national and cultural—of demeanor and behaviour to be observed.

In the process of observation, we take mental notes of what the other person does or does not do, what is said or not said. All these are a part of the relationship-building process, and they are influenced to a large extent by the observations and interpretations of each person in the relationship.

**Relationship Fact 6:**
**Human relationships generate notifiers.**

Behavioral indicators, cues, hints and signals put together are called *notifiers.* Notifiers send alerts or messages telling how a person could, or might not be able to manage different dynamics in relationships, if the trends or patterns of his or her mind do not change.

It is worth taking note that in standard English, *notifier* as a noun does not seem to enjoy as full usage as its sister noun, *notice*, or the verb *notify.* All have the same Latin etymology: *notus* = "known" + *facere* = "make". *Notifier,* however, has an international acclaim beyond its English usage, it being the name brand for one of the world's largest fire alarm systems, Honeywell, according to https://esd.notifier.com/.

Family Relational Health Services International (FRHSI) and Honeywell are different types of businesses but have a common purpose in engaging the noun *notifier* to send an alarm—a signal to arrest attention. In the case of Honeywell, notifier is to call attention to actual, physical fire that has the potential to destroy life and property. For FRHSI, notifier calls attention to a potential relational fire in the form of an emotion, which can be either good or bad, love or hate, desirable or undesirable, acceptable or unacceptable, with the potential to make or break family relational health (See pp. 123–124 & 138).

The Bible is not silent about the potential fiery impact of the mind on relationships. God uses James to set off the notifier in chapter 3. Consider verses 5–6: "Even so the tongue is a little member, and boasteth great things. Behold, how great a matter a little fire kindleth! And the tongue is a fire, a world of iniquity: so is the tongue among our members, that it defileth the whole body, and setteth on fire the course of nature; and it is set on fire of hell." The tongue is used metaphorically, representing the relational mind.

The relational fire, usually negative in nature, emanating from the mind and sparking and crackling through the tongue, has a potentially devastating force on relationships if not contained, smothered, and extinguished. At best, every stubble and stock (unresolved and residual relational issues) should be put out—that is to say, they should be addressed and resolved, so that no embers (little unnoticed issues) with the likelihood or ability to start another fire, will remain.

### Basic Description and Categorization of Notifiers

Here arc two important facts about *notifiers* in terms of their basic description and categorization in the context of family relational health:

1.  **Description**: The *notifier* is a simple yet complex combination of verbal and nonverbal responses or reactions produced in the brain from the impressions gathered by the senses from the person's social and geographic or physical environments. This is part of the process of the developing mind. (See definition of *mind* in the Glossary as well as the difference between *reaction* and *response*).

2.  **Categorization**: *Notifiers* are manifested behaviors, conduct, or deportment grouped into two main categories for simple, easy (nonclinical) processing. They are either:

    *   positive, desirable or acceptable (generous, courteous, altruistic, kind, respectful, sharing, behaved, willing, patient, controlled)
    *   negative, undesirable, or unacceptable (mean, rude, selfish, unkind, feisty, demanding, defiant, unwilling, impatient, impulsive)

The treatment for both categories of *notifiers* will be determined by the study of their patterns, trends, frequency and intensity. It is this early study that Solomon was alluding to in Proverbs 20: 11 & 12: "Even a child is known by his doings, whether his work be pure, and whether it be right. The hearing ear, and the seeing eye, the Lord hath made even both of them."

It is worth observing that in the preceding verses, Solomon mentioned that mature and even leading societal figures such as kings are to be observed by the trend and pattern of their behaviour and transactions. To drive home the seriousness of not taking the issue of observing behaviors lightly, the wise man came right down to the least likely of society to behave questionably and fraudulently: a child. Then he made the arresting comparison that "Even a child is known by his doings." Pay keen attention to the *notifiers* early!

**Relationship Fact 7:**
**Human relationships are relational.**

When *notifiers* are carefully observed, they give an indication of the state of the four vital signs of family relational health in the person's mind. They suggest how one person *connects* with, *interacts* with, *bonds* with, and *supports* the other person.

*Relational* means being connected to, belonging to; having to do with; being a part of. Merriam-Webster Dictionary uses the term *kinship*, which offers additional explanation on the critical nature of the term *relational*. Kinship refers to having affiliation, tie, link, likeness, similarity. In a healthy family relationship, the parties experience the deepest possible sentiments of these descriptions.

*Relational* refers to a state of like-mindedness, as Paul admonished the Philippians in chapter 2:2: "Fulfill ye my joy, that ye be likeminded, having the same love, being of one accord, of one mind."

**Relationship Fact 8:**
**Human relationships have markers.**

As relationships grow and develop, there are directional markers along the path that can tell about the quality of the *notifiers*. Those markers are the trends of the relationship. This means that we can observe the tendencies, the inclinations, the drifts, the leanings, and the movements of the *notifiers*.

*From these directional markers of emotions, we can see if the relationship is going up or down if we use a typical linear measuring line graduated from 1 to 10. The techniques and principles for developing, applying, and interpreting this directional measuring are addressed in Appendix 2 p. 459,* which covers instruments for assessing and treating family relational health.

### *Differentiating Being Able, Capable, and Teachable*

Markers can reveal how able, how capable, and how teachable a person could be in order to keep a healthy relationship. Being *able* means that the person has the natural capability, the necessary knowledge, and the skills for a healthy relationship. According to Quora, this person has *realized potential*; hence, he is able.

Being *capable* means this person has *recognized potential.* That implies that there is evidence that he or she will be able to do what is required or necessary, if given the opportunity to do so in the right relational atmosphere. It could be considered as *capability perceived but untried or unproven.*

Being *teachable* applies to a case where none of the above exists— when there is no immediate evidence that he is able or capable, but there is the demonstrable, expressed, rational interest and desire to be so equipped. Such a person unquestionably admits his limitation(s) but speaks of the inspiration, drive, and motivation to be so engaged.

Thessalonica, in that they received the word with all readiness of mind, and searched the scriptures daily, whether those things were so." *Readiness* of mind could be seen as *openness* of mind. They clearly wanted to learn, and they did not depend only on what was preached unto them; they also did their homework (research) for reinforcement and deeper understanding. Any family member who adopts that principle towards the acquisition of knowledge and skills is more than likely to enjoy a healthy family relational experience.

## Attitude

We cannot do justice to the subject of *aptitude* without reference to its cousin, *attitude*. Attitude is a reflection of a person's character—who he or she is by nature and virtues. One's attitude is essentially the quality that he or she is, hence his or her virtues. It is suggested that the desirable virtues of healthy relationships are courage, honesty, compassion, pride, friendliness, truthfulness, sense of humor, temperance and liberality, and magnificence. One can be fit and possess the natural capability to learn but might not have the right attitude toward learning. It can be a thin line between the two, but they are not necessarily identical.

## Altitude

"Ladies and gentlemen, this is your captain speaking. We are now heading for our cruising altitude of 38,000 feet. As soon as we have reached that level, we will turn off the seat belt signs, and you will be free to move about the cabin if you need to do so."

That announcement, coming from the cockpit of the plane, brings some additional sense of comfort for the flying passengers. Achieving that desirable cruising altitude is the result of a combination of man and his machine. On the man's part—that is, the captain/pilot—the achievement is the combination of knowledge, skills, experience, and competence to operate the aircraft. On the part of the machine—that is, the airplane—it is as a result of the perfect calibration of the complex mechanisms of the aircraft, traffic pattern altitude, stand-and-day model of temperature and pressure, aerodynamics drag, engine thrust and efficiency, and other performance criteria of the laws and principles of aerodynamics, all influenced by the engineers and technicians of the aviation industry.

Altitude, commonly understood, has to do with the height to be achieved. In the context of family relational health, the altitude in terms of the highest quality of the relationship to be achieved is a combination of one's aptitude and attitude. There can be no good takeoff, sustained lift, and achievement of a desired cruising level in a relationship if there is not an equally sustained calibration of those healthy states of mind by the parties involved.

Emulatable, attitudinal, healthy relationship can be discerned early if the *notifiers* are not taken for granted—where the positive ones are cherished and the negative, undesirable ones are carefully treated and/or replaced (correlate with simplified summary, p. 175).

## Healthy *DNRA* from Creation

The ten basic facts about human relationship above show that one's family of origin contains the DNRA of one's potential family relationship. DNRA indicates the potential or probable quality of family relationship that the individual can develop and maintain. We reiterate that from as early as conception, the relational atmosphere of the home begins to influence the child's relational health and aptitude and all the foregoing factors addressed.

When God created the first two human beings, He established a relationship with them individually before they met each other. Adam knew and related with his God before he knew and related with Eve. Similarly, before Eve knew and related with Adam, she knew and related with her God. The impact of the *God-human* relationship on their minds was so healthy and positive that it naturally spilled over into the *human-to-human* relationship they forged afterward. God's image was stamped into their minds; they had the choice to sustain that through loving obedience to His counsels and guidelines for their lives. Alas! They failed but all is not last!

### Differentiating Between God's Image and God's Likeness on the Mind

The record says that humans were made in God's *likeness*. This means that God implanted in them a small portion of Who He is—nature and virtues—with the understanding that they would progressively grow more and more like Him (Matt. 5:48). They were made conditionally perfect and could choose to cherish His *image* and His *likeness* in them. They had a perfect home atmosphere in which they to begin life.

These two words—*likeness* and *image*—can be taken apart and studied separately. *Image* is understood to be the impact on the mind. God passed on to His children His character, His qualities, and His attributes. By breathing His breath into them, He quickened (which means to bring to life) their total being: body + mind. "And the Lord God formed man of the dust of the ground, and breathed into his nostrils the breath of life; and man became a living soul" (Gen. 2:7). They were energized and enlivened to be like Him.

The first thought process that Adam and Eve experienced was akin to that of God, their Father purity, holiness, goodness, love etc. However, like children who are born to Christian parents but have to grow and hone their path of the faith for themselves, Adam and Eve had to hone and happily practice the characteristics established in their 'young' new minds at creation. Their Father empowered them with the choice to keep His image undistorted in their minds.

When the image of God stays in the mind, it infuses the entire being, and the likeness of God is exuded from within. The likeness is not merely the appearance or form, which indeed it is. *Likeness* also means that which exudes from your being as a result of the image in your mind.

### Christ-likeness

To be Christ-like does not mean to resemble Christ - having His complexion, height, body mass, etc. It is behavioural—manifesting the character and bearing of Christ, so that we become like Him. God made the human mind as His appointed media center of the universe. This means that man, His masterpiece of Creation, would yield his willing, obedient mind for the fullness of the Godhead to be beamed through the vast universe. O! How far we have fallen!

*Image* and *likeness* are the total fullness, the combination of God, His character and form or appearance. This is what Jesus meant when He said: "Have I been so long time with you, and yet hast thou not known me, Philip? He that hath seen me hath seen the Father; and how sayest thou then, Shew us the Father?" Jesus was the *theanthropos*—the *God-man*. "Behold, a virgin shall be with child, and shall bring forth a son, and they shall call his name Emmanuel, which being interpreted is, God with us" (Matt. 1:23).

While Adam could not claim to be the *first* theanthropos, because he was *not* God, he was certainly the first fully human representation of the image and likeness of God, because God (Father, Son, and Holy Spirit) said so as they agreed to make man: "And God said, Let *us* make man in *our* image, after *our* likeness" (Gen. 1:26).

When sin struck, it distorted the image of God in man. The distortion was not in his physical form or appearance; it was in his mind. "And God saw that the wickedness of man was great in the earth, and that every imagination of the thoughts of his heart was only evil continually" (Gen. 6:5). His thoughts were so corrupted, he no longer reasoned in constant harmony with God. The infusion of the Holy Spirit was intercepted by another source, which Adam let in by his choice. That impairment of mind naturally impaired the body (See Psychosomatic health, pp. 47, 60, 410 & 463).

## Holy Sexual Procreation Plan— Conceived in the Mind of God

Adam and Eve's children were conceived after the Fall. Their sexual relationship, which resulted in Eve's pregnancy was in harmony with God's plan for procreation (See p. 326). That was not sin. However, with their minds having been corrupted by sin, and consequently the whole being, the children were the product of their sinful bodies.

The procreation plan and method (sexual intercourse), having been conceived in the mind of God, remained holy, but unfortunately it had to be carried out in no-longer-holy vessels, His now-sinful children. He still kept them in the scheme of the procreation plan and initiated the redemption plan as His rescue mission, the Protoevangelium for them (Gen. 3:15; John 3:16; Rev. 13:8; 1 Peter 1:20).

Against this fact, their children were indeed "shapen in iniquity; and in sin did their mother conceive them" (Ps. 51:5, paraphrased). But the children were not without hope. Inasmuch as each child was born sinless, being born of sinful parents and inheriting the genes therefrom, they had the predisposed propensity and proclivity to sin and were therefore born with the need for a Saviour. As the sinful nature began to be acted out in their minds and lives, the Holy Spirit balanced that experience by activating their sense of the need for the Saviour as they grew more and more conscious of good and evil, right and wrong (See John 16: 8).

## Sin-Affected DNA: There Is Hope

Despite sin being in their DNA, and the sinful home atmosphere in which they were born setting the pace for their DNRA, they were not without hope, because they, too, were born with the power of choice. It is no doubt that in addition to the impressions of the Holy Spirit upon their hearts/mind, their parents, Adam and Eve, must have not only taught and reminded them of where they were (in the paradise of the Garden) and of how they came to be on the outside, albeit temporarily, but also about God's assurance of redemption through the protoevangelium (Gen. 3:15).

Cain and Abel, by their individual power of choice, literally set the trajectory for their siblings to follow down through the ages, until the protoevangelium would be fulfilled:

> Seeing then that all these things shall be dissolved, what manner of persons ought ye to be in all holy conversation and godliness; Looking for and hasting unto the coming of the day of God, wherein the heavens being on fire shall be dissolved, and the elements shall melt with fervent heat? Nevertheless we, according to his promise, look for new heavens and a new earth, wherein dwelleth righteousness." (2 Pet. 3:11–13)

Cain chose the path of disobedience, while Abel chose the path of obedience. We conclude, therefore, that our paraphrased version of the Anchor Text holds perfectly to the foundation and principle of the theory of the DNRA of family relational health. It is based on our chosen relationship with God:

> Be aware that the quality of the relationship that you have with Me, your God, whether it be a loving one through obedience, or a hateful one through disobedience, and consequently, the relationship that you have with your family members, have far-reaching effects and results, which do not end with your present family or generation,

but that it has the potential to affect many more families and their off-springs after you, and could even go on to influence your third and fourth generations, long after you are gone.

## Suggestions for Action

1. Do a self-introspection; consider some of your behaviors and qualities and what aspect of your family of origin has influenced it or them. Cherish the acceptable ones, and if there are undesirable ones, make every effort by God's grace, and if needs be that of a professional Christian family therapist, to get rid of those.

2. Be conscious of the company and relationships you cherish. Aim to shed negative influences always, and be alert and do not allow any unhealthy influence to overpower your mind.

3. Guard well the thoughts of your mind and carefully watch your utterances. It is not your tongue that is the source of what you say wrong or incorrectly; it is your mind from which the utterances are generated.

4. Know your abilities and capabilities. Improve on them and have a spirit of teachable-ness. Be willing to learn always.

5. Pray for continued evidence of Christlike-ness and that the image of God is seen in you as you mature as a Christian.

# Chapter 9

# Demons of the Past Meet the God of the Present

**Anchor Text: Psalm 42:5**

"Why art thou cast down, O my soul? And why art thou disquieted in me? Hope thou in God: for I shall yet praise him for the help of his countenance."

**Paraphrased for Families**

Why am I feeling so low in spirit, and why am I so depressed? I do not have to be like this, despite what might have happened in my distant or immediate past. I can exercise hope in God and give praise to Him; because His presence in me will inspire, brighten, and heal my mind.

Among the many effects of sin on the human mind is the feeling of disconnection and despair. For different persons, this sense of utter alienation and disengagement can affect our relationships with all those around us and definitely with God. That is what David was experiencing when the Holy Spirit healed him and inspired him to make a record of that experience in the interest of others who would come after Him and feel that way. "For whatsoever things were written aforetime were written for our learning, that we through patience and comfort of the scriptures might have hope" (Rom. 15:4).

The Holy Spirit had David record his gloomy and dark state of mind for the benefit of those who will go through similar moments in these days, so that they can have patience and hope. We are to have the assurance that such feelings do not mean that all is lost or that we have come to the end of life. It is simply human! Adam and Eve must have had their bouts of feelings of disconnection, detachment, and despair, all anchored in guilt and shame, as they sought to settle down to life outside of the Garden of Eden.

## Chemical and Hormonal Imbalance

Just about all human beings since then, at some time in life, experience that melancholic, gloomy, forlorn feeling (See p. 230). From a psychological/clinical perspective, there are many reasons for those sensations or moods. Hormonal or chemical imbalance are the most common diagnosis for these mood swings, which manifest themselves in many different ways. Thyroxin, serotonin, dopamine, norepinephrine, and many other chemicals and hormones are on the top of the list of the deficiencies and imbalances that are named in these circumstances.

There is a multiplicity of mental illnesses and disorders that have been diagnosed and continue to be discovered and labeled as man tries to account for his disheveled and disturbed state of mind. The continuous revision and increase of the APA publications since the 1800's to the present DSM-5(2013) and the newest ICD-10-cm codes of October 2021, is the perfect example here. Undue or bad stress, fatigue, and plain tiredness are among the layman's and in some instances, the professional's common explanations for such potentially debilitating feelings.

While the Bible does not engage the scientific/psychological account into a controversy, it states authoritatively that these feelings of disconnection, disquietude and emptiness of mind are the result of sin. (Isaiah 59: 1- 2). Jesus Himself said in John 15:5: "I am the vine, ye are the branches: He that abideth in me, and I in him, the same bringeth forth much fruit: for without me ye can do nothing." Disconnection from God is the beginning of disconnection from life itself, and the deterioration will continue, unabated, until man's connection with God is fully and completely restored. (See more on: Disconnection - page 332).

Thanks be to the God of Families, God of the Christian, and the Bible. We have the answer for such downcast, downtrodden feelings, spirit, and moods. We know the origin and we are given the healing therapy to counteract the adverse effects that they can have on us. That is why this work refers to the Bible as God's family book for His children. And we can further add: His therapy book.

Until the full and complete restoration to the paradise experience in the Garden of Eden, we will have to do more than, as the song says, "go on singing." Until then, we have to live. Until then, we have to find the healthy way to relate with and manage the natural experiences of the "disturbing Ds": disconnection, discouragement, disquietude, dejection, despair, depression, detachment, disengagement, desperation, despondency. These are the feelings of being laid bare, exposed, and vulnerable, as a result of sin on the mind.

All human beings face this conundrum of negative emotions which can be cancelled with a therapy of hope. It is the intention of providing such assurance therapy that has motivated the format for this chapter of two sharp contrasts: demons of the past and the God of the present. (See **Mental Illness – A General Biblical Description**. P. 230)

The purpose of this potentially disturbing chapter is to identify some of the deep psychological wounds and scars—mental, emotional, social, and spiritual—that persons might experience, and the potential impact these experiences can have on their relationships. The deeper purpose of the chapter is to present some of God's psychotherapy for hope and healing from His Healing Book, the Holy Bible, there by helping us to live quality lives now and ultimately to prepare us for the Soon Return of Christ.

# Demons Defined

*Disclaimer: The definitions and explanations below are not intended to be a theological discourse on the subject. What is offered here is limited to the purpose of basic information in the context of family relational health care.*

The first key word here is *demon*. The word itself strikes up fear and trepidation in the average, uninformed, nonclinical mind. It is registered in the social, superstitious psyche that *demon* is antihuman, so it naturally conjures up dread, terror, and emotional consternation to think of demons being in our sphere of existence.

The English Oxford Living Dictionaries offer the following definitions and examples for demons:

1.  An evil spirit or devil, especially one thought to possess a person or act as a tormentor in hell

    *   "He was possessed by an evil demon."
    *   "Each of the damned souls was guarded by a group of hideous demons."

2.  A cruel, evil, or unmanageable person

    *   "I was a little demon, I can tell you."

3.  A powerful, often destructive compulsion or obsession.

    *   "He is plagued by demons which go back to his childhood."

The term *demon* is used to describe a wide variety of spiritual beings. The word is derived from the Greek term *daimōn*, which refers to all sorts of beings, not only ones that are evil. The conventional definition of *demon* refers to malignant, supernatural entities who seek to harm humans. Among the synonyms offered are *fiend, ogre, devil, imp, monster, sprite,* and *goblin.*

From a Biblical account, demons are really the opposite of angels in terms of their mission. The angel is a messenger of care, protection, and salvation from the Lord of Life and Light (Ps. 91:11, Matt. 16:27, Luke 4:10); the other is an agent of evil, insecurity, and destruction from Satan, the Chief of darkness and sin. Another Biblical reference to demons is *unclean spirit.* In Mark 5:2–13 we actually see the interchangeable use of *unclean spirits* and *devils,* clearly indicating that they are one and the same.

According to Mark 5:5, demons identified themselves with the corporate name, *legions,* their being a part of the one-third of the angelic force that sided with Lucifer during their insurrection in heaven (Rev. 12:4). According to the ancient Greek army record, a legion was about five or six thousand. Legions of evil angels would clearly be a formidable force for humans to contend with. Elisha's assurance to his young attendant alludes to the retinue of angels that God has at his command and will also deploy for our protection: "And he answered, Fear not: for they that be with us are more than they that be with them" (2 Kgs. 6:16).

The Bible offers one account for the origin of sin. Isaiah 14 and Ezekiel 28 tell us that sin originated mysteriously in the heart (mind) of the chief of angels, Lucifer, the covering cherubim. With his iniquitous state of mind, he galvanized an ideological rebellion in heaven with the intention of staging a coup to overthrow God, but he was defeated by Michael, Jesus Himself (Rev. 12:7). The nature of his coup was more ideological than it was physical. (Ephesian 6: 10–12)

Upon his utter defeat, the angel Lucifer became the devil, Satan. Devil has one letter more than evil, which was the newly acquired nature of Lucifer. Then the one-third of the angelic host which sided with the devil, Satan, was cast out of heaven with him. They all fell from their angelic status to their new devilish, demonic status. *Demonic,* because their newly assumed work was to be the terror and haunting force of all who would choose to be on the side of God; their chief target of course is human beings, over whom they already had supremacy in nature (Ps. 8:5).

It was against this background that Satan attacked Adam and Eve, the first human family. After being created by God, they were to be the icons of His creation, through loving obedience to Him. Satan decided it would not go that way, so he marshaled his host of angels who had fallen out of favor and grace with God. They were to be his agents to attack and harass all of Adam and Eve's children. They were to terrorize men and women, husbands and wives, fathers and mothers, boys and girls, sons and daughters, and all subsequent categories of the human family, and everything belonging to them, whether made and provided directly by God for them or they designed for themselves.

These angels, who became demons, were correctly referred to as *fallen angels.* Unfortunately, through ignorance, many persons have mispronounced the term, and instead of saying *fallen*, they say *falling* angels, thus creating the impression that these beings are in a constant suspended posture, looking down and dropping on us human beings. They exist as invisibly as Satan, and in the same way that God did not strip Satan of his original angelic capabilities, he and the others exist in real spirit form and do make their evil presence felt among men, who were created in physical form.

## Demon-Possession

Since angels exist among humans, it is important that we address a commonly used term which speaks to their impact on us. The term is *demon-possessed.* What does it mean? When God created human beings, the brain/mind was to be His dwelling place. The mind of man was created with the capacity for God to communicate directly with His children. "Come now, and let us reason together, saith the LORD: though your sins be as scarlet, they shall be as white as snow; though they be red like crimson, they shall be as wool" (Isa. 1:18).

God made humans as physical beings, and God would remain the Supreme, self-existing Spirit. Therefore, human beings would have communion with Him through the spiritual aspect of their existence, definitely so after the fall. *Spirituality* is one of the God-given characteristics of our humanity, existing in the mind, as do our emotions, values, relationships, and sociality. These attributes and qualities of our being are as intangible as they are real.

**Five Salient Facts about Spirit**

*Fact 1:*
*God exists in spirit form.*

"God is a Spirit: and they that worship him must worship him in spirit and in truth" (John 4: 24). That is the opposite of human or physical form, as Jesus aptly taught: "Behold my hands and my feet, that it is I myself: handle me, and see; for a spirit hath not flesh and bones, as ye see me have (Luke 24:39). In our limited humanity, we cannot fully comprehend the Spirit form existence of God, hence Jesus came to connect directly with us. He is the God-man, the *theanthropos*, God in human form. "Behold, a virgin shall be with child, and shall bring forth a son, and they shall call his name Emmanuel, which being interpreted is, God with us" (Matt. 1:21).

*Fact 2:*
*Angels exist in spirit form.*

God created them in spirit form and man in physical form: "For thou hast made him a little lower than the angels, and hast crowned him with glory and honor (Ps. 8:5). The angels were assigned the role of messengers (Gen. 19:1), meaning they could not be bound in flesh or physical form as humans, whom God designed for a different role—that is, to have dominion over the earth (Gen. 1:26–28). Angels had the attribute of invisibility which God did not invest in human beings. Angels live with God in heaven, while humans live on earth. Before sin, however, God did relate directly with the physical man (Gen. 3:8).

*Fact 3:*
*Angels have oversight of humans.*

By virtue of their supernatural status, God evidently gave angels some amount of access to, and oversight of, man, subject to His divine approval and permission. "For he shall give his angels charge over thee, to keep thee in all thy ways" (Ps. 91:11; see also Mark 4:6 and Luke 4:10). Angels could therefore speak to, guide, and direct humans. "And he shewed us how he had seen an angel in his house, which stood and said unto him, Send men to Joppa, and call for Simon, whose surname is Peter" (Acts 11:13).

*Fact 4:*
*Fallen angels retain their original attributes.*

In the same way that God did not strip Satan of his original angelic attributes and capabilities, so it is that those angels whom he influenced with his treachery exist in spirit form with their original capabilities, and do make their evil presence felt among men. "And no marvel; for Satan himself is transformed into an angel of light. Therefore, it is no great thing if his ministers also be transformed as the ministers of righteousness; whose end shall be according to their work" (2 Cor. 11:14–15).

## Why Didn't God Divest Satan of His Powers and Not Permit Sin?

One worrying question that some Christians face regarding the power of Satan and his demonic cohorts is: Why did God not take away the power from Satan and his fallen cronies, seeing that they would have been hell-bent to bring down His kingdom, with His created human beings as their prime target? The answer is that God did not use His power arbitrarily to defend or vindicate Himself. He, in His divine omniscience, had to allow the accusation of Satan that He was unfair and arbitrary, to run its course so that the entire universe could see the folly in the accusation.

At the same time, it was necessary for all to see God's unquestionable justice, His long-suffering, and the window of opportunity that He made available for the erring ones to repent and return to their former relationship with Him. Had He taken away their attributes and capabilities, they could justifiably accuse Him of being vindictive and malicious, as are some earthly rulers who feel threatened by some of their subordinates and, in defense of their position, divest their accusers or rivals of whatever fighting power they would have had before in their former positions.

Instead of fighting back for Himself, God created another set of rational beings—humans—on earth and invested them with His love and care, as He had done to Lucifer. He granted them conditional immortality, subject to their chosen obedience to His love and principles of righteousness. When Michael and His angels fought with the then-Lucifer and the angels who sided with him, and prevailed, the rebellious group was cast out from heaven (Ezek. 28:12–19).

## Living Up to God's Standards of Righteousness—His Ten Commandments

Earth therefore became the testing ground for Satan's accusation, and the human mind the battlefield, as the forces of evil sought to capture this set of God's intelligent ones to their side. This is a part of the cosmic warfare referred to in Ephesians 6 and paraphrased in Chapter 2 of this book, "The Family Under Attack."

The human family is honored by God to be part of the jury, as it were, to vindicate His character, justice, and fair play. This they would do by living in accordance with His loving guidelines of righteousness, which Satan labeled as unfair, and up to which none of God's created beings could truly live (the ideology – p. 214). There is a germ of truth in that suggestion, because in our sinful state, we cannot measure up to the standards of God's righteousness. However, God never intended it to be so, because He reminded us that it is "not by might, nor by power, but by my spirit, saith the LORD of hosts" (Zech. 4:6). And Jesus Himself said, "for without me ye can do nothing." Paul added his human experiential testimony in Phil. 4:13: "I can do all things through Christ which strengtheneth me."

Unfortunately, there are subtle echoes of that accusation continuing even today, when some preachers of the Word are suggesting that human beings cannot live up to the expectations of all of God's Ten Commandments, His royal law (Jas. 2:8–12). This is a continuation of Satan's malevolent attack on God, which he began in the Garden of Eden when he suggested to Eve that what God said about the fruit of the Tree of Knowledge of Good and Evil was not true or correct, hence she could decide to disobey Him (Gen. 3:2–5).

In the case of the attack on God's Ten Commandments and their requirements and expectations of God's faithful children, the apostle John retorted in God's defense: "By this we know that we love the children of God, when we love God, and keep his commandments. For this is the love of God, that we keep his commandments: and his commandments are not grievous. For whatsoever is born of God overcometh the world: and this is the victory that overcometh the world, even our faith" (1 John 5:2–4). And it is by this same faith that every human being can live by grace in accordance to all of God's Ten Commandments, in the originally expressed wording from Mount Sinai.

## How Do Demons "Possess" Human Beings?

Returning to Fact 4, the question still remains: How do they (demons) "possess" us? Where and how does their "possessing" us take place? Spiritual beings primarily make spiritual connections. For a connection to be made there has to be receptivity, and receptivity means an opening or access to that place where the communication can be received and processed. That place in the human is the *mind*.

Here we see another marked difference between human beings and animals. Animals cannot sin because God never invested them with the power of an intelligent mind for the processing of right and wrong, or obedience and disobedience to His moral laws. God gave animals instincts influenced by nature and gave man dominion over them to care for, rule, and direct them (Gen. 1:26–28).

As stated earlier, we are reminded that we human beings are part of the cosmic warfare between good and evil, light and darkness, which warfare was initiated by Lucifer (Satan) in heaven against the Most High (Isa. 14 and Ezek. 28). Here is the reminder from Chapter 2: "Put on the whole armour of God that ye may be able to stand against the wiles of the devil. For we wrestle not against flesh and blood, but against principalities, against powers, against the rulers of the darkness of this world, against spiritual wickedness in high places" (Ephesians 6:11–12).

We understand that the cosmic warfare in which we humans are engaged is not as physical as it is spiritual. Since our spirituality is anchored in our minds, and the access or avenues to the mind are the senses, this suggests that we should have careful guard over them. While it is true that Satan does not have direct access to our minds, it is also true that he reads what the avenues to the mind—the senses—are focused upon.

The acts of the senses are laid bare for everyone, including satanic forces, to see, analyze, monitor, and interpret: what we love to look at, view, and admire; what we love to listen and respond to; what we love to sample, taste, and eat; what aroma captivates and commandeers our sense of smell and consequently creates desire which we will seek to fulfill; what we seek after to grasp and lay hold on literally or figuratively and which consequently move us into action. The technology of the internet now has us under surveillance, making pop-ups on our devices based on what our expressed interests are.

When Satan intelligently does his work of observing, analyzing, and interpreting the activities of the senses, he automatically has access to the mind. He knows that it is the mind that does the processing of what the senses send it to, and he further takes note of the frequency and intensity of the resultant actions, behaviors, and lifestyles consistent with the engagement of the senses.

Satan capitalizes upon that perception, creating more of the negatives to which the senses are drawn and which are not good for the well-being of the soul. At the same time, he calculatedly does all that he can to reduce the positive scenes and activities that are elevating to the soul, and even seeks to render them unattractive and boring.

Satan and the evil, demonic angels have taken on the work of accentuating the evil and undesirable that attract the senses, and denunciating and downplaying that which is noble and elevating to the same senses and ultimately for the well-being of the soul. As human beings yield progressively to the allurement and temptation of demonic forces, so do their minds become possessed, even to the final point of their rejection of the impressions of the Holy Spirit upon them. It is not only by seeing or beholding that we become changed, but equally so by hearing, smelling, tasting, feeling and definitely doing.

## Fact 5:
### Angels can be detected by humans.

It is not in every case when angels bore messages from God that they were *seen* by the recipient human. This is so because their encampment might not be revealed (Ps. 34:7). They spoke, and their spiritual presence was felt and could be acknowledged by the human, given that his mind has the God-built-in capacity to sense and connect with such spiritual presences around him.

So it is that evil angels, demons, are always targeting human beings to influence their minds toward evil. The human whose mind is not alert and kept vigilant by the indwelling Holy Spirit will not be able to detect that it is under attack until the devil has infiltrated it with devilish thoughts, imaginations, and schemes toward evil all through the avenues of the senses.

When the avenues to the mind are not gainfully occupied and in harmony with God's will, that mind becomes vulnerable to the entrance of the forces of evil which are always on the prowl for access. "Be sober, be vigilant; because your adversary the devil, as a roaring lion, walketh about, seeking whom he may devour" (1 Pet. 5:8).

Sobriety and vigilance are healthy, active states of the mind that is stayed on the Lord. Such minds cannot be possessed by the devil, because "Thou wilt keep him in perfect peace, whose mind is stayed on thee: because he trusteth in thee" (Isa. 26:3). "Stayed" as used in the text means that the mind is in constant connection with God, via the Holy Spirit, Who dwells in us by our choice (John 14:17, Rom. 8:11, and 1 Cor. 3:16).

## Consequences of the Idle Mind: Home for Demons

To be possessed by demons means that the mind that is not occupied by the Spirit of the Living God is left vacant for its spiritual capacity to be filled by any other spiritual force that is seeking space for dwelling. Today's Living Bible renders Proverbs 16:27 thus: "Idle hands are the devil's workshop; idle lips are his mouthpiece."

The *Phrase Finder* offers some interesting interpretations and applications of the original proverb from Solomon:

> "Nothing good comes from boredom. It's said that idle hands are the devil's workshop, an old saying dating at least as far back as Chaucer in the twelfth century who called idle hands the devil's tools."

> "In Works of Labor or of Skill I would be busy too: For Satan finds some mischief still for idle Hands to do." (I. Watts, Divine Songs for Children, 1715)

> "If the Devil finds a Man idle, he'll set him at Work." (J. Kelly, Scottish Proverbs, 1721)

> "If the devil catches a man idle, he'll set him at work." (T. Fuller, Gnomologia, 1732)

> "The Turks have a proverb, which says, that the devil tempts all other men, but that idle men tempt the devil." (Colton, Lacon, 1820)

> "An idle brain is the devil's workshop." (H. G. Bohn, Hand-Book of Proverbs, 1855)

When the avenues (the senses) to the soul or the mind are not guarded by the standards which the Creator has established, the forces of evil can create scenes, situations, and conditions to attract their attention, enter through the least opening, and take up residence. When we merge the counsels of Jesus found in Matt. 12:43–45, Luke 11:24–26, and John 5:14, a solemn warning is issued against a vacant mind, void of the presence and impressions of the Holy Spirit.

Here is the summary from Luke: "When the unclean spirit is gone out of a man, he walketh through dry places, seeking rest; and finding none, he saith, I will return unto my house whence I came out. And when he cometh, he findeth it swept and garnished. Then goeth he, and taketh to him seven other spirits more wicked than himself; and they enter in, and dwell there: and the last state of that man is worse than the first."

In His wisdom, God, our Creator, commands us to keep our minds stayed on Him. This is a counsel we should obey. Disobedience to it has its natural consequence: "Know ye not, that to whom ye yield yourselves servants to obey, his servants ye are to whom ye obey; whether of sin unto death, or of obedience unto righteousness?" (Rom. 6:16).

## Differentiating Demon-Possessed and Demon-Influenced.

### Demon-Possessed

To be *possessed* means to be taken charge of. One can only truly be *possessed* when one yields oneself to the superimposition of the other. This further means one has to surrender and give up to the powers that be. It means to open the doors of the mind and allow full access and manipulation. Consider some ways that this can happen:

- **Selling One's Soul**—Satanic forces can influence, to some extent, the outcome of some of our efforts, activities and enterprises. It is said that in the celebrity world, and among ordinary persons as well, bargains are made with demonic forces, organizations, and societies in an effort to secure success. The common expression is the transactional term "selling one's soul." There are cases in which it is said that success does come, but so do the after effects of derangement of mind and behaviour; "losing it" indeed. If this happens it is an example of getting what you want but losing what you have.

- **Literature and games**—Satanic forces are cunning and devise means to captivate the mind. Literature and gaming activities that are built around superstitious, delusionary, and fictitious scenes and characters, giving glory and homage to extraterrestrial beings and occurrences, are unquestionably satanic. When the mind becomes absorbed and subsumed with such activities, innocent as some appear to be, the end result is loss of one's control over the rational mental processes. The thinking is devilish, and so the speech and behavior follow suit.

  Parents with growing children ought to be especially cautious in this regard. The modern, apparently innocent gaming consoles ought to be carefully selected and monitored. Even mobile phones and tablets and laptops are loaded with these sensational and captivating activities, many of which are to the peril of young minds.

  Parents who allow these modern gadgets to do the babysitting for them need to be conscious of the possibility of potential harm that is being subtly done to their children. Some of the best-selling storybooks are to be listed among these sources of evil infiltration of young minds.

- **Practicing deception**—When persons make lying, dishonesty, trickery, and duplicity a way of life, they are simply giving evidence of Satan's paternity in them. Said Jesus: "Ye are of your father the devil, and the lusts of your father ye will do. He was a murderer from the beginning, and abode not in the truth, because there is no truth in him. When he speaketh a lie, he speaketh of his own: for he is a liar, and the father of it" (John 8:44). After the sweet taste of success is experienced from one pernicious act to another, they end up "having their conscience seared with a hot iron" (1 Tim. 4:2), and the devil becomes master of their minds (See p. 293).

We only need to look again at the present Russian-Ukraine War ( February 2022) to see one of the greatest, daring evidences of how the sweet taste of success of a pernicious act can embolden the design and execution of others, even more destructive than the one before.

When Russian President, Vladimir Putin invaded and annexed the Federal Republic of Crimea and the city of Sevastopol on March 18, 2014, (just about the same time when this work began) amidst the international outcry against his violation, he never retreated. Instead he ramped up and escalated the military presence in the area. With that sweet taste of his political strongman-ship, eight years later, he carried out his ultimate ambition of invading Ukraine. This was after he made several denials, political maneuverings and claims that his army was merely carrying out routine practice on the peninsula and on the Black Sea, and that he had no such intention of invasion.

We see the same ploy in many day-to-day inter-personal, marital and familial relationships. Baby-steps of so called little white lies or fibbing are told among children, friends, husbands and wives, business partners and other collegial relationships. When continued unchecked and unrepented of, the sweet taste of their success slowly but progressively escalate into full blown deceit, deception and ultimately, destruction of the relationships and sometimes, even lives. Such is the final work of the demonic nature of deception in the human relational mind. (See: **Putin and Zelenskyy – Modern Example of Cain and Abel**? page 151).

## Demon-Influenced

This can be viewed as somewhat lighter than demon-possessed, but the end result can be the same. Satan is constantly in the creative, innovative business of development, albeit negative and evil. Here are some means of his negative influence:

- **Observation of our past and proclivity**—He observes our tendencies, proclivity, and inclinations and builds scenes and opportunities to cater to them. He capitalizes on our failed pasts and amplifies such failures before our eyes. He watches, analyzes, and records our responses and reactions, and he exploits any manifested weakness that he picks up. Influence is his mastery game, and with all that commandeering accumulated knowledge that he has of us from our birth, he is not devoid of means and trickeries to influence us.

- **Intimidation for the future**—Not only does Satan keep focusing on our past, but he also uses those experiences to influence our attitude to the future. By amplifying our weaknesses and challenges, he creates apparently insurmountable circumstances to daunt us from getting ahead. Intimidation is an influential tactic to keep us from going forward.

- **Fear of success**—Some persons are not only afraid of failures; Satan creates influential circumstances that make some afraid of success. He uses family members, friends, colleagues and associates to dampen our drive and motivation. Such influences are demonic, contrary to the visionary counsel by Augustus Hopkins Strong (1836 -1921): "Couldst thou in vision see thyself the man God meant, thou never then could be, the man thou art content."

  To ward off Satan's demon-influencing power intended to prevent us from striving for success, we need to heed Paul's admonition to Timothy: "… stir up the gift of God, which is in thee …" (2 Tim. 1:6). That gift does not have to be pastoral ministry but any of those listed in 1 Corinthians 12:1-31 and Ephesians 4:6–11.

## Job: A Testing Case and Lesson

To be demon-possessed or demon-influenced is not an event. A person is not instantly "out of one's mind" and suddenly becomes possessed. Such occupancy of one's mind by the devil or his demons is a result of a process of neglect, recalcitrance, and carelessness in not taking heed to the words and counsels of the Lord. The mystery of iniquity and lawlessness does work (2 Thess. 2:7), and there could be the times when an "innocent" soul ends up being the 'abode' of evil forces. Some can end up being placed under severe, unprecedented, and inexplicable tests by the devil, as was the poignant case of Job (Job 1–42).

When such situations occur under the permissive will of God, if we keep our faith anchored in the Lord, although we cannot understand how the situation fell upon us, there is assurance in God's words that we will eventually come out of it victorious. "There hath no temptation taken you but such as is common to man: but God is faithful, who will not suffer you to be tempted above that ye are able; but will with the temptation also make a way to escape, that ye may be able to bear it" (1 Cor. 10:13). (See paraphrase in Chapter 12).

An important lesson that we get from Job when going through adversity that we cannot account for, is to maintain the knowledge of our integrity. As in the case of his friends, who themselves were bewildered by his dramatic calamity, there will be those who, out of the ignorance and yet sincerity of heart, attempt to push the suffering one against an unnecessary wall of confession and guilt. "Search your heart my brother, there must be something terribly wrong that you did for which God is punishing you!" (See pp.273 -275)

Others put it very bluntly: "Your sins are now catching up on you!" In their spiritual exuberance, yet ignorance, they will quote Numbers 32:23: "But if ye will not do so, behold, ye have sinned against the LORD: and be sure your sin will find you out." Even further, others will dismiss any hope that the ailing person might be holding on to by denunciating them as now experiencing the "retribution" of the Lord, anchoring their 'certainty' on Galatians 6:7: "Be not deceived; God is not mocked: for whatsoever a man soweth, that shall he also reap."

In such times of being in the relational wilderness, when all those in your world, possibly even your closest friend and life partner (as in the case of Job's wife, chapter 2:9) give up on you as a result of the indescribable catastrophe that you are experiencing, your only hope of survival rests upon your own inner conviction of your faithfulness to God. This includes your faithful repentance for past sins.

Job survived upon his assurance that he was faithful, as he was inspired by the Holy Spirit all along his path of life. He did not consider himself perfect, but he knew of his sincerity and faithfulness. He must have checked and found no unconfessed sin. It is upon such clear conscience that he anchored his faith: "For I know that my redeemer liveth, and that he shall stand at the latter day upon the earth" (Job 19:25). He ultimately became an example of the fulfillment of God's assurance: "… but God is faithful, who will not suffer you to be tempted above that ye are able; but will with the temptation also make a way to escape, that ye may be able to bear it."

Demons, correctly understood, are those angels that fell from their high and lofty status as God's agents to minister to human beings. They are the diametric opposite of that—agents of Satan sent to mesmerize and demonize in every way they can. They attack everything that is good for human beings with the ultimate goal of having them (humans) to share in their (demons') fate of eternal hellfire. "Then shall he say also unto them on the left hand, Depart from me, ye cursed, into everlasting fire, prepared for the devil and his angels" (Matt. 25:41).

# Mental and Relational Illnesses Compared: DSM-5 and FRH

At this stage of our study, it is important to mention two other terms that, at times, can be confused with the subject of demon possession. They are *mental illness* and one that is probably unique to this book, *relational illness.*

Too often in some Christian communities, if an individual is behaving contrary to expected norms, there are those who are ready to label the unacceptable or concerned behavior as demon possession without any attempt to get professional help. Sometimes they engage in intense, prolonged fasting and prayer services and sometimes even rituals of exorcism in their effort to cast out the demon. Alas! Woeful ignorance is rife.

An outstanding case was reported by the BBC from Nigeria in early November 2019 stated: "Police in Nigeria have opened investigations after they rescued 15 people detained in a prayer house in the main city of Lagos. The male and female victims, who were between ages of 19 and 50, were in chains, Bala Elkana, the police public relations officer in Lagos state, said in a statement on Thursday. Some of them were taken to the prayer house by their families to seek spiritual help from mental illness and other diseases, he added." The family member who is clinically or relationally unwell, with one of the illnesses listed below, should benefit from professional diagnosis and treatment (See p. 249).

## Mental Illness – A General, Biblical Description

There is a prevailing level of ignorance, misunderstandings and the resultant taboos and stigmas that are attached to mental illness in many areas of the society. Before we look at the scientific/medical/clinical description of the subject and the comparative description of family relational illnesses below, let us consider a general description of mental illness, anchored in the teachings of the Bible.

Stated simply at the layman's level, mental illness could be summarized as a state of mind that, at any time, is characterised by varying degrees and possible combinations of sadness, anxiety, disquietude, worry, feeling depressed, edginess, agitation, dyspathy, ferment, restlessness, dysphoria and a host of other comparative unwelcomed, troubling mental experiences.

All human beings, from the very opulent, living in splendour and grandeur to those living in squalor and abject poverty, experience some degree of mental illness at some time in their lives. No one is immuned. From a biblical perspective, sin is a mental disease with its resultant manifestation as mental illness. This is so because all have sinned (Rom. 3: 23) and there is none that does (total) good (Psa. 14: 1 -3, Rom 3: 10-12). Mental illness is ingrained in the human psyche (our "being born in sin" – Psalm 51:5) It could be said to be in our DNA and is therefore a "natural" part of our sinful experience. (See p. 327 re: Chemical Imbalance).

Such inherent conditions and experiences are then exacerbated by different life-styles and practices, unhealthy relational dynamics, and physiological health malfunctions, among others, all further resulting in the exponential complexity of mental illnesses.

Therefore, in the context of our definition, delineation and differentiation of the active, sound mind, it is still understood that there is not a totally sound, relational mind among us human beings. We are best seen as conditionally sound. Throughout this book however, we will only refer to the sound mind, while keeping the reality of conditionality in mind. (See the Glossary p. 395 & 397 for the active, sound and conditionally sound mind). The ideal, desirable level or state of soundness that we need in order to obtain optimum family relational health is only possible through Christ, in Whom we can do all things, because He strengthens us. (Phil. 4: 13)

In addition to His strengthening grace, God has blessed us with medical knowledge and skills to offer professional care (psychiatric, psychological, psychotherapy, sociological) for those mental disorders until He comes again with healing in His wings. (Malachi 4:2) It is only at that time when the afflictions that assail the human family, inclusive of mental illness, will not rise a second time. (Nahum 1: 9)

*Disclaimer: The issues addressed below are not described exclusively from a mainstream scientific/clinical perspective but from the perspective of family relational health, the difference and commonality between which two this book makes a continuous efforts to establish. There is room and recommendation for further study in the books that are written to address the deeper, clinical, medical, and related perspectives on the subject.*

**Mental Illness – A Scientific/Medical/Clinical Description**

*Mental illness* or *mental disorder* is a clinical/physiological/hormonal/ chemical malfunctioning of sections of the brain, some glands, organs and the central nervous system. The illness, which is manifested in a person's thoughts, expressions, and behaviors, can range from a mild state to a chronic, debilitating one. Examples include schizophrenia, paranoia, bipolar disorder, hypervigilance, dementia, depression, ADHD, GAD, and over two hundred others are listed in the *Diagnostic Statistical Manual of Mental Disorders* (*DSM-5*). In most cases, medical and psychiatric treatments, inclusive of drugs and psychotherapy, have to be administered to stabilize, and where possible correct, these conditions.

**Relational Illness** (In the active, sound mind)

*Relational illness* describes culturally and socially acquired undesirable and normally unacceptable conditions, behaviors, and practices of the active, sound relational mind that directly and negatively affect relationships. These illnesses include, but are not limited to, unkindness, harshness, insensitivity, disrespect, insolence, arrogance, selfishness, meanness, callousness, defiance, conceit, and rudeness. Some could be picked up in one's DNRA.

Relational illnesses are in the impaired active, sound mind, (and are not to be confused with mental illness as defined by the DSM-5.) Mental illness on the other hand is anchored in the partially-active, conditionally sound mind manifested at varying degrees. It is important to note that a conditionally sound mind is not necessarily the same as a deranged mind, the latter implying a state of insanity or lunacy. (Review again, if necessary, the Glossary on the active, sound mind and the conditionally sound mind (pp. 395–397).)

The DSM-5, one of the major comprehensive works of the psychological and psychiatric professional community, lists those mentioned above as relational illnesses and others similar to them as: "Conduct Disorder—a repetitive and persistent pattern of behaviour in which basic rights of others or major age-appropriate societal norms or rules are violated" (p. 469). *Disorder* is one of the key overarching terms used by mental health clinicians to describe behaviors and practices considered outside the norm of the society in which the individual exists and operates.

Further, the *DSM-5* on page 715, in the banner caption for the chapter on "Other Conditions That May Be a Focus of Clinical Attention," states in part, "The conditions and problems listed in this chapter, are not mental disorders. Their inclusion in DSM-5 is meant to draw attention to the scope of additional issues that may be encountered in routine, clinical practice and to provide a systematic listing that may be useful to clinicians in documenting these issues." It further used the term *relational problems* and states:

> Key relationships, especially intimate adult partner relationships and parent/caregivers child relationships have a *significant impact on the health* of the individuals in these relationships. These relationships can be *health promoting and protective*, neutral or *detrimental to health* outcomes.

In the extreme, these close relationships can be associated with maltreatment or neglect which has *significant medical and psychological consequences* for the affected individual. A *relational problem may come to clinical attention* either as the reason that *the individual seeks health care* or as a problem that affects the course, prognosis, or treatment of the individual's mental or other medical disorder." (*DSM-5*, page 715; emphasis supplied)

In the context of family relational health, there are a number of analyses that we will do on these two important statements from the DSM-5, with emphasis on the six italicized sections. These analyses will be fully presented in book 2 in the series, *Family Relational Health: A Missing Dimension in Comprehensive Health Care.* For the limited purpose of this chapter, we will note the following:

- The *DSM-5* does concur with the position of this book that mental illness and relational illness (although it did not name the latter) are not one and the same: "The conditions and problems listed in this chapter, are not mental disorders."

- It would appear, however, that the *DSM-5* does not see relational issues as health issues but that they are, as it were, appendages to health, hence they "may be a focus ...". It would appear therefore that the *DSM-5* would not subscribe to the perspective of family relational health the same way it does to the term *mental health*. The probability exists further that the *DSM-5* would not subscribe to the term *illness* being used to describe the conditions that it referred to as relational *problems*, in the same way that it describes mental health conditions that are not considered healthy as mental *illness*. The operative words here are *health* and *illness*. In the analysis in the other forth-coming book, focus will be placed on their fullest meanings/definitions and applications from the perspective of the World Health Organization (WHO).

Again, for the limited purpose of this chapter, we will look at the working definitions of five key terms from a family relational health perspective:

1. **Health**—the overall combined and interrelated conditions of one's physiological (referring to the state and functions of the body) and psychological (referring to the state and functions of the active, sound mind) state of existence. This is in harmony with the WHO definition: "Health is a state of complete physical, mental and social well-being and not merely the absence of disease or infirmity."

2. **Illness**—a temporary impairment of health functionality, physiologically or psychologically (inclusive of relationally), with the potential or prospect of repair and restoration, depending on the correct diagnosis and treatment; or it can be prolonged, even beyond being able to respond to treatment

3. **Impairment**—a damaged or affected state at possible different levels of severity. An impairment does not have to be the same as a disorder, inasmuch as there is commonality between them and the difference could at times be blurred to the non-clinical eye. The manifestations of an impairment can be less impacting on functionality.

4. **Disorder**—the advanced, even to incurable, state of an impairment of health functionality (illness) that was not professionally diagnosed and treated; or an impairment of health functionality acquired either congenitally, incidentally, or developmentally and for which no corrective or curative clinical or medical treatment protocol is known. In nontechnical layman's language, a *disorder* would simply be any behavior or activity (in whichever form it comes) that is not according to the established, acceptable, or ideal order where the individual who has and shows them exists and operates.

5. **Relational Problems** - We express concern with the DSM-5 describing relational issues as 'problems.' From a family relational health psychotherapy perspective, when family relationship misunderstandings, disagreements and conflicts are perceived, described and labelled as 'problems' the attitude of mind tends to be negative and evokes the 'flight' instinct. No one really wants to live with 'problems' inasmuch as such experiences are as concomitant to life as any other routine and vicissitudes of family members living together (Review p. 30 & 31).

The healthier, euphemistic and psychotherapeutic labels for such relationship matters are 'challenges' and 'issues'. Properly taught and used, these concepts of the mind will result in a lower level of adrenalin rush into the blood stream than that which the harsh impact of 'problem' will produce. Better management and resolutions of the issues are more likely to result when the thought processes are healthy and result in words and expressions that are less adversarial and problematic in their implications. Given how the state of many relationships today can be tenuous and fragile, professional caregivers need to be careful and conscious of the words that they use in attempting to treat relational illnesses.

When the term 'challenge' is properly used with reference to relationship disquietude, a combination of discomforts, strains, tensions, or struggles, it can summon the inner emotional grit, tenacity and perseverance than its emotionally shocking and unwelcomed opposite - 'problem' will do. 'Challenge' can be used to ignite the positive 'fight' instinct and see the confronting issue(s) as a trial, a test and a task to be healthily defied and overcome in the interest of all concerned.

It should not be taken for granted the impact that the right choice of word has on our human relational mind. There's no denying that left untreated, family relational issues and challenges can deteriorate to 'problems' and the relationship becomes a disorder. (See Family Problems Versus Challenges: A Mind-set p. 30).

*Mental illness* and *relational illness* do have commonalities which can be identified and diagnosed by competent practitioners in the disciplines of medicine, psychiatry, psychology, and sociology, and especially by those who subscribe to the need for professional balance between the practices of physiological and psychological health care, inclusive of family relational health.

## Relational Illness Mutating Into Mental Illness

The DSM-5 and similar medical/psychological publications list most if not all of the following (mentioned from pp. 238-247) as mental illness and/or comorbidities, clinically attributing their existence to various chemical and hormonal malfunctions of the brain, glandular and other systems of the body. Such clinical analyses and diagnoses are unquestionably correct. What is seemingly not taken in account many times, is that some cases of mental illness did not begin with a straight physiological/chemical malfunction, but that they began as a relational impairment based on some attitudinal, social, cultural, religious and other unhealthy behaviours. This could be extrapolated as the negative, sinful aspect of our being "fearfully and wonderfully made" (Psalm 139:14), when the mind (i.e. the soul that ought to "know right well"), which is the engine of our being, superimposes the wrong that it knows/gathers/accumulates (cognitive) on the body (behaviour and psychomotor—actions/doings).

When such are not treated with proper relational, education and skills, they can mutate and metastasise into brain, glandular and organic impairments and malfunctions and ultimately are correctly diagnosed as mental illness. From a Christian and more so family relational health psychological perspective, the genesis of the chemical, hormonal, electrical and all combined physiological malfunctions of the human system began when the relational mind created by the Creator chose to sever connection with Him, partially and gradually completely. (See p. 327 re: Chemical Imbalance).

The same principle applies in the plant and animal worlds. If the plants are uprooted from the soil, they die but the soil remains. If the fish is taken out of the water it dies, but the river or sea remains. When man disconnects himself from God, he dies, but God is eternal - "… from everlasting to everlasting thou art God." (Psalm 90: 2; Isaiah 43: 13). Man severs from God at his own perils.

## Relational Demons of the Past

In the context of human and family relationships, and based on the definitions and examples offered above, demons could also be regarded as a state of mind filled with fear, anxiety, torment, trouble, and worry, all related to past experiences and situations. The reality is, every human being has a past!

As each member of the human family grows and matures, there is a natural accumulation of memories in the process of development (Revisit p. 195). Regrettably, as a result of sin, some of those memories are colored by different shades of darkness, representing a preponderance of negative emotions such as regret, remorse, sorrow, guilt, shame, denial, pain, and anxiety, among others. Whether self-inflicted or imposed on us by others, these negative emotions can have demonic, devastating results on the affected persons, and on their relationships, if not professionally treated and managed.

The negative emotions can be grouped as:

- painful reflections
- annoying recollections
- residual pains

- haunting memories
- regretful memories
- hateful memories.

Inasmuch as they all have the common denominator of being from the past, each of these groupings has a different impact and intensity on the person experiencing it, depending on its origin and the management and relational skills of the person relating to the case.

In her book *The Inheritors: Moving Forward from Generational Trauma*, Gita Arian Baak, PhD, categorizes the various memories as:

- inherited memory
- memories as family stories
- silent memory
- phantom memory
- diasporic memory
- absent memory
- postmemory
- photographs and art as memory

Baak writes, "Inheritors of trauma can be defined as the generations of people who, consciously or unconsciously, have thoughts and feelings about devastating events that happened when they were very young or before they were born or that may even go back to earlier generations." This concurs with the Anchor Text of Chapter 8.

**Subgrouping of Negative Emotions**

Another possible subgrouping of negative emotions could be secret fears, hang-ups, and flashbacks. Let us briefly consider them:

*Secret Fears*

Each human being, as he or she grows, develops some form of fear known to others, while some remain unknown and become secret fears. These are states of mind that no other person knows except the victim. In many instances, these secret fears live in the subconscious and only pop up when an external stimulus makes its way from the conscious and awakens them in the subconscious mind. Secret fears could be categorized among those things that Paul referred to in Hebrews 12:1 as "the sin which doth so easily beset us", and we could add, "about which nobody knows."

Secret fears are not to be arbitrarily labeled as phobias. They are not necessarily the same. Phobias are persistent abnormal fears which intensify with time. The irrational nature of a phobia can cause panic and disorder once it is triggered; as such, phobias are correctly categorized as mental illness. Secret fears, from the family relational health perspective, do not necessarily have such dramatic manifestations and can be easily treated with the correction of the source of the concern from which the fear has developed. Untreated, a secret fear could develop into a phobia depending on its source, nature, and the intensity of its impact.

### Hang-ups

A hang-up is a type of personal idiosyncratic fascination or inhibition. It is a private opinion, position, belief, or way of viewing situations, different from almost all other persons. A hang-up is not necessarily rational, but it is held with a conviction that makes it true to the person. "For some reason, I just do not like when he holds the glass that way. Yes, I know nothing is wrong, as all other persons say, but it irks me and jars on my nerve every time he does it."

Correctly analyzed, there could be an antecedent that sets off that hang-up, but like the secret fear, it is buried deep in the subconscious and is brought back to life by the process of association with anything that stimulates the memory deeply enough. Left untreated, hang-ups have the potential to impair relationships as they manifest themselves in sometimes awkward, strange behaviors without explanations. There is every possibility that left untreated, they can become antagonistic, antisocial or could mutate into depression or related conditions such as PTSD (See p. 392).

### *Flashbacks*

This is probably the most potentially intense and dangerous of the three. That is so because of the very nature of its name. It can happen in a *flash*, even dramatically, without notice! It could be described as an emotional earthquake. A flashback can come in the form of a panic attack the moment the negative memory is stimulated. Equally so, the person can go into a freeze of emotion and response, with no one in the immediate company understanding why that traumatic display. An emotional convulsion can be experienced and have a devastating impact on the person and the relationships in which that person is engaged. Again, a demonstrable evidence of PTSD.

The sources from which these potentially demonic emotions can come are as varied and numerous as the emotions themselves. Consider the following, limited examples:

- bitter family conflicts and feuds
- infidelity/unfaithfulness
- being duped/conned/swindled
- sexual molestation
- rape
- embarrassment as a result of a family member committing suicide
- imprisonment
- neglect
- deception
- betrayal
- personal sense of failure
- being mobbed/robbed
- false accusation
- sibling rivalry

Again, this is a general note and listing, limited to the family relational health perspective. Deeper analytical study on each is available.

**Treatment Protocol**

It is understood that these experiences can, and in many cases, cause changes in the chemistry of the brain and section of the glandular system and give rise to mental illnesses. The danger, as stated repeatedly in this book, is that too often, the family relational origin of the condition gets lost in the society's rush and treatment protocol to call it mental illness and offer, in most cases, only drug therapy without balancing it with the necessary psychotherapy.

The primary issue in considering these uncomfortable, painful situations (secret fears, hang-ups, and flashbacks) is not to determine who is wrong or right; it is not whether the pain is acquired by the hurting one or inflicted by someone else. Given the fact that pain and hurt are being experienced, the preferred order of professional response is to stabilize and treat the hurting person, then address the sources of pain and manage their effects to avoid reoccurrence as part of an ongoing care regimen. This method is not absolute, and the preferred order can be changed through careful analysis of the case at hand.

It is interesting to note that medical or physiological conditions are treated in that order. In fact, that is one of the ethical principles of medical practice: to care for the sick and suffering without prejudice and with unconditional positive regard. A suffering wrongdoer from a robbery or even a murder scene is attended to first and admitted to hospital as a *patient*, although he or she is kept there secondarily under police guard as a person of interest, suspect, or *criminal*. It is unethical not to treat him or her for the wounds, although it is known that he or she is a victim of his or her own questionable or criminal activity.

# Negative Intrigue of Relational Illness

Although the *positive, unconditional regard* clause is expressed as an undergirding principle in the practices of psychotherapy and counseling, it is not always adhered to in some family cases. This is so, given the sometimes mysterious nature of relational issues between husbands and wives, parents and children, and the many other combinations into which relational conflicts are experienced.

The lack of that positive unconditional regard is due to the sometimes baffling and humanly intriguing nature of some of the relational issues that assail people from time to time. Unfortunately, too, some caregivers are not experienced and competent to manage relationally sensitive matters, worse yet when they themselves might have had similar relational challenges from which they have not healed.

In many cases, these relational challenges end up becoming human-interest stories for novels, movies, TV and Radio Talk Shows, and theatrical presentations (Revisit p. 64). Cases from other professional practices do end up on the big screen, but because matters of the mind are not visibly and tangibly experienced, they, by nature, carry some amount of fascination, curiosity, suspicion, and temptation to serialize them. In that regard, the question of reality versus imagination tends be asked in relation to misunderstood, misinterpreted, and incorrectly undiagnosed relational illness.

# Critical Need for Professional Competence

Whereas the body, including the brain, is tangible, and the manifestations of most of the illnesses that affect it can be visibly observed, diagnosed, physically manipulated, operated upon, and treated, the mind offers no such accessibility. Note that inclusion of the brain here is referring to it specifically from the neurological perspective and not from the mental illness perspective, inasmuch as there are commonalities between them. A neurologist or neurosurgeon treating a disease of the brain (meningitis, encephalitis, cancer, tumors) is not the same as a psychiatrist or psychologist treating mental illness or disorders even with a drug therapy regimen (CPH$^2$).

Illnesses of the mind are far more difficult to diagnose and treat than those of the body, and sometimes the process can be fraught with hypothesis, speculation, inference, and assumption. Of course, we know that such instances do occur in the medical practice, but with fewer occurrences and possibilities. Certainly, there are imaging and other techniques that are available for mental health clinicians to make better assessment and treatment of some mental illnesses.

Despite such advancing technologies, however, and more so where such facilities are not available, there remain elements of questioning, probing, conjecturing, intrigue, and even unhealthy suspicions and accusations about mental and relational challenges, treatments, and results. Professionals in fields that offer psychotherapy and related treatments ought to raise the bar and offer care that represents understanding of the potential devastating nature of these "demonic" conditions of the relational mind. Each case is to be treated by a clinical, caring professional, one whose practice is free of the intrigue, enthrall, and fascination of the case story. The professional assessment must differ from that of an ignorant layperson or a frustrated family member. Remember relational illness.

## Mutating Relational Illness

When family relational illnesses are not treated, like illnesses of the body, they intensify and possibly mutate and go through the same stages—acute, severe, chronic, debilitating—and ultimately become a disorder. At this final stage, the individual's quality of life can become totally disoriented, thrown out of kilter, with disrupted normalcy and total disorder. The effect becomes relationally contagious as other family members and those within the affected individual's sphere of influence are affected (CPH$^2$) (Review p. 85).

Relational mayhem, turmoil, and chaos can set in and throw the entire family, and sometimes a whole community, into disarray. When the effects are clinically diagnosed, the person could be suffering from any one or a combination of the following conditions:

- posttraumatic stress disorder
- suspicion
- mistrust
- hypervigilance
- paranoia
- impaired relationships
- maladaptive and maladjustable lifestyle

Some aspects of psychosomatic conditions grow out of these states of health, as the following brief outline will show.

**Effects on the Body**

The following and other related manifestations at varying frequencies and intensities may be noticeable:

- fatigue
- tiredness
- lethargy
- lassitude
- weakness
- feebleness
- fragility
- defenselessness
- vulnerability
- susceptibility
- liability
- proneness

## Effects on Mental Ability

These may include the following:

- impaired judgment
- negativity
- pessimism
- cynicism
- distrust
- hopelessness
- glumness
- worrying
- fretting
- beleaguering
- hounding
- contempt

## Effects on Emotions

One who used to be affectionate, bright, and gregarious could descend into bouts of:

- alienation
- disaffection
- estrangement
- unfriendliness
- distancing
- apathy
- dispiritedness
- indifference
- irritability
- cantankerousness
- resentment

**Effects on Behavior**

The conduct, performance, and comportment of persons affected could be marked by:

- insomnia
- restlessness
- accidents
- agitation
- edginess
- smoking
- drinking inordinately
- eating disorder
- extremes with sexual interest
- mild to severe tendency to be damaging, detrimental, and destructive.

# Treating Relational Illnesses

We must painstakingly make two key observations and reminders here.

**Observation 1**

The prevalence of the manifestations under the four headings above can be family relational illness as well as mental illness. Treatment requires professional consultation and cooperation between practitioners in the related fields to do careful teamwork in the interest of the affected persons. Because family relational issues often go undiagnosed specifically and untreated, there is a tendency to generalize and label them as mental illness. There are numerous cases of misdiagnosis when the dichotomy between the two illnesses is not clinically established.

The worst-case scenario is when the family member, lacking relational skills, causes an unhealthy situation or even a major disturbance and is prescribed medication and even hospitalized for a mental condition which technically is nonexistent. Such persons sometimes go into a state of disbelief, shock, and eventually depression or other forms of mental illness for having been so labeled.

This is a case of imposed self-fulfilling prophecy and make-believe. The person is made to believe that he or she is mentally ill, and in so many cases begins to behave accordingly. This is similar to the case of a child who is wrongly accused of stealing cookies and who therefore goes on to commit the act. The subconscious reasoning is: "After all, why bear the accusation for nothing?"

Such patients become victims of professional ignorance and nothing short of malpractice. Gross errors like these do happen in medical practice, right into the operating theater. The British Broadcasting Corporation (BBC) reported on March 7, 2018, of a patient having brain surgery performed on him at a hospital in Nairobi, Kenya. During the surgery, the staff discovered that they were operating on the wrong patient. Facts can indeed be stranger than fiction!

Let us be clear. This book is not advocating that when a family member causes disturbance and disruption in the family and the community, he or she is to be given a mere rap on the knuckles. The wrongdoer cannot be exonerated on the premise of not knowing better, true as that might be sometimes. He or she must be held accountable for the wrong committed because "Ignorance of the law is no excuse" (see Chapter 4, pp. 62-63). Depending on the magnitude, intensity, and trend of the behavior, the situation might necessitate some amount of medical assessment and treatment.

The treatment, however, does not have to be drug therapy (alone), depending on the diagnosis. Relational wrongdoings and developed illnesses are not necessarily the result of physiological, chemical, or hormonal imbalances in the strictest, clinical sense of the word. Some psychosocial behaviors need psychotherapy that will help the one at fault to firstly shed any ignorance that might have influenced the misdemeanor. A treatment for behavior modification with disciplinary measures, which ideally should not be punitive but redemptive, might be advisable. Awakening of one's sense of responsibility and accountability are to be prescribed into the treatment program.

The challenge with this recommended treatment for the kind of relational disturbance that might have been committed is that mental illness is so easily diagnosed and drug therapy is equally easily prescribed and administered; whereas psychotherapy and behavior modification are much more demanding and time-consuming. Against this harsh reality, this work postures the need for a clear distinction between *relational illness* as defined herein (see the Glossary) and *mental illness* as extensively covered in the *DSM-5* and other professional documentations. And beyond the distinctions, it is necessary that the appropriate differentiation of treatment be factored in.

**Observation 2**

When a family member behaves outside the family norm, the ignorant others, in their desperation and many times utter embarrassment, resort to either their religiosity or their pseudo-sociality to find answers to the family member's behaviour. From a religious perspective, they "know" that the person is demon-possessed and that his or her sin is telling on him or her. There are those who resort to intense and prolonged fasting and even painful, embarrassing exorcism (the Nigerian case cited, p. 230). Too often, the person is treated with ostracism, banishment, or even excommunication.

Among family members with a false sense of social pride, the victim is treated as an outcast and misfit. He or she naturally loses social status among the group. No one "knows" them anymore, and they become social exiles. It is not rare to see some straggling vagrant who, when enquired about, turns out to be a member of some well-to-do family in the immediate, nearby, or distant community. The reason for his or her being disconnected? Some behaviour or attitude that might have not been in harmony with family's expectations or desires, and he or she was cast out.

Who knows, Nebuchadnezzar of Daniel 4 could have had both treatment experiences from the religious and social communities when he became ill. We know from the development of the record that his was a case of intervention from God, in the interest of humbling, but not humiliating the king for his blasphemy, and in the interest of his salvation. It was also to provide reassurance to the people that God was ultimately in charge. Here is a summary of the record from Daniel 5:20–21:

> But when his heart was lifted up, and his mind hardened in pride, he was deposed from his kingly throne, and they took his glory from him: And he was driven from the sons of men; and his heart was made like the beasts, and his dwelling was with the wild asses: they fed him with grass like oxen, and his body was wet with the dew of heaven; till he knew that the most high God ruled in the kingdom of men, and that he appointeth over it whomsoever he will.

The outcome is that the pompous king regained his sanity, repented of his blasphemy, was restored, and eventually will be among the redeemed.

Relational "demonic" behaviors (not mental illnesses as identified earlier) can have catastrophic effects on the individual and the family unit. The logical question, therefore, is: How do we manage—or, better still, rid our minds of—the demons of the past? Let's see how some family members try to release themselves from the powers of their demons.

Firstly, here is the hard fact that all of us human beings must face as it relates to any demons of our past: We simply cannot wish them away. They are part of who we have become; indeed, they are part of who we are. They are the records and facts of our lives.

From a psychological perspective, we are not conceding that relational challenges and even disorders are of the same nature as demons. Identified in the Bible as fallen angels, demons do have potential negative impact on the human mind that is not being influenced and directed by the indwelling Holy Spirit, as we have already established earlier in this chapter. They are definitely not the same.

*Demon* is used to describe these relational challenges, difficulties, and even complications because of the sometimes mysterious, inexplicable, or baffling nature of their manifestations. Relational strains, troubles, and problems are primarily due to a combination of ignorance and indiscipline, calculated and inadvertent wrongdoing, hypocrisy and hatred. Regardless of the source of the relational illnesses, they are to be professionally treated with a clear understanding of how the active, sound mind in which they exist responds to treatment (Review p. 243).

## Mind and Body: Voluntary and Involuntary Responses to Treatment

To a large extent, the body responds involuntarily to treatment, primarily when drug therapy is administered to it. Once the medication gets into the bloodstream (the main carrier of the body), the organ, gland, or tissue that is targeted does not have any choice as to the effect the drug will have on it (See p. 435). That is why the physician who is making the prescription has to follow clinical and administrative protocol with a sense of professional accountability, because once medication is in the body system, the patient has virtually no control over its effects, because the body's response is involuntary (CPH²).

The very opposite is the case of the response of the mind to treatment in the form of psychotherapy/counseling. The active, sound mind responds voluntarily—that is to say, the person exercises the power of choice as to whether or not he or she will accept and implement the prescriptions of advice, counsels, directives, or recommendations from the therapist/counselor (See pp. 76, 208, 325, 367, 386). That explains why the result of psychotherapy is not always predictable, and a relational health prognosis is not easily made, as is the case with physiological and drug treatment.

The fact of the voluntary response nature of the mind to treatment does not mean that the therapist/counselor is without professional accountability for the advice, counsels, directives, or recommendations offered as treatment. To the same extent that the therapist/counselor will exult and be happy and even take credit for the positive outcome if the client's case is improved, so should she or he be prepared to accept liability for any negative outcome - *conditions applied.* So the fact that the client *chose* to accept and carry out that offered treatment does not automatically render the therapist/counselor unaccountable. Professional ethics require all practitioners to practice within their boundaries, preparation, training, experience, and competence.

## Spiritism and Witchcraft: Used to Deal with Demons of the Past

Two major methods used to manage the demons of the past, are in actuality tantamount to being one and the same, given the commonality of their nature. Those methods are *spiritism* and *witchcraft.* Since one of them is so close in name to *spiritualism*, we must also have the differentiation in their definitions.

Those of us who had the blessing of attending foundational Bible classes in a fundamental Bible-believing church would remember learning that in the non-Christian system, the belief is in extra-terrestrial powers, influenced and driven by forces and intelligence beyond our normal human understanding. The intrigue and fascination further drive such minds into 'studying' the existence and work of such super human, spiritual forces (Review pp.87, 166).

Many who became captivated and engaged into pursuing the eerie messages, elevate their 'knowledge' to the status of worship, their being mesmerised into believing that they are in touch with the higher powers, whom some even refer to as God or who they conceive God to be. From the many biblical references to these spurious beliefs and practices, are those who Paul encountered on Mars Hill, worshipping the Unknown God. (Acts 17:23 See also 1 Tim. 4:1)

In a basic search outside of the Christian sources, we came upon several references and distinctions between spiritualism and spiritism, both of which encapsulate versions of the results mentioned above. Two of them worth considering are the following from Wikipedia:

"Spiritualism is a system of belief or religious practice based on communication with the spirits of the deceased, through mediums. It is also the doctrine or philosophy that the spirit exists as distinct from matter, or that spirit is the only reality."

"Spiritism is a spiritualistic philosophy and religion codified in the 19th century by the French educator Hippolyte Léon Denizard Rivail, under the pen name Allan Kardec. It proposed the study of 'the nature, origin, and destiny of spirits, and their relation with the corporeal world.'"

## Satan's Fundamental Deception

Without much extrapolation and biblical exegesis, it is clear that *spiritualism* and *spiritism* are beliefs, practices and philosophies that go totally contrary to the teachings, principles, and practices of the Holy Bible and are therefore opposed to God and godliness, and consequently, to family relational health. Their focal point is an extension of the first lie that Satan told to Eve: "Thou shall not surely die" (Gen. 3:4). This is the beginning of the false teaching of the "never-dying soul." The renowned Charles Wesley (1707–1788) even wrote a song about it: "A Charge to keep I have, a God to glorify, a never-dying soul to save and fit it for the sky" This song is sung so earnestly in many Christian churches, but it is scripturally incorrect. (Read further: The Soul = The Man, pp. 285-287).

*Spiritualism* also promotes the idea that the departed person still exists, suggesting that there would still be some access to, and communication with, the "spirit" of departed loved ones. All of this contradicts Psalm 146:4: "His breath goeth forth, he returneth to his earth; in that very day his thoughts perish."

Consider this rationale: Since relational strains, troubles, and problems that families have to contend with emanate from the mysterious mind and are perceived as demonic in nature and are therefore *spiritual*, we may understand why millions around the world, both in religious and nonreligious communities, resort to various forms of spiritualism and spiritism to find answers to their relational distresses, despairs, disasters, and calamities.

"Coast to Coast AM" host George Noory, supported by Rosemary Ellen Guiley in his book *Talking to the Dead*, had no question in his mind about the reality of communicating with the dead when he wrote:

The developments in spirit communications over the recent decades have been nothing short of astonishing. Whether you can accept the evidence or not, the results are impossible to dismiss. To us, the evidence is clear: we already have the tools for establishing real-time, two-way contact with the dead, as well as entities who perhaps live in parallel worlds to ours, and possibly with versions of ourselves in parallel dimensions. My own personal spiritual search has led me to the unshakable conclusion that we do not die. I am absolutely convinced that there is an afterlife and that we carry on in our new ways after we are done on Earth.

Noory is not the only public, influential voice that is preaching such spurious, antibiblical doctrine and leading millions down the path of spiritualism. Albeit, he seems convinced!

### Spiritism vs Witchcraft and Fortune-Telling

*Spiritism* purports to be able to give a powerful shield and mental restoration to those who are affected by demons. It brings back mental powers that have been touched and disturbed. Where the mental state has been weakened by spiritual attacks (naturally by "demons") in the form of curses, hexes, or spells, spiritism can fix it. The answer is to fortify oneself spiritually. This is not the same as the positive transforming power of the Holy Spirit on the heart-mind of the person who is surrendered to Christ. It is a crafty move to deceive and smear the mind further with satanic vices.

Witchcraft and spiritism say the same thing in essence, except that the senior one, spiritism, seems to appeal to the upper echelon of society, while the junior appeals mostly to the 'lower' class. Here we find the less-sophisticated practices of obeah and voodoism. These are rituals that claim to heal any condition or trouble in a family. The practitioners or masters claim to be able to reunite estranged family members, fix relationships between parents and children, and restore the harmony and balance in any family's life. They can bring back unity and even foretell the future for persons who comply with their directives and divinations.

The Witch of Endor whose assistance Saul sought falls into this category (1 Sam. 28). Equally so are the modern practitioners of palmistry or chiromancy (palm readers), tasseography (tea-leaf readers), taromancy or cartomancy (card reading), horary astrology (horoscope), and crystal ball gazing. The work *Les Prophèties* of the historically world-renowned French physician and astrologer Michel Nostradamus (1503–1556), a collection of over nine hundred poetic quatrains predicting the future, are among the more intellectually respected and acclaimed versions of the satanic sophistries designed to capture and commandeer the mind of human beings.

But the likes of Nostradamus and many after him are not the beginning of such false teachings. We can go back as early as the study of Egyptians Old Kingdoms (3700-2150 BCE); It is about in those times that we would meet figures like Hermes Tismegistus and the teaching of Hermeticism. We would also have to consider developments during the Renaissance (14th-17th Century) with focus on personalities such as Cosimico de Medici (1389 - 1464) of Florence, Italy. We would need to factor in Greek and other scholars and philosophers who purported the theories of the spiritual communications with the underworld. We could go on with the never-ending list of those who were either exponents or opponents of divergent views and positions about the spirit world.

One of the greatest attractions in the resort paradise of Jamaica, Montego Bay in the western parish of St. James is the Rose Hall Great House made famous by the 18th century legend of the White Witch of Rose Hall, Annie Palmer. The former brutal plantation owner was murdered by one of her slaves, because of what she did to a slave relative of his. The 'spirit' of Annie Palmer is said to have been palpably present and much has been the lurid stories about her, part of which has formed the treasure of the property up to this day, attracting thousands of local and international visitors annually.

We would want to fast-forward to Room 217 of the Stanley Hotel in Estes, Colorado, USA, that once presidential suite considered to be the haunted room on the property. The 'spirit' of long-time housekeeper, Elizabeth Wilson is said to abide there since she died in 1950. The place has been dubbed the Disneyland of Ghost because it is said that her 'spirit' has made its presence felt in no ordinary way so that many who have ventured to stay there have encountered her in more ways than one.

Back to Jamaica, this time to the quiet rural community of Font Hill in the eastern parish of St. Thomas. Font Hill became nationally and to some extent internationally abuzz in 1974, when the infamous spirit (duppy and jumbie in Jamaican dialect), under the name Copie, commandeered attention. Legend had it that the spirit was trapped in a bottle which was accidentally broken by one of the members of the Isaac and Adina Brown's family. Another account is that Copie came to the community from England. As a result of the spooky and bizarre happenings over several weeks, the Brown's home and the entire community was transformed into a 'tourist destination', because thousands of curious visitors came from near and far to experience the mysterious demonstrations of the spirit.

The common thread that runs through all these historical cases and stories mentioned above, and the myriad of others that could be garnered around the world, is the relentless efforts of Satan to use his deceptions and lies to spread false teachings about the state of the dead and more so, about God and His loving, patient management of the malady of sin. In all these we see the combination of the 7 S's mentioned or alluded to between Genesis 3: 1-24 and about which we need to be fully aware in contemplation of our quality of life in the here and now and our eternal destination. These 7 S's are: Satan, Serpent, Subtlety, Sin, Soul, State of the Dead and Salvation in Christ,

Through a systematic study of the Holy Bible following the recommended procedure in Isaiah 28:9 &10: "Whom shall he teach knowledge? and whom shall he make to understand doctrine? Them that are weaned from the milk, and drawn from the breasts. For precept must be upon precept, precept upon precept; line upon line, line upon line; here a little, and there a little" we can be safe in getting a full and clear knowledge of those S's.

And, Jesus, Himself added: "Search the scriptures; for in them ye think ye have eternal life: and they are they which testify of me." (John 5:39) With that diligent study pattern, and complete reliance upon the Holy Spirit for full understanding, we can all find the truth unto salvation and be spared from the wiles of the devil. (Eph. 6: 11)

## Negative Emotional Reflective Fixation Syndrome (NERFS)

None of the above means of spiritualism can help the human being to effectively deal with or manage painful reflections, annoying recollections, residual pains, haunting memories, regretful memories, and hateful memories. Many continue to gaze and live in the shadow of their past and are suffering from what we will call negative emotional reflective fixation syndrome (NERFS). This is an inordinate, helpless feeling of being stuck or trapped in the experience of the past; a feeling of being condemned; and the consequential need to be punished for misdemeanors or sins of the past.

Some manifestations of NERFS are self-flagellation, voluntary (self-imposed) isolation and ostracism, and extreme and even painful acts of remorse and contrition. Regrettably, some go on to the nth-degree of committing suicide. None of the potential life-threatening acts of mortification, humiliation, and punishment helps in any substantial way to manage the effects of the various negative descriptions of one's past.

# Meet the God of the Present

The answer to managing the effects of the demons of the past is to meet the God of the present. That was the glorious and redemptive inspiration that rescued David's mind immediately as he expressed his sense of depression and helplessness. Here again is our Anchor Text from Psalm 42:5: "Why art thou cast down, O my soul? and why art thou disquieted in me? Hope thou in God: for I shall yet praise him for the help of his countenance." Paraphrased and applied to families: "Why am I feeling so low in spirit, and why am I feeling so depressed? I do not have to be like this despite what might have happened in my distant or immediate past. I can exercise hope in God and give praise to Him; because His presence in me will inspire, brighten, and heal my mind."

Paul, the great apostle to the Gentiles, went through David's experience when he evidently reflected on his past and tried to grapple with the demons of both his past and present. He recorded his feeling of desperation and utter helplessness in Romans chapter 7. Between verses 15 and 22, he listed his litany of failure as he saw his dismal state of mind when measured in harmony with God's standard of judgment—His Holy Law. In verse 24, Paul gave out his yelp of loss, degradation, and despondency: "O wretched man that I am! who shall deliver me from the body of this death?"

# Reflecting on Our Checkered Past

It is at such points when we face the gravity and deadliness of our demonic past and present, and then respond to the illuminating power of the Holy Spirit, that we find hope. One of the healing assurances from God for such times of lowliness and contrition is found in Isaiah 30:21: "And thine ears shall hear a word behind thee, saying: 'This is the way, walk ye in it, when ye turn to the right hand, and when ye turn to the left.'"

Left to ourselves, we would become overwhelmed and get drowned under the weight of the past. The demons of the past lifestyle and behavior would shred some persons to pieces, as in the attempted case of the demoniac in Mark 5. But we do not have to continue to harm or mutilate ourselves physically and mentally, emotionally, or spiritually, because there is Jesus! He is the God of the past, present, and future: "Jesus Christ the same yesterday, and today, and forever" (Heb. 13:8).

Against this guarantee of grace and power for victory available from the God of treacherous men like Jacob and David—men who had such checkered pasts—those of us upon whom the ends of the world have come (1 Cor. 10:11) can have hope. If we gaze into our painful, regrettable, and remorseful pasts; if we allow those who know of our tainted and unsavory pasts to keep reminding us of them; we will be ensnared and imprisoned therein.

**Healing from the Past: Regardless of Satan's Contention**

Speaking of those who know of our past and will keep us living there, we consider two encounters recorded in Zechariah 3 and Jude 9. We are assured that all is not lost, regardless of the issues and challenges of our past life.

In both instances, we see Satan positioning himself as the accuser of the people of God (see Rev. 12: 10). When God sets out to reward the faithful, Satan assumes the role of prosecutor to hold up any evidence of the past that he succeeded in leading them to do contrary to God's will. Here we see the chief demon, Satan, protesting that God's people should not be credited with eternal life. "And he shewed me Joshua the high priest standing before the angel of the LORD, and Satan standing at his right hand to resist him" (Zech. 3:1).

What was Satan's point of contention? Their past! "Now Joshua was clothed with filthy garments, and stood before the angel. And he answered and spake unto those that stood before him, saying, Take away the filthy garments from him. And unto him he said, Behold, I have caused thine iniquity to pass from thee, and I will clothe thee with change of raiment" (verses 3–4). As human beings, they had challenges in their past lives. Look at Moses; he disobeyed the Lord and struck the rock instead of speaking as he was instructed, hence he could not enter the Promised Land and died at Mount Nebo (Deut. 32:48–52 and 34:4–6).

What the arch-demon does not know is what we know from God's word: "Moreover the law entered, that the offence might abound. But where sin abounded, grace did much more abound" (Rom. 5:20). Paraphrased and interpreted: "The presence of God's law, which is the standard of His righteousness, shows up the demonic offences committed in the mind. But as many demons of the past that might be affecting you, God's grace is much more available to cover them and make you whole and free from their effects."

Then Paul captures and repeats Jesus's reaffirmation: "And he said unto me, My grace is sufficient for thee: for my strength is made perfect in weakness. Most gladly therefore will I rather glory in my infirmities, that the power of Christ may rest upon me" (2 Cor. 12:9).

**Satan's Limitation**

Satan and his demonic forces are limited; they can only see the misdeeds and sins that we commit in response to his temptations. What they cannot see is the repentant heart as the Holy Spirit does His work of conviction and healing (Review p. 220). Satan cannot understand how the heart repudiates his temptations and enticements as the Holy Spirit produces that genuine sorrow for the demons of the past.

With his fallen nature like ours, he, too, is limited to the outside as stated in 1 Samuel 16:7: "But the LORD said unto Samuel, Look not on his countenance, or on the height of his stature; because I have refused him: for the LORD seeth not as man seeth; for man looketh on the outward appearance, but the LORD looketh on the heart."

Thanks be to God, He can and does look beyond our faults and see our needs. In the context of this chapter, that great need of ours that God sees and provides for is the relief of our minds from the negative impact of the relational demons of our past. We cannot erase the records, but there are no perpetual sins. All can be forgiven. "If we confess our sins, he is faithful and just to forgive us our sins, and to cleanse us from ALL unrighteousness" (1 John 1:9).

## The Role of Forgiveness

As we rejoice in the assured forgiveness of the Lord, we need to remember that there are two important roles we have to play in the forgiveness process:

1. **Forgive ourselves**—In accepting forgiveness from the Lord, we must internalize it and forgive ourselves. That is the only way to rejoice in God's full and free salvation. We are counseled and invited to "come boldly unto the throne of grace, that we may obtain mercy, and find grace to help in time of need" (Heb. 4:16).

2. **Forgive others**—We cannot experience the joy of God's forgiveness for the demons of our past if we do not forgive those who trespassed against us: "And forgive us our debts, as we forgive our debtors" (Matt. 6: 12). Among those who we will need to forgive are they who influenced some of our past demons. An unforgiving heart is a demon that will haunt us even unto the grave.

The demons of the past do not have to hold us captive. By abounding, growing faith in the God of the present, we can live and experience quality relational health in this life and in preparation for the life to come.

## Suggestions for Action

1.  Guard well the avenues to your mind; build a fence around your senses.

2.  Be encouraged in your moments of low feelings. Like David, look up to the hills from whence comes your help.

3.  Constant meditation on God's words is one sure way of preventing your mind from going idle and thereby providing an entrance to satanic forces.

4.  Anchor your faith in God. Know the truth about the quality of the relationship that you have with Him.

5.  Live a happy, forgiving life. Take seriously the prerequisite for your forgiveness in the Lord's Prayer.

# Chapter 10

# Fearfully and Wonderfully Made
## 1 + 1 = 1; M+M=M

**Anchor Text 1: Psalm 139:14**

"I will praise thee; for I am fearfully *and* wonderfully made: marvelous *are* thy works; and *that* my soul knoweth right well."

**Paraphrased for Families**

I will give you praise always, Lord, because I know how whole and perfect you have made me. All of your creation is filled with wonder and marvel. Above all is my intelligent mind, which knows well what is right in your sight.

**Anchor Text 2: Ephesians 5:31–33**

"For this cause shall a man leave his father and mother, and shall be joined unto his wife, and they two shall be one flesh. This is a great mystery: but I speak concerning Christ and the church. Nevertheless, let every one of you in particular so love his wife even as himself; and the wife see that she reverence her husband."

**Paraphrased for Families:**

When a man and a woman get married, with their hearts being joined together as husband and wife, they individually should leave the overshadowing and protection of their parents' home and live their new life together as one family. This is a mysterious experience, but it is beyond the mere union of a man and a woman, because God designed their human union to be a symbol and object lesson of

Christ joining Himself with the Church so that it becomes one with Him. However, in the marriage, it is important that the husband especially loves his wife in the same way that he loves himself, and the wife is to reciprocate with honor toward her husband.

*What Will They Think of Next?* Global Television Network, a Canadian television station, retitled its program originally named *Science International* (1976–1979) to this rather intriguing title, evidently to make it more appealing and to hold its viewers in preparation for the next episode. That decision is a part of the exercise called *rebranding* of the product or service or program in the business world, and it is done in order to hold and increase the company's market share.

This same captivating question—*What Will They Think of Next?*—has also been used many times to close some educational documentaries seen on some television channels (such as the Discovery Channel) that report on recent discoveries and inventions, especially in the scientific, technological, and industrial world. The question is intended to leave the listener in awe and amazement and in an anticipatory mode of mind, looking forward with bated breath to the next episode.

## The Creation

James Weldon Johnson (1871–1938), writing about the Creation in his epic poem of the same name, seemed to have employed the same technique of intrigue and suspense as he portrayed how God called the various forms of life into being. In stanzas 1–8, Johnson painted a picture of the orderly development of the world from the firmament to the animal kingdom, about which God continuously declared: "That's good!" (See p. 336)

According to Johnson at the end of stanza 9, God did the review of His creation and, as satisfied as He was with all that He had brought into being, there seemed to have been something seriously missing, hence His bemoaning: "I am lonely still!" That must have been the "What-can-I (or preferably We)-think-of-next? moment, and indeed it was.

In a classic artistic style, Johnson painted a captivating picture of God sitting down by a river and, in deep contemplation, reviewing all of His creation. He considered them in the order they were brought into being. He affirmed each one for the purpose that He had created it.

However, at the end of His review, according to the poet, God felt that there was something, preferably someone, that was missing. Of all His created works, He had not yet made any close enough to Himself with whom He could have dialogue and a face-to-face relationship.

Johnson went on to portray a very human scene of a mother tending to her baby by suggesting that God gathered clay and knelt on the ground, where He formed the human body. Then, as the Bible gave the final account, God blew His breath of life into the body He had formed, thereby bringing to life His crowning act of creation, a human being.

What did He (preferably *They*) think of next? Of course, it was the masterpiece, indeed the crowning act of creation: *man*! Johnson's elaborate depiction and exposé was summed up in God's own words: "And God said, Let us make man in our image, after our likeness: and let them have dominion over the fish of the sea, and over the fowl of the air, and over the cattle, and over all the earth, and over every creeping thing that creepeth upon the earth. So God created man in his own image, in the image of God created he him; male and female created he them" (Gen. 1: 26). "And the LORD God formed man of the dust of the ground, and breathed into his nostrils the breath of life; and man became a living soul" (Gen. 2:7).

# The Creation of Man: God's Intelligent Design

We did not use the popular intriguing and enthralling question *What will they think of next?* to suggest that the Godhead, like human inventors, was on an evolving, discovering process during the Creation Week. Nor is our use of Johnson's tenth stanza, which portrays the creation of man, intended to suggest that man was a grandiose idea that the Trinity came up with, much to their own surprise.

Not at all! Instead of "What did they *think* of next?" in the context of the Creation on the sixth day, it would correctly be "What did they *do* next?" The fact is that the creation of man was God's intelligent, intentional, and designed final act of His creation plan.

Why was that so? Because man was, to an extent, an extension of God Himself. God reproduced Himself—or, more appropriately and accurately expressed, God made an authentic yet partial representation of Himself when He made man. Here again is His own statement of account: "And God said, Let us make man in our image, after our likeness" (Gen. 1:26). This is as close as one can get to self-replication.

This was cloning and meiosis and mitosis all in one, not just at the biological but also at the divine level. He chose to reproduce Himself and give His "offspring" (Acts 17:29) representative portions of His own quality. It was by intentional, intelligent design. It was not an afterthought. It was not a case of an inventor bumping or stumbling into a great idea and bringing it to reality (See p. 320).

The creation of the human was not a case of God experiencing a "eureka" moment, as with the famed mathematician Archimedes, who is credited with having shouted the Latin for "I have found it" and running naked down the street when he discovered the mathematical formula that he had been conceptualizing for some time. The creation of man by God was a part of the plan that was made *before* the Creation.

Paul cites proof of that to the Ephesians: "Blessed be the God and Father of our Lord Jesus Christ, who hath blessed us with all spiritual blessings in heavenly places in Christ: According as he hath chosen us in him before the foundation of the world, that we should be holy and without blame before him in love" (Eph. 1:3–4).

We suggest that David's exultation, recorded in our Anchor Text, was a result of designed inspiration from God who made him. We say *designed* because, while David was not told directly like John on the Isle of Patmos to "write" (Rev. 21:5), it is clear that his poetic gift from the same God was not only for his present readers but also for posterity, indeed for generations after. Some of those who were to benefit from David's inspiring and affirming statement of the marvelous creation of man are those of us upon whom the ends of the world have come (1 Cor. 10:11).

## Fools Deny Creation

Some people find themselves in a quandary concerning their origin, their purpose here on earth, and ultimately, their destiny. There are those persons who hold and teach that the human being has been on a path of evolving and is seemingly getting better. Then there are the agnostics, atheists, skeptics, humanists, pantheists, and freethinkers, with their versions of intelligence about creation.

These, put together, are they whom David called *fools*, because they deny their marvelous creation by firstly denying the existence and creatorship of God: "The fool hath said in his heart, there is no God. Corrupt are they, and have done abominable iniquity: there is none that doeth good" (Ps. 53:1). Such persons end up with reprobate and degenerate minds. "And even as they did not like to retain God in their knowledge, God gave them over to a reprobate mind, to do those things which are not convenient" (Rom. 1:28).

It is not only in the non-Christian or secular world that versions of such beliefs and creation skepticism are held. In the over 4,200 religions in the world, there are various beliefs as to who God is. Even in Christianity, there is the occasional and even convenient reference to God as "whoever you conceive him to be." This nebulous concept of God has given rise to the nonspecific, all-encompassing category "people of faith" or "the faith community".

There is that societal caution not to offend anyone by appearing to be specific in reference to God, so we use politically correct terms with which everyone is comfortable as to his or her idea of God. In this regard, faith is the common tie, since faith is considered as just belief, and whosoever one believes in, that is fine. You respect my belief or faith and I do yours, so at the end of the day, we are people of faith and belong to the faith community.

This all sounds good and accommodating for all creeds and practices on the surface, but it is a tool of Satan nonetheless to negate and question the existence of the Creator God. Peter spoke about their existence in his time and prophesied about their continuation unto this twenty-first century and until the Lord returns: "But there were false prophets also among the people, even as there shall be false teachers among you, who privily shall bring in damnable heresies, even denying the Lord that bought them, and bring upon themselves swift destruction" (2 Pet. 2:1).

## The Sex/Gender Controversy

Given the nature of the following sections the reader is advised to read again the explanations of **Whomsoever May Read** in the Preface.

We would not have done justice to the issue of denying and questioning God's creation of human beings if we did not address those surging controversies over sexual and gender identities. There are those who are questioning and are discontented with the sex (male or female) into which they were conceived. To make their case, they do not attribute the sex into which they are born to the natural biological work at conception; they label it as being "assigned," implying that their being considered male or female is a discretionary and even subjective decision by their parents (See p. 298).

So much so that the California Department of Education on January 19, 2019, published a position on the issue that: "California kindergartners could soon learn all about the 'gender stereotypes' plaguing society, the importance of accepting transgender lifestyles, a kaleidoscope of 15 different genders to choose from, and other 'health guidelines.'" (See more on the issue - p. 347). Yet God's law of human life beginning from conception, which He established at Creation, has not and will not change. "For I am the LORD, I change not; therefore ye sons of Jacob are not consumed" (Mal. 3:6).

## Intersex, Congenital and Life Variations

God remains in control of nature, and there is fundamental constancy and perpetuity in said nature regarding the conception and birth of human (and animal) life. These laws remain so despite the impact of sin, even as manifested in congenital adrenal hyperplasia (CAH) and many other genetic variations resulting in cases like intersex traits among others. God has blessed the medical professionals led by those in the field of endocrinology and related disciplines to offer clinical explanations with reference to the chemical and hormonal changes for such congenital and developmental differences.

With the correct teaching, acceptance and understanding of these findings, those born with such differences such as inconclusive definitiveness of their biological and physiological sexual identity as male or female, and their families, should be able to lead more comfortable and appreciative lives. Their self-construal should be healthy as they accept who they are and not to be in competition with whom they are not. The word of the Lord of Life about our conception, recorded by the Prophet Isaiah (49:1-2) and Jeremiah (1:5) still stands today. Despite it all, God is still in control and sees the end from the beginning.

While maintaining the conviction in the original two biological sexes of male and female from Creation, the Christian acknowledges that the biological paradigm of life has shifted and many variations, alterations and changes have taken place in the human body and mind, even from conception. As a result of new discoveries and endless medical, biological, other scientific and related issues, researchers in the various fields do not have a dull moment. As viruses mutate, develop new strains and boggle the minds of virologists and epidemiologists to study and find answers to control and treat them, (as is the case of Covid19), so do new discoveries and maladies about the human body arrest and commandeer the knowledge and skills of the various medical professionals to find answers and treatments.

Operating strictly from a scientific and clinical perspective, these professionals, many of them Bible-believing Christians, owe it to the world community to offer impressions, interpretations, and explanations of whatever variations they encounter in their researches and findings. Such correct actions will protect the dignity and self-esteem of all persons whose physiological and functional characteristics are different from those of the majority of the world population. One researcher, Kaity Lynn, (2019) posted via Quora that of the world population, "1.7% of all births is the last figure I am aware of. It is good to keep in mind that "Intersex" covers more than a single condition. There are many people effected (sic) by an intersex condition that will never know it."

It is understood that stigmas and labels that dehumanize and speak pejoratively and uncomplimentarily of such fellow human beings are unhealthy and should not be accommodated. It is the same principle that applies to persons with mental challenges. Labelling and calling them disparaging names such as mad, crazy, numb skulls are intolerable. They deserve respect and acceptance as children of the one God of Creation, despite the differences in their beings – body or mind. This is the epitome of Christ-likeness that every sincere, Bible-believing Christian ought to lovingly embrace and follow.

**Biblical Answers**

While the Bible does not in every way, speak in biological, physiological, chemical, hormonal or scientific terms, it does offer clear explanations for the variations from the original that God made at Creation. David reminds us that since the fall (Gen. 3:15) we are all born in sin and shapen in iniquity (Psalm 51:5). This is certainly not complimentary and at the same time it is not condemnatory, but it strikes reality. Jesus' parable of the sower (Matt. 13: 24-28) helps to shed more light on the mystery of the changes in God's Creation which He declared as 'good' 6 times between the record of Genesis 1:4-25, and He strengthened the description with the intensifier 'very' in the 7th declaration in verse 31.

The first sentence of Matthew 13: 28 "… an enemy hath done this," is the succinct answer to the entire human dilemma, physiologically and psychologically, that God's children have experienced, and for which we humans are relentlessly seeking and suggesting answers. There are several other biblical references or allusions to the human dilemma of congenital and development challenges. Then there are cases of instantaneous changes in health and life functions. Job's mysterious and traumatic experience (chapter 1-42) is a archetypal case and was recorded to give those of us now, millennia later, hope that despite it all, God is still in charge and will one day bring it to an end when 'affliction will not rise a second time. (Nahum 1: 9)

In a different story this time recorded in John 9:1-41, Jesus addressed the matter of congenital defects (preferably 'difference') in the case of the man born blind. The truth is that no one in the medical, scientific, philosophical or sociological disciplines will consider it as insensitive or dehumanizing to call blindness from birth a defect, impairment or abnormality and therefore suggest instead that the man was born with 'sight variation' or 'visuality difference.' His physical and physiological condition was that he was simply blind. How subjective we can be in determining what is socially sensitive, pejorative and uncomplimentary, depending on who is calling what! Again, this observation does not negate the fact that we need to be sensitive in descriptions that we make of various conditions that are not the same as the biological and physiological majority, nor are we to strenuously deny or euphemize away the differences.

In summary, Jesus rose to the defence of the parents and especially the mother, since mothers are always carrying the brunt of the accusations when it comes to congenital or prenatal issues, including whether it is a son or daughter who is born. Jesus spoke against the speculative accusations as to why the son was born blind. He suggested that there are times when God in His divine providence, permits these phenomena in our human experience to help us to remember and turn to Him even amidst the heavy toll of sin in our beings. Let us be clear. God did not manipulate the mother's womb in order to bring about the child's blindness. Sin had its mysterious impact as it has always manifested itself in abnormalities of various kinds. But God intervened providentially and showed His supreme power over sin and its consequences (Review p. 188).

## God's Decision, Permission and Action – Different Times and Circumstances

Let us quickly remember that God does not inflict these conditions on His children as suggested by Satan that He should. (Job 2: 4 & 5)

Instead, God permitted him (Satan) to go ahead with yet another of his devious acts aimed at discrediting God's love and care for His children. That permission by God for Satan to carry out his temptation is an investment in His children's faith in Him. Their endurance and overcoming will be trophies of His grace and testimonies of His keeping power and vindication of God's character against the accusations of the evil one.

Sure, the Bible does record cases of phenomenal and even catastrophic events that happen to some people as God's doing. These are stand-alone events and served very specific purposes such as discipline and punishment for defiance, recalcitrance and behaviours breathed in them by Satan, himself. Those behaviours would corrupt others and lead them to destruction, had swift discipline not been administered commensurate to their deeds. God knows when and how to act after giving ample time for the wayward and rebellious to repent. Cases in point: The Flood (Genesis 6 - 9:29); Pharaoh (Exodus 1:8 - 14:30); Korah, Dathan and Abiram (Numbers 16:20-35); Nebuchadnezzar (Daniel 4:1- 37) and Herod (Acts 12: 21-23). Consider the very opposite experience in the case of the King and nation of Nineveh – page 444.

While God did not stop the archenemy in Job's case, He made sure that the temptation was done under His watchful eyes and He kept His hands on the ultimate control of our wellbeing in fulfilment of His assurance that: "There hath no temptation taken you but such as is common to man: but God is faithful, who will not suffer you to be tempted above that ye are able; but will with the temptation also make a way to escape, that ye may be able to bear it." (1 Cor. 10:13).

In His love and wisdom, as He sees that we will benefit from His eventual miraculous intervention, He will act as is best in our individual cases. It is also true that it is not every condition that assails us, congenitally, developmentally or accidentally, for which God will provide a miraculous intervention, correction or cure. Job's faith remained alive on this assurance, hence he was able to declare: "For I know that my redeemer liveth, and that he shall stand at the latter day upon the earth: And though after my skin worms destroy this body, yet in my flesh shall I see God: Whom I shall see for myself, and mine eyes shall behold, and not another; though my reins be consumed within me." (Job 19:25-27) God assures us further that His "grace is sufficient to keep us. (2 Cor. 12:9)

**The Change of Changes to Come**

It is this solid, unmoveable faith that has kept many Christians, born with variances and differences, or who suffered catastrophic and life-changing incidents and accidents, firmly anchored in the love of God and the fervent hope in Christ soon return. Then, they will experience the change in their bodies that they longed for and deserved. "In a moment, in the twinkling of an eye, at the last trump: for the trumpet shall sound, and the dead shall be raised incorruptible, and we shall be *changed*." (1 Cor. 15:52)

Certainly, there are many like Job who have experienced the life-turning events and become witnesses of God's immediate power to change things as His divine wisdom sees fit. See evidence of this in the unfolding events in the latter part of Job's experience: his repentance (42:1-6) and his restoration (42: 10-17). Read the added discussion on the story in Chapter 9 - "Job: A Testing Case and Study" (See p. 228)

It is also important not to miss how God addressed Job's friends who, in good intention, albeit wrong, interpreted his trauma and dilemma as evidence of his sins catching upon him. (Num. 32:23) God required their repentance as He forgave them and exonerated Job from their accusations – a sound lesson for us today!

## Variations and Subtleties of the Sex/Gender Controversy

Those who do voluntary genital mutilation and those who impose it on others, as in the case of the Texas mother who wanted to have her young son's genitals removed and transform him into the girl she desired, all do so in their quest to "find" their sexual identity. Note that female genital mutilation (FGM) is not done on the basis of gender identity but for "femininity and modesty", a cultural ritual which subtlety redounds to the subjugation of the female for the sexual satisfaction of the male. There are those who even suggest that the procedure will make her 'perform' better. The physiological/ anatomical fact is that removal of the clitoris reduces one of the major God-given erogenous sensitivity of the wife for sexual satisfaction, which satisfaction ought to be a balancing experience with that of her husband in a healthy marriage.

The controversy continues with those who are teaching that parents should not "assign" the sex (male or female) of their children at birth but should leave it to the children to determine their preference as they grow. Those who are heralding the idea that there is a multiplicity of sexes or genders based on the medically established cases as addressed above (intersex, inter-alia), as politically correct and inclusive as they might want to be in light of the present movements, have one common objective: to erase from the mind of man the connection with God as Creator. This is Satan's original goal from the time he staged the attempted ideological coup in heaven (Isa. 14:11–14 and Ezek. 28:12–18).

It is worth noting that in the human management of the animal kingdom (which was part of the original assignment from God in Genesis 1:26–28), there is generally no controversy about sexual identity; no displeasure or dissatisfaction with the biologically developed sex from conception; nor is there any concern or felt need in the veterinarian or animal husbandry community to change the sexual orientation of animals. There is no observation that the male or female animal's behavior seems opposite to that of its biological birth sex and should therefore be administered the various forms of surgical treatment to help it to be "its preferred sex."

This general observation should not be confused with the practice of castration of some male animals in the interest of what some producers refer to as the preferred quality and taste. Tom Barthel, owner/operator at Snake River Farm in Becker, Minnesota, in the United States, shares this position:

> Males of many domestic animal species are castrated at an early age. There are at least two good reasons for early castration. One is that early castration is less stressful for the animal; the other is that early castration minimizes the effects of male hormones. Those hormones affect animal behavior, physical characteristics and meat quality. Males are frequently more aggressive and more active. They have a greater muscle mass that results in generally a leaner carcass. In some species, male hormones affect taste. Those taste effects are generally negative. Males that have not been castrated are referred to as "intact."

This practice of castration of the male animal is an economic and (a scientifically manipulative) business decision by farmers. However, it is not suggesting that there is a preference of the female over the male. It is not a case of the farmers expressing dissatisfaction and preferring to have this set of animals be outrightly changed from one sex to the other. Given the extremity to which humans are going, it might not be surprising to hear of some animal pet lovers wanting to change the sex of their favorite animal, instead of simply purchasing another of the desired sex (See p. 298).

The emphatic point here is that it is only the human, the intelligent being of God's creation, who questions the acts of nature regarding sexual identity, functionality, and purpose. As stated emphatically earlier, we do understand that there are bio-physiological and genetic congenital developmental issues and challenges that can affect a person's sexuality in more ways than one. Medical science continues to discover and address these issues. The focus of our concern is what sometimes is the clearly orchestrated hype about gender and sexual preferences that would all of a sudden leave one to question if all down through the centuries, what was known and accepted about the basic male and female sexes, was wrong.

Some of us might remember the days when coconut oil went under severe stress and question about its potential dangerous cholesterol content and negative impact on health. Its place on the shelves of the shops and supermarkets was visibly empty or overrun by the newfound idols of the cooking industry. However, it seems that once whomever the piper was that blew the tune for those who wanted a share in the cooking oil market got his pay, and they felt that they had a stable share, coconut oil was back to its original exalted position as one of the oils of preference for human consumption.

It would appear that there is a new societal light bulb that has gone off in so many heads about the "correct understanding" of human sexuality, way beyond mere male and female, which safely accounted for the development of the human race from time memorial. From a Biblical, Christian, prophetic perspective, we can only see this whistle-blowing and piping tune being danced to as the new sexual order of society as being a masterful work of the opposing forces to the God-inspired teachings of the Bible. On the surface these efforts are presented as promoting equality and respect of personal choices in a free and liberal society, a posture, standing on its own, one would be hard pressed to question (Ref. to Item 3, p. 40).

## Wonderfully Made for Relationship

One key question we need to address is: What does our being "fearfully and wonderfully made" have to do with the subject of this book—family relational health? Of all the differences between the two main biological forms of animate life that God made, animals and human beings, the most outstanding is the human's ability to forge and keep relationships. That capability is the work of the active, sound mind which is akin to that of the Creator. The first understanding here is that God made man (male and female) to be in a relationship with Him. Let us consult our Glossary for the working definition of *relationship*:

> The conscious process of ongoing intrapersonal awareness in one's mind, and the engagement of that conscious mind *with* or *against* another mind (interpersonal) in an effort to produce a desired result. This is based on the understanding that all human relationships begin and continue to exist in the active, sound mind. Once engagement of minds is established, the resulting relationship can be mostly and purposefully positive (with), or negative (against) and rarely ever neutral.

Also, read again the definition in the Glossary of the *active, sound mind*. Active sound-mindedness is a physiological and psychological attribute that is unique to humans. David's inspiration led him to realize that in his *soul,* meaning his *mind,* he "knows well what is right in your sight." Nothing else in God's vast creation here on earth possesses that quality or characteristic of being—the relational mind.

### God's CPRI: Differentiated Animal and Human Mind Consciousness

Let us go for some simple, clear, visible facts to substantiate that position:

1.  God *called* the animals into being (Gen. 1:20–21, 24–25).

2.  God *created/made* man instead (Gen. 1:26–27).

3.  The creation of man was a consultation of Minds, those of the Godhead—Father, Son, and Holy Spirit: "Let *Us* make man" (Gen. 1:26).

4. God was intimate with man in that He breathed into the nostril of man (Gen. 2:7).

Fact 4 involves the first CPR (cardiopulmonary resuscitation) performed on earth. However, by virtue of the fact that man was not dead, having not yet come to life, the CPR act would be better seen as CPRI (Creator's procreative relationship initiative or Creator's personalized relationship initiative). This means that God's intimate act in bringing man (Adam and Eve separately) into being was the first demonstrable evidence of relationship-building.

God did not merely call them into being. He was divinely gregarious as He touched, made, and molded them. He was up close, upfront, and personal as He replicated Himself in this new being of His creation. This was God's love first performed on earth, an exemplary love which was to permeate the minds of all members of the human family who would come after, beginning with the marriage relationship.

## The Esteemed Value of Face-to-Face Relationship and Kiss

Seeing that healthy emotional feeling is a part of the love relationship gift from God, it might be little wonder why the memory of that first physical touch beyond the holding of the hands, that kiss, in a healthy relationship between a fledgling husband and wife, is such a cherished memory. That kind of physical and emotional contact, generated from the affective domain of the mind and not merely from the cognitive, is to be highly valued and not taken lightly, as is portrayed in the movie scenes of the entertainment industry.

Inasmuch as lip-kissing between husband and wife in our sinful existence cannot be paralleled with the Holy God breathing in the nostrils of Adam and Eve, the comparative evidence of facial, physical intimacy is the point of reference here. To bring Adam and Eve to life, God initiated a face-to-face relationship by breathing into their nostrils His breath which is life. He could have simply *spoken* it as He did for the animals, but he *did* it!

We have no record to specify how Adam expressed his first physical contact with Eve, but upon seeing her face-to-face, he exulted, "This is now bone of my bone and flesh of my flesh." He did not speak in only spiritual terms but in the physical as well. Since the Fall, face-to-face contact with God has been no longer possible, and one of the desires of human beings is to see God face-to-face again (Gen. 3:6–10, 22–24). Such was the expressed desire of Moses recorded in Exodus 33:16–23.

Despite how we might admire the physique or physical formation of a romantic partner, that physiognomic face-to-face contact is indispensable. The sustained, developmental admiration and approval of the messages from the face generally generate that emotional desire and subsequent magnetic pull to bring the faces together and seal with that sensitive and healthily sensual kiss.

The value and esteem of that first kiss has been the record in the testimony of thousands of couples husbands and wives throughout the centuries of human conjugal relationship. It is even one of the celebrated high points in a Christian marriage ceremony; when the marriage officer pronounces them as "now husband and wife," he tells the husband, "You may now kiss the bride!"

This kiss is usually anticipated and generally greeted with cheers of affirmation from the onlooking family members, friends, and well-wishers. The husband and wife are now sealed and united as one. This does not always imply that they might not have kissed each other before, but "In the mouth of two or three witnesses shall every word be established" (2 Cor. 13:1). Paraphrased: "In the eyes of all these witnesses, our love is now publicly established for each other." And this is verily borne out in a section of the marriage vows: "I now call upon these persons here present to witness …"

This value and esteem about a first kiss was the evident experience of former US First Lady Michelle Obama, as she recorded that cherished memory between her and Barack in her book *Becoming Michelle Obama*, chapter 9, page 111: "Any worries I'd been harboring about my life and career and even about Barack himself seemed to fall away with that first kiss, replaced by a driving need to know him better, to explore and experience everything about him as fast as I could." A plaque marking the location for their first kiss has been installed on the corner of Dorchester Avenue and 53rd Street in Chicago, USA.

We affirm that this intimate and positively healthy emotional act should be engaged in by a man and a woman with the understanding that that level of intimacy is ushering in the one-fleshedness as they begin to recreate themselves, individually, into each other's mind. Correctly understood, this loving act between husbands and wives, although in their sinful, human state, this is a miniscule symbolic reflection of when the Holy God of Creation breathed His love and image into the human body and mind, individually; brought them together; and declared that they were not twain, but one.

Further, they understand that the ultimate combined result of their being one—mentally, physically, emotionally, spiritually, and socially—is to be symbolic of the relationship between Christ and His bride-church (Eph. 5:22–32). We need to keep the bar raised on the esteem of the marriage relationship without minimizing any aspect of it: mental, physical, sexual, emotional, spiritual, or social.

The raising of the bar of our healthy emotional relationship, inclusive of the physical kiss, is not limited to the married couple— but the apostle, under inspiration of the Holy Spirit, entreats the members of the church to "Greet ye one another with an holy kiss" (Rom. 16:16; 1 Cor. 16:20; 2 Cor. 13:12; 1 Thess. 5:26). We, in our human realm, understand that there is kiss and there is *kiss*. Not all kissing is the same! A conjugal kiss between a husband and his wife is understandably not the same as a simple social brotherly and sisterly kiss between two nonconjugal members of the Church.

As we mature toward that fullness in Christ, the differentiation between such emotional and indeed spiritual greetings will be clear: "And they shall not teach every man his neighbor, and every man his brother, saying, Know the Lord: for all shall know me, from the least to the greatest" (Heb. 8:11). Paraphrased in the context of the issue being studied: "As we mature in Christ, no one will need to explain to the other the meaning and boundaries of kissing each other, whether it be in the conjugal relationship between husband and wife or in the social and spiritual relationship between brothers and sisters in the Church." This takes us back to the paraphrased Anchor Text of Chapter 8:

> Be aware that the quality of the relationship that you have with Me, your God, whether it be a loving one through obedience or a hateful one through disobedience, and consequently, the relationship that you have with your family members, has far-reaching effects, which do not end with your present family or generation; it has the potential to affect many more families and their offspring after you, and could even go on to influence your third and fourth generations, long after you are gone.

## God Initiated and Demonstrated Relationship

A healthy relationship with God is a prerequisite for healthy relationships with all fellow human beings: spouses, parents, children, siblings, and all other relatives. (See the spiritual reciprocity in the (See Para. 1 Introduction p. xxv). Relationship is God's nature. The Godhead (Father, Son, Holy Spirit) epitomizes and exemplifies this relationship, as seen in all the records available to us from Genesis to Revelation. For Them it has always been *Us*. The One does not work without the Other.

From a philosophical perspective, we can attribute to God the first philosophy of the universe which we will call 'Letusism'. –ism as a suffix means a practice, a deeply entrenched belief and quality, or a motivating characteristic and hallmark of being. Such is the attribute of Us in the Godhead, hence Their absolute and infinite Oneness. This was the supreme example of relationship which They wanted to implant in the relational mind of Their masterpiece of Creation, man – male and female together. (See the Glossary p. 407 for a finer definition of 'Letusism').

Let us consider three outstanding times when They demonstrated visible, exemplary team relationships:

## 1. At the Creation

"And God said, Let US make man in OUR image, after OUR likeness" (Gen. 1:26). They made man in Their Own image (note: not *images* but one *image*) and infused in him/them (male and female, Adam and Eve) the relationship quality of Their Being. God did not first *tell* man *how* to demonstrate relationship, He *showed* him how. He began intimately—one-to-one with each of them.

God did not require or demand of man to love Him. He initiated love at Creation and continued to do so as part of the redemption plan: "But God commendeth his love toward us, in that, while we were yet sinners, Christ died for us" (Rom. 5:8). "We love him, because he first loved us" (1 John 4:19).

## 2. At Jesus's baptism

"Now when all the people were baptized, it came to pass, that Jesus also being baptized, and praying, the heaven was opened, And the Holy Ghost descended in a bodily shape like a dove upon him, and a voice came from heaven, which said, Thou art my beloved Son; in thee I am well pleased" (Luke

3:21 & 22). Here at the early stage of His earthly ministry, the team relationship was demonstrated in three distinct parts:

- **The Son's part**—Jesus demonstrates for us the importance of baptism by being baptized Himself, even though He did not need to go through that rite, seeing He was without sin (Heb. 4:15).
- **The Spirit's part**—The Holy Spirit made His presence felt and seen in the form a dove hovering over Jesus with a blessing.
- **The Father's part**—The Father made the grand announcement of affirmation: "This is my beloved Son, in whom I am well pleased" (Matt. 17:5; Mark 1:11; Luke 3:22).

### 3.  At the Crucifixion for our redemption

"To wit, that God was in Christ, reconciling the world unto himself, not imputing their trespasses unto them; and hath committed unto us the word of reconciliation" (2 Cor. 5:19). While Jesus was visibly on the cross, the Team was carrying out the redemption plan together through Him.

## The Soul = The Man (The Entire Being, See p. 58)

Earlier, we asked the very deep, intense question: "What does our being 'fearfully and wonderfully made' have to do with the subject of this book—family relational health?" Then we gave a partial answer: "Of all the differences between the two main biological forms of animate life that God made, animals and human beings, the most outstanding is the human's ability to forge and keep relationships."

While there are studies showing that some members of the animal kingdom do demonstrate evidence of relational affinity and bonding, this generally lasts for a time, especially between birth and young adulthood. Even in those cases where there are apparently established clans, the developmental and sustained relationship does not last for relational posterity to be kept and identified. That capability in humans is the work of the active, sound mind, which is akin to that of the Creator (See again pp. 205, 279).

Let us put some fullness to that answer by going back to our Anchor Text and, this time, picking up one key word that David used to refer to his intelligence: *soul*. He said: "and that my soul *knoweth* right well." And our paraphrased version reads, "above all is my intelligent mind which knows well what is right in your sight."

## Concurrence of the Prophets

In order to identify with David's sense of esteem and reverence of whom he recognizes himself to be, we need to establish the biblical understanding of that key word, *soul*. Let us begin by saying what it is *not*, as is wrongly portrayed in many Christian/religious circles. The Bible does not teach anywhere that there is an entity or part of the man that is called his "soul."

The first reference to *soul* is the Genesis record of God breathing His breath into the man's nostril: "And the LORD God formed man of the dust of the ground, and breathed into his nostrils the breath of life; and man became a living soul" (Gen. 2:7). This immediately suggests that prior to God breathing His breath into the nostrils, that which was lying on the ground was a dead or nonliving soul or entity, because after the body was quickened by the breath of God, it became a *living soul*. God did not put a soul in the body, He placed His breath—the breath of life—and the body came to life.

This clear understanding was reestablished in the book of Ezekiel. This is what the prophet, under the inspiration of the God of Creation, said with reference to *soul*:

Behold, all souls are mine; as the soul of the father, so also
the soul of the son is mine: the soul that sinneth, it shall
die. The soul that sinneth, it shall die. The son shall not
bear the iniquity of the father, neither shall the father bear
the iniquity of the son: the righteousness of the righteous
shall be upon him, and the wickedness of the wicked shall
be upon him." (Ezek. 18:4–20)

Even before Ezekiel, Moses wrote to the Children of Israel in the
fourth book of the Pentateuch, Numbers 15:28: "And the priest shall
make an atonement for the soul that sinneth ignorantly, when he
sinneth by ignorance before the LORD, to make an atonement for
him; and it shall be forgiven him." Moses was not addressing a part
of the sinner that is named his soul, for which part the priest was to
intercede, leaving the other part(s) for the sinner.

Notice the consistency throughout the Bible with reference to
the use of *soul*—the soul that sinneth, shall die. He was addressing
the whole existing being, the man, the person, the *whole* person. It
was not speaking of a part of the man that will die and leave the
remaining part to go on living, visibly or invisibly.

Let us quickly remind ourselves that the first lie and deception
of Satan recorded in the Bible made the diametric opposite
pronouncement regarding death: "And the serpent said unto the
woman, Ye shall not surely die: For God doth know that in the day
ye eat thereof, then your eyes shall be opened, and ye shall be as gods,
knowing good and evil" (Gen. 3:4–5). Here, Satan was establishing
the false teaching that has been perpetuated through the centuries
unto this day: the never-dying soul. The soul is seen as an entity
or a separate, distinct part of man that lives on after the tangible,
visible body part of him ceases to exist. (Review Satan's Fundamental
Deception, p. 254).

In the last book of the Bible comes what could be considered the
final definitive understanding of *soul* as the complete being. This was

brought out when John, also under divine inspiration, prophetically warned: "And the second angel poured out his vial upon the sea; and it became as the blood of a dead man: and every living soul died in the sea" (Rev. 16:3). Applied to that disaster on April 15, 1912, when the Titanic sank in the Atlantic Ocean, it was 1,500-plus souls or persons who died and another 700-plus souls or persons who survived.

Correctly understood, then, when David said "my soul knoweth right well," he did not use the term to refer to a section or part of his being; he used it as an intensifier to capture the wholeness of his existence, anchored and manifested in the relational mind. Hence, the mind is the man! Put simply and comprehensively, David said: "And that I know right well!" Our paraphrased version says: "my intelligent mind which knows well what is right in your sight."

*Soul* is the entire being made alive by the breath of the Living God. When that breath leaves the body, that which remains is a dead soul, and the relational quality of the mind ceases to exist. David, coming face-to-face with the fragility of man and the ultimate cessation of life due to the effect of sin that will cause the soul (the man) to die, cautioned: "Put not your trust in princes, nor in the son of man, in whom there is no help. His breath goeth forth, he returneth to his earth; in that very day his thoughts perish" (Ps. 146:3–4).

## The "Knowing" Soul

Having established our working understanding of *soul*, let us proceed with looking at the intransitive action word that says what the soul does: It *knows*. To *know* is to be familiar with; to be au fait, to be acquainted with. Still deeper, to *know* means to be able to distinguish, to recognize, to identify, to discern, to understand, to appreciate, to experience, and to comprehend.

Questions: With what aspect of his being does the man *know*? Do we know with our hands, our feet, our stomach, our genitals, our skin, any part of our anatomy? The obvious answer to this second question is No! And based on our working definition in the Glossary (See p. 399 & 408), the answer to the first part is not the brain (alone) but the *mind,* which is the composite working and functioning of the brain in coordination with its avenues or connections to the outside (of the cranium/skull) world—the senses—resulting in a complexity of thoughts, perceptions, emotions, imaginations, and actions, affecting the quality of one's total existence and that of those in one's sphere of influence in an equally complex variety of ways.

David, in expressing his sense of responsibility and accountability for whatever he does, challenged himself, and those who would eventually read his writings, to remember those teachings and principles and right-doings to which we have been exposed. Those guidelines and values that we have come to know and understand, and are familiar with, and have experienced and embraced and appreciated, are expected to shape our relational minds toward right behaviour and living. And we are to remember also that our being able to think of, and to do right, comes because we are fearfully and wonderfully made in God's image.

## Human Multifaceted-ness Distinct from Animals

One of the outstanding characteristics of the relational mind that separates humans from the animal kingdom, and gives more evidence that he/she alone of God's Creation is made in the image of the Creator, is its multifaceted-ness. Multitasking, rationalizing, conceptualizing, theorizing, hypothesizing, and intellectualizing are all skills that are unique to man (Review p. 279).

## Mind, Soul, Spirit, and Conscience

In accounting for those six and other skills, the Bible uses at least four terms for the different functionalities of the marvelous mind that God has placed in His masterpiece of Creation, human. These terms are heart, soul, spirit, and conscience. While there are commonalities between each term, each one accounts for a different aspect of the multifaceted, multidimensional, multifunctional, multitalented, multivariant, polymorphous mind. Consider this list and the number of times each one appears in the King James version, as supplied by Sword Searcher 4.5.

*Disclaimer: The brief explanation that is offered after each term is not considered to be a study or even a detailed explanation of the term. Nor are the quoted Bible passages intended to be regarded as the major ones that support the usage of the term in the Holy Scriptures. At best, these comments and Bible references are intended to stimulate the mind and inspire further reading and research on each one, following the example of the Bereans (Acts 17:11).*

### Mind—99 Times

The Mind is seen as the seat of intelligence. This is where the intellectual, cognitive, perceptive, reasoning, and rational functions take place. Major decision-making occurs in this aspect or the *cognitive domain* of the man. Isaiah 1:18 records the Lord's appeal to the mind to accept forgiveness and grace and maintain the relationship with his God. "Come now, and let us reason together, saith the LORD: though your sins be as scarlet, they shall be as white as snow; though they be red like crimson, they shall be as wool."

### Heart—823 Times

The heart is used to refer to the *affective domain* aspect of the mind and is portrayed as the softer, emotional, feeling side of the person.

It is from here that compassion, empathy, sympathy, kindness, and care emanate. One of the best examples of the heart being moved with compassion is recorded of Jesus in Mark 1:41: "And Jesus, moved with compassion, put forth his hand, and touched him, and saith unto him, I will; be thou clean." Another example of heart being used to refer to the emotionally responsive aspect of the mind is: "A merry heart maketh a cheerful countenance: but by sorrow of the heart the spirit is broken" (Prov. 17:22).

### Soul—473 Times

The soul is referred to as that aspect that responds to the appeal of salvation. Consider, for example, Proverbs 23:26: "My son, give me thine heart, and let thine eyes observe my ways." There are the times when *soul* and *heart* are used interchangeably and as an intensifier for each other. "Now set your heart and your soul to seek the LORD your God; arise therefore, and build ye the sanctuary of the LORD God, to bring the ark of the covenant of the LORD, and the holy vessels of God, into the house that is to be built to the name of the LORD" (1 Chr. 22:19). (See also Biblical Understanding of Soul p. 58).

### Spirit—464 Times

Reference to the spirit tends to focus on the aspect of direct connection with the Divine and the Supernatural—God Himself. It is the straight line, as it were, to God. It is the spiritual intuitive aspect of the mind. The prime example of this was God's own bemoaning over the evil of His main Creation, human beings: "And the LORD said, My spirit shall not always strive with man, for that he also is flesh: yet his days shall be an hundred and twenty years" (Gen. 6:3). Then, in verse 5, the clear reason is given: "And GOD saw that the wickedness of man was great in the earth, and that every imagination of the thoughts of his heart was only evil continually."

## The Unpardonable Sin

Specifically, God (in Gen. 6:3), made God made reference to the spiritual connection between Himself and man: "My spirit shall not always strive with man." Paul, in counseling the Ephesians, made reference to the personhood of the Spirit and cautioned against grieving Him because there comes a point when He will leave; that is, He will stop appealing to you to do right. "And grieve not the Holy Spirit of God, whereby ye are sealed unto the day of redemption" (Eph. 4:30).

When He leaves, that closes your possibility to be saved, because He, the Holy Spirit, will cease to be in touch with you spiritually, and you will then be permanently excommunicated from God. That is when one would have committed the unpardonable sin or blasphemy against the Holy Spirit. "Wherefore I say unto you, All manner of sin and blasphemy shall be forgiven unto men: but the blasphemy against the Holy Ghost shall not be forgiven unto men" (Matt. 12:31). The blasphemy takes on three characteristics:

1.  Denying the work of the Spirit on the heart
2.  Attributing the manifested work of the Spirit to either demons or human ingenuity, whichever is more convenient, depending on the work being focused upon at the time of criticism
3.  Resisting and fighting off the impressions of the Spirit to make changes

### *Conscience—30 Times*

The conscience is like the radar that is designed to keep track of movements and to ensure that one stays on course. It gives off a signal if one is veering off the correct path. That signal may vary in strength and sometimes come as guilt, remorse, shame or regret. The conscience is that aspect of the mind created by God to help us keep integrity, scruples, principles, and morality intact. It is the GPS or preferably the MPS – Mind Positioning System of our being (See p. 408).

The most condemnatory state for one's conscience is for it to be *seared*, as mentioned in 1 Timothy 4:2: "Speaking lies in hypocrisy; having their conscience seared with a hot iron." A seared conscience is one that is scorched, bone-dry, parched, and lacking sensitivity toward right or wrong. In Romans 9:1, Paul points out that the conscience responds to the impressions of the Holy Spirit and bears witness to His work on the mind: "I say the truth in Christ; I lie not, my conscience also bearing me witness in the Holy Ghost."

## The Unfathomable Relational Mind

The intricate, complex, and mysterious combination and coordination of mind, soul, spirit, and conscience make up the *relational mind*, which David succinctly describes as *marvelous*. (See the differentiation of *mind* and *relational mind* in the Glossary pp. 408 & 413.) It is unfathomable because it is made by the Creator, Who is omnipotent, omniscient, omnipresent, and eternal. He simply cannot be explained. This same Creator challenged one of His faithful children, Job: "Canst thou by searching find out God? canst thou find out the Almighty unto perfection?" (Job 11:7). The answer is simply, and profoundly, No!

It should be understood, then, that the part of His Creation that is closest to Himself, man, would have been made a close representation of His own unfathomable and incomprehensible nature, so that not even the man can understand himself. Outside of God, and within himself by himself, man can do nothing (John 15:5). Then Paul reaffirms in Philippians 4:13 that the very opposite is equally true: "I can do all things through Christ which strengtheneth me."

In speaking of the immeasurable, inexplicable nature of God's creative work, the man to whom God gave wisdom as a special gift, Solomon, said: "Then I beheld all the work of God, that a man cannot find out the work that is done under the sun: because though a man labor to seek it out, yet he shall not find it; yea further; though a wise man think to know it, yet shall he not be able to find it" (Eccles. 8:17).

## Limited Human Effort to Research the Mind

We cite the above references to the Creator's work in order to anchor our position regarding the human relational mind. The summary of the position is that by virtue of it being akin to that of his Creator's, it cannot be measured and explained by anyone or any power in the universe, including man himself.

So, with all the research and studies that human anthropologists, psychologists, sociologists, behaviorists, and their counterparts will attempt, they all are seeking to do the impossible—that is, to explain the power of the mind. They would merely scratch the surface, as God permits them through revelation. Of course, in their ignorance and attempt to deny the existence of God, they will take the credit as the result of their research and label it as their discovery. (See **Affirmation/Claim and Declaration** p. xxxv).

For the third time in this chapter, the dominant and all-pervading question continues to evoke a deeper answer. The question is: "What does our being 'fearfully and wonderfully made' have to do with the subject of this book—family relational health?" Let us progress toward the fullness of the answer by reminding ourselves about God and the relationship that He established with His creatures, primarily man. In His omniscience and omnipresence, He keeps a perfect relationship with all His children, especially those who come to Him by faith.

# Assurances of God's Caring Relationship

Here is Jesus's assurance on that matter: "All that the Father giveth me shall come to me; and him that cometh to me I will in no wise cast out" (John 6:37). In an effort to express the guaranteed nature of the caring relationship of the Godhead for the human family, Jesus taught the Model Prayer (Luke 11:1–4). He compares the relationship of earthly, human fathers with that of God in verses 5–12 and sealed it with a very poignant assuring question in verse 13: "If ye then, being evil, know how to give good gifts unto your children: how much more shall your heavenly Father give the Holy Spirit to them that ask him?"

Before the Savior's assurance, the messianic prophet Isaiah taught about God's caring relationship this way: "And it shall come to pass, that before they call, I will answer; and while they are yet speaking, I will hear" (Isaiah 65:24). David, our 'anchor speaker' for this chapter, would not be left out: "Like as a father pitieth his children, so the LORD pitieth them that fear him" (Ps. 103: 13). Paul echoes that assurance in Hebrews 11:6: "But without faith it is impossible to please him: for he that cometh to God must believe that he is, and that he is a rewarder of them that diligently seek him." Across the length and breadth of the world, God maintains a relationship with all His children, and understandably more so with those who call upon Him.

# God's Multifunctional Mind Implanted in Man

Let us now apply this exemplary caring relationship of God to the human family and relational health. To do this, we will compose a partial paraphrase of God's pro-creational command to the first family in the Garden of Eden: "So God created man in His own image, and blessed his mind with the ability to forge and keep a healthy, multifunctional family relationship with all those in his household" (Gen. 1:27) (Revisit p. 106).

Interpreted, this means that to the same extent that God in His omnipotence and omniscience can keep a healthy relationship with all His children, He has equipped the human mind with an adequate portion of His multirelational power to forge and keep healthy relationships with all those in his sphere of influence, beginning with those in his household.

This explains how a man who is led by the God of Families can multifunction as *a* good man; a faithful husband; a caring father for as many children as his quiver can hold (Ps. 127:5); and a supporter of other relatives, and still identify with the life of the community and therefore be seen as a model citizen. This is all possible because of his relationship with God, from whom he draws relational skills to help in his time of need. (Heb. 4:16).

## God's Earth-Population Strategic Plan

This chapter can be safely concluded with the understanding that one of the chief functions God had in mind when He made the male and female was for them to continue for Him where He left off or stopped in creating the human family. This means that He had already populated the air, land, and seas with animals and created in them the natural biological instinct for procreation. When He made the pronouncement upon them "Be fruitful and multiply, and fill the waters in the seas, and let fowl multiply in the earth" (Gen. 1:22), He was simply inaugurating the fertility and functionality of their bodies.

Their biological procreative system would operate instinctively within the confines of their various classifications: kingdom, division or phylum, class, order, family, genus, and species. God did not invest the animal with the kind of intelligence in any way akin to His. He blessed them with relational instinct, not relational minds. The supervision and management of the environment for their well-being was assigned to man by the Creator (Gen. 2:26).

Man (male and female) was to have dominion—note carefully, not dominance—over them. This means that he was God's steward who was to care and protect them. They would be subjected to him. His loving, caring attitude toward them would bond them to him in a way that would represent God's care, as God Himself would inspire the man's mind to study and understand them.

This fact of man being placed in charge of the animal kingdom and the environment in general was evident from the beginning, when God gave Adam the privilege and responsibility to name the animals (Gen. 2:19) and to care for and dress the garden (Gen. 2:15). That evidence remains to this day, inasmuch as it is so grievously tainted by his sins, as the whole of Creation groans (Rom. 8:22) through various forms of degradation under man's ignorance, mismanagement, and selfish exploitation.

## God's Loftiest Role for Man

But as vast, diverse, and extensive as man's role and responsibility was in his supervision and management of the environment and the animal kingdom, God had yet a larger, higher, loftier, and more comprehensive role for him. That role was to model and represent the Godhead. Man (male and female) was to be the extension of the Trinity in this section of Their limitless universal domain and existence—that is, here on earth.

Here the Godhead decided to extend Themselves through a process of Their devising: Creation. That extension was not in the animals, sun, moon, stars, planets, seas, trees, or nature in general, but in two special beings, akin to Them in nature and character (See p. 337).

Let us remind ourselves that *akin* as used here does not mean *equal* or *same as*. Instead, it means similar; to an extent; bearing characteristic marks and traits of the Original. By extension, akin implies being similar but subjective to the Original.

So man (human beings, male and female) was created by God to be the closest piece of Creation to Himself. There are those, especially in the feminist movement, who express concern over the generic use of the term *man* to represent both male and female. It should be noted that the Godhead—Father, Son, and Holy Spirit—do speak of Themselves at times in the one generic term: God, or He, or Him. There is no record that God has taken on any sexual attribute, hence God is neither male or female.

The Bible tells us that God exists in Spirit form (John 4:24), which form is not manifested in flesh or blood (Luke 24:39). Existence in flesh and blood, as God Himself created it, is manifested in two complementary biological characteristics, male and female. In the human form of life which is the highest of God's Creation, the sexes are further identified as man and woman.

Then, the human being, in exercising the God-assigned role of dominion over the animal kingdom, went on to assign distinguishing names for the animals in their equal biological sexual designations of male and female. Hence the male bovine, whale, and others being called *bull* and the female being called *cow*; the male bird in general called *cock* and the female *hen*; the male sheep called a *ram* and the female called *ewe*. There are various designations in different classifications of animals, but the pattern of identifying the only two distinct complementary sexes of male and female remains constant since Creation to this day (Revisit p. 277).

When Jesus, a member of the Godhead, took on human form in order to be with us (Matt. 1:22–23), it is to be carefully noted that He was born of a woman, the female of the human species. This miraculous act was consistent with His own plan at Creation as well as a fulfillment of the specific promise that He made to Eve (Gen. 3:15). That promise was prophetically codified and later revealed as the Redeemer–Saviour who would engage in a life-long battle with Satan, the deceiver, and free us to salvation.

## Jesus, the Saviour, Could Have Come in Adult Form

It is not far-fetched to think that God, through a vision, could have instructed Joseph (and Mary) to gather clay, take it to a certain place, and do whatever else He would have instructed them to do, and that He, God, would have eventually appeared. He could also choose to appear as an angel in the retinue of a legion of angels, and then assumed human form at whichever place He would have chosen. He is the self-existing God of omnipotence and all the other accompanying attributes.

In that very miraculous process, (by-passing the biological law He, Himself designed) from the conception to birth of the Saviour, we see God demonstrating balance and respect for the female (Gal. 4:4). He, Jesus, took on the male sex, seeing that He was coming to be the exemplary second Adam/male, (1 Cor. 15:45–48). There was no sex-gender prejudice with God. There is no need for speculation with even thinking about attributing Jesus' conception to parthenogenesis. Out faith is anchored in the God of Creation.

In His divine wisdom, He came without the aid of the male, thus further demonstrating that the female has fully a part in the redemption plan, as does the male, represented by Him the man-child (Gen. 3:15; Rev. 12:5). However, the representative earthly (male) father was not to be left out and was influential in the life of the growing child, Jesus. The record is that He, Jesus, was subject to *them*—Joseph, earthly male father, and Mary, earthly female mother (Luke 2:51).

## Marriage—God's Prerequisite to Procreation

As stated earlier, when God fearfully and wonderfully made the human family (male and female), He had an extensive, all-encompassing role for them to play in the continuation of His Creation plan. One of the major aspects of that role was, and still remains, continuing to make other human beings. As a prerequisite to continue that elevated and esteemed role, they both had to be completely and exclusively committed to each other as a man-husband and woman-wife.

God Himself said it definitively and conclusively at the very beginning: "Therefore shall a man leave his father and his mother, and shall cleave unto his wife: and they shall be one flesh" (Genesis 2:24). Then Jesus reiterated it some four thousand years later as recorded in Matthew 19:4–5 and Mark 10:8. The simple straightforward summary is: "And they twain shall be one flesh."

Paul, the apostle to the Gentiles of the New Testament Church, caught the strain, and in the fifth chapter of his letter to the Ephesians, he elaborated on the sacredness and sanctity of the marriage relationship. The Holy Spirit inspired Paul to take it several notches higher by citing the marriage relationship between a husband and wife as a mystery (Eph. 5:22–32). Then he elevates it to the highest possible esteem, that of it being a symbol of the relationship between Christ and the Church. So we see the man and the woman firstly symbolizing and representing the Godhead at their Creation, and secondly now symbolizing and representing Christ in the redemption plan.

Having reaffirmed that marriage is God's prerequisite for parenting, it evokes the question about God's response to children of unmarried parents. Each human being born on this earth is breathing the life-giving breath of God. God knows each child from conception. He has called and engaged countless thousand times thousands into His Service. God does not condone or countenance any violation of the laws, commandments, or guidelines that He has established. At the same time, His divine providence and mercy is always balanced with laws and judgment as He sees fit.

He expects parents to cease and desist from engaging in any activity that He expressly forbids, such as sexual intercourse, which He indicates is to be reserved within the sacred boundary of marriage (Heb. 13:4). Equally so, He does not condone that the offspring of those parents should be treated with derision or social and church ostracism. The child is breathing His breath and therefore a potential in His hand, and certainly a candidate for heaven.

God expects all sinners, including fornicators and adulterers and every other form of departure from His ideal, to repent. But children born out of wedlock, at no choice of their own, will, during growth, development, and maturity, be exposed to knowledge and God's ideal, and be able to choose to order their lives and lifestyle in harmony with God's ideal (See pp. 307, 308). If they choose not that ideal, God-established way of life, they will have to account to God for their chosen path of violation of His principles and cannot refer to their parents, who went wrong when they violated God's requirements.

We know that there is at least one instance in the Bible when God, in His divine wisdom, did not permit the child of a pregnancy out of wedlock to live (2 Sam. chapters 11–12). That case with David and Bathsheba was of a specific nature, and God knew the intensely wrong message that could be perpetuated had He not taken a decision that only He is entitled to take where the ending of life is concerned.

## The Mystery of the Marriage Relationship

With more emphasis on the mystery that Paul referred to in Ephesians, we return to the first equation in what could be considered the mysterious line in the topic of this chapter: $1 + 1 = 1$. That equation evokes the simple question: How? It is not humanly and mathematically correct. It is not normally or naturally correct, hence its mysterious nature. So it is with God. He, Himself, is mysterious, and His ways are past finding out (Rom. 11:33; see also Ps. 72:5, Isa. 40:28, and Eccl. 11:5), and that nature He has passed on, in part, to the human whom He has made in His likeness.

But God, the designer of marriage, did not leave this mystery of marriage totally inexplicable to His children. Seeing that the relationship is the highest that the human can experience on earth (after their relationship with Him), God made provision to open man's relational mind to understand and thereby enjoy the bliss of that relationship.

The quality of that marriage relationship between husband and wife, based on God's original divine plan, would set the tone, pace, and quality for all other relationships that would flow from it. Those out-flowing relationships would be the father-mother relationship, the parent-child relationship, the sibling relationship, and all the other multifaceted ones to emerge from these (See Categories p. 466). This complex out-working itself is mysterious, and understandably so, to the mind that is not led by the Spirit of God (1 Cor. 2:14).

Keeping the focus of the mysterious mathematical equation on the two individuals around whom it is constructed, that is the husband and the wife, let us see its immediate application in the context of their being fearfully and wonderfully made. To do this, let us review ten of the general, basic facts about them as spouses, individually:

1.   They were born separately.

2.   He is male; she is female.

3.   They were born to different parents.

4. Their location, community, nationality, and culture could be quite different in more ways than one.

5. While there are commonalities with their biology and physiology, there are equally stark differences—skeletally, structurally, and in some instances, anatomically, hormonally, and chemically.

6. Their temperaments and personalities can be distinct and separate.

7. Their mind-processing of the same issue can be patently different and even opposite at times.

8. Their ordinary tastes, desires, likes, and dislikes, among many others personal dynamics, could be palpably different.

9. Their internal family culture and practices can be not only different but potentially diverse.

10. Their perspectives, outlook on life, and consequently worldview could also be not only different but potentially diverse.

Just a cursory nonclinical glance at this list of differences between potential spouses in the intended marriage is enough to boggle the mind! How can they live happily committed together in love and harmony for one, five, ten, twenty, forty, sixty, and even more years, until death do them part? That is clearly a mysterious goal. But again, as we repeat in this book, God's biddings are His enablings. He bids it, He says it is possible, and therefore it is.

The possibility of this accomplishment lies in the very key word that describes the relationship: mystery. Here we see that $1 + 1 = 1$ works out to be what Jesus said in Matthew 19:5, that at marriage the two are no longer two but *one*. This oneness takes place in their minds before it is demonstrated in their bodies. Their two minds are mysteriously bonded in one, while maintaining their distinct individuality.

Here the two exemplify the mysterious Godhead, three distinct persons—the Father, Son, and Holy Spirit. This is the Trinity, the three-in-one God that distinguished them (the Godhead) from polytheism that the Israelites were exposed to in their four hundred years of slavery in Egypt. That is why He instructed Moses to teach that as one of their first post-slavery lessons on their way to freedom of worship en route to the Promised Land. "Hear, O Israel: The LORD our God is one LORD: And thou shalt love the LORD thy God with all thine heart, and with all thy soul, and with all thy might" (Deuteronomy 6:4–6; see also Mark 12:29).

This is God who designed the unfathomable mind of the man and the woman. He also conceptualized the marriage bond for them, and it is the omnipresent, omniscient Holy Spirit who keeps their minds together in perfect peace as long as they stay on Him (Isaiah 26:3). With the indwelling, keeping power of the Holy Spirit in his and her heart, the husband and the wife will be empowered to do their part in keeping the mystery alive in their minds.

Keep the mystery of your wife, of your husband in mind. Do not take him or her for granted. M + M = M, that is to say, *Marriage + Mystery = Mastery*. Both are to strive for the mastery of the relationship and not to master, meaning to subjugate or dominate the other one.

Give respect for the mysterious individuality of his or her being. Always keep your mind open to study and understand the other one. When you do, you will have the bonus experience of the third equation of the marriage mystery: PSS = PMM. As the husband and the wife maintain the study of each other in their family lab, they will happily discover that *Progressive Spousal Study* will result in *Progressive Marriage Mastery.*

Finally, the husband and wife, fearfully and wonderfully made to engage in the mysterious bond of marriage, can go on to live together until death do them part, temporarily. They will reunite at the Second Coming of the Lord Jesus. And, at that mysterious, cataclysmic event, the ultimate symbol of their marriage will be realized, that is the marriage of Christ and His Church (Revelation 19:7). This was the final mystery about which Paul wrote to the Ephesians.

## Suggestions for Action

1. Pray each day asking God to perform His CPRI (Creator's personalized relationship initiative) on your mind, keeping you quickened and alive in His service.

2. Practice being a good steward of family life. Be accountable, faithful, and answerable for the small or big responsibilities that you have to assume as a member of your family.

3. Learn to show full respect and appreciation for members of the opposite sex; remember that God made only the two of us to be a full representation of Him.

4. The greatest sense of self-esteem you can have is the fact that God made you in His own image. Live and behave as evidence that His image is firmly stamped in your relational mind.

5. If you are married, by God's grace remain committed to your vows. If you are not married, pray for the marriages in your family, in the Church, and in the community.

# Chapter 11

# Mysteriously and Grievously Divided
# 1 - 1 = 2; M-M=M

**Anchor Text 1: Genesis 3:16**

"Unto the woman he said, I will greatly multiply thy sorrow and thy conception; in sorrow thou shalt bring forth children; and thy desire shall be to thy husband, *and he shall rule over thee.*"

**Paraphrased for Families**

God explained to Eve: As a result of your yielding to the temptation of Satan, the role of childbearing for which I have equipped your body is now going to be uncomfortable and painful from conception to delivery. And further yet, because you strayed from your husband into temptation, you will need to seek his permission and support for whatever major decisions you consider. As a result of your joint sin, your husband is going to laud his leadership over you (See p. 333).

**Anchor Text 2: 1 Peter 3:7**

"Likewise, ye husbands, dwell with them according to knowledge, giving honour unto the wife, as unto the weaker vessel, and as being heirs together of the grace of life; that your prayers be not hindered."

**Paraphrased for Families**

In the same way you husbands, learn to relate with your wives with knowledge and understanding, showing honor and due respect to them, knowing that their makeup is different from yours, their being of a more delicate and comely nature (see Jer. 6:2), and that at the end of it all, you are both to be recipients of God's grace. Be sure to follow this counsel so that your prayers will not go unanswered by God as a result of the way that you treat your wives.

Maybe one of the most sobering and reassuring thoughts that can be used to begin this chapter is this: Despite the mayhem and grievous divisions of sin have wreaked upon God's original family blueprint, all is not lost. There is an advancing battalion of the enemies against God; against His word, the Bible; and understandably against His children who choose to be led by His Spirit in observing His ideal pattern for family life. Our twenty-first century pluralistic society is clearly hell-bent on dismantling and obliterating every remaining vestige and semblance of the ancient landmarks of good, Bible-based family life.

Bible-believing Christians cannot turn a blind eye to these forces and their threats. We cannot wish them away, nor does it help to play the proverbial ostrich on the seashore poking its head in the sand in order to convince itself that the lightning is not flashing. Instead, we need to adopt the New International Version translation of Luke 1:17, "And he will go on before the Lord, in the spirit and power of Elijah, to turn the hearts of the parents to their children and the disobedient to the wisdom of the righteous—to make ready a people prepared for the Lord." We need to vigorously study to find the truth as to why our world in general and our families in particular, are so mysteriously divided. With that knowledge we will be able to live and speak the truth and beauty of God's ideal for family relational health.

## An Informing but Non-confrontational Approach

As has been repeatedly established in several places in this book, in addressing a number of these present-day issues that are making unrelenting efforts to question and discredit God's original ideal for family life, we do not want to come across as being confrontational or adversarial against those who have opposing perspectives. At the same time, we must speak with conviction and the sense of responsibility, so as to to bring balance to the subject that is slowly but surely shifting from the original path upon which God established it. (Revisit the Preface, p. ix).

Our intention therefore, is twofold: firstly, it is to strengthen and stabilize the faith of Bible-believing Christians that God's original words still stand amidst the mounting challenges against them. Secondly, it is to offer those of the now millennial generation (Generation 7 and beyond) a balancing, Bible-based teaching to compare with that which is captivating and commandeering their attention. With that knowledge, they can make balanced and informed decisions as to how they will heed or reject the teachings in God's words for their family life.

By writing this way we intend to look objectively at the perspectives of those who are declaring that the Biblical plan for family life is obsolete. The aim is to understand such frames of thinking, to present God's ideal, and to offer counsel and assurance to those who are still open to finding the old landmarks upon which quality family life has been established, built, and lived over millennia unto this day.

In the process, an attempt will be made, with the aid of the illuminating power of the Holy Spirit, to identify where and how the deterioration of the quality of family relational health took place, and how those who desire, can get back to God's original plan. (Review The Genesis Foundation, p. xviii).

## Emphasis on the Male Man – God's Strategic Move

It is to be noted that in some of the subtopics of the previous chapters, the emphasis has been on the relational mind of the *man*, the male in the family. That has been very intentional as we build our deeper understanding of family relational health. This emphasis is basic, fundamental, and original as we study God's structure and development of the human family. The focus is on the *male man*, the *ish* (Hebrew) of Genesis 1:26–27, first part of the verses: "And God said, Let us make man in our image, after our likeness … So God created man in his own image …"

Also, in chapter 2 of Genesis, which gives more details of the Creation record that began in chapter 1, the *male man* is the first focal point of the establishment of the family, as noted from verses 7–9: "And the LORD God formed man of the dust of the ground, and breathed into his nostrils the breath of life; and man became a living soul. And the LORD God planted a garden eastward in Eden; and there he put the man whom he had formed. And out of the ground made the LORD God to grow every tree that is pleasant to the sight, and good for food; the tree of life also in the midst of the garden, and the tree of knowledge of good and evil."

In verse 15, we see the Lord made another significant move in the development of the family by establishing the *home*—the garden home. It unequivocally states that the *man* was the first to begin domestic home life: "And the LORD God took the man, and put him into the garden of Eden to *dress* it and to *keep* it." This strategic move by God cannot, and ought not to be taken for granted. God has never made a mistake. He moves by forethought and deliberate design. Between verses 15 and 17, we see God developmentally setting up the structure, operation, and government of the family on earth.

There was no such structuring of the animal family. He simply formed them; set them free in the air, land, and water; and then subjected them to the dominion of the *man*. In His forming them, He evidently built instinct, *not* sense, into them, so that among themselves, there would be the natural instinctive relationship that would govern their relational existence.

Inasmuch as zoological studies show that some animals demonstrate calculated and even strategic intelligent moves, there is no evidence that any of them possesses the multifunctional and relational mind of the human family. That's the way God, the Creator, designed it, making the man "fearfully and wonderfully."

## The Stewardship and Leadership of the Family

The stewardship of family life was established with the key elements of responsibility and accountability being laid squarely at the feet of the *man*. The key words in those verses are *dress, keep,* and *commanded*— all three directed to the *male man*. The status of precedence and preeminence in the human family are also not to be taken lightly.

In the establishment of a company, the minimum number of persons required is two. One of them has to be either accorded or has to assume leadership. Where that is not clearly established, there could be mayhem, chaos, and no sense of orderly development. Everyone could end up being a law to himself and will do what is right in his own eyes (Judg. 17:6 and 21:25). It was not God's plan for the human family to operate in such a chaotic manner, so He clearly established an order in the beginning at Creation. From the Creation, it is seen that God is "not the author of confusion" (1 Cor. 14: 33) or divisions as our topic is now screaming at us.

Even in the animal kingdom, leadership is clearly established. The senior or older male is in many cases, especially in wildlife (safari), the leader of the pack. It is from him that the others take their cue to charge or retreat, especially in the event of an attack. It is interesting to look at a flock of flying birds, how they crisscross and change directions along their journey. Ornithology tells us that every formation we see is led or directed by a leader, and there is no doubt that that leader is a senior, experienced one.

If God equipped the animals with such instinctive leadership plan, would He not have done more for those He created to share in relationship with Himself and among themselves? God in His divine wisdom, knowing His endowment in the mind of the *male* man, accorded him the leadership of the family. There was and still is no need for drawing of lots, spinning a coin, or any form of toss-up to determine who should lead the family. That was God's original family blueprint which He unquestionably demonstrated at the very beginning. He made the home, then made the *male* man and commissioned him with leadership responsibility.

We either believe and accept the Genesis record or we don't!! (Revisit The Genesis Foundation, p xviii). The relational health of the family began deteriorating at the Fall in the Garden of Eden (Gen. 3). With the entrance of sin, the man's leadership role was compromised but not obliterated, because "the gates of hell shall not prevail" against God's original plan (Mark 16:18), and His word (directives, instructions, and guidelines) "shall not return unto (Me) him void"; they shall accomplish what He wills (Isa. 55:11).

## Home and Family Leadership – Differentiated from Societal Leadership – Old Guard Patriarchalism?

Given the high, current international sensitivity that exists on unisexism and the general call for and drift towards homogenism within and outside of the Church, it is understood that almost any statement that is made in support of the fundamental, biblical teaching on male leadership in the home, will be met with questions, concerns and even accusations of old guard patriarchalism (See p. 323).

Therefore, against this understanding and before attempting to develop the subject further, let us try to split, not just the proverbial but the real 'leadership hair' between what the Bible unequivocally teaches about male leadership in the home and what it does not teach about leadership in the society outside of the home.

Firstly, the Bible does not address the evolutionary and revolutionary societal leadership in general as a subject. There are many references and allusions to civil and political leadership, because God's people for whom it is written, live in the world and must relate to some extent, with what goes on in it including governmental matters. It talks about kings and queens, autocracies and bureaucracies, democracies and totalitarianisms in human government and administration of communities, countries and across the wide world.

The Bible also addresses how God will relate with those leaders who force their way against His supreme leadership as Creator. (Dan. 4:32 & 5:21) It balances that position of God reigning in demagogues (religious, political or social) and at the same time, admonishes God's followers to obey the instructions, laws and decrees of even despotic leaders, as long as their requirements are not in contravention of His holy laws and principles. (See the exemplary state leadership of one king – p. 443).

There are virtually endless leadership guidelines and best practices that many non-committed Christian scholars, politicians, motivational speakers and coaches among others, have made with Bible passages. Depending on how they are presented, they continue to be well received, with the Bible being portrayed as an authoritative source of knowledge and wisdom on general/human and societal leadership. There are some of those presenters who, based on their own biases, do cite or make allusions to Bible verses that they say support absolute male gender and sexism leadership in the political or other sectors of the society. They are those who use the Bible to lambast itself by citing what they perceive as contradicting lessons, for so they think.

In instances like these, the Bible itself is its own defence. Study it properly and thoroughly (Isa. 28:10) with an open mind, and it will be seen that no such teaching exists in it. Where it might appear to be so, there is the inspired counter-balance somewhere else in the same Bible with reference to God's ideal. There are also cases that imply as absolute male dictatorial family leadership. They are recorded to show man's folly in not abiding by God words, and they are also recorded to show that the Bible does not cover faults and weaknesses, even among God's chosen people and appointed leaders.

## Husband-Father Foundation

Certainly, the Bible which represents God's ideal for His children in their homes, upholds positive, healthy husband-father leadership as the foundation of the society. There will always be those who, unfortunately, have had poor or bad men and husband-father leadership experience, and others with hidden agendas, will passionately and vehemently oppose that posture for male home leadership in the Bible. They can cite anecdotal stories, records and certainly Bible texts that they will posit as evidence that the Bible is chauvinistic, patriarchal and written against women.

It is not the intent of this book to bring all those possible skewed references to the table and defend the Bible against them. Instead, let us consider six salient differentiations between Bible-based advocacy of male leadership in the home, and the general non-Bible-based leadership in the society:

1. *Nucleus of Society* – The Bible presents and upholds the home as the social and spiritual nucleus of the society, ideally headed by the male husband-father, *when he is present*. Ever since God in His divine wisdom instituted that form of home and family leadership at Creation, it has remained the time-tested

and accepted pattern of family life cross-culturally and universally.

The same Bible also records cases where the ideal male leadership of the family was absent and the wife/mother leadership held the family together not only the home, but communities. There are countless laudable cases of those today, and such ought not to be patronizingly acknowledged. At the same time such acknowledgments are not to be done with sweeping generalizations at the expense of continuing to preach, teach and live the foundational Edenic ideal.

Over the centuries, there have been small groups which have tried the exact opposite or male leadership, matriarchialism or matrilineality (with a slight difference between the two). Among the little-known and documented present female-led societies according to Madaus, S. (2019, August 15) are: the Mosuos of China, Bibri of Costa Rica, Umoja of Kenya, Minangkabau of Indonesia, Akan of Ghana and Khasi of India.

Despite these and other pockets of differing views and practices, inclusive of states or countries run by religious beliefs that advocate absolute male leadership over the female, to which views and practices this work does not subscribe, it is safe to observe that there is no major culture, community, country, nation, race, creed or any other demographic group which does not embrace the practice of healthy, stable husband-father led homes as taught in the Bible, even among non-Christians, albeit with their own tweaks and variations.

2. *Family and Church* – **Divine Origin** The family assembled at home and the congregation assembled in the church/temple are of divine origin, with their operational principles and mandate manual being essentially, one and the same – The

Holy Bible. One underpinning principle in this divinely-appointed husband-father leadership in the home is that of the priest or the spiritual leader. It is to be noted that where this role is solidly and healthily in place, family stability is more secured and children tend to come out better with rounded, positive impact and influence on the society. (See Chapter 5, **Extrapolation 8**, p. 109, 349).

3. *The Church – An Extension of the Home* -The Church is an extension of the home. It is reasonable to think that it ought to operate under the same God-inspired leadership principle that He established for their individual (single home) and institutional (group of homes) team spirit, man-woman operation.

4. *Home and Church – Same Base Principle Operation* - The home and Church are dove-tailed into each other and are therefore inseparable. It stands to reason further that the multiplier effect of the number of homes (single units) coming together to form the Church, (institutional/group) will not take away from the base operational principles and practices of the original group despite the multiplier effect. God would guard the dynamics of their togetherness.

5. *School, An Outgrowth, NOT An Extension of the Home* - The school (from Kindergarten to University) which is the out-growth (not necessarily expansion) from the home, is primarily designed to take up where the homes left off in educating the children to become productive, good citizens of the society outside of the home. They are not seen as an extension of the home as the Church is. They are not dove-tailed and are therefore not seen as a continuation of the home.

This observation is primarily referring to educational institutions in the public system. And even in Church-operated schools, the programs change and so do the dynamics in leadership. There is never an intention to have the Church or denominational school to stand out as an extension or even more specific, a continuation of the home.

Such schools are to reflect and teach the Christian, Bible-based behavioural patterns and Christ-likeness that would have been established in the homes and Church. In addition to those base criteria, there would be all the necessary educational and academic curricular, with the institutional leadership criteria being focused on qualification, experience, competence, commitment to Christian values, and not sex-gender preference.

6. ***Home-Church and School Leadership – Different*** - In our dynamic and evolving society, the training and preparation for leaders in schools, other institutional and organizational entities are done in designated/specialized places, depending on their areas of disciplines, emphasis and competence. Hopefully, there are not constitutions or company portfolios that stipulate that women cannot occupy leadership roles in them, given that ideally leadership roles at the workplace, in general are to be performance-criteria based, seniority and demonstrable institutional and organizational requirements and standards.

On the other hand, it is the organized Church that is to prepare and conduct training for the various categories of its leadership and consequently for the general membership. It would appear that while there will be the necessary diversification in the sectional, departmental or other structural leadership in its operation and incorporating every member (brothers and sisters), the DNA of its core leadership should follow the divinely established pattern as taught in the Bible. Leadership and Followership are NOT the same.

To the same extend to which the Church continues to use the Bible as its sword to ward off all societal infiltrations, dogmas, ideologies and philosophies that go contrary to its teachings, it would appear prudent that it resists any temptation, even to be socially/societally and politically correct, that will lead it to make any compromise in the operations of the two main institutions that it proclaims as God-inspired, God-ordained and God-organized – the Home and the Church. Do we need to advocate for a separation of not just Church and state, but for non-separation of Home and Church?

Against the development of the foregoing six pointers, it might be worth exploring if there pros and cons to be considered in an effort to conclude the growing potentially divisive issue of leadership as presented. Are there foundational, fundamental (not clichéd societal status quo's) but biblical directives to be strengthened and kept? And what is there (if any) to be dispensed with?

## Modern Threats to God's Original Home and Family Operational Plan

The fundamental words, directives, instructions, and guidelines from God which are under threat today are those having to do directly with the establishment and leadership of the home and family. The negative effects are not only felt in the home from which they come but in the Church, in the school, in the workplace, and in the broader society. This is so because the home is the nucleus of them all. It produces the leadership and team members in those institutions to which it gives birth. What happens in it, and goes out from it, will definitely influence the quality of life everywhere.

Interestingly, there is also the reverberation factor. Although it is the home from which the other institutions of society come, and they will understandably bear marks of the quality of life that the leaders from it bring into them, the dynamics of life in them (school, Church, workplace) have their reverberating impact on the home.

This is definitely not the case of the proverbial chicken and the egg as to which one comes first. We know for sure that the home comes before the societal institutions. But it is equally true that there is an influential reciprocity between them, both negative and positive. As to which one is more dominant and therefore more influential, the research is yet to declare—depending, of course, on who is conducting the research.

Today, in our twenty-first-century society, this position and teaching about male leadership beginning in the home is severely questioned and tested, even in the very Church which God has appointed to protect, proclaim, and live His words and teachings regarding the family as He originally established it. This questioning and wondering and even conjecturing is a result of the distortions and varying versions of what is right about the structure and operation of the family. Let us consider some of these distortions.

## Distortion 1: Dissonance Between Equality and Sameness

When God made the first two members of the human family, man and woman, Adam and Eve, He made them *equal*; yet individually, they represented an equal but different aspect of His image, His very being. None was more valuable to Him, because without one of them, He would not have been fully represented. It took the two of them equally to procreate and continue where He stopped at the Creation of the human family. That was and still remains His immutable plan.

It is equally clear that God did not make them the same or uniform. The difference in their physical features and identifying marks is as clear as the daylight that preceded their creation. Their physiological and functional construction was not identical either, as God's revelation through the study of biology and physiology has established (Review Some Differences pp.302-303).

Consider, for example, the comparative effects of two of the base hormones that establish and develop their biological and sexual characteristics: testosterone and estrogen. Without delving into the clinical studies of the morphological, physiological, and behavioral effects of the two hormones, it is established that the male's testes produce more testosterone and less estrogen than the female's ovaries. Both bodies produce the two hormones, but not in the same proportion.

Apart from the sexual libido, which is stronger in the male due to his higher level of testosterone, that hormone accounts for the texture of his skin, the brawniness of his muscles, and the competitiveness and even "toughness" of his mind. Comparatively, estrogen accounts in part for the obviously opposite but complementary characteristics of the female. Note carefully how Anchor Text 2 at the start of this chapter addressed the differences alluded to here. Both were indeed fearfully and wonderfully made, but not of the identical construct. God made them complementary in body, and made their minds to be complimentary to each other, hence their equality but not sameness.

## Distortion 2: The Scourge of Male Dominance

From the very beginning, the Creator made the *male man* (*ish*) before and different from the *female man* (*isha*). Notice the distinction, and at the same time the combination of the reference to the two of them in Genesis 1:26–27. Notice, too, that in Genesis chapter 2, which gives the more detailed version of the Creation, no more was reference made to the combination of *him*, meaning both of them (generic), but from thereon, it was always distinctly and pointedly the *man* (the male) in verses 7–8 and 15–21.

That picture changed, however, in verses 21–22, when God positively answered the two negatives that He, in His divine wisdom, expressed about the man, as recorded in verses 18–20. "It is not good that the man should be alone …" and "but for Adam there was not found an help meet for him." Let us reiterate that God never makes a mistake, because He does not slumber or sleep (Ps. 121:4). The order of His Creation was not evolutionary or progressively developed as a result of discovery through evaluation, monitoring, and modification (Revisit p. 267). His original plan, including the order and timing of the structure of the human family, was by intentional, intelligent design.

**God's Positive Negatives about Adam's Aloneness**

Therefore, His pronouncement of "not good" and "not found" with reference to Adam being alone was evidently one way for His children in posterity to see the critical importance of the one to the other in the human family. It clearly was more intended for the *male man* (Adam) to appreciate the care that His God had for him in providing him with a partner and companion. The interjection in verse 20 should be carefully observed and noted. Adam had a leadership and dominion interaction with the animals. He named them and no doubt moved about with and among them, maybe even giving some directives and commands: "Come!" "Sit!" "Go!"

The "not" expressed by God suggests that Adam could and would *not* be able to find interactive, reciprocating companionship with the animals. While he named them and gave them directives and they followed him accordingly, there was no mutuality in their participation, so his benefit from interacting with them was limited and could not be satisfying.

It is safe to suggest that God, in His divine wisdom, used that negative *not* for a positive outcome. This happened when Adam's built-in sensitivity for companionship would be naturally 'aroused' as he discovered his 'incompleteness' from a human-relationship perspective and therefore the need for a partner of his kind. Adam was complete as a stand-alone individual but incomplete as a family and as a company. God's timing was perfect (See pp. 357-358).

It is not far-fetched to believe that Adam might have made the observation to his God that he noticed that the animals were paired off, but that he was alone. It is reasonable, therefore, to expect that when his longing desire for a mate and companion was met, he would have treated her with utmost respect and appreciation for the completeness that she would have brought into his life.

### Adam's Costectomy and Body-Part 'Donorship'

There is every reason to believe that this sense of respect and appreciation was Adam's state of mind and response when he awoke out of the "anesthesia" that God administered on him in order to perform the first surgery: *costectomy*, or rib removal. Here, Adam became the first body-part donor, involuntary though it was, because it was part of God's original design. He certainly would have had it no other way when he realized the great use to which it (his rib) was put, redounding to his personal benefit and happiness through a companion.

It is important to note that contrary to a popular suggestion, that each male is born with a missing rib as a result of the first man's (Adam) costectomy, each male is born with his 12 pairs as do the female. Interestingly, medical and physiological study does show that a damage or removed rib does regrow. (https//elifesciences.org/digests/40715/ribs-hold-the-key-to-better-bone-healing). So Adam did not go about lacking a rib from his thoracic cage. God did make him and subsequently all of us fearfully and wonderfully" (Ps. 139:14)

Adam did not experience the grogginess, wooziness, and dizziness that is now characteristic of patients who survive surgery in this sin-cursed world of sickness and ill health. Instead, he came out with a bout of exhilarating joy and excitement, plus a feeling of completeness that inspired his exclamation: "This is now bone of my bones, and flesh of my flesh: she shall be called Woman, because she was taken out of Man" (Gen. 2:23). Adam experienced identity, commonality, and relational camaraderie that was impossible for him to have had with the animals.

Alas! That was substantively short-lived. The Bible has not told us how long the first couple basked in the bliss of their garden home. We do not know the period that existed between chapters 2 and 3 of Genesis. For the record of our faith in the unquestionable authenticity of the Bible, we reaffirm our understanding that the Genesis record of the first week of Creation was seven days of 24 hours each, beginning from the evening unto the morning (Genesis 1:5, 8, 13, 14, 18, 19, 23, 31 & 2: 1 – 3). In our sin-affected finite minds now, we cannot comprehend the virtual infinity of time then, because as it is with God (Psalm 90: 4, & 2 Peter 3:8) He had implanted that sense of time in Adam and Eve. They lost it with the advent of sin in their minds, and that loss we have inherited from them.

The Bible does not offer a day-by-day countdown record of developments after the all-time important first seven days of Creation. Clearly God did not see it fit to inspire Moses with any more details because: "The secret things belong unto the LORD our God: but those things which are revealed belong unto us and to our children for ever, that we may do all the words of this law." (Deut. 29:29) And: "And he said unto them, it is not for you to know the times or the seasons, which the Father hath put in his own power." (Acts 1:7)

It is important to note that in addition to the weekly cycle of seven days, the other three outgrowing cycles of nature: the four seasons; cold and heat; planting and reaping (Gen.3:28) that God put in place, have not ceased despite the advent and effects of sin on them. We believe that that element of perpetuity is consistent will all of the foundational plans that God instituted at Creation.

One fact that we have is that with Eve's falling to the temptation of Satan, through the serpent, and with Adam's failure to live by the directive and command that were given to him, first and directly by God, regarding the eating of the fruit in the middle of the garden, the mystery of iniquity did work, and their relational health became permanently impaired.

### Beginning of Male Dominance

Undoubtedly, the greatest, deepest, and most prolonged impairment of their relationship is *male dominance*. Apart from his blaming Eve (and subtly God) for his failure when he said, "The woman whom thou gavest to be with me, she gave me of the tree, and I did eat" (Gen. 3:12), there is no other evidence that Adam treated Eve in any abusive way. One thing is sure: the relationship impairment was not healed, and it definitely became relationally genetic (Ps. 51:5).

Ever since then, there has not been a perfect couple on earth. All marriages and subsequent human relationships—parent-child, sibling—have been fraught with challenges and problems of every kind, and unfortunately, there seems to be no abatement to this day.

But the saddest and worst part of the sordid account in the dilemma of the human family is that the impairment is caused to a large degree by the unbridled, unguarded, testosteronic effect of the aggressive *male man*. The knowledge and sense of his original failure, and the genetic/hereditary effect of the blame of his first father, Adam, against Eve his first mother, has resulted in an inexplicable behavior of dominance that males in general, and more so the unconverted ones, display toward the female.

As the toll of sin began to set in, the relationship gap between man and woman got wider. He began to subjugate her. Abuse and battering slowly crept in. Down through the centuries, humiliation through molestation and rape became one of his ways to control her. And the Bible is not silent on the matter that it would have happened.

"Did God not say that the man shall rule over the woman and that her desires shall be unto him?" This question is often asked in reference to Genesis 3:16 and cited by overbearing and domineering men as their license, as it were, to keep the woman under not just submission but subjugation.

In retaliation, women in general, and feminists in particular, cite the very text (and others) as evidence that the Bible is essentially chauvinistic, written by men against women (Review p. 311). The sinful, negative aspects of some of the cultural practices of patriarchalism are blown up. There is no question as to whether some such negatives do exist, and such is the overall nature of sin. However, neither of the two positions cited above is correct. The Bible itself offers clear explanation of the facts.

In His omniscience, God looked down the corridors of time, as He alone can, and saw the ultimate impact that sin would have, firstly on Eve and Adam, and then upon their children's children. He saw that the impact would even be to the last generation, (See Chapter 8, "The DNRA of Family Relational Health") and until the final restoration plan for which He, Himself, has made provision from the foundation of the world (John 17:24; Eph. 1:4).

The law of action and consequence has existed from the creation of man in the Garden of Eden. There is also the caution about it that God made to Adam as recorded in Genesis 2:17: "But of the tree of the knowledge of good and evil, thou shalt not eat of it: for in the day that thou eatest thereof thou shalt surely die." Let us analyze and apply that verse against that law:

- **Caution**—"thou shalt not eat of it" (verse 17, second phrase)

- **Implied choice**—"You may eat of it" (by virtue of the exercise of the power of choice)
- **Understood consequence**—"thou shalt surely die" (verse 17, third phrase)
- **Consequence**—"surely died" (after living a mere 930 years, according to Genesis 5:5, out of his conditional immortality)

Ellen G. White writes in *Education* (page 15):

> When Adam came from the Creator's hand, he bore, in his physical, mental, and spiritual nature, a likeness to his Maker. "God created man in His own image" (Genesis 1:27), and it was His purpose that the longer man lived the more fully he should reveal this image—the more fully reflect the glory of the Creator. All his faculties were capable of development; their capacity and vigor were continually to increase. Vast was the scope offered for their exercise, glorious the field opened to their research. The mysteries of the visible universe—the "wondrous works of Him which is perfect in knowledge" (Job 37:16)—invited man's study. Face-to-face, heart-to-heart communion with his Maker was his high privilege. Had he remained loyal to God, all this would have been his forever. Throughout eternal ages he would have continued to gain new treasures of knowledge, to discover fresh springs of happiness, and to obtain clearer and yet clearer conceptions of the wisdom, the power, and the love of God. More and more fully would he have fulfilled the object of his creation, more and more fully have reflected the Creator's glory.

Alas! The consequence of disobedience through the wrong exercise of the power of choice (See pp. 366 & 384).

## Pain: the Consequence of Sin

Before sin or had sin not come, Adam would have taken care of the garden without pain, seeing that it was a part of his divinely appointed, happy activity as he connected with and took care of his environment and benefited therefrom by enjoying the fruits of his work. Eve would have borne children without pain, because such was her divinely appointed happy privilege to be God's agent for continuing where He left off or stopped at Creation when He made them. The difference would be that the children would come from their joint coming together (mind and body), as was God's functional design of their bodies, representing Him (See p. 207).

Pain is the consequence of sin. The first pain that the first family would experience as a consequence of their sin was a relational one on their minds. They could not see and relate with each other as usual. Sin had imposed a posthoneymoon dark glow and uncomfortable experience on their minds. It is clear that Eve began the estrangement when she strayed from Adam's protective side from which she came, and where she should have remained. They were to know of each other's whereabouts, and Eve seemed not to have told Adam where she was going, or even what she might have intended.

There might be those who want to suggest that this expectation of Eve was the subtle beginning of female subjugation. That is patently incorrect. Both husband and wife are to share with each other their whereabouts. Straying from her husband was simply, and proven consequentially, wrong. Equally so, if Adam had left her for any questionable and extended distance or time, that would equally be unhealthy and wrong. The record is that she made the wrong move.

In his inability to have direct access to our minds, Satan watches our behaviors, which are indicators of our thoughts and desires. He knows how best to capitalize on them and how to create the means for their fulfillment, especially when they are not in harmony with God's will for our lives. (See p.220 - How Demons "Possess" Human Beings?). As Adam and Eve toured the garden, he might have passed on to her the caution God had given him before she was created.

Eve could not, therefore, plead ignorance to what could have happened in the vicinity of the tree in the midst of the garden. Bear in mind that Satan had ulterior motives toward them, given his sordid behavior in heaven where he influenced a third of the angelic forces to take sides with him. He undoubtedly had Adam and Eve under behavioral and indicative surveillance. That is his nature (1 Pet. 5:8), so for Eve and all of us, her children, it remains true that to be forewarned is to be forearmed.

Upon sensing his failure and weakness to abide by God's instruction to him, and yielding to his wife's coercion to participate in the act of disobedience to God, Adam reacted in self-defense by blaming Eve. He could have chosen to go it alone in obeying God. It is safe to reason that if Adam had remained faithful to God, Who directly gave him the instruction, God would have accounted his faithfulness for righteousness and on his merit, forgive, redeem and restore Eve. Thus he would have foreshadowed Christ, our ultimate Redeemer. Unfortunately, his own sense of failure was developing in his mind; he evidently rationalized in his already weakening sense of responsibility and accountability, and he went along with her.

Sounds like so many cases today. Certainly, nothing is new under the sun. Eve's was an act of disobedience, firstly to her husband and consequently to God, and Adam's was an act of putting his wife before God. Demonstrating faithlessness, he acted in disobedience to God.

### Beginning of Psychosomatic Illness and Chemical Imbalance

From thenceforth, it was no longer natural for Adam and Eve to be always good and nice with each other. That emotionally charged relational pain would work its way into their bodies and be reflected particularly in the two major activities of their physiological functions and endeavors, which God had outlined to them. This was the beginning of psychosomatic illness. For Adam, that major activity was working in the garden for the sustenance of life for the family (Gen. 3:17–19), and for Eve, that major activity was working her body for the production of life for increasing the family (Gen. 3:16).

None of the two major activities would be done with the ease, comfort, and enjoyment that they should have experienced before they sinned. (NB. Eve's first pregnancy was after the fall). To a large extent, the quality of any work in which we get engaged is influenced by the health of the mind. Unquestionably, the state of mind is the engine, the driver, and the motivator behind everything that we do.

Pain would be the consequential sign of their deteriorating bodies until they returned to the ground from which the structural material of their being (their body) was taken. The ultimate consequence of sin had to run its course so that the entire universe could see its folly and not blame God for arbitrarily bringing it to an end, an accusation which Satan would want to make.

Sin produced the first chemical and hormonal imbalance in their brains, which imbalance was acted out in their relational minds. The production of serotonin, dopamine, norepinephrine, endorphin, oxytocin, and all those healthy hormones and chemicals would be compromised. ***Clinical Update:*** Joseph Gutzman, writing in the Hill | Changing America, (July 21, 2022) quoted researchers from University College of London that: "Many people take antidepressants because they have been led to believe that their depression has a biochemical cause, but this new research suggests this belief is not grounded in evidence." The study went on to exonerate the imbalance of serotonin as the "culprit for depression." Their sense of failure and disappointment would raise the level of adrenaline and cortisol in their bloodstream to an unhealthy level. Fluctuating emotions would pave the way for bipolar behaviour and depression. Their perceptions would be impaired, and their relational outlook would not be as lofty and ideal. The marvel of their being fearfully and wonderfully made would be affected, and the natural degeneration of the quality of their lives would inexorably follow.

### Sentenced to Hard Labor

God saw the sinful kaleidoscope of man's action and in mercy to them, He described the future as it would be individually, and consequently on them as a couple and family. By describing it to them, He raised their awareness of the consequence of their sin, and at the same time, lovingly preparing them for what was to come.

It is important to note that before He mentioned the gloom of despair that was about to descend upon them, He mentioned the bloom of hope that would come after. This is our exemplary, caring God and Father showing us how we should relate with the erring members of our families in the face of the imminent consequence of their wrongdoing. Hope is always the antidote for despair.

He gave them the assurance that all is not going to be ultimately and eternally lost. He explained the redemption plan that He had put in place in order to restore the broken relationship that they, by their chosen disobedience, had caused. That redemption plan was the protoevangelium, the First Gospel, that He, God, in the Person of the Son, will come in the fullness of time (Gal. 4:4–5) and bring relational healing and restoration (Gen. 3:15 and Mal. 4:2–3).

For Adam (and subsequently all men), the consequence would be pain working on the ground. Food production would be strenuous and difficult, as he would encounter briers, thorns, and other factors of impediment. God told him, "Thorns also and thistles shall it bring forth to thee; and thou shalt eat the herb of the field; In the sweat of thy face shalt thou eat bread, till thou return unto the ground; for out of it wast thou taken: for dust thou art, and unto dust shalt thou return" (Gen. 3:18–19).

Muscular aches and tiredness would occasionally wear him down, in providing for all aspects of family needs. Time and season for most of his plans and activities would sometimes be problematic, and he would have the experience of being frustrated. Providing for the family not only materially but more so relationally could become daunting sometimes and reduce his sense of patience and tolerance in responding to the various needs of his family.

One of the most despicable evidences of that effect on many men today is their abdication of their God-appointed roles as husbands and fathers. Their sense of responsibility has descended to an alarming depth, leaving bewildered wives and mothers strenuously bearing the burden of providing for the family and growing up the children singlehandedly. Sin has pushed the boundaries of single mothering to the point where in some cultures, parenting is devolved upon the mothers only, while fathers stay in the fields, the offices, boardrooms or among other out-of-the home engagements.

Many children have been deprived of their sense of paternal and family identity, resulting in truancy and maladaptive and maladjusted youngsters. In so many cases, the vicious cycle continues, especially with boys growing up without the example of good, responsible husbands and fathers. They are deprived of the needed demonstration of establishing care and providing for a family. (See GEDM in Glossary p. 40). Many end up drifting into the hands and arms of unscrupulous fellow males who themselves are victims of the same situation, and they forge relationships that are detestable and totally against nature. And many are those others who end up in hotbeds of crime and violence.

Painfully, so many of these otherwise potentially good young men seem to mount the same horse and ride down the same road of absenteeism and irresponsibility. Here we have a partial fulfillment of the prophecy by Ezekiel: "the fathers have eaten sour grapes, and the children's teeth are set on edge?" (Ezek. 18:2). Girls have not escaped the ills of the absence of a positive, healthy, father figure in their lives. Unwanted and teenage pregnancies and immoral lifestyles of many young women are the result of their not having the early exposure to the one who is supposed to be the first man and male model in their lives: their father. From him, she should see how a healthy husband-father cares for his wife and children.

Daughters should know what it feels like to be healthily hugged and cradled by a man without the impression that the sexual aspects of their bodies are the price to pay for such comfort and care. When they mature into women, they would have been able to use that positive experience to measure the scruples of the man with whom they associate and who might even become their future husbands and fathers of their children.

## Eve's Dependence upon Adam

For Eve, (and subsequently all women), one of the consequence of sin would be pain in childbirth. "Unto the woman he said, I will greatly multiply thy sorrow and thy conception; in sorrow thou shalt bring forth children (Gen. 3:16, first part). The throes and travails of delivery would range from uncomfortable to excruciating. And even before those, there would be the nauseated feelings (morning sickness), the potential spike in blood pressure, her body falling out of shape, among other experiences. Her female and childbearing hormones, such as estrogen and progesterone, would not always be at their normal levels. They would begin their fearful manifestation in menarche and could even get worse if she becomes the victim of dysmenorrhea (painful monthly periods).

Her gynecological and obstetric body functions, the calibration during the nine-month gestation period, and the experience at delivery would not go as they were designed before the Fall. Twelve times in the King James Version of the Bible have her pain and anguish been referred to analogically to emphasize that sin is, by all account, intolerable: "For I have heard a voice as of a woman in travail, and the anguish as of her that bringeth forth her first child ..." (Jer. 4:31).

Then there would be the natural dependence on her husband for support, including the feeling of security and protection that she will truly need, but which unfortunately might not be forthcoming as she desires and deserves: "... and thy desire shall be to thy husband, and he shall rule over thee" (Genesis 3:16, last part). Eve would undoubtedly have symptoms of posttraumatic stress disorder (PTSD) from the negative flashbacks of her encounter with the serpent, as she had to grapple with the painful consequences. There would also be guilt feelings from the reminder from her husband that they are going through those difficulties because of her weakness in yielding to the temptation of the evil one.

The negative back and forth of verbal accusations, emotional alienation, her occasional disillusionment, and constant unfulfilled expectations will weaken her sense of self-esteem and weigh her down. Not least among these times of disillusionment will be her sense of unfulfilled sexual desire and satisfaction. Look again at the paraphrase of Anchor Text 1 at the beginning of the chapter.

Given the biological and physiological complexity of her sexual physiology over that of her husband, including her much lower level of the sex libido hormone, testosterone, and given his ignorance of such facts, and his own impatience and inexperience, she could end up feeling sexually frustrated and even used by him at times. Thus, her desires will be to her husband in so many ways, not dictated and inflicted by God, but by the sinful falling-out of the natural, healthy circuitry of their relational minds.

And his feeling of being bothered by what he will regard as her nagging, will bring out the sinful, negative, hardening effect of testosterone on his brain and into his relational mind. He could become insensitive and distanced from her feelings. He asks: "What is wrong with her? Why can't she think otherwise?" All this for both of them because their minds, the engine of their beings, were already in pain due to their disconnection from the source of life, God, their Creator.

## Did God Design Their Punishment?

There are many who interpret the pain that Adam and Eve, and consequently all of us, their descendants, experience as a punishment inflicted by God, based on the statement: "*I will* greatly multiply thy sorrow." We know that God is not a sadist, and therefore He takes "… no pleasure in the death of him that dieth …" (Ezek. 18:32 and 33:11), and therefore not in their pain either.

He appeals to His children who are heading towards untimely and eternal death to "turn yourselves, and live." And Paul summarized it to the Romans thus: "For the wages of sin is death; but the gift of God is eternal life through Jesus Christ our Lord" (Rom. 6:23). Wages used in Romans is the same as consequence, payment, or result.

In the language of the Bible writers, every act is attributed to God, without distinction between His designed will and His permissive will. At the end of every major segment of His Creation, He declared it was good (Gen. 1:4, 10, 12, and so on). Being good is God's nature, and He cannot be otherwise. At the same time, that same nature does not condone or overlook sin (Psalm 5:4; Hab. 1:13).

In His permitting it to run it consequential course, He is seen as causing it to happen. But that is where the distinction between *causing, permitting*, and *doing* comes in. In order to make the correct attribution, we need to know and understand the character of God, and that is fully summed up in a simple but profound expression of the praise "God is good all the time, and all the time God is good, and that's His nature."

We can conclude that what God said to Adam and Eve was a description of what He saw and would permit, in love, to happen to them, as against it being a prescription of His for their punitive annihilation. It is a consequence that He would permit, but for which He would provide them with grace to endure (1 Cor. 10:13) until the fullness of the protoevangelium is realized (Gen. 3:15).

## Sinful Impact on the Male Relationship

The unregenerate male in many cases disparages women and treats them like second-class human beings. He treats them like chattels, as Adam was to positively and healthily relate to the animals over which God gave him, and by extension, Eve, dominion. His sons, in so many parts of the world, are treating their Eves as though they are the animals over which their father, Adam, was to have dominion, and they now inherit that 'ownership' status. They exercise merciless lordship and ownership of the ladies in their lives and in society, as in the 2021 case of international outcry in an Asian country where the rights of girls and women to study and work are cases of concern.

Sexploitation in the form of the sex trade or, as correctly called, human trafficking is a big business. In most modern cases, the female is the main commodity. One of the most despicable and disgraceful accounts of male sexual violation and abuse of the female was an atrocity in David's family. It was committed by his son, Amnon, on his half-sister Tamar (1 Sam. 13).

We would not have done justice to the listing of the evils of the male against the female if we did not reflect on another Bible story. This is the case of the dethroning of Queen Vashti by the drunken, power-mad king Ahasuerus. (Esther 1–2). This is a record that could be inadvertently overlooked in the context of the dominance of the male over the female.

In Ahasuerus, we find a typical overbearing male ruler, backed up by his cronies and lackeys, who decided that to the same extent he showed off his material acquisitions, he could also parade what was to him another of this 'possessions,' this time a fellow human, his queen/wife (verses 10 & 11). When Vashti protested in the interest of maintaining her dignity, self-esteem, and self-respect, she was punished with dethronement and banishment (verses 12-19).

The crowning of Esther as Vashti's replacement must not be seen as God sanctioning such a travesty of gender manipulation and ill-treatment. Instead, this is a classic case of how God, in His providential way, brings good out of humanly calculated evil, beyond human comprehension (See Joseph's case, Gen. 37-50). The focal point of the story is that Vashti was disbanded from the monarchy because she would not submit to the will and fancy of a despotic, domineering male. Alas! There are still many modern Vashtis today, and they are to be lauded and supported for the valiant stance against ruthless men.

Today, no well-thinking male, beginning with husbands and more so the Christian husband, should conveniently capitalize on the statement that God made to Eve in Genesis 3:16 and go on to ask, "Did God not say that the man shall rule over the woman?" Any man and husband so inclined would do well to earnestly and prayerfully read again the paraphrase of Anchor Text 2 in this chapter and see the healthy change of mind that the Holy Spirit will work in him.

## Women's Ordination to the Pastorate
## A Foundational Complementing and Balancing Perspective

This segment of this chapter would be incomplete without addressing in part, the current, potentially divisive issue of Women's Ordination to the pastorate in some Christian denominations. The subject incites controversy and even contention between the two main groups of believers: the liberal and the conservative thinkers, based on their modern contemporary scholarly biblical interpretations and fundamental biblical perspectives, respectively.

Disclaimer: Inasmuch as the subject is raised beside the discussion on male dominance, from a biblical family relational health point of view, it is not seen as a part of the dominance discussed above. Secondly, it is known that volumes of material on the subject have been produced and published in various media, so the Reader is not short of divergent views and perspectives. It is further understood that the subjects of women's total involvement in the life of the Church, including preaching, and Women's Ordination to the pastorate are not one and the same, and that in this article, the former is not focused upon or addressed in any way whatsoever.

The comments, questions and suggestions that will be raised below are not influenced by any of the published material alluded to above, nor have any been previewed in preparation for this writing. This is original and posited in keeping with the premise of family relational health, and is intended to lead to an objective, open-minded reasoning, thereby trying to influence the extent to which the differing postures will take the subject and to help, where possible in mitigating the potential, devastating impact that the debate could have if it goes unchecked. It is not a pros and cons approach. The forces of evil will exult as the debate rages on at the expense of more energy being spent on the spreading of the Gospel, healing relationships and the ushering in of the soon return of our Lord and Saviour.

**God Declared All "Good" at Creation**
**Balanced and Complementary**

We remind ourselves that in the beginning, after each major point, and at the end of His Creation, God declared that everything was "good!" "Good" declared by God, was and is still understood to means impeccable, flawless, and perfect and cannot be improved upon. We believe that that was the complete and eternal description of the plans and provisions that He made and handed down to His masterpiece of Creation—male and female, man and woman. He made them equally but distinctly, to complementarily represent Him and to carry on from where He stopped at Creation (Revisit p. 297). That is to say, they were to effectively manage the provisions made for them and at the same time to meet His expectations of faithful worship and glory from them.

It is safe to believe further that the principles and relational practices, both for their work, fellowship and worship which He taught and implanted in them individually and together, were to be as constant and perpetual as His further declaration about some perpetuities in nature (Gen. 8:22), inasmuch as this particular declaration was made long after their creation.

It would be correct to observe that the priesthood and pastoral leadership (the issue of concern here) were understandably not directly mentioned or addressed in the garden home directives from God to Adam and Eve. Would it be equally safe to suggest that the microcosmic leadership in the home-church worship in the Edenic setting (inasmuch as we do not know how long that lasted) was a fore-shadow of the macrocosmic leadership in the post-Edenic congregational home-church, and that the multiplier effects would naturally be maintained with the exponential expansion of congregations? What leadership dynamics, if any, would have remained, and what, if any, would have been changed in the growing number of congregations which would eventually be grouped into districts, dioceses, parishes, conferences and territorial management arrangements?

Let's engage the Socratic Method: Do we need to distinguish between the originally-intended home and church leadership? Was the Eden home motif of home life, inclusive of worship, intended to be continued as homes multiplied? Or, was that motif changed, adjusted, or modified after the family was expelled from Eden due to their disobedience to God? Are leadership roles and the different roles of followership/participant-ship the same or interchangeable? Could anyone assume any role at any time? What provisions or conditions or even inspiration might have been put in place for unforeseen prophetic or developmental eventualities or probabilities in the leadership and administration of the home-church groups?

A quick fast-forward from Eden to, and a cursory glance at the days of the Levitical (Old Testament) priesthood/pastorate could elicit the question whether that pattern of the male gender appointment and leadership was in any way a continuation of the simple pattern established in Eden (See Addendum, p. 446). Further, to what extent if any, was that established Edenic leadership principle mirrored or continued in the Apostolic (New Testament) Church (the ekklesia) established by Christ? Changes? Modifications? Adjustments? Where? How? By whom and When? Certainly there are answers for these and more intrusive and analytical and ecclesiastical questions and queries, that could be influenced by the nuances in language (Old Testament Hebrew/Aramaic and New Testament Greek) and translations, and their correct interpretations which might result in different meaning of which the unlearned minds would not be aware.

Despite the probabilities of such nuances in etymologies, derivatives, phase history, etc., that some of the above questions and concerns might bring, we maintain the reassurance and reaffirmation of our faith and conviction in the perfection of God's original plan for the human family and their relationship with Him. It is safe to suggest that any relational, operational or leadership questions that are of a flashpoint or hot potato nature in our present, sinful existence, over the subject under study and all others of disquietudes and contentions, would be advisably analyzed in the context of the following probabilities and realities:

## Forces Arraigned against God's Original Ideal

Given that the forces that are arraigned against God's original design operate with the strategic plan to divide, weaken and conquer: to what extent could those forces have set out covertly and overtly, to marshal our growing human relational intolerance, ignorance, unbridled ambitions, convenient misinterpretations of Bible passages, scholarly works proffered as lower or higher criticism of the Bible, misguided and unscriptural cultural practices to our own relational and spiritual demise? (compare lines 1 and 2, p. 40 Item 3)

Could a part of the subtle (Gen. 3:1) master plan for our human relational downfall and failure be the combination of all in the above paragraph so as to breed infighting, theological and academic wranglings and disputes into the two houses of the Lord—the Home and the Church? (See p. 316) What lessons could we possibly learn from the various contentions among God's people? Two poignant examples as recorded in Numbers 12:1-15 & Acts 15:36-40 - albeit the issues were different, but contention is contention.

The goal of such forces is to bring the Word of the Lord into disrepute; distract the Church from its mission of fulfilling the Great Commission of Matthew 28: 19 & 20, and from heeding the Elijah Message of Malachi 4:5 & 6. In the end, the accomplishment will be the defeat of the plan of salvation. (See Songs nos. 8 & 38 of FRH Songs of Praise and Bible Verses Paraphrase). This is a program which Satan began from the Garden of Eden, having lost his (Lucifer's) attempted insurrection and coup in heaven. (Isaiah 14:12-14) and Ezekiel 28:12-15). His was a war of ideology based in pride.

On the assumption that all the parties in the present doctrinal debacle have a vested interest in the fulfilment of the mission of the Church, and that no one is subtly (Gen. 3:1) holding a proverbial hard-end towards gender supremacy and inferiority, then on the premise of family relational health, and in the interest of honouring the God of Creation and not to fall prey to the forces that are against God's original ideal, consider the following introspectives, from a Socratic Method rational approach in addition to the sustained objectivity that would have influenced the position on the subject.

What is/are the driving force(s) and motivation(s) behind the contention of Women's Ordination? What has not been accomplished? What is not being accomplished? What needs to be accomplished? And, what is not likely to be accomplished in the Church due to the position of the majority of those who are of the conservative, fundamental position on the subject? What has been, what is being and what will be lost? And, what will be or what could be gained with the acquiescence or lack thereof of the majority to that of the minority, vice versa, on the issue? What has changed or what needs to be changed about the "good" that God declared at creation? Or, what aspect, if any, about the present controversy that was not covered under God's "good" declaration? We need objective responses.

From the days of the early Church, corporate responsibility and support for the sincere, prayerful majority has always been the success story of the body of Christ. (See the Cenacle –Upper Room Experience, Acts 1:12-14; the Jerusalem Council, Acts 15: 1-35). On this premise and on the genuine response to the pointers above, could that combination under the guidance of the Holy Spirit resolve the subject at hand? (Revisit the Genesis Foundation, p. xviii).

In the study of home and church leadership, the roles and duties among other related matters, should be differentiated, defined, delineated, compared and contrasted based on the Bible, historical and developmental records and what healthily pertains in the context for family relational health. Reaffirmation should always be made of God's original ideal of the complementary and complimentary leadership of the male and the female in the home and in the Church, with no need or question about rivalry, superiority or inferiority.

**God Designed Sex/Gender Harmony**

We reaffirm that in God's original plan, Eve was not made subject to Adam's dominion as were the animals made to him first and by extension to her equally. She was equally human as Adam, both being made to complementarily represent the image of God. Complementary as used here suggests that they were intrinsically not identical but compatible to represent and fulfil different aspects of the image of God. Eve was to identify with Adam's leadership, and Adam was to respect and incorporate her into the operations (work and worship) of the home and family that they would build together, under his God-appointed leadership. Was that pattern of operation to have been continued towards and until Eden is restored?

The Bible is replete from Genesis to Revelation with the ideal alluded to and implied above, despite the impact of sin, and it is all ours for the full understanding even in this age of the sex-gender controversy, as we individually and together, men and women, males and females seek the guidance of the indwelling Holy Spirit.

The preeminence in terms of order and timing (not the same as predominance) of the male outside of his God-given positive responsibility, accountability, and answerability for the well-being of his family cannot and should not be tolerated. Family relational health will never be experienced if this scourge is not eradicated and healed. The husband is the head of the wife, as he, the man, submits to the headship of Christ (Eph. 5:22–23), Who has the well-being of both of them at His heart. As long as He is in charge of them, all should be well.

# Distortion 3: The Extremism of Feminism

It is a general observation in life that nothing good happens when we move from one extreme to the other. Of course, there are exceptions to this rule. There can be nothing unsafe about moving from falsehood to truth, nor does caution need to be exercised for moving from near death to prolonged or extended life. With those and other exceptional cases, the caution is appropriate. Swinging the proverbial pendulum from one extreme to the other has potential problems.

It is unhealthy to move from an extreme hot condition into extreme cold except under carefully guided therapeutic knowledge and management. Almost all such drastic changes can be health- and life-threatening. The caution to avoid extremes holds good even as we consider the subject of family relational health, with specific focus on the troubled issue of gender imbalance caused by sin.

The writing of this section of the chapter seems to be providentially timed, for today, March 8, is being observed as International Women's Day. It is a day designated annually to bring attention to the wide gamut of imbalance between the two sexes across the world in a general sense. The day is also set apart to focus on the achievements women have made and continue to make in society without any reference to ethnic, cultural, religious, economic, and political affiliations.

Without getting into the historical background of the day (which information is readily available in libraries and on the internet), we may assume that something went awry in the relationship between the two sexes, resulting in one having the need for an international day to be declared for the specific purpose of highlighting the issues, concerns, and challenges of that compared to one the other. There evidently has been, or there remains, some infighting, unhealthy competitiveness, disparaging, putting-down, denying and discrediting, and even disenfranchising, and all the other possible negative characterizations of the relationship between the two.

## Satan, the Master Divider

Although it is just the two of us—male and female, man and woman (incorporating the biological issues mentioned on p. 270)— who were fearfully and wonderfully made at Creation, not with sameness or uniformity but with complementary and complimentary equality, the ideal goal of sustained harmonious coexistence has yet to be realized. The house, and consequently the home, have become and have remained divided.

Not only is Satan the master divider in the human family (beginning in Eden), but he is also the master manipulator. His strategy is to divide and conquer by pitting one family member against the other. He incited separation, distrust, and disloyalty, then manipulated them into the blame game and then into rivalry. That is the genesis of the relational debacle between the two sexes. With the deterioration over time, it has now become known as the culturally and socially based gender battle or the battle of the sexes.

This we believe subtly accounts for the feminist movement. Good and plausible as it appears on the surface having served some good purposes, it is unhealthy in its depth, strategy, and ultimate outcome. Rebecca Traister, in her work *Good and Mad—The Revolutionary Power of Women's Anger*, captures it very eloquently:

> The contemporary re-emergence of women's rage as a mass impulse comes after decades of feminist deep freeze. What used to be called "the feminist movement" had found energetic new life in the first decades of the twenty-first century. After years of backlash, feminists, journalists and bloggers had received a conversation about gender, and many of us who participated in the conversation were angry—angry about sexism, and racism and economic inequality and how all of these injustices were woven together. But, perhaps anxious to differentiate ourselves from the spitting-mad forebears, many contemporary feminists (including me), had worked to make the expression of our frustrations sound agreeable, relatable and inviting to others, including to the very men who might have a hand in oppressing us.

The ultimate outcome of the movement is the infighting and wrangling and power struggle of the sexes/genders. It is the classic case of the pendulum being swung from one extreme to the other.

Rivalry between the sexes and the evolving gender imbalance as a result of the social characterization of the roles and expectations of the sexes, were not a part of God's plan for the human family. To the same extent, it was not His plan to have more focus placed on our physiological health, the state and function of the body, at the expense of the psychological, the state and function of the mind (CPH$^2$). Being fearfully and wonderfully made meant that symmetry and purposeful balance would be maintained as the hallmark of healthy development of both male and female, as was exemplified in Jesus's growth and development (Luke 2:52).

## Satan's Sex-Gender Attack Strategy

There is in the title and anchor verse of Chapter 2 an implied message worth revisiting:

- **The Title**: "The Family Under Attack!"

  That is the battle cry, and somewhere in the chapter is the commanding, rallying response, "Let Us Fight Back!"

- **The Anchor Verses**

  *Original*: "For we wrestle not against flesh and blood, but against principalities, against powers, against the rulers of the darkness of this world, against spiritual wickedness in high places."

  *Paraphrased*: "For we wrestle not against ordinary marital, parental, and general family relational challenges, but against the continuous deteriorating standards of this world; against the subtle forces set at destroying God's original family ideals; and against the corrupt, immoral practices of this age, operating from high academic, religious, social, and other influential stages in society."

In analyzing those headers, we see there is an attack, which itself raises three questions:

1. On whom is the attack made?
2. By whom is the attack made?
3. How is the attack made?

We already know the answers to the first two questions, which in order are "the family" and "Satan." The third question requires some concentration in the context of the issue under study. Earlier, we said that Satan's strategy against the family is "to divide and conquer, by pitting one family member against the other." In the commanding rallying response, we are told to "Fight Back!" That too now raises the question: "With whom do we fight?" And, for that too, Satan had it all worked out: simply fight back at each other!

That is actually how he established the dividing line in the human family beginning in the Garden of Eden. He set Adam and Eve to fight against each other to determine who was responsible for the introduction of sin. This we see in Adam's blame-game response to God in Genesis 3:12: "The woman whom thou gavest to be with me, she gave me of the tree, and I did eat."

Down through the centuries, the multiplier effects of that infighting remain evident in families. And who do we see, hear, and feel in the fight? Our husbands, wives, parents, children, relatives, colleagues, and even those we call our friends. And, very specifically, again in the context of this chapter: Who are the females having to be fighting against? The males of course! And: How is the fight or the war being fought?

## Six Far-reaching Verbal Feminist Fight-backs

Let us begin by looking at the war of words and some subtle innuendoes as the females engage in the fight-backs.

### Fight-back 1

"The *head* rules, but it is the neck that turns the head!"

In this context, head = the man and neck = the woman. *Headship* here naturally questions the direct lessons in Ephesians 5 among other references that God inspired toward male leadership of the home and family. Satan has succeeded in placing home and church leadership under severe pressure and question, as is being played out in society today.

He begins by influencing the wrong and inept ways by which many home leaders, that is the husbands-fathers, are carrying out their responsibilities. We find so many men in and outside of the Church either overdoing their roles or reneging on them. Both extremes evoke adverse reactions from women, and the forces of evil are the final winners.

### Fight-back 2

"At the Creation of the human, God made the trial effort first, and then made the perfect model after."

Here, the trial one = the man and the perfect one = the woman. This statement is a retort aimed at squelching the general societal male's perspective of the female as inferior.

Unfortunately, it seems ingrained in the psyche of so many men that the female is inferior and therefore subservient to meet men's needs and fancies not least of which is the sexual. The truth is that God did not wire their relational minds with any such sense of inferiority or superiority, but with total mutuality in love and harmony. Satan planted that seed and as we have already noted, it has grown into the monstrosity of gender imbalance and infighting. (Review Bible Answers on p. 272 with direct reference to Matt. 13:28)

### Fight-back 3
"Anything a man can do, we can do it better."

The subtle message here is that there is really no difference between the sexes, regardless of what the Creator has said and which is indisputably attested to biologically and physiologically. Uniformity, sameness, evenness, and equality end up being one and the same. That proposition is expressed in the present movement in many countries where it is said that at birth, no sex type should be ascribed to the newborn, but that choice is to be reserved for the child to make upon growing up. The implication is that there is no difference between the sexes. The suggestion is that difference is merely the result of socialization. This is simply not natural or biblical.

Here we repeat, for emphasis, an item of news referred to in chapter 10. An EAG News.org headline screamed on January 20, 2019, "CA schools to teach kindergartners about 15 genders under new guidelines." The story continued:

> "The California Department of Education's proposed Health Education Framework for K-3 students, which would be mandatory with no opt-out option for parents, promotes a decidedly liberal perspective on gender and sexuality many parents would likely disagree with, and some educators are speaking up, Christian Headlines reports."

While we respect and uphold the Education Department's right to make such proclamation in the public domain, in which all views are free to be expressed, we expect that they will respect and uphold the inalienable right of the Bible-believing Christian community to differ and maintain their faith conviction in the original male-female biological facts of life, given that those convictions, maintained and practiced, will pose no threats whatsoever, to public safety, law and order. Ultimately, are we likely to declare that there is no such identity as male or female? The trend is potentially alarming and disturbing.

This book is not advocating a 'sex-caste' system and therefore subscribing to sex/gender stereotyping. Both men and women have clearly demonstrated in many cases, that there are some engagements and endeavours of life such as home chores and responsibilities, professional work among other possibilities, that were once thought to be sex/gender sacrosanct, and for which many glass ceilings have been necessarily shattered. Pendulum-swinging extremity is our cautious watchword here, where such extreme actions question God's parameters in the biologically complementary distinctions (physio-biologically/psychologically, functionally and otherwise) of the two sexes that He established at Creation. (Matt.19:4).

Sin has undoubtedly thwarted and confused such distinctions as it has done, and continues to do in many other aspects of life. It is the responsibility of sincere Bible-believing Christians to apply to the Holy Spirit to give them discernment to sift through the heaping rubbles of philosophies and sophistries, even religious ones, and keep to God's original family blueprint, despite the mounting versions of our modern society.

### Fight-back 4
"The *best man* for the job is a *woman.*"

This gender-driven retort might not be merely alluding to thoroughness, efficiency, and proficiency of performance of any given task. On the surface, the statement would appear to be portraying the female as more reliable and dependable and therefore always the ideal candidate to produce satisfaction and completeness. There might even be statistically researched 'evidence' to substantiate. That exaggeration has the gender battle as its undertone. Caution in applauding the statement ought to be exercised by all well-thinking Christian women and men, in an effort to avoid the subtlety of the trap against maintaining our God-given, unique biological sexual identities.

Wherever a more dependable female workforce exists, it ought to be lauded for its positive efforts, and it ought to be carefully analyzed and studied. All dependable, quality performing workers are to be lauded, praised, and compensated equally, be that person male of female. It is grossly unconscionable, dishonest, and wrong for a woman to do the same job as a man but be paid less because she is female. Archaic as it is, it was wrong from the beginning, and there should be no place for that gender-basis discrimination today.

It is worth noting that in many tertiary institutions especially in the west, females not only outnumber males in enrollment and completing the study program but also perform, on the average, higher. As a society, we continue to laud these facts at our expense, if we do nothing in a sustained way to improve the imbalance. If we do not study the reasons and be proactive regarding the factors that are producing such unbalanced sex/gender performance results, we will simply continue with one sex exulting and the other lamenting, and the two ultimately regretting, based on the existing trends.

The discipline of study and academic performance is just another aspect of the imbalance that needs to be addressed. In the final social analysis, some of the better academically performing females do not always end up in intimate and, or work-related relationships with males of similar academic and performance quality. And the vicious cycle of the gender infighting continues. With the picture remaining so socially bleak, both will continue to lose until the ills of sin are addressed, and both males and females see themselves and each other as God, their Creator, intended it to be when He made them—equal but not the same. (See effects of GEDM in Glossary p. 403).

### Fight-back 5
"I don't need a *man*; all I wanted was a *baby* in order to prove my biological maternal capability."

And the decadence in the quality of family life and responsible parenting gets worse. God's original design was that children should be conceived, born, nurtured, and grown by a responsible father and a responsible mother, both as coparents. While that ideal has been affected and has not been fully maintained down through the ages, the reminder is, all is not lost.

There remains in this society healthy families, built and sustained by supporting husbands and wives who go on to be exemplary fathers and mothers. The ideal home atmosphere in which children are to grow and develop is still the one built and managed jointly by the husband-father and wife-mother (Revisit p. 314).

Women who echo such fighting-back sentiments suggesting that the male is merely a convenience and a sperm donor are, knowingly or unknowingly, making a preparation to disenfranchise such children from their God-appointed and designed ideal of effective parenting. By virtue of genetic makeup, a child is predisposed to the need of a father and a mother. We are all aware of the devastating problems of irresponsible parents, so we should be careful not to go from one extreme to the other. We should always work toward the ideal while facing the reality and improving where we can.

We also remember that there are those who suggest that all a child needs is love and care, and that any combination of adults can provide for and meet those needs. On the surface, that position may appear plausible, but if it is correct in total, then it renders God's Creation ideal for a female mother and a male father questionable and even unnecessary. And they are not.

There are countless thousands of successful adults who are products of single-parent households, but equally so are the many out of that group who, when clinically and socially analyzed, do show how much more they could achieve, in one or more aspects of life, had they got their inalienable, biological right to healthy coparenting of father and mother. This belief and posture that exalt single parenting, primarily mothering, over and beyond what God instituted in establishing the family (Gen.2: 24), is anti-God's ideal. It must be debunked on the premise of the healthy coparenting practices based on the Word of God, and on the countless evidences down through the centuries, to our present time, of those who practice healthy coparenting with outstanding, exemplary results.

While we know the evils that can affect children who grow up in a toxic father-and-mother home atmosphere—a condition that is unacceptable and to be prevented, we ought to be wary of sweeping generalizations, lest we end up fulfilling the proverbial saying of "throwing away the baby with the bathwater." Good, outstanding single parenting is to be lauded. Some of the great contributions to society today are the products of such single mothers and fathers too, the Author not being exempted. (see the Dedication page 'Loving Memories'). At the same time, we should aim toward God's ideal while we work toward possible improvement of the current reality.

### Fight-back 6
"At the beginning of all women's trouble is *men*: *men*arche, *men*struation, *men*opause."

According to women who express this sarcasm, "men" are at the beginning of their misery at those three main biological stages of their lives and, most times those changes are accompanied by varying degrees of discomfort and pain. Of course, men fight back by saying that at the beginning of man's problems is wo(e)man. He is doomed, he can't escape because wo(e) is always ahead of him! This could be reasoned as beginning with Adam, because Eve really stepped before him, hence his response to God "... the wo-man who You gave to be with me ..." (Gen. 3:12) inasmuch as it was he who named her in Gen. 2: 23. "She shall be called Woman..."

As comical and hilarious as of these (and others not mentioned) attacks and counterattacks may seem, their individual and combined uses, depending on the circumstances, do carry some amount of subtlety that aggravates, compounds, and prolongs the sex-gender tension, adds fuel to the fire, and keeps the battle raging.

## Women's Misuse of Their Sexual Prowess

There is another subtle way that the woman, in general, fights back—a way that is as uncanny as it is controversial, and that is the use of her body, primarily her sexual prowess. While the male rapes her and demoralizes her, as was already discussed and unequivocally condemned (p. 323), she also subtly uses her sexual powers as a weapon against him. She flaunts her body at or before him, capitalizing on his sinful testosteronic sexual weakness, and even traps him to his demise and in many cases, to his death. Probably the best-known Bible story, even among nonbelievers, to illustrate this female prowess over the male is that of Samson and Delilah (Judg. 16).

The summary of this all-time classic, deceptive, treacherous betrayal of a man by a woman is between verses 18 and 21 of Judges 16:

> And she said unto him, How canst thou say, I love thee, when thine heart is not with me? thou hast mocked me these three times, and hast not told me wherein thy great strength lieth. And it came to pass, when she pressed him daily with her words, and urged him, so that his soul was vexed unto death; That he told her all his heart, and said

unto her, There hath not come a razor upon mine head; for I have been a Nazarite unto God from my mother's womb: if I be shaven, then my strength will go from me, and I shall become weak, and be like any other man.

And when Delilah saw that he had told her all his heart, she sent and called for the lords of the Philistines, saying, come up this once, for he hath shewed me all his heart. Then the lords of the Philistines came up unto her, and brought money in their hand. And she made him sleep upon her knees; and she called for a man, and she caused him to shave off the seven locks of his head; and she began to afflict him, and his strength went from him. And she said, The Philistines be upon thee, Samson. And he awoke out of his sleep, and said, I will go out as at other times before, and shake myself. And he wist not that the LORD was departed from him. But the Philistines took him, and put out his eyes, and brought him down to Gaza, and bound him with fetters of brass; and he did grind in the prison house.

Down through the centuries, countless men have fallen victims to unscrupulous women, in marriage and outside of marriage. Such devious women use their feminine charm to lead men into their sphere of influence and on to demise and destruction. Then there are those women who will not do such despicable acts, but applaud their sisters who do so by suggesting, "Good for him! After all, think of what some men, his brothers, have done to women!" And again, the battle rages unabated.

## The #MeToo Movement

The present #MeToo movement, which was started around 2006 by Tarana Burke on the Myspace social network, has proven to be one of the greatest vehicles to vindicate women against the violent and outrageous sexual abuse to which some men of might and means have subjected them. Whether it is against a legal, political, entertainment, royal or business luminary, or just the unscrupulous man on the street, decent, unsuspecting women have now been helped to come out from under the social pressure of hiding and expose the man who demeaned them for selfish male gratification at the expense of their pride, dignity, and self-esteem.

Thank goodness, many genuinely hurting women have even gotten their redress because they have gained the courage to come out and speak up; thus they experience their needed catharsis and closure. Also, some notable assailants have gotten their due punishment and are even now reaping their just rewards at a place they would never have imagined possible for them to be living, given the luxurious lifestyle that some had before their just conviction.

This book does not rejoice at the fate of any transgressor, especially those who are proven to be contrite and repentant. While such contrite and genuinely repentant men cannot be exonerated from their evil, horrendous, and immoral deeds, and must accept their penalties, opportunity and provision should be made for those who might be genuinely desirous to make whatever social restitution that might be acceptable, to do so. This, of course, is subject to the due process of the law with reference to the gravity of the offence, regardless of the contrition and penitence.

## The Potentially Vulnerable Male

Not to be missed, however, is the subtle vulnerability to which men in general are now exposed. This happens when the #MeToo Movement is capitalized upon by some vicious women in an effort to get back at men in general. Given the trend in sexual assault cases and interpretation of sexual harassment against women, any hitherto before consenting woman who wishes to change her mind, can simply do so and cry foul at her behest, and the man is going down! It is suggested that sexual blackmailing has been perpetrated against some men by unscrupulous women, but so many cases go unreported for obvious reasons.

In most cases the onus now is on the man to prove his innocence in terms of the charge of harassment, and yet it is more difficult for him to show that, in the case of sexual intercourse, it was consensual. The odds are biologically and physiologically skewed against him, since in order for him to perform the sexual act, his mind has to be engaged (except in extreme cases such as Lot's – Gen. 19:30-36) in order to have an erection and proceed with intromission and penetration. On the other hand, the female does not need any comparable visible physical evidence that she is ready and in agreement to the sexual act (The absence of which readiness is almost always to her physical and emotional disadvantage). Her defense can even be pushed to the limit; maybe she was originally in agreement for the coitus act but changed her mind midway. Even at the heightened stage for his intromission that she participated in, he is expected to respect her decision to cease and desist.

This expectation implies that he ought to be able to exercise restraint and constraint regardless of the electrochemical changes in the hypothalamus, the sexual center of the male brain that now produces the point-of-no-return in the whole anatomy and physiology of his sexual state. It suggests that he is to be able to 'flick that switch' to the off position even if it means that he has to become emotionally robotic, meaning without sensation. When going into the sexual act, maybe all men should have that 'Plan B' to retreat at the beck and call of the woman. Understandably, this caution would not apply to a husband who is in a faithful and healthy commitment with his wife. Oh! How sin has impaired this healthily ecstatic bonding gift from God to husbands and wives, alluded to in 1 Cor. 7: 2 - 5; Hebrews 13: 4. Alas!!

At this stage of her declaration to: "Stop! I do not want to go any further," the woman has no obligation to say what really motivated her decision to call it off. Whether it be genuine fear, concern, or simply her time to trigger her premeditated manipulation and the thrill of her sexual controlling power. The call is always hers for virtually all rational physical, physiological, and potentially futuristic reason. In this regard, the man is always at her mercy where the truth of the sensitivity of the time is concerned.

While a woman can accuse a man of provocatively exposing himself, thus making her uncomfortable and feeling sexually harassed, it seems socially acceptable for the woman to be skimpily dressed, top to bottom, with no one knowing when her behavior is a calculated act to get his attention. But it would be considered unthinkable for the man to equally complain of feeling sexually harassed. Any such complaint from him is more likely to be met with ridicule and in some places, even with a question as to whether he is really a man! Rejecting the advances of a woman!? The same attitude of ridicule is generally expressed at men who report being domestically abused by women!!

There are also the subtle cases of female bosses who sexually harass men under their jurisdiction, and there is hardly any place of recourse or redress for the man. Because the woman knows this, she can almost always make good her vicious ploy against the man. Such was the case of young Joseph when he was attacked by his mistress, Mrs Potiphar (Gen. 39:7–23). Ultimately and as always, God honored sincerity, and Joseph was not only exonerated but exalted. Unfortunately, there is no record of what became of that abuser of a brilliant, decent young man. And there are many present-day cases of a similar nature, although many go unreported and unheard.

Another extreme case of the vulnerable male is the situation where the woman was hurt or abused by a man and did not get the redress she deserved. She sets out to get it at all cost, and sometimes preys on an unsuspecting man who, in many instances, did not have his mental and moral guards up. Once he is trapped inside, he cannot claim ignorance or innocence. Here he sounds pretty much like his vulnerable brother described by Solomon in Proverbs 6:20-35 and 7:1-27, and ends up paying the full cost of his ignorance.

## All Is Not Lost

Inasmuch as the raging battle of the sexes/genders goes on, and the war that Satan is fighting on so many fronts against God's original plan for the family continues, his loss is already guaranteed. The final application of our Anchor Text, that we are fearfully and wonderfully made, is one of hope and assurance from God, our Creator. Despite the drama and trauma of the ages as a result of sin; despite the divisions and distortions in the family; despite the abuse and dominance of the male over the female; and despite the extremism of feminism, all is not lost.

One of the effects of the grace of God upon the human mind is the provision for renewal: "And he said unto me, My grace is sufficient for thee: for my strength is made perfect in weakness. Most gladly therefore will I rather glory in my infirmities, that the power of Christ may rest upon me" (2 Cor. 12:9). Here God assures Paul and all of us who are caught up in the cosmic warfare initiated by Satan, that He is still in control and has the final decision. God's grace is still available today, and many families, many husbands and wives, many fathers and mothers, many brothers and sisters, indeed many males and females are reaching out and accepting it.

Impaired family relationships can be repaired, healed, and restored. To the same extent that the body can regenerate and replace dead cells, so can the mind, the relational mind, regenerate and replace damaged, even dead emotions (CPH²).

Husbands and wives, and all the other categories of the male and female combinations of the family, can and will, until Jesus comes again, experience strong disagreement, but they can equally solve their conflicts and get back healthily together again. This is only made possible because in God's original, intelligent design, He fearfully and wonderfully made us both, male and female, in His own image.

The sustained distortion of God's image in the mind of the husband and the wife will result in the equally mysterious subtitle of this chapter: 1 – 1 = 2; M – M = M. It is to be noted that this equation is the very opposite of the one in the preceding chapter: 1 + 1 =1; M + M = M.

When a marriage that was supposed to be healthy gets so damaged and distorted, and one spouse pulls away from the other, the two visible discordant individuals stand in the full view of all onlookers. The oneness becomes dismantled, fully divided, and two unhealthy individuals result from what was supposed to be one healthy couple. So 1 - 1 = 2, i.e., 1 Hurting Couple - 1 Hurting Spouse = 2 Hurting Spouses.

In their unfortunate case, marriage – mystery = misery (See pp. 303-304). Clearly, there is the loss of the charming pull of the mystery of each other in their individual minds. Their individuality becomes commonplace, and the novelty of the newness that might have brought them together gets worn out. The novelty of the new was replaced with the routine of the regular; there was nothing more about each other to study, know, understand, desire, and cherish. Forcing them to stay together could be a miserable experience, save for divine intervention.

## Singlehood

This new experience brings to light another critical aspect of family relational health that has not been given much attention before in this book—Singlehood!

Up to forty years ago and before, the focus on family life was primarily on husbands and wives, and parents and children, so much so that the Scripture Readings for most family life presentations were a choice between Ephesians 5: 22, 23 (most times verse 21 is left off); 1 Corinthians 7:1-16. Sometimes verse 25-40 is used, depending on the subject being addressed. Added to the above popular selections would be Genesis 2:18-24; Exodus 20: 12; Proverbs 22: 6; Matthew 19: 3-15 and Ephesians 6: 1-4.

Although some of these passages and others not listed here make mention of, or allusion to other members of the family, the main reason they were read was with reference to marriage and parenting. Sometimes, comments would be 'patronizingly' made about singles. A full presentation on singles in those times would be a novel experience, except one of the most popular topics: "Sex and the Single Girl" which usually emphasized the negative issues of fornication and adultery.

One arresting fact that Church leadership now has to face is that Singlehood is the fastest growing category of family members in the Church. The influential factors behind this phenomenon are many and varied. While we will not address them here, it is important that we identify the four main categories of singles in the Church and community. They are: 1. The Once-married Single; 2. The Not-yet Married Single; 3. The Never-married Single; and 4. The hybrid 'Married' - Single.

The Bible teaches five fundamental lessons that could be incorporated under the three subtopics of: Being Single, Singleness and Singlehood. As will be noted at Lessons 4 and 5 below, it is stated that extrapolations and conditions are applied. This means that, due to the complexity and complications of sin on our human relationships, some matters are not always as simple and straight-forward as others. Some studies, as in the cases of Lessons 4 and 5, will require much detailed analyses, taking into account the historical, cultural and other factors. The detailed studies of family relational health cover all these wide areas of Singlehood including the definitions and characteristics of the above four categories. The studies are made possible through various seminars, counsels and therapies available in other FRH publications.

**Lesson #1– We Were All Created/Born Singly**

Adam and Eve were created singly. We may assume that subsequently, all their children, and their children's children were to have been born singly. This is based on the biological knowledge that only a single oocyte from one of the woman's ovary is released during each menstrual cycle. We can deduce therefore that the two ovaries were designed by God for alternate single ovulation. The Bible is silent on that biological issue, except the record of the birth of the well-known twin, Jacob and Esau to Isaac and Rebecca. Genesis 25:19-26).

Since that first biblical reference, we know that there have been the continued exceptional cases of multiple pregnancies: twins (this Author, himself, being one!), triplets, quadruplets, quintuplets, and even more. These can be due to the woman's multiple ovulations—hyper-ovulation—and consequently those ova being fertilized. Multiple pregnancies can also result from Assisted Reproductive Technology (ART) such as invitro-fertilization (IVF) or the use of fertility drugs. And, even in these cases, the babies are born singly except in the rare instances of conjoined twins.

Miraculously, and as evidence that all is not lost in God's original intent for humans, even in the cases of multiple births, each child is born with his or her unique individuality as a single person. This is even true of conjoined twins as was the case of Iranian sisters, Ladan and Laleh Bijani (1974 – 2003) who expressed the desire to pursue different careers, as evidence of each one having a mind of her own. There have been others like them. Inasmuch as we are not comparing humans with animals, it is noteworthy that even with their multiple births, such kid, calf, lamb, fool, cub, etc. shows some amount of individuality and unique characteristics.

The above comments on multiple pregnancies are not intended to be perceived as any authoritative lesson on genetics, heredity, fertility or about the two types of twins – identical (or monozygotic), fraternal (or dizygotic) or of any gynaecological or obstetric nature. Such information and lessons are available from the practitioners and experts in the various branches of medicine, genetics and heredity.

**Lesson #2 – Not Intended to Live Singly**

Singlehood or living singly was not a part of God's plan for His children inasmuch as we were apparently intended to be born singly. He expressed this at the very beginning by introducing the first negative (expressed in the record of humanity) in a healthy, positive way when He established the family. (See Distortion 2, p. 319–320)

"It is not good!" (Gen. 2: 18) Ideally in God's plan, after being born and matured singly, each man should marry a woman, who then becomes his wife and consequently, each woman would be married to a man, who then becomes her husband. (Gen. 2: 24; Eccl. 4: 9 -12; Matt 19: 1- 6; 1 Cor. 7: 8)

**Lesson #3 – Singleness Understood and Accepted**

Singlehood became an understood reality as a result of sin, and should only be experienced due to the natural death of a spouse. (Rom. 7: 2; 1 Cor. 7: 39; Matt. 19: 6; Mark 10: 11-12), hence the correct wording of the marriage vows: "Until death do us part."

Despite this understood reality, the mission of the Church should remain focused on preserving marriage unto its originally intended permanence. Thanks be to God all is not lost, and some who have experienced the lost before, through divorce, have regained the experience through healthy remarriage.

### Lesson #4 – Singleness after Marriage

Singlehood after marriage and before natural death is a manifestation of the multiplied effects of sin on the human heart/mind – Separation and Divorce. (Matt. 19: 7-9; 1 Cor. 7: 10-15).

For members who have fallen into this experience, the Church needs to provide an equally good ministry for them as to all other struggling saints, so that they can regain and maintain their sense of self-esteem, sanity and value (depending on the experience they would have had) as they continue in preparation for the Lord's return. (Extrapolations and conditions applied).

### Lesson #5 – The Ministry of Singlehood

Singlehood for life (celibacy) can be a choice and is understood and acceptable. (1 Cor. 7: 25-40) In this case, healthy singlehood can be seen as a ministry in which these members (See single men and single women) engage, not out of resignation, that is to say, giving up because they can't, or are fearful to get married.

Instead they are resolved and live happy single lives including a positive impression of, and a support for marriage. However, they have chosen to devote their lives to the service of the Lord in the Church and community. (Extrapolations and conditions applied).

As in the case of the three-tiers inter-dynamic categories of family relationships outlined in Appendix 2 (p. 466), the four categories of singles mentioned earlier have many sub-categories to each one.

Family relational health practitioners need to know each by itself in order to do justice in treating the relational challenges that they face. (See Song Number 39 "Single But Not Alone" in *FRH Songs of Praise and Bible Verses Paraphrase*).

We close this chapter as we started, not on the gloomy fact of being mysteriously and grievously divided, but on the repeated assurance that all is not lost. God's grace is still sufficient (2 Cor. 12:9) and still has the power to heal broken hearts.

Ideally, the marriage should remain intact and the husband and wife should grow old gracefully together until death do them part. But where the mystery of sin had its toll on the marriage before natural death, they can experience healing, and even if the union is not restored, they can live honorably and civilly apart, still in the blessed hope of the second coming of Christ when He will make all things new (See Rev. 21:5).

## Suggestions for Action

1. Remember that the stewardship of family life includes responsibility and accountability. Pray for God to help you to be responsible and accountable for your aspect of the life of your family.

2. God has made us male and female, equal but not the same. Spend time to understand, celebrate, and affirm what that means for the members of the opposite sex of your family.

3. As male and female in the family, God expects us to learn to complement and compliment each other. Learn the difference and do everything in your power to genuinely practice both.

4. The first and worst pain that family members experience is the relational one in their minds. Pray that God will help you

as a family member to be sensitive to the relational pain that might be in the mind of your family and do what you can to help to relieve and heal it.

5.  Do not allow Satan to engage your mind in the sex-gender battle in your home or in society. Value and support each member of the opposite sex, firstly in your family, and take that same spirit and attitude to your Church and society wherever you are.

# Chapter 12

# The Healing Plan

**Anchor Text: 1 Corinthians 10:13**

"There hath no temptation taken YOU but such as is common to man: but God is faithful, who will not suffer YOU to be tempted above that ye are able; but will, with the temptation, also make a way to escape, that ye may be able to bear it."

**Paraphrased for Families**

Be assured that no relational challenges you face are unique to your family, but that all marital, parental, or other issues are common to families everywhere. The God of families is faithful and will not leave your family to be hurt and suffer beyond that which you can endure. He will, with the relational challenges, also provide His approved human professional way to help, so that you may be able to manage and improve your relationships.

## The Early Detection Counsel

Maybe the most fundamental, arresting, and yet assuring counsel of medical care is "Early detection saves lives." Inasmuch as death is inevitable, life and health can be prolonged and enjoyed if this warning is obeyed. With continuously advancing research, study, and knowledge in the field of medicine and physiological health, there is hardly any good excuse for anyone to suffer from the debilitating diseases, maladies, and disorders that still assail many in the population today.

Research is proving more and more that so many of the illnesses affecting us are caused by our patterns of life and behaviors, hence they are correctly labeled as lifestyle diseases. Improved quality of health is becoming more and more possible for most people in the developed and developing world.

In the context of family relational health as covered in this volume, there is the parallel counsel to that of the medical care cited above. "Early detection and professional treatment save relationships and lives too." Even though all human relationships will end at death, quality relationships in marriage, parenting, and all other familial bonds can last for a lifetime. Unfortunately, this is not the experience in countless families in the past and will continue not to be so in the future (Review Paraphrased Anchor, p. 62).

To the same extent that there are great advances in medical care as mentioned above, so too are the continuous studies, research, theories, recommendations, and treatment plans in the related fields of psychology, sociology, and human behavior (CPH²). Amidst all this advancement and development in knowledge and professional skills, there is so much mayhem and social dislocation in the homes and the institutions that come out of them—schools, churches, clubs, associations, and the workplace. What is it that is hindering or preventing the preponderance of such professional skill-sets from having the desired positive impact on the quality of relational health in society?

From a Christian, Bible-based perspective, we can engage the cliché that "it doesn't take a rocket scientist to find the answer." From His throne in heaven, the God of Families had already provided the answer in another of His bemoaning cries, warnings, and challenges, and at the same time an invitation to His people: "For my people have committed two evils; they have forsaken me the fountain of living waters, and hewed them out cisterns, broken cisterns, that can hold no water" (Jer. 2:13).

In Chapter 3, we raised a similar concern as in the questions above regarding the unabated prevalence and continuous outbreak of family relational illnesses. Among the illnesses are: unkindness, harshness, insensitivity, disrespect, unfaithfulness, debauchery, insolence, arrogance, selfishness, meanness, callousness, defiance, conceit, and narcissism. The biblical and psychosocial diagnosis that we made then was based on a detailed clinical analysis of "lack of knowledge," or ignorance, anchored on Hosea 4:6.

In the study for this chapter, focusing primarily on the healing for the above and more relational illnesses and disorders, the attention will not be on mere *ignorance* but on the blatant denial, refusal, and substitutionary action of many families toward God's provision for their relational health and well-being. It will not be the case of ignorance at which God promises to wink (Acts 17:30). Instead, it will be focused on the case of man's calculated choice and decision to go contrary to God's expressed blueprints for family relational health and happiness, and His provisions for healing when such health is impaired (Review Impairment, pp. xvi & 235).

## God's Biddings Are His Enablings

We repeat our conviction that God's biddings are His enablings. This means that whatsoever God bids, instructs, or directs, He means just that because He would have already put everything in place to ensure that our obedience to His biddings is honored and rewarded. His assurance is guaranteed.

He says that marriage can work successfully, until death do them part, and it has happened, is happening, and will continue to happen until Christ comes the second time. He says that despite the failure of multitudes of parents, as in the case of Priest Eli (1 Sam. 2: 28–36 and 3:11–14), effective parenting and parent-child relationships are still possible today and will continue to be realized even to His coming.

Let us emphasize a salient point here: our conviction and persuasion about God's biddings being His enablings is based on the guarantee and assurance in His Word, because He cannot lie (Titus 1:2). He says: "And he said unto me, My grace is sufficient for thee: for my strength is made perfect in weakness. Most gladly therefore will I rather glory in my infirmities, that the power of Christ may rest upon me" (2 Cor. 12:9).

There is also the supporting fact for that conviction based on our understanding of how He created us. It is He who made the human relational mind, akin to His, having made man in His own image. He equipped and fortified the mind with the inherent skills and ability to forge and keep healthy relationships. Conditions applied, however. They would only be able to experience success in their relationships as long as they would be willing to abide in Him and follow His guidance and instructions. He said it definitively, "for without me ye can do nothing." (John 15:5), and Paul testifies, "I can do all things through Christ which strengtheneth me." (Phil. 4:13).

This is not a case of God making humans into robots in order to manipulate them for His selfish joy and pleasure. It is, instead, an exercise of their free will. When He created them, in addition to making them in His own image, He also endowed them with the power of choice. Man can choose to disobey Him with the understanding that obedience and disobedience have their individual rewards/consequences (Deut. 30:15–20).

## Two Reasons for Terminal Relational Illness

Despite the advances in medical and psychological care, family and general human relationships are clearly not getting better. In fact, we can cite yet another disturbing discovery that accounts for this woeful and discouraging picture of family relational health. There are two major reasons, maybe hitherto unforeseen, that family relational illnesses which go untreated can become relationally cancerous and ultimately terminal.

The first reason is biblically based: drawing from broken cisterns. The other is psychosocially based: reliance on home remedy or Band-Aid treatment

**Reason 1: Drawing from Broken Cisterns**

We have more than once referred to the Bible as God's family book, or better still, God's family manual. In searching through its pages, we learn that when God made the human family, He provided them, over a period, with five ways to receive instructions and guidance from Him. Those directives that sometimes came as decrees and commandments were given to families in order for them to live and enjoy quality family relationships, for His glory, the blessing of others, and their individual and family improvement.

The five sources through which God communicates His family directives are:

1. Direct inspiration via the Holy Spirit
2. Through nature or from nature's lesson book
3. His Inspired Word, the first of which is the Bible itself, which in turn is amplified and supported by other inspired writings which He gave
4. Through dreams and visions
5. Through shared human experience

Together, these sources constitute God's fountain of living water for family relational healing.

The description "quality family life" will be consciously and deliberately repeated in this chapter as we seek to raise the bar to a higher level of family life. The healing which we are advocating is not for mere recovery from physical maladies but more so from the traumas of the experiences of this present life in preparation for the restored Edenic family life that God intended at Creation. We are seeking to have a foretaste of the quality family life prophesied in Isa. 65:17–25. Inasmuch as that quality life is in the future, practice for it begins in the present, because eternal life begins in this present life.

As we seek to develop this new focus on the desirable quality family life against the background of the existing long list of relational illnesses (Review p. 365) from which we need healing, let us repeat, for the purpose of comparison, two opposing answers to achieve that healing:

1. God's biddings are His enablings.
2. The applauded advances in human knowledge.

A simple analysis of the two will reveal that they are diametrically opposed.

### Genuine and Nongenuine Relational Healing

In the first one, here is God, the Creator speaking: "When I created you, I made complete provision for you to experience quality family life." Then, here is man, the created being: "We will devise our own means by which we will experience quality family life." The first offering is original, while the second effort is contrived. As in the case of purchasing some auto parts for vehicular repair sometimes, there is a choice between the genuine and the nongenuine (or not made by the originator). In the interest of durability and reliability, the choice is clear. The genuine.

Applied: God's biddings are lovingly wrapped in the sources that make up His fountain, and are ours for the taking and they immediate usage, which will bear the evidences of His enablings. On the other hand, man's devised answers, thrown together as a collage of ideas and concepts, are like a maze through which we must meander to find our way out. These are his cisterns that can hold no water.

A fountain is portrayed here as an original source of water, while a cistern is a catchment or reservoir for water from whichever source it might be available. It goes without saying that, ideally, the better and preferred water should be that from the fountain. One regrettable characteristic of the fallen mind of man is the rejection of the ideal, and more specifically, the sources of truth that do not resonate with his wayward thinking. God said it in no uncertain terms: "… because thou hast rejected knowledge, I will also reject thee, that thou shalt be no priest to me: seeing thou hast forgotten the law of thy God, I will also forget thy children" (Hos. 4:6).

The natural consequences of this rejection and recalcitrance are that we are allowed to have our own way:

> Wherefore God also gave them up to uncleanness through the lusts of their own hearts, to dishonor their own bodies between themselves: Who changed the truth of God into a lie, and worshipped and served the creature more than the Creator, who is blessed forever. Amen. For this cause God gave them up unto vile affections: for even their women did change the natural use into that which is against nature. (Rom. 1:24–26)

Paul, in the above verses, spoke specifically of the practice that is opposite to what God established in Eden for the male husband and female wife, and similar behaviors, but the pronouncements are not only for those questionable sexual behaviors. All sins have the same consequences if they are not repented of, and the sinner seeks forgiveness and healing from God.

### God Honors Our Choices

There comes a time when God honors our choices, even when they are to our detriment and demise. His love will constrain us to do good (2 Cor. 5:14) but will not force us against our will if we adamantly prefer to do wrong (Rom. 1: 26). "And for this cause God shall send them strong delusion, that they should believe a lie: That they all might be damned who believed not the truth, but had pleasure in unrighteousness" (2 Thessalonians 2:11–12).

Through Solomon, God spells out that He has the desire, will, and resources to heal us from our errors, mistakes, and faults—but again, conditions applied. He will not force us; He will respect our choices, with the understanding that we will suffer the consequences of those choices. Here is the litany of His reasoning, arguments, complaints and concession:

> How long, ye simple ones, will ye love simplicity? and the scorners delight in their scorning, and fools hate knowledge? Turn you at my reproof: behold, I will pour out my spirit unto you, I will make known my words unto you. Because I have called, and ye refused; I have stretched out my hand, and no man regarded; But ye have set at nought all my counsel, and would none of my reproof: I also will laugh at your calamity; I will mock when your fear cometh; When your fear cometh as desolation, and your destruction cometh as a whirlwind; when distress and anguish cometh upon you.
>
> Then shall they call upon me, but I will not answer; they shall seek me early, but they shall not find me: For that they hated knowledge, and did not choose the fear of the LORD: They would none of my counsel: they despised all my reproof. Therefore shall they eat of the fruit of their own way, and be filled with their own devices. For the turning away of the simple shall slay them, and the prosperity of fools shall destroy them. (Prov. 1:22–32)

### God Is Not Sadistic

God is not a sadist or one who delights in seeing punishment inflicted. When God says, "I also will laugh at your calamity; I will mock when your fear cometh," He is seeking to arrest our attention to the potential magnitude and gravity of our stubbornness, waywardness, and disobedience. As human beings, we know what it is like to be mocked and derided when one is in a state of weakness and failure. Therefore, we understand how earnestly God wants us to abide by His biddings. So, He uses the imagery (ridicule and derision), which we know, as a means to help us to desist from doing wrong.

Such utter rejection by man of God's wooing and persuading leads to an impoverished, substandard state (not *quality*) of relational health. Elsewhere, God made a similar appeal through the Prophet Ezekiel:

> Therefore, O thou son of man, speak unto the house of Israel; Thus ye speak, saying, If our transgressions and our sins be upon us, and we pine away in them, how should we then live? Say unto them, As I live, saith the Lord GOD, I have no pleasure in the death of the wicked; but that the wicked turn from his way and live: turn ye, turn ye from your evil ways; for why will ye die, O house of Israel? (Ezek. 33:10–11)

God took it so seriously that He called the heavens to bear witness to the foolishness and unwarranted behavior of His children. "Be astonished, O ye heavens, at this, and be horribly afraid, be ye very desolate, saith the LORD" (Jer. 2:12). That was the way He introduced His comparison between His fountain and man's cisterns, and not mere cisterns, but *broken* cisterns.

Sounds similar to Jesus's expressed disappointment when Jerusalem rejected Him: "O Jerusalem, Jerusalem, which killest the prophets, and stonest them that are sent unto thee; how often would I have gathered thy children together, as a hen doth gather her brood under her wings, and ye would not!" (Matt. 23:37 and Luke 13:34). God is always appealing, trying to heal and restore the broken relationship between Him and His created beings. (See Paraphrases #14,40,41 and 46 applied to husband and wife in FRH *Songs of Praise and Bible Verses Paraphrase*).

## Cisterns of Philosophies and Theories

In a state of mockery, and to intensify his rejection of God's prescription for his relational healing, fallen man has improvised his own sources of water to keep his family. These are the cisterns of human philosophies, theories, hypotheses, and conjectures which are not in harmony with God's will for His people.

We must acknowledge that to a large extent, all knowledge comes from God. Paul alluded to this fact when he said, "In whom are hid all the treasures of wisdom and knowledge" (Col. 2:3). In the original sense of the word, whether the researchers, philosophers and propounders of the various schools of thought want to admit it or not, their mental and intellectual powers are the result of the unfathomable brain with which God endowed man at Creation. (See **Affirmation/Claim and Declaration** p. xxxiv).

Therefore, it should be understood that "He maketh his sun to rise on the evil and on the good, and sendeth rain on the just and on the unjust." God equally allows the "sun" and "rain" of intellect and knowledge and, by extension, professionalism and skills, to fall on all His children, without prejudice.

So many of their philosophical and scholarly theories and works are designed against God, as in the case of the Big Bang Theory, Theory of Evolution, the Eternal Inflation Theory, and the Oscillating Universe Theory, among others. But He does not retaliate with a strong arm against them but allows them time to run the course of their folly (2 Tim. 3:7–9), or even to change as they allow His light to shine into their minds.

It is important also for us to observe balance in our critique or criticism of some of these works that are not necessarily from those who acknowledge and give due credit to God for what they have produced. As long as their pronouncements and promulgations and treatment plans for family relational behaviors and issues do not violate God's standards of righteousness and can serve the purpose of education and relational care, they may be incorporated into the plan for improving family relational health.

On the negative and foolish end, we find feeble, imperfect, fallible man refusing to listen to his Creator, devising his own theories and treatment programs for his sin-devastated relational mind. Some of them will just not work and will be among the cisterns that hold no water. A prime example of such cisterns is the Humanistic Learning Theory in Education. It teaches in essence, that natural good is inherent in us human beings, and that all we need to do is to evoke such good by educational, psychological and sociological endeavours and there is therefore no need for any divine intervention. Psychologists Abraham Maslow (1908-1970), Carl Rogers (1902-1987) and James Bugental (1915-2008) are among some of the celebrated propounders of this theory, springing from the Greek through Latin eras on to our present day. In the end theirs will be a classic and specific application of the satirical proverb: "Physician, heal thyself!" (Luke 4:23). This just does not happen.

**Reason 2: Reliance on Home Remedy and Band-Aid Treatment**

To compound the intensity of his rejection of God's gracious and providential sources of healing and strengthening for family relationship, man moves to a lower stage of cistern construction. We refer to this effort as reliance upon home remedy or the Band-Aid treatment. You might hear, "I do not want anybody to tell me anything about my relationship" or "This is my life and my family, and I will run it in the way that I know best and as it pleases me to do."

This sounds very much like the person described as a fool in Luke 12:20: "But God said unto him, Thou fool, this night thy soul shall be required of thee: then whose shall those things be, which thou hast provided?" Earlier in Proverbs, Solomon offers this caution: "Seest thou a man wise in his own conceit? There is more hope of a fool than of him" (Prov. 26:12).

This reliance upon home remedy is considered even lower than the first because this family leader or member rejects the care that is offered by professionals (Christians or non-Christians), in addition to rejecting the counsels of God. As long as the treatment program does not violate God's principles of righteousness and can help with the relational challenges with which the family is faced, such treatment should be accepted and taken.

To the same extent that there are good non-Christian medical doctors and other professionals, so are there good non-Christian psychologists, family counselors, therapists, and social workers who can and do make meaningful contributions to family life, and their skills should not be rejected on the mere premise of religion or ideology (CPH[2]).

Let us put the concern about reliance on home remedy into a sharper perspective. It is not intended to create the impression that in every instance of a family relational challenge—whether of a marital, parental, or other nature—the parties involved should immediately seek professional counseling and therapy. There is a respectful provision made for self-help, as discussed in Chapter 3 under the DIY Principle: do it yourself (Review p. 73). That is not being discouraged here.

### *Importance of the Family Altar*

We must affirm, however, that the Christian family's first response to family relational challenges is earnest, individual, and family prayer. This is to be accompanied with equally earnest searching and study of God's Words for counsels, guidance, inspiration, and action. Let us also take caution not to treat God as we normally treat the fire department: we only tend to remember their services at times of crisis. The family altar should always be lit and burning bright. Family worship should be a daily staple in the menu of their relationship. Then, when any unusual challenge arises, building up the flames of the altar with more intense prayer, even family fasting, would be understood. (See Number 29 of FRH Songs of Praise and Bible Verses Paraphrase).

In family crisis management, God is always the First Responder; we must first and always take it to the Lord in prayer. In His divine wisdom and as a part of His answer to our prayer, He will direct us to the human support team that He will continue to supervise as they work on His behalf. This is where the paraphrasing of our Anchor Text comes in: "He will, with the relational challenges, also provide His approved human professional way to help, so that you may be able to manage and improve your relationships."

That is why, when the Christian is to see the medical practitioner for any major treatment program, we continue to place it into the hands of the Great Physician, the Balm in Gilead (Jer. 8:22). We go and follow all the instructions and directives of the earthly professional as Jesus instructed by implication in Matthew 9:12: "But when Jesus heard that, he said unto them, They that be whole need not a physician, but they that are sick." See also Mark 2:17; Luke 5:31.

### Professional Family Relational Treatment

It is the same approach we are to take when the matter of concern is a relational one. We should genuinely seek the Wonderful Counselor (Isa. 9:6) first, Who counsels through His servants: "Let nothing be done through strife or vainglory; but in lowliness of mind let each esteem other better than themselves. Look not every man on his own things, but every man also on the things of others. Let this mind be in you, which was also in Christ Jesus" (Phil. 2:2–5).

This is as wise and thorough a family relational counseling as one could get. And through Solomon, we get an endorsement to seek counseling/therapy as the need arises: "Where no counsel is, the people fall: but in the multitude of counsellors there is safety" (Prov. 11:14). See also chapter 15:22.

In apportioning the gifts for the administration of the affairs of the Church, which affairs would understandably include ministering to family relational matters, the Holy Spirit gave the gifts of wisdom and knowledge (1 Cor. 12:8). In Hebrews 5:14, we are told, "But strong meat belongeth to them that are of full age, even those who by reason of use have their senses exercised to discern both good and evil." *Full age* and *use of their senses* could be interpreted as alluding to maturity, experience, and even competence gained from training and preparation, long practice peer review and consultation.

This record is reminiscent of the preparation that God gave to Solomon at the beginning of his reign, and in answer to his prayer:

> And God said unto him, Because thou hast asked this thing, and hast not asked for thyself long life; neither hast asked riches for thyself, nor hast asked the life of thine enemies; but hast asked for thyself understanding to discern judgment; Behold, I have done according to thy words: lo, I have given thee a wise and an understanding heart; so that there was none like thee before thee, neither after thee shall any arise like unto thee. (1 Kgs. 3:11–12)

When all of the above and additional Biblical counsels are put together, we see clearly that God made ample provision and gave guidance and directives for the effective treatment of the relational challenges that He knew would assail families in the process of time.

Implied and understood in these injunctions from the Lord is the need for proper, professional preparation, given that the issues of life would become more complex and demanding, and the relationships that will be formed will become equally challenging and potentially exhausting. Undoubtedly, family relational health is a biblical, psycho-social priority—God's priority for His children.

### Potential Folly of Home Remedy and Band-Aid Efforts

With reference to the *home remedy* and *Band-Aid* approach to family relational health issues, let us express this caution: Continuous application of home remedy/first aid and, worse yet, Band-Aid treatment for relational illnesses in utter and calculated denial and defiance of professional care as mentioned above, is not only foolish but relationally suicidal. We have already acknowledged that there is room for these home-style efforts and treatments, but again—conditions applied.

Ignoring the amber light of relational issues will only be pushing oneself and one's family life and well-being through the red light. Inevitably, that will end up in an accident, crash, and woefully, untimely loss of life. "The way of a fool is right in his own eyes: but he that hearkeneth unto counsel is wise" (Prov. 12:15). "There is a way which seemeth right unto a man, but the end thereof are the ways of death" (Prov. 14:12 and 16:25).

### Descriptions of Home Remedy/First Aid/Band-Aid

There is a subtle danger in the use of home remedy/first aid or Band-Aid treatments for family relational challenges—or, as we have clinically labeled them, illnesses. On the surface, it could appear to be a non-issue, but it is more than meets the eye. Let us give the working definitions for each, then by use of another analogy and parallel between physiological and psychological health care, address the potential danger in them.

- **First aid**—This is immediate treatment or care or attention given in the case of an emergency when professional medical service is not immediately available. First aid is like an on-the-spot first responder and is therefore an acceptable stopgap with the understanding that its usage is temporary and should ideally not be repeated since it might not provide the clinical answer to the condition.

- **Band-Aid**—The Band-Aid was invented in 1920 by a Johnson & Johnson employee, Earle Dickson, in Highland Park, New Jersey for his wife, Josephine, who frequently cut and burned herself while cooking. The prototype allowed her to dress her wounds without assistance.

  Inasmuch as Band-Aid is a patented name, sometimes it is used loosely and even interchangeably with first-aid, in the same way that Xerox, although a patented name, has often been used simultaneously as copying. "I am going to Xerox this document in order to keep a copy before submitting the original to the office." So, the original use or concept of Band-Aid was that of taking care of oneself without assistance.

- **Home remedy**—This is a home-grown version of first aid. Whereas first aid, correctly understood, could and should have some formal knowledge and preparation into its packaging, preparation, and administering, home remedy is generally the result of trial and error in addressing a particular health challenge. It is a layperson's concoction, or at best, a thought and discovery that some hitherto unknown treatment works. Home remedy comes most times by well-intentioned family members or friends sharing what they have tried and what works for them. Sometimes, home remedy could be described as folklore remedy.

## *An Analogy of Physiological-Psychological Care*

In medical care, a family member cannot go to the pharmacy, order, and be sold any drug that he or she might have used before, heard about, or researched and learned is the treatment for a certain illness. Only an OTC can be purchased that way without a professional prescription. It would not only be unethical, but illegal for the pharmacist to conduct that sale. Equally so, if that family member were to find a way to obtain the drug and administer it to an ailing family member, he or she would be liable for prosecution, regardless of the result.

The ethical and clinical issue has to do with the diagnosis of the illness to be treated, the proportion, administering protocol, and all the other data and factors to be taken into consideration. That is why the dispensing pharmacist is ethically bound to ascertain evidence that a registered physician made the prescription before dispensing it. It should also be noted that before the medical doctor writes the prescription, there are at least two clinical protocols that he or she is ethically bound to follow:

1. Depending on the potency of the drug, the doctor must enquire about

   a. any drug or medication or treatment that the patient is on presently, or in the recent past;
   b. any allergy to, or known reaction to, certain chemicals or components in the drug to be prescribed;
   c. any food or lifestyle practice that could possibly adversely interact with, or could produce adverse reaction with the drug about to be prescribed.

2. Potential side-effects—The patient should be informed on any likely side effect(s) that the new drug could produce and how the patient should relate with such probability.

Even in the case of OTC medication, much care needs to be exercised in following the directions of use as provided by the manufacturers. Care must be taken not to adopt a home remedy spin and interpretation, and ultimately mix and concoct formulation on different medications, not knowing their chemical compositions and potential reactions and impact on the various organs of the body.

### Examples of First-Aid Relational Treatment

The treatment for family relational illnesses is not taken as seriously. Let us remind ourselves again that we are not addressing mental illness but relational health and, consequently, relational illness as defined in the Glossary (See p. 412). Relational challenges are not taken as seriously as physiological issues. When relationships begin to hurt, there seems to be total dependence on a combination of home remedy and first aid. Examples of first aid could be:

- "OK, just apologize to him and go back!"

- "Come on, hug and kiss each other. Tell each other that you love the other and you won't hurt each other again!"

- "Pray together and forgive each other."

As with the concern that was raised above about prescription, proportion, and the administering protocol in the case of medication for physiological illnesses, so often some family members make suggestions and give advice on relational issues that they had, or that they knew some other person had, but such recommendations do not serve the case in point. In many instances, they can even exacerbate and worsen the relationship.

- "I just told him that I did not care what he wanted to do, and I just walked away!"

- "When she comes back, do not make any apology, just be firm and let her decide what she wants to do. That was what I told mine last year, and see, it went exactly as I wanted it to!"

Many times, those who offer their "treatment" are not qualified to speak to the issue that is affecting the individual or family. They do not know the relational antecedents or anything much about the family dynamics. However, out of their sincere, good intention to help, as well as out of the exuberance of their ignorance, they make the relationship worse by offering their "tried and proven" home remedy. The combination of their home remedy and first aid treatment sometimes results in a glorified Band-Aid.

To make the situation worse, unlike the medical doctor, who had to be guided by ethical and clinical protocols in the administration of the drug and therefore remains accountable (to some extent) for the outcome of its usage, those who give relational health treatment cannot always be held responsible for any adverse outcome.

### Danger of Covering Up Relational Wounds

With reference to family relational treatment, *Band-Aid* really means a camouflage or a cover-up, hoping that the issues, pain, and wound would be carefully concealed as life goes on. Band-Aid treatment in relational health is not necessarily seen as first aid, because whereas first aid is applied with the hope that healing will take place, a Band-Aid is applied with an intent to conceal and move on.

- "Look at the fine gift that I have brought for you. Just forget what happened and let's move on!"

- "OK, whatever you want me to do, I will do even more, as long as you will just not mention what happened again."

- "Look, I think we are wasting time trying to talk about what is done and over. Let us forget and move on!"

When a figurative Band-Aid is applied to family relational issues, the intention is not to work through and resolve the challenges;

instead, the intention is to bury them alive. Let us remember, however, that unresolved issues buried alive *remain* alive in the subconscious and will eventually float back to the conscious and demand to be properly dealt with. Healing is not the goal as much as covering or glossing over or just plain hiding from the facts that need to be properly addressed.

## Solomon's Epilogue on Life's Relationships

After looking at the wide panorama of life and reviewing the escapades he had gone through, Solomon, under inspiration, wrote in the book of Ecclesiastes, what is regarded in many circles, both Christian and non-Christian, as the most profound, authoritative summary of lifestyle. Solomon's life was a real example of a conundrum, as he experienced the extremes of the ups and downs and ins and outs of risk-taking, exploratory, and audacious living.

At the end of that checkered, colorful life, God's original promise to Solomon prevailed. His wisdom outshone his foolish, disreputable life. Here is his epilogue on his adventures as he concluded his discourse on life, stated in his simplistic yet profound, characteristic manner: "Let us hear the conclusion of the whole matter: Fear God, and keep his commandments: for this is the whole duty of man. For God shall bring every work into judgment, with every secret thing, whether it be good, or whether it be evil." (Eccles.12:13–14).

Let us borrow from Solomon's wide experience and draw a conclusion on our discourse in this book. If we want healing from the relational issues, challenges, problems, and ultimately illnesses of life, we must go to the original source, the fountain that God has provided. All our efforts will continue to yield but little if we continue to reject the counsels, guidelines, admonitions, and directives from the One who made the relational mind.

We could interpret and accept God's loving upbraiding of His people through Haggai as applicable to us today as we seek to deal with our relational health challenges: "Ye have sown much, and bring in little; ye eat, but ye have not enough; ye drink, but ye are not filled with drink; ye clothe you, but there is none warm; and he that earneth wages earneth wages to put it into a bag with holes" (Hag. 1:6).

## Successful Relationships: Mission Possible

Here is the paraphrase of Solomon's conclusion in the context of family relational health: "Let us hear the final discussion on family relational health: reverence the God of Families and give due obedience to Him, for this is our complete responsibility and accountability to Him. Remember, all our human relationships will be judged by Him, inclusive of every secret and private one, whether they be healthy or unhealthy."

With that resolved consciousness of mind, let us revisit and conclude with our paraphrased Anchor Text: "Be assured that no relational challenges you face are unique to your family, but that all marital, parental, or other issues are common to families everywhere. The God of Families is faithful and will not leave your family to be hurt and suffer beyond that which you can endure. He will, with the relational challenges, also provide His approved human professional way to help, so that you may be able to manage and improve your relationships."

We reaffirm that God's biddings are His enablings. He says that good human relationships are possible because He has already put in place what we need to make it possible. Successful relationships are ours for the asking. "And it shall come to pass, that before they call, I will answer; and while they are yet speaking, I will hear" (Isa. 65:24). Inasmuch as that prophecy was primarily focused on the life in the new earth, the blessing is available today. That is why Jesus gave the assurance in Luke 11:9–10: "And I say unto you, Ask, and it shall be given you; seek, and ye shall find; knock, and it shall be opened unto you. For every one that asketh receiveth; and he that seeketh findeth; and to him that knocketh it shall be opened."

God's assurance of successful marriages, parenting, and other forms of human relationships are not the same as granting us immunity from the harsh realities of this sinful life. The foundation of the assurance is: "My grace is sufficient for thee" (2 Cor. 12:9) to keep you amidst all the vicissitudes and fluctuations of life.

The truth is that none of us has any sound basis to expect protection against and exception from the challenges and problems of life, given the fact that each of us has made our 'contribution' to the sinful records of nature. All have sinned (Rom. 3:23). But the same Paul later echoes this conviction despite our exposure to these harsh realities: "… in all these things we are more than conquerors through him that loved us" (Rom. 8:37).

One aspect of the power of choice with which God has endowed us is the responsibility to choose to do good, and to always keep our eyes fixed on that ideal. "Let us therefore, as many as be perfect, be thus minded: and if in anything ye be otherwise minded, God shall reveal even this unto you" (Phil. 3:15). We cannot experience optimum family relational health if we do not consciously, conscientiously, and consistently keep our eyes on Jesus, the Author and Finisher of our faith (Heb. 12:2). This requires discipline, self-control, and honesty on our part. (Read again the 3 C's on p. 157).

## Seven Steps Toward Relational Healing

As with healing for damaged tissues of the body, which can take a considerable amount of time depending on the intensity and complexity of the damage, so does the healing of relational impairment take time, depending also on the nature and severity of the situation (CPR²). The relational mind has to be channeled and focused in order to experience good, quality relationships at home, in the Church, at school, at the workplace, and in society.

There are recommended Seven Steps that each family member needs to take as he or she strives toward the mastery of relationships in Christ, and thereby to experience healing and restoration where there might have been damage in the relationship. Note the repetitive and apparently overlapping element in each step, simply because they are not disjointed. Each one grows into the other and progressively strengthens the resolve of the mind.

Consider committing yourself and being prepared and willing to do the following:

1.  **Acknowledge your lack of the needed relational skills**. This means to be honest with yourself. Be humble and face the reality that "I do not know everything, and there is stark evidence that I need to be more knowledgeable." Your mind will then go in a desirable searching mode to find the answer.

2.  **Admit and expose your ignorance** in order to improve. This means that you are willing to simply say "I do not know" or "I do not understand" or "I would like to know or understand." An old proverb says, "The humblest calf sucks the most milk." One unhealthy fact of life is that it is hard to be humble. Let your mind become healthily penetrable.

3.  **Be specific** about the hows, whens, whys, and whats of relational skills that you have not mastered at this time. Avoid glossing over the facts. Be pointed and specific as to our area of ignorance: "I am not sure when to …" or "So how do I …?" or "Why doesn't it work when I …?" or "What is the best way to …?" Be vulnerable when vulnerability is needed. Your

mind becomes teachable. (Review the teachable markers, p. 200).

4. **Display a genuine desire to acquire the necessary relational skills**. This means that you are not to pretend. Learning is best done in a childlike state of mind. Be simply sweet and show keen interest in learning. "The truth is that I do not know it and I really want to learn and understand" or "I have a genuine, open mind to learn!" Consider the positive learning attitude of the mind in the fourth stanza of "Live Out Thy Life Within Me" (Hymn #316 of SDA Hymnal, adventisthymns.com): "But restful, calm and pliant from bend and bias free, awaiting thy decision when thou has need of me; Live out thy life within me, O Jesus king of kings, be thou the glorious answer to all my questionings." Your mind becomes unguardedly, positively open after questionings.

5. **Make the necessary adjustments** and practice the necessary new relational skills in order to improve the relationship. This means that your adjustment will not be expressed as, "OK, since that is how it is to be done, well, let me do it!" or "There it is. I have adjusted now. Hope that makes you happy."

Instead, you are the first to be happy with yourself that you have made the needed adjustment. "OK, I have really done it, and I can see why it was necessary" or "OK, I am happy that I could make this adjustment, and I know they will be so happy too. We will all be better." Your mind becomes actively and positively engaged.

6. **Be patient** with yourself and other(s) in practicing the needed and necessary relational skills. This means that you know that it will take time for you to reach your expected or desirable level of relationship. It takes time to change and

grow progressively. The relational mind does not change like the flick of a light switch. Some changes take time.

Avoid such attitudes as "OK, I do not know how long I can keep trying to improve on this matter. Do I really need to go through all this!?" or "You say that you are trying; is this all you can do? Are you sure that you are not just wasting time?" Instead, acknowledge every step, however small, as a stepping-stone: "Well, at least I was able to do that. Amen! Next time I am going to ..." or "I saw the effort that you made and wish that more could be accomplished. Do not give up! Every little effort makes the way for another one!" Your mind becomes progressive, even with 'baby steps'.

Let us be clear: This counsel is not supporting procrastination and those who are inclined to joke around and drag their feet in making changes to their behavior. Such attitudes are to be discouraged and stopped. It can be very disconcerting and discouraging when a family member makes light of important adjustments and changes to be made. Those who are so inclined need additional professional help to assess their temperaments and discover the causes for any such nonchalant, laid-back, procrastinating, or similar attitudes to making healthy adjustments in good time.

7. **Learn and use affirmation, encouragement, and challenge as motivation for continuation and improvement of the relationship.** This means that for every time that an accomplishment or an improvement, however small, is made, you are to acknowledge it. Do not take it for-granted. Say "Good, I am so happy that I did that!" or "I notice that you did it better this time. That is good. Keep it up!" or "I can see that you are making an effort to do better. I know you will be able to. Keep it up!" Remember, encouragement sweetens labor. The mind will sense and go into development mode.

The above Seven Steps can be best taken *after completing* the necessary analysis of the relational dynamics. Such analyses and evaluations of the relationship will be done as each individual of the family team cooperates with the professional help toward which God directs them, and their continued, total reliance upon the inspiration the Holy Spirit. Family relational health is definitely a biblical, psycho-social priority, and the God of Families has made all the provisions for its full and complete realization.

## Suggestions for Action

1.  Ensure that your family altar is burning bright daily. Remember that your personal prayer life sets and influences the quality of your family and group worship together.

2.  Heed the early signs of family relational illness. After you have sincerely tried to address the challenge, if it is not improving, seek professional help.

3.  Be careful about giving suggestions to others about how to treat their relational issues—and also, watch what suggestions you take from others. Not every home remedy works exactly the same for everyone, even with the same condition.

4.  Do not pretend that issues are solved and settled if they are not. Remember that unresolved issues buried alive remain alive down there in the subconscious mind and will likely pop back up at some time when we least expect it to happen.

5.  Practice and apply the **Seven Steps Towards Relational Healing** and share them with others.

# Epilogue

# Respitals—Treating Relationships the Healthy Way

And they built *Respitals* across the land,
They believed both healths should go hand in hand:
Health for the body, health for the mind,
None, they believed, should be left behind.
They all agreed on hospitals and *Respitals,* too,
Health for the body and health for the mind.
They lived in a balanced healthy land!

This sounds like a utopia. Here is portrayed a dreamland where equal attention is paid to both major aspects of health: hospitals for physiological health and *Respitals* for psychological and, more specifically, family relational health.

*Respital*? What is that? Large governmental, private-sector, and philanthropic organizations and agencies have invested billions of dollars in sociological, anthropological, and philosophical research and projects aimed at addressing the alarming state of moral decadence, virtual mayhem from crime and violence, social dislocation, and destabilization in mainstream society worldwide. Unfortunately, too many of these investments have not yielded the desired or expected returns. The continuous decline in family relational health is rife.

One factor that has caused diminishing returns and ultimate loss on these investments is seemingly evading the evaluation of these meaningful projects. At the same time this factor is subtly and viciously eating away at the human and economic capital and destroying the quality of life in the home, workplace, and society at large. This all-time evasive factor is poor human and family relational health.

## Potential Clients for FRH Respital Care

There are countless hurting, distraught and traumatized persons of every demographic grouping—ethnic, race, nationality and other backgrounds, world-wide. They are victims of natural and man-made disasters, crimes and other human and family relational illnesses. Some have been exposed to, or have experienced wars, ethnic cleansing, human trafficking and a host of such ills, resulting in a plethora of conditions and disorders that did not begin in the truest, clinical diagnostic category of mental illness. Review the differentiation of mental and relational illnesses from p. 230–233.

Among these hurting and distraught persons are ex-members of the military, navy, army, constabulary, security and other high-risk professions. Many of them are experiencing post-traumatic stress disorder (PTSD) and related psychosomatic conditions that in some cases, mutated from the relational illness mentioned above.

It is a fact that by virtue of the nature of some of their jobs and other exposures, the chemistry of their brain and glandular functions would have been impaired. Added to that is the fact that their family relational health had been severely affected and disrupted, making their recovery from the trauma to which they have been exposed even more challenging and difficult. Sadly, many of them are not professionally treated and rehabilitated into an acceptable state of family relational health.

With such lack of the needed care and treatment, some continue to pose an unprecedented threat to their own well-being and that of those around them, after they would have been correctly diagnosed with mental illnesses of varying degrees from mild to debilitating.

The Respital, which could also be described as the Family Relational Health and Restoration Centre (FamRest), is conceived as a rural not-for-profit grant-supported state-of-the-art world-class villa-resort, environmentally friendly complex, fully equipped and professionally staffed with local and international experts. The resort and institution is to provide curative, corrective, restorative, affirming, and preventive services needed by family groups and individuals towards returning to help building and maintaining a relationally healthy society.

The Respital is to provide a customized, blended range of services for psychosocial (non-medical/physiological, non-psychiatric) care and treatment, inclusive of assessment, diagnostic, evaluative, counseling, and therapy; human and relational education; enrichment; wholesome and morally sound fun and recreation; and healthy and delectable cuisines for local, regional, and international patrons and clients such as:

- referrals from family relational health caregivers, including counselors, psychologists, therapists, pastors, social workers, chaplains, and physicians

- surviving family members from traumatic experiences such as murders, disasters, and accidents

- traumatized ex-members of the army, military, navy, police, security companies, and other high-risk employments

- parents and students of the clinical category *troubled child*, as referred from schools and social care-based institutions

- retirees and ex-workers seeking a caring, therapeutic experience

- patrons from tour operators, travel agencies, and convention planners who embrace the Respital values

- married/estranged husbands and wives for strengthening, healing, and restoring relationships;

- companies' HR staff development toward healthy work relationship

The tag-line for Family Relational Health is "Treating relationships the healthy way." That "healthy way" will be realized when some of the billions of dirhams, dollars, euros, francs, niras, pounds, rands, rubles, shillings, yens, yuans, etc that are invested into scientific and medical research and the development of state-of-the-art facilities correctly providing physiological healthcare for the body, are equally invested into projects like the Family Relational Health Respitals. Such investments will bring balance and attention to the critical aspect of family relational healthcare for which the society is in dire need. (CPH2) (See pp. 13, 472)

Then and only then will society be able to 'live happily ever after', because body and mind will be harmonized and balanced. That will happen when, as a society, we go about treating relationships the healthy way, thereby removing the socially stigmatized and taboo attitude from family relational issues and challenges.

The comprehensive Draft Proposal for the establishment of the world's first Respital in the context of Family Relational Health is completed and will be the subject of another publication in the family relational health series. (See list in the end of this book).

The Reader who is convinced about the principles of family relational health as presented in this volume, and who can envision the establishment of the world's first Respital, and who is therefore desirous of getting more information on its proposal, may send an enquiry and expressed interest to heartbonding@gmail.com.

# Glossary

*Limitation and disclaimer:* In keeping with "What This Book *Is Not* and What *It Is*," as stated in the Preface, the definitions and explanations below are originally written in the context of family relational health and arriving out of work in the family relational health laboratory, and are therefore limited to their usage in this book. We do not claim to give other clinical, medical, psychiatric, social, or other analyses and details for the pursuit of academic or other studies outside of family relational health as presented herein.

These definitions are specifically referred to as *working definitions* because they are expressed in this unique context to harmonize with the posture of this work, while maintaining, as close as possible, similarities with their wider usage in general contexts.

**active, sound mind:** The normal, healthy, coordinated processing and functional relationship between the brain and the senses (see differentiation between both in this Glossary) where both are free from any known incapacitating conditions physically, physiologically, hormonally, chemically, neurologically, or otherwise.

**active mind:** An active mind is not necessarily a sound mind. A mentally ill, mentally deranged person, a senile person, and one who suffers from degenerative brain disorders (dementia or Alzheimers, for example), in most cases is still able to experience and demonstrate some amount of physiological and neurological sensitivity. Such persons, depending on the intensity or the advanced stage of the condition, can, at most times, be aware of their state of hunger, thirst, tiredness, other needs, and even some amount of security and environmental issues.

However, such persons might not be able to subscribe to or keep a relationship as ideally as would be desirable and acceptable. Their recognition of, identity with, and acceptance of their relationship with spouses, children, relatives, friends, or coworkers can be compromised because the prefrontal cortex, amygdala, and hippocampus, among others, are impaired. So although the senses are picking up the stimuli/sensations, the processing in the brain is not going as normal hence the mind (composite working of the brain and senses) will not be as sound as is necessary.

One distressing experience of family members whose relatives suffer from any of the illnesses mentioned above are those times when the suffering one asks questions such as: "Who are you?" or "Who says that you are my husband (or wife, son, mother)?" or "I do not know you." Clearly, there is some amount of activity going on in the brain/mind (see differentiation between *brain* and *mind* in this Glossary), but it is devoid of soundness as stated above. Memory has been affected because the coordination between the frontal lobe (the seat of relationship) and the temporal lobe (the memory bank) is impaired.

This double description (active, sound mind) is therefore like an intensifier in English grammar: "That deed was very good." The deed was already evaluated or appraised as being good, but the good was emphasized and intensified as *very*. It is further understood that a sound mind cannot be inactive; it is engaged manifestly or not. That mind, being a functionality of the brain, is always doing some amount of processing or some interplay, directly or indirectly, consciously or subconsciously.

**sound mind:** This description means that there is total and complete functionality of the relational aspect of the frontal lobe in coordination with the parietal, occipital, and temporal lobes. The cognitive, affective, and psychomotor characteristics are demonstrably intact. The person with a *sound* mind is able to rationally decide for or against a relationship, depending on his or her own expectations and desirable qualities, criteria, or standards.

The sound mind is able to judge, appraise, evaluate, calculate, critique, analyze, rationalize, and exercise all other such means of measuring, gauging, and reaching a conclusion. "For God hath not given us the spirit of fear; but of power, and of love, and of a sound mind" (2 Timothy 1:7). Fear is indicative of an active mind that might sense some amount of security or safety issue but lacks soundness in processing and will therefore resort to a *reaction* instead of a *response* (see differentiation between these two Rs pp. 411 & 414).

**conditionally sound mind:** As stated in **Mental Illness – A General Biblical Description**, p. 230, as a result of the combination of the results of sin, different life-styles, unhealthy relational dynamics, and the state of our physiological health, no human being can be considered to have a totally sound mind as described above, at all times. While we will not suggest an outline of the various degrees or stages of soundness of mind, we will suggest that at most times, for the best of us, we are conditionally sound in mind.

This could be considered as a case of slippage in consistency of soundness, which slippage is experienced by the person as a result of lapse in one or more of the parameters or characteristics of the sound mind such as the ability to judge, critique, analyse and rationalize—mentioned above.

The lapse could be precipitated by ignorance and a lack in certain relational skills at the time when they are needed to be used. Continuous failure to acquire, maintain and properly utilize such skills and thereby reduce the instances of such slippages, could set the pace for deterioration of the person' rationality and his or her continued fall into a state of unsoundness of mind.

Derangement, idiocity, (idocity/stupidness), and lunacy are advance stages of the unsound mind, the care and treatment of which are outside of the purview of family relational health, and therefore are not addressed in the context of family relational illness. Conditions like those and their variations fall under the care and treatment of psychiatrists and other mental health clinicians.

\* \* \*

**altitude:** The high, desirable quality of the relationship to be achieved as a combination of one's relational aptitude and attitude. "How high on a scale of 1–10 do you rate the quality of your relationship?" Review the aeroplane flight analogy on p. 203.

**aptitude:** The manifested or latent evidence of one's ability, capability, and teachableness to do, learn, or acquire relational knowledge and skills.

**attitude:** The manifested or demonstrated reflection of a person's character; the *who* he or she is by nature, vices, or virtues in any aspect of any relationship. It is the manifested behaviour reflecting the state or process of mind.

**attributes:** The qualities, assets, traits, or characteristics of a person that he or she brings as contribution into a relationship. Attributes are what you have to contribute or offer toward a goal and they can be dynamic and developmental.

**bond:** One of the four vital signs of family relational health anchored in the affective domain of the mind. It produces the sense of emotional affinity, tie, kinship, intimacy, familiarity, and relatedness between persons. It is considered as the glue or adhesive that holds family and other group members together regardless of the challenges they might encounter.

**brain:** The major section of the central nervous system encased in the cranium or skull with the two main human existential functionalities:

- *physiological*—the management and regulation of the major functions of the organs (including the sense organs), glands, and various systems of the body.

- *psychological*—the processing, interpretation, management, and regulation of the raw data gathered/produced by the senses from the external environment of the cranium. As indicated in the parentheses above, the brain not only receives the messages from the senses, it also modifies and reshapes the same senses as they interact with the world on its behalf.

**connection:** One of the four vital signs of family relational health anchored in the cognitive domain of the mind. It produces the sense of acknowledgement, recognition, acceptance, and the sense of belonging between persons. (NB: Relational *connection* can be acknowledged but may be devoid of *bond*, which is anchored in the affective domain.)

**conscience:** This is the radar of the active, sound mind. It keeps track of the movements of relationships in the mind to ensure that one stays on course. It gives off a certain signal if one is veering off the "relational" path (See MPS p. 408). That signal may vary in intensity and can at times come as guilt, remorse, shame, regret, and contrition. The conscience is that aspect of the mind that helps us to keep integrity, scruples, principles, and morality intact. The most condemnatory state for one's conscience is for it to be psychosocially seared or scorched, hence one becomes irresponsive to established principles of right or wrong, good or bad, healthy or unhealthy.

**(CPH²):** A code used to denote a statement of the double comparison of physiological and psychological health, which comparison is one of the seven foundation pillars of family relational health. The statement of comparison usually begins with the phrase *to the same extent that.* This is one of the underpinning premises of family relational health to bring balance to the value that society places on physiological/medical healthcare and psychological health care inclusive of family relational health care.

**CPRI:** This acronym stands for Creator's procreative relationship initiative or Creator's personalized relationship initiative and refers to the first intimate relational act of God in breathing into the nostrils of Adam and Eve and bringing them to life (Gen. 2:7). A precursor to human CPR (cardiopulmonary resuscitation), the difference being that mouth-to-mouth in CPR as performed by the human to help in stabilizing or restoring fleeting life of a seriously ill person while CPRI was carried out by God at Creation to give life.

**developing:** Manifested ongoing evidence of development; non-stagnating; evidently or visibly taking place or happening gradually on an upward trajectory; opposite of deteriorating.

**developmental:** Established, acceptable, and desirable process of movement or graduated order; an adverb of manner suggesting motion or movement in a positive, healthy, desirable and acceptable way.

**disorder:** An advanced, even to an incurable state, impairment of health functionality (illness) that was not professionally diagnosed and treated; or, an impairment of health functionality either congenital or acquired incidentally or developmentally and for which no corrective or curative clinical or medical treatment protocol is known. *Disorder* can refer to any behavior or activity (in whichever form it comes) that is not according to the established, acceptable, or ideal order (norm) where the individual who has and demonstrates it exists and operates, in which case it would be considered a social or behavioural disorder.

**developmental notifiers of health attributes (DNHA):** The established, acceptable, and desirable basic evidences or manifestations of normal, healthy physiological development from conception through to young adulthood, such as are observed, measured, evaluated and recorded, beginning at the antenatal through postnatal clinics and to school life. This is a complementary physiological subset of the DNRA.

**developmental notifiers of relational aptitude (DNRA):** the study of the dynamic impact of the psychosocial impressions of human relationships which are continuously and imperceptively gathered and accumulated in a person's mind, beginning from conception in one's family of origin and progressively incorporating all other environmental exposures and experiences throughout the developmental years to young adulthood (approximately 25–30). They are manifested in various combinations of actions, conduct, demeanor, bearing, and deportment.

The DNRA are the skills, competences, proficiencies, and knacks formed in part from the family of origin in the frontal lobe of the brain (the primary seat of relationship).and is a major antecedent (subject to sociological and environmental factors) to the kind of relationship that one can forge and keep through the lifespan.

**developing notifiers of relationship potential (DNRP):** The sustained manifested and demonstrated evidence of the effects and results of the coordinated established, acceptable, desirable DNRA and DNHA predicating the quality of relationship that might be forged and kept, maintaining the same trend and pattern or the relational health trajectory.

**emotion:** A physio-psychological experience resulting from the chemical and electrical interactions in different cells of the brain as a result of the stimulus produced in them by the complex messages received from the senses.

From its Latin etymology, where *e* = "out" and *movere* = "to move," an emotion is literally the *out-movement* or *motions* of the interaction or charges of the electrical and chemical properties in various cells of the brain, which interactions or charges are stimulated by the different messages received from the optical, auditory, glossopharyngeal, and olfactory nerves and the spinal cord. Those out-movements or out-motions are manifested in a further complexity of perceptions and feelings, resulting in responses or reactions in the person, expressed in different actions or words. (See the differentiation between *response* and *reaction* in this Glossary pp. 411 & 414).

**family:** The original, biological, historical, and biblical basic communal unit of human society, beginning with the marriage of the male and female as husband and wife (Gen. 2:24), and expanding with said husband and wife becoming parents as father and mother, having produced another or others of their kind: offsprings child(ren) as son(s)/daughter(s).

This grouping is sociologically referred to as the *nuclear family* (see *household* p. 404). The generic use of the term *family* goes beyond the biological, bloodline perspective and incorporates the theological, which is also called the ecclesiastical (Matt. 12:46–50), anthropological, sociological, psychological, analytical definitions, concepts, and perspectives based on the composition and operations of the group (See p. 465).

**family relational health:** The quality of the intra- and interpersonal relationship that exists in the active, sound mind of an individual indicated by the strength, intensity, trend, and patterns of the four psychological vital signs of connection (be it firm or fragile), rapport (be it mutual or selfish), bond (be it positive or negative), and support (be it conditional or unconditional) that affects and influences the individual's overall existence.

The quality of those vital signs are manifested in his or her thoughts, words, perceptions, actions, and general worldview on a daily basis, at home between husband and wife, father and mother, parents and child/children, siblings and relatives, providing an index to that which could be demonstrated at school, church, the workplace, and in society at large.

**family-of-origin impact (FOOI):** The key psychosocial data and information from one's biological family and/or household members (parents, siblings, relatives, etc.) influencing the formation of one's DNRA.

**general educational and developmental malaise (GEDM):** A low-keyed apparent lack of interest in, and nonchalant attitude toward, the pursuit of educational and personal development seen among many young men who did not do well at the secondary level of schooling. GEDM is a nonmotivational spirit of "whatever" comes; a resignation to the unskilled labor force, and in most cases, a lack of intention to establish a family. One major reason for this malaise among those young males is a weak and faulty upbringing which, in most cases, can be traced back to their family of origin and very likely the absence of a positive, healthy father image in their childhood. Faulty socialization is the overarching factor that needs to be addressed.

**health:** The overall, combined, and interrelated condition of one's physiological (referring to the state and functions of the body) and psychological (referring to the state and functions of the active, sound mind) state of existence. This is in harmony with the World Health Organization's definition of health as "a state of complete physical, mental, and social well-being and not merely the absence of disease or infirmity."

**household:** The communal unit of any combination of persons sharing one house as home, ideally but not necessarily beginning as a family (as defined on p. 402), but definitely headed by one who is accorded or one who assumes leadership by virtue of his or her seniority, maturity, and experience (Revisit p. 313). The household can be an expansion of the family to include relatives such as cousins, in-laws, and others, and is therefore sometimes used interchangeably with its predecessor, *family*.

**idiosyncratic inhibition (II):** A somewhat secret fear that a person has, but one that does not necessarily have any negative or traumatic antecedents; a kind of personal temperament-based social withdrawal syndrome that does not necessarily have a rational supportive basis, but which the person holds and believes in and 'healthily' enjoys, and which might not pose any threat to those in his or her sphere of influence.

**internal family attention deficit disorder (IFADD):** Whereas ADHD and similar mental health disorders, primarily have genetic, biological and chemical origins and are clinically the result of a combination of impairment or malfunctionality of the brain (such as chairi malformation), some glands, organs and the central nervous system, *IFADD* is primarily a psycho-socially acquired behavioural impairment of family relationship.

This relational disorder is due to the unfulfilled predisposed needs, (established from conception) for healthy interaction when there is a balanced combination of the *five*

*A's* for internal family identity and stability: admiration, affection, appreciation, attention and affirmation. The combination of these *five A's* in turn are to enhance the building and stabilization of the four family relational vital signs: connection, rapport, bond and support.

Deprivation of the above combined experiences can lead to emotional disconnection, estrangement and ostracism from those in one's immediate sphere of influence. Continuous registration of such negative encounters in the brain, as picked up by the senses, reduces the production of the feel-good/happy hormones/chemicals such as dopamine, endorphin, oxytocin and serotonin, the absence of which could be considered as a secondary or psycho-socially and developmentally induced chemical imbalance resulting in, and influencing the lack of family relational identity, low self-esteem and a poor sense of self-construal.

When these healthy, emotionally-based states of mind are not present, they further result in relational reactions and the triggering of the defence mechanisms against the sensed deprivation. The resultant fight impulse then stimulates undue level of adrenaline and cortisol which, when interacted with testosterone (already high in males) can be manifested in relational confrontation, calculated attention-drawing hyperactivity, callousness and family relational dysfunction.

**illness:** A temporary impairment of health functionality, physiologically or psychologically (inclusive of relationally), with the potential or prospect of repair and restoration, depending on the correct diagnosis and treatment; or it can be prolonged, even beyond being able to respond to treatment, in which case it could become a disorder. (See *relational illness* pp. 410 & 412, with a differentiation between itself and *mental illness*.)

**impulsive corrective disorder (ICD):** An inordinate, pedantic sense of self-importance and exaltation characterized by the affected one always seeing and pointing out the faults, errors, and weakness in others; an attitude of correcting, modifying, and offering one's own spin on what was already clearly stated, even to repeating and claiming the already established point without offering credit to the originator of the thought or idea.

ICD could be the result of self-esteem and confidence deficiency from one's family of origin or from the experience of being in an overpowering socialization where there might have been a lack of affirmation and encouragement, resulting in the fight-back mentality to be seen and heard.

On a possible opposite side, ICD could stem from an experience of growing up in an environment where one was unduly exalted and placed on a socio-emotional pedestal, thereby developing a sense of indispensability and self-importance, and a feeling that one must always be consulted for input or to make one's voice heard. (See TRI p. 417)

**laboratory (family):** *Biological*—The family relational health laboratory is a testing and research facility called home in which one hones his or her intra- and interpersonal skills in the dynamics of family relationships in preparation to making a meaningful contribution to the quality of life in the society. From there with the necessary consent and support of the team members (fellow researchers and practitioners i.e. family members), an individual can make an experiential proclamation as to the discoveries made and affirmed. Among such main discoveries will be what works and what does not work in a relationship; even with specific reference to possible hows, what's, when's, where's and why's of family relationships. All these are to be supported by external studies (literature, anecdotes and narratives) with similar and different family dynamics and perspectives.

*General:* The familial unit at home, or the social, collegial, transactional, ecclesiastical (Church), or other grouping(s) (Review family p. 402) to which one belongs, and in which one sincerely, purposefully, and consciously studies, embraces, practices, models, observes, appraises, evaluates, tests, analyses, and contributes to the guidelines, principles, values, beliefs, ethics, disciplines, standards, norms, patterns, qualities, behaviors, directives, and all other parameters of healthy relationship. From those combinations of activities, one can experientially attest to the findings, impact, and influence on him or her.

**letusism:** A family relational health philosophy characterized and demonstrated by reciprocal mutuality, and is the expressed verbalization of oneness in any relationship, beginning with the marriage of the husband and wife. It is the epitome of healthy teamship and is agreeably summarised in the principle of one-for-all-and-all-for-one. Letusism is anchored in the supreme example of the work of the Godhead (Father, Son and Holy Spirit) as manifested in the Creation, Salvation and Redemption of man. Letusism does not dispense with one's individuality but abhors the practice of individualism.

**mental health:** Whereas *health* in summary is the overall combined and interrelated condition of one's physiological and psychological state of existence, the mental aspect of that existence is specifically the overall, combined, balanced functions of the brain in coordination with the senses (together constituting the mind), where the brain and the senses are free from any known seriously incapacitating conditions physically, physiologically, hormonally, chemically, neurologically, or otherwise. That working combination is manifested in a generally acceptable, positive perception, action, and worldview on a daily basis in the mutual interest of the individual and those within his or her sphere of influence.

As defined by the World Health Organization (March 2018): "Mental health is a state of well-being in which an individual realizes his or her own abilities, can cope with the normal stresses of life, can work productively and is able to make a contribution to his or her community." (See Addendum to the Glossary - 1, p. 420) "Mental Health on Tokyo Olympic Stage"

**mental illnesses and disorders:** A possible combination of physiological, chemical, and hormonal malfunctionality of the brain resulting in imbalances in the different aspects of the glandular and organic systems of the body. Manifestations of such malfunctionality result in clinically diagnosed conditions such as schizophrenia, paranoia, bipolar disorder, hypervigilance, dementia, depression, ADHD, GAD, and over two hundred others covered in the *Diagnostic and Statistical Manual of Mental Disorders (DSM-5).*

**mind:** The composite working and functioning of the brain in coordination with its avenues or connections to the outside (of the cranium/skull) world—the *senses*—resulting in a complexity of emotions manifested in thoughts, perceptions, imaginations, and actions, affecting the quality of one's total existence and that of those in his or her sphere of influence in an equally complex variety of ways. One collective name for the processed output of thoughts, perceptions, imaginations, etc. is *emotions* (See definition for *emotion* Glossary p. 402).

**mind position system (MPS):** An analogical parallel of the conscience with the GPS- Global Positioning System. Whereas the GPS is fed by different satellites/radars, **MPS** is fed by many spiritual, emotional and social 'radars' – sensitivities, scruples, standards, norms, etc. which in turn are registered into the conscience for action to be taken (See Conscience, pp. 293 & 399).

**negative emotional reflective fixation syndrome (NERFS):** An inordinate, helpless feeling of being stuck or trapped in an experience of the past; a feeling of being condemned, and the consequential need to be punished for misdemeanors or sins of the past. The feeling is produced by continuous fixed gazing on the past failure(s) instead of looking ahead of the wrong and healthily committing not to return.

**notifiers:** Signs, signals, indicators, cues, or hints of what is taking place. A *notifier* is a simple yet complex combination of verbal and nonverbal responses or reactions (pp. 411 & 414) produced in the relational mind from the impressions of relationships gathered by the senses from one's social and physical environment. When properly monitored, observed, and evaluated, notifiers can provide a cue or indication of the quality of relationship that such a person will be able to forge and keep. These are tell-tale signs of what relational perspectives are being formed in the mind—the major observational factor of one's DNRA (See Chapter 8).

**physical health:** The evident/visible state of the body from what is immediately seen, heard, or felt of by the individual. Views or opinions on one's physical health tend to be limited to the physique or physical appearance but cannot be relied upon without factoring in the physiological.

**physiological health:** The overall state and function of the body—physically, anatomically, hormonally, chemically, and neurologically—and all the substructures of each having to do with the physical and functional aspect of the person.

**potential** (noun): possibility; that which is evidently likely; that which can be reasonably expected of a person; known or assumed attributes/abilities.

**psychological:** The functional aspect of the brain having to do with the processing of data received from the external environment of the cranium or skull via the senses (See definition of *senses* Glossary p. 415). The processed data becomes the information and knowledge which influence the behaviors and activities of life. Psychology is the umbrella aspect of the function of the brain that covers such features as mental, emotional, spiritual, social, relational, behavioral (and any other) which are the features of our being.

Due to our being "fearfully and wonderfully made" (Ps. 139:14) and therefore mysteriously by God, Who Himself is mysterious and cannot be fathomed (Job 11:7), the intricate functionality and dichotomy of the brain cannot be fully understood. This work therefore simplifies its functions as *physiological* and *psychological* as succinctly defined elsewhere in this Glossary, and as presented through the various discourses in the chapters.

**psychological health:** The overall combined state and function of the mind—spiritually, mentally, emotionally, socially, and relationally—having to do with the immediately nonphysiological functional aspect of the person (but not excluding it), more so in relation to him or herself (intrapersonal) and others in his or her sphere of influence (interpersonal).

**psychosomatic health:** The impact (negative or positive) of the active sound, mind on the body, hence the mind is referred to as the engine of our being, thus the equation body + mind = being, succinctly referred to by David in Psalm 139:14. Psychosomatic health could be seen as the potential superimposition of the psychological health over the physiological. A critical factor of psychosomatic health is the intricately woven and often less-observed *relational* aspect of a person's life, hence the position of this work to place family relational health on its own platform for study and appreciation. (See the companion book *Family Relational Health, A Missing Dimension in Comprehensive Health Care*). Review also the brief discussion on Takotsubo cardiomyopathy or broken-heart syndrome in Chapter 5 p. 97.

**rapport:** One of the four vital signs of family relational health anchored in the cognitive and affective domains of the mind. It produces the sense of reciprocal communication between family members for mutual benefit. This vital sign reflects the combined action of the intelligence (cognitive) and the affective (feeling) in the way that verbalization or relational expressions are made. (NB. *Connection* can be acknowledged but devoid of *healthy rapport*.)

**reaction** (noun; *react*, verb): The impulsive or defensive retort, snap, or 'bite-back' that is made to a comment or an action that does not go in sync with one's expectation, idea or perspective on an issue; a sharp, uncalculated counterattack intended to squelch or crush and dispose of that which is considered as opposing. An instinctive defence state of mind in the face of perceived opposition.

**reactive emotional acceleration rate and speed *(REARS)*:** In the context of family relational health and primarily with reference to unhealthy or questionable relationships, *REARS* is the rate and speed between which a person hears, sees or feels an attack coming from another towards him or her, and where he or she perceives, believes, thinks or knows that he or she needs to act, verbally, physically or both, in defence or protection against the other.

In *REARS,* three significant elements to take into consideration are 1. The Rate – this is the 'distance' covered between two opposing states of mind in a given period, example - from love to hatred; from admiration to detestation;

2. Acceleration - This is the intensity of the mental energy summoned and used for the execution of the decided action; 3. The Speed or (Perceptual Speed) refers to the length of time taken to execute a decided action. *REARS* can be seen as a type of bipolaric behaviour given the rapidity of the combination of the three factors, without notice.

Those three elements of the reactive emotion are influenced or determined by at least six factors: 1. The quality of the relationship between the parties involved; 2. Pre-existing conditions such as unresolved issues; 3. The premium that he or she places on the relationship especially with futuristic thinking. This thinking could be further influenced by one of two factors – where there is a genuine love for the other, or where there is a dependence or felt need for support from the opposing person; 4. The maturity and relational skills especially in conflict management; 5. The perceived or assumed intensity of the attack; 6. The place and setting of the atmosphere at the time of the incident.

**relational:** Being connected to, belonging to, having to do with, and being a part of.

**relational health (general):** The quality of the intra- and interpersonal relationship that exists in the active, sound mind of an individual, indicated by the strength, intensity, trend, and patterns of the four psychological vital signs of *connection, rapport, bond,* and *support* that affect and influence the individual's daily overall existence as manifested in thoughts, words, perceptions, actions, and general world view. (Review the applicational extension on family relational health p. 403).

**relational illness:** Psycho-socio-culturally acquired impairment of the active, sound relational mind, in many cases calculatedly and consciously manifested in undesirable and unacceptable conditions, behaviors, and practices that negatively affect relationships temporarily, for a prolonged time, or terminally depending on the timing of the diagnosis and the treatment regimen. Illnesses include, but are not limited to, unkindness, heartlessness, spitefulness, ruthlessness, harshness, insensitivity, hypersensitivity, disrespect, insolence, arrogance, selfishness, greediness, self-centeredness, egoism, meanness, callousness, defiance, conceit, and narcissism.

Some untreated relational illnesses can eventually mutate into, and/or be confused with, mental illnesses and disorders, such as schizophrenia, paranoia, bipolar disorder, hypervigilance, dementia, depression, ADHD, and GAD, these being due primarily to physiological, chemical/hormonal malfunctions and imbalances in the brain and aspects of the glandular system. Some relational illnesses can be manifested by persons with mental illness and vice versa, hence the need for careful, clinical diagnosis.

**relational mind:** The composite and complex working of soul, spirit, heart and conscience anchored in the frontal lobe (or pre-frontal cortex) of the brain, where the major intra- and interpersonal data from one's social environment is processed, in coordination with the parietal, occipital, and temporal lobes. The nerve centre of our relational existence.

**relationship:** The conscious process of ongoing intrapersonal awareness in one's mind, and the engagement of that conscious active, sound mind *with* or *against* another mind (interpersonal) in an effort to produce a desired result. This is based on the understanding that all human relationships begin and continue to exist in the active, sound mind. Once engagement of minds is established, the resulting relationship can be mostly and purposefully positive (with) or negative (against) and rarely ever neutral.

**response** (noun; *respond*, verb) The diametric opposite of *reaction*. The measured, composed, analytical comment or action to that which comes contrary (or consistent) to the expectation or perspective on the issue being addressed. A response tends to be clinical and analytical and seeks to immediately account for possible causes and sources for that which is heard, felt, or experienced from another person especially who is adversarial, upset, or angry. Ideally, a response seeks understanding and clarity with a view to mitigating confrontation and hostility. It is the means of taking the healthy 'high road' not of superiority but of emotional control in the face of imminent unhealthy conflict.

**scan/X-ray (relational):** The deep, honest, unbiased, unqualified, and objective opening of the relational mind to any psychometric assessment, evaluation, or survey to which it is subjected, with a view to ascertaining, as close as possible, the person's state of thinking and perspective on the relationship matter or issue in question.

A relational mind scan or X-ray is firstly intended to help a person to be in touch with him or herself under a guided exercise, to which he or she would not necessarily subject him or herself on his or her own volition. Such exercises are also intended to provide the therapist with as clear a picture as to where the person's mind/perspective is on a particular issue, so as to make the professional treatment plan as informed as possible.

A scan or X-ray in the medical laboratory provides an image of the *tissue* of the body so that the trained eyes (mind) of the radiologist can interpret normalcies and abnormalities in the structure under study. The relational mind scan or X-ray provides the client, who him/herself is the radiographer, an opportunity to examine the *issue* of the mind. Here we find a simple but profound analogy: *Tissue* is to *body* as *issue* is to *mind*.

When the radiographer (the client) completes the relational scan or X-ray, the radiologist (the therapist) does the interpretation of the results that the exercise shows. The reliability, validity, and ultimate value of the examination depends totally upon the integrity of the radiographer.

In the medical lab, the radiographer might have to intravenously infuse a contrast or dye into the tissue or blood vessel to help highlight the area being examined. In relational scanning or x-raying of the mind, and especially from a Christian perspective, the contrast to be infused is Prayer to the Holy Spirit, inviting Him to illuminate the mind of the client, thereby helping him or her to see deeper and wider into the issue being addressed, and therefore produce an honest and true picture of how the matter exists in the mind. For the non-Christian (who might not engage in Prayer), the contrast to be infused is a positive appeal to the conscience to be true and honest in responding to the exercise.

**sense(s):** The descriptive functions of awareness and connection of the five organs (eyes, ears, nose, tongue, and skin) that link the body with its environment. The organs themselves act as receivers of environmental and existential stimuli for the brain, which processes that raw data from them into information that ends up forming one's body of knowledge that drives choices and decisions and actions or inactions in life. The manifestation of this combined working of the senses and the brain constitutes the psychological function of said brain, which function is demonstrated through the faculty called the *mind*. Hence, the mind is the coordinated, composite working of the brain with its outside connections to the world, the senses.

**specimen (laboratory):** With the home being the *family relational health* laboratory (Review pp. 406 & 407), as discussed in Chapter 1, the *active, sound relational mind*, from a family relational health practitioner's perspective, is the whole person, the specimen in the lab on which all the studies are conducted. Isaac Watts (1674–1748) said: "The mind's the standard of the man," and Solomon said in Proverbs 23:1, "For as he thinketh in his heart, so is he."

In the family relational health laboratory, all family members are specimens upon whom each one practices and studies. By opening the mind to each other, we learn to understand each other and become a healthier and better family. In the professional practitioner's laboratory, the clients consenting to and availing their minds to be addressed and worked upon on become the specimens (Review pp. 17 – 22).

One professional ethical principle that might be unique to family relational health practice is that ideally, one of the prerequisite qualifications of the practitioner should be that he or she, by experience, has a healthy family relationship. Treatment for family relational illness should not be limited to book/academic/professional knowledge and some classroom practicum exercises.

The relational mind is the most private part of our being and should only be opened to one who is experiencing a healthy relational mind, so that the proffered treatment is, to some extent, tested and proven by "lab exercises" backed up by the academic, scholastic preparation.

The healthy family lab experience referred to here as a prerequisite to practice is not alluding to a healthy marriage only. A single person can have a healthy family relationship, and is therefore qualified to offer treatment, understandably with some ethical boundaries. He or she will have a limit in treating very intense marital challenges—not just sexual, as some might be inclined to conjecture. There are other dynamics of the marital relationship which will require a competent, experienced practitioner to treat. In the field of family relational health practice, there will be graduated orders of competencies and specialties up to the level of consultancy, thus making provision for caregivers to focus on different tiers in the family structure and the accompanying, various challenges and needs. Details in the coming FRHS Training Manual (See Specialization, p. 468).

**standard laboratory instruments notes (SLIN):** The composite 12-point clinical data that provides the specifications of each professional, evaluative, and assessment instrument used in family relational health care. These specifications are ethical prerequisites for practitioners in order to professionally utilize such instruments (See p. 464).

**support:** The fourth of the four vital signs of family relational health anchored in the psychomotor/behavioral domain of the mind. It produces demonstrable, practical, doable evidences of the quality of the previous three vital signs. This vital sign manifests itself in both material and emotional forms.

    The ultimate evidence of *support* is being there; at hand or even a thousand miles away; when needed, as much humanly possible, 24/7; being available, accessible, and reachable when needed.

**terminal relational incorrigibility (TRI):** A state of being terminally relationally ill, because the victim has conditioned his or her mind with no capacity to receive and accept correction. This person who reaches the mental state of "my way or the highway" could be considered as the ultimate relational narcissist—the kind of relational despot who listens to no one but him/herself and expects everyone to listen to and abide by his/her dictates. (See ICD p. 406).

**vital signs:** The four indicators—family *connection*, *rapport*, *bond*, and *support* of the relational mind, give the therapist suggestions, intimations, or *notifier* of the possible health status of the relationship. These vital signs were gradually identified, developed, studied, and tested in the family and professional relational labs described in Chapter 1, and have been subjected to assessments and appraisals by scores of peer reviews in the wide international scope over the last thirty years.

## Gordon's 2022 C=rt² Law of Relational Interaction and Conflict Management

-A Psychological Adaptation of Einstein's 1905 $E=mc^2$ Theory of Relativity

Based on the family relational health theory of the two basic states of mind during an interaction/conflict - *Response* and *Reaction* - as defined in the Glossary, (pp. 411 & 414), the following four equations of outcome are constructed:

1. Reaction + Reaction = Conflagration ($R^2$=C 1)

2. Reaction + Response = Confrontation ($R^2$=C 2)

3. Response + Reaction = Consultation ($R^2$=C 3)

4. Response + Response = Collaboration ($R^2$=C 4)

**Background to the Law**

The law is built on the premise of two minds involved in an interaction/conflict: One or both of them could either be in a *Reactive* or a *Responsive* mode as explained in the demonstrations below. The order in which they appear indicates who leads, *Reactor* or *Responder,* in the interaction/conflict, thereby influencing the outcome.

## Demonstrations/Scenarios of the 4 C's

1. **Conflagration** – A consuming fire! When two negatively-charged minds meet head-on, they tend to head-off into a furnace of antagonism, aggression and hostility which can result in the maiming/destruction of one or both parties.

2. **Confrontation** – A stand-off state of mind believing that one has the upper hand. It is negative when it begins in the reactive mode of mind, but it can be positive when initiated in the responsive mode by the *Responder* who tries to help the *Reactor* to improve his or her approach. The *Responder* who keeps the right, healthy frame of mind can lead the *Reactor* into consultation.

3. **Consultation** – The positive engagement of two minds aimed at a mutually beneficial outcome. Objectivity, communication, negotiation, compromise, and adjustment are healthy states of mind in which a consultation takes place.

4. **Collaboration** – The ideal experience when both parties interact with the responsive state of mind. They reciprocate in their exchange resulting in the win-win outcome, with understanding and management for the common good.

The above is the synopsis of the Law. The comprehensive Paper will be published separately.

# Addendum to Glossary - 1

## Mental Health on Tokyo
## 2020 Olympic Stage
Compliments of Naomi Osaka & Simone Biles

Surprise, shock and disbelief were some of the emotions that greeted Naomi Osaka's untimely announcement that she would not be available for the French Open at the Tokyo 2020 Olympics Games. To no less extent was the emotional upheaval as USA Gymnast, Simone Biles made it known that she was pulling out of the Gymnastic Team right there in Tokyo. Two different countries, two different games, two different Olympians but one common reason: their felt need to protect their mental health.

The issue that the ladies independent decisions brought to the fore resonated with deeper gravity than the general perspectives on emotions that the majority of the thousands of participants in Tokyo had. When the 2020 Tokyo planners selected the motto of "United by Emotions", it is safe to assume that their minds were focused on the euphoric sentiments of excitement, jubilation, the triumph of victory and the sense of achievement of sportsman/womanship and the camaraderie that would follow. All good and desirable and cherished expressions of emotions, but we should not be mesmerised into thinking that those sentiments are all that celebrities and all other human beings experience in the reality of their mental health.

It is important to note that if Naomi and Simone had reported their inability to take part in the games due to any muscular strain or other physical injury (as Biles indicated that such was not her case), it would immediately evoke emotions of sympathy, understanding and compassion. Such is the society's contrasting attitude to physiological illness over the psychological. The former is seemingly more understandable and even acceptable over the latter, which at times can be met with unkind queries of the validity of the complaints, conjectures and even suspicions and hurtful innuendos.

In the simple, but profound words of Naomi: "It is ok to be not ok." she heralded another fact about our emotions and human reality that we generally seem to be wishing away. We are not and cannot be always ok, and it is not abnormal to be "not ok". Those emotions mentioned at the top of this article are among the multiplicity of others that we need to grow and mature to face, accept, manage and live with, as we grapple with life and its realities.

Naomi and Simone expressed their deep inner feelings and in doing so, without being aware, they forcefully brought balance to the one-sided perspective of the motto that would probably prevail at the games. Their unashamedly, bold decision brought psychological calibration to our understanding of the need to be 'united' not only by the euphoric 'emotions' but by the dysphoric ones when we experience them. Just by being themselves, the ladies helped to highlight another fact of life regarding the true state of the human mind.

The celebrated young women were willing to make themselves vulnerable, dismount from the pedestal of society's super expectations of them, and state how they truly felt inside. That is one sign of good mental health – to be in touch with one's inner feeling and be assertive enough to express it and take the necessary action to address and manage it. This is an aspect of self-construal, which is being able to define oneself and what one is experiencing inside, even if such definition is not in sync with those in one's immediate sphere of influence.

Stressed and feeling pressured to disclose everything about oneself to everyone, via the probing and scrutinizing press; grappling with the residual effects of some of the emotional traumas in the training camps, among other unsettling emotional experiences, were some of the untold feelings that they, in their unique way, were smothering inside.

Their united, yet unplanned call could probably sound like: 'Give me time to connect with the private individual who I am.' This is a critical stabilizing factor in maintaining good mental health. The constant glare of the limelight can interfere with the emotions and the individual's need for some intra-personal time to be with him/herself. Simone expressed it fully: "I felt like it would be a little better to take a back seat, and work on my mindfulness."

In summary, they each could say: I need to protect my mental health which is my sense of who I am for me. This is not selfish, it is 'healthish'. This is part of my inalienable right. Biles again had it: "I was shaking, and barely napped. I've never felt like this going into a competition before. I tried to go out, have fun and after warming up in the back I felt a little better, but once I came out here, I felt, no, the mental is not there. I need to let the girls do it and focus on myself."

Naomi and Simone provided an invaluable lesson that hopefully was not lost in all the elation and exhilaration of Tokyo 2020. Our mental health must not be taken for granted. And in connection with the focus of this book, family relational health – a complementary functionality to mental health of the active, sound mind - it is understood that regardless how healthy one's relationship might be with those at home and elsewhere, we are all subject to changing emotions.

At the end of the day, our mental health is ours to safeguard. The world owes Naomi and Simone a debt of gratitude for the timely reminder of the importance to value one's mental health, even before and beyond fame and fortune.

# Addendum to Glossary - 2

# Blur Between Mental and Family Relational Illness

-Will Smith/Chris Rock Academy Award
Debacle (2022) - A Case in Point.

In chapter 7, p. 148, **Timely International Promotion of Emotions** and in Addendum to Glossary No. 1, **Mental Health on Tokyo 2020 Olympic Stage**, p. 420, in keeping with the importance that this work places on our God-given gift of emotions in family relational health, we highlighted two instances when human emotions were healthily demonstrated on the international stage. At the Olympic Games, the world saw emotions flowed uninhibitedly in a healthy way, as the victorious Olympians displayed unity and camaraderie among themselves, thereby fulfilling the theme of the Games, "United by Emotions."

In a different but equally a healthy way, we saw Naomi Osaka and Simone Biles teaching the world, in their own personal way, the importance of staying in touch with, and preserving one's emotional system, even if it means stepping aside, as they individually did, from the limelight of the glitz and glory of showmanship.

Just about one year later, the world again witnessed another demonstration of emotions, but this time it was raw and unbridled, done in a fit of rage that sent shock waves of violence and disunity ricocheting across the international stage. Occasion was on March 27, 2022 at the prestigious Academy Award Ceremony (The Oscars) when the world watched what was probably the most recent public, untenable demonstration of human emotional reaction, offered believably unscripted, by one of the most celebrated stars/actors in the entertainment industry, Will Smith.

Earlier, we stated under the **General Biblical Description of Mental Illness** (p. 230) that all human beings, from the very opulent, living in splendour and grandeur to those living in squalor and abject poverty, experience some degree of mental illness at some time in their lives. No one is immuned. Several efforts have been made in this book to differentiate between mental illness and relational illness, and our subtopic here brings it out again, that it can be difficult to do sometimes. Which could be considered as Will Smith's case – mental illness or family relational illness? The blur between the two could not be more obvious and captivating.

It is clear that Will's reactive emotional acceleration rate and speed (*REAR* p. 428) picked so fast from an eye signal of disapproval from Jada Pinket Smith, his wife. He seemingly went into rapid fast forward, (rff above fast-forward ff) from what seemed to be his relaxed smile of approval for Chris Rock's joke at Jada's baldness, to a violent demonstration of rage, ending up with him walking to the stage and planting a slap in Rock's face, resulting in him committing virtual career suicide. His moving from one apparent state of relaxation to the opposite extreme of paroxysm could probably be well labelled as bipolar emotional reaction.

Again, the difficulty of differentiating between mental illness and family relational illness! Another lesson to be learned about our marvellous, mysterious minds from the non-verbal exchange between Will and Jada during what was clearly an awkward moment for both, is that facial and body languages are the physiogmatic and psychosomatic out-working of the thought processing function of the mind. However, Will said Jada did not influence his action.

Based on the unsavoury spillings of comments and reactions to his action, many of which are said to be coming from inside the Smith's family, it can be deduced that Will's behaviour could have been triggered from, maybe, a long bout of his suffering from *Internal Family Attention Deficit Disorder* (IFFAD).

**Clinical Description** (See Glossary p. 404 for detailed description)

***Internal Family Attention Deficit Disorder*** (*IFADD*) is a family relational illness (not to be confused with mainstream clinical *mental illness*), resulting from continuous deprivation or lack of expressed approbation, appreciation, commendation and celebration of one's abilities, achievements and accomplishments by those in one's immediate sphere of influence. The disorder is more pronounced and potentially familially devastating when it is lacking from those with whom one shares life behind those sacred closed doors of that place called ***home***. This is where home ought to be a citadel of peace a practicing lab (pp. 4, 12), instead of where there is strife and contempt for any member's ambitions and efforts.

## Manifestations

***IFADD*** may be seen as a continuum from mild, non-threatening to tantrumatic behaviour, and can escalate to being extreme and even bizarre, weird, detestable and traumatic conduct and deportment in children and adults alike. Sometimes these behaviours are done privately (at home) and publicly to get attention and acceptance for the "***who I am***" and the "***what I can do***" from those who are expected to be one's supporters, admirers and cheerleaders. Comments, expressions and actions can be extreme and disruptive. ***IFADD*** shows up in the form of emotional restlessness and agitation based on the natural desire and humanly predisposed need for emotional anchorage in healthy family relationship.

## Treatment – Short and Long-term

Treatment for ***IFADD*** can be both a short and long-term procedure. On the immediate to short-term level, the effects of ***IFADD*** can be assuaged and relieved by loved ones giving the evidence and genuine, sustained assurance of the healthy family relational *four vital signs* of: *connection, rapport, bond and support.* (Review Studying of Family Members, pp. 4, 12). The characteristics and principles of these vital signs are planted and nurtured in one's active, sound mind by those in whom one invests trust and love, and from whom one therefore has a justified, reasonable expectation for similar returns.

The individual, him or herself, has to take responsibility for his or her own emotional wellbeing. One has to build one's self-assurance in one's ability to set out and accomplish that which is to be done. While the support and affirmation from family, friends, fraternity, fans and followers are important to a person's sense of accomplishment, it is indispensible that we do not make ourselves dependent on the applauds and praises of those around us. There can be no justification in blaming those in our world for the 'who I am' and more so the 'who I will turn out to be.'

In the final analysis, each person is ultimately accountable for him/herself and for what he or she did or did not do. Interpreted in the context of one's accountability for one's deeds, Ezekiel 18: 19-20 gives God's position on the issue: "Yet say ye, Why? doth not the son bear the iniquity of the father? When the son hath done that which is lawful and right, and hath kept all my statutes, and hath done them, he shall surely live. The soul that sinneth, it shall die. The son shall not bear the iniquity of the father; neither shall the father bear the iniquity of the son: the righteousness of the righteous shall be upon him, and the wickedness of the wicked shall be upon him."

Even where the family has failed to give us the foundation upon which to build and feel emotional strength, the onus is still the individual to address his or her mind to be the best he or she can be. This is the epitome of self-construal in which one addresses the mind to careful self-definition intra-dependently, and working well with that which comes interdependently from those in the various *f-groups* that we have identified.

On the long-term clinical, treatment for **IFADD** involves careful analyses of one's family-of-origin impact (FOOI); other possible developmental and experiential traumas; the present family relational and social issues and dynamics; one's perspective and world-view of life. These and other factors will need to be packaged into a carefully-designed treatment program.

The quality of our human healthy emotional growth system influenced by self-esteem, self-worth and self-construal is established firstly in what one receives (or does not receive) from the *five 'f's'* in one's immediate sphere of influence: family, friends, fraternity, fans and followers - in that important order of development. "No man is an island, no man stands alone..." said 16th Century British Writer, John Doone. And in 1972, American Song Writer, "Bill" Harrison William Withers composed his song "Lean on me" which has now become an international anthem, inspiring support for each other in times of crisis. In 1908 American Composer, James David Vaughn captured the spiritual sentiments of our need for each other in his song: "I need the prayers of those I love." We need the support of those we love in order to thrive healthily in any pursuit in life. The immediate family unit at home ideally should be the first and most reliable and trust-worthy source of such support and encouragement.

The clinical impression is that Will's **IFADD** had reached catastrophic proportion (based on the comments on social media from many familial and collegial insiders), hence his desperate bid for approval and appreciation primarily from she to whom he has been said to be pandering for such, for a long time. Upon seeing her disapproval and discomfort from Rock's poked joke at her, Smith seemingly seized the opportunity, swung into action for her public defence and a demonstration of '*the who I am, and can be!*' for her. This assumption and interpretation of his speedy action can be considered reasonable, given that there was no precedence of altercation between him and Chris Rock, at least as has been made public.

## Take Away/Application

While we bemoan and loathe (and hopefully no one will gloat) about Will Smith's career 'suicidal' act, given his resignation from the Academy, and the Academy ten-year suspension on him, and the natural ripple effects that these will have down the road, there are two profound lessons for all onlookers to take from it.

Beginning with Chris Rock, the obvious victim of Will's out-burst, then to Jada, on to the members of the Academy, other luminaries in the entertainment industry and other professional/vocational fields, pastors, politicians, and all who aspire for, and live on the public stage: Take heed of the biblical counsel in Proverbs 16:32 "He that is slow to anger is better than the mighty; and he that ruleth his spirit than he that taketh a city." (The Stage!) Practice healthy family relationship and be the genuine support and cheerleader for those you love and those who love you, beginning firstly with those of your own household.

In addition to the recommended treatment for *IFADD*, a deeper, more clinical assessment could help us to understand more possible reasons for the inexplicable cases of flare and blow-ups, fits-frenzies of rages and temper, throes and spasms, emotional fireworks and explosions, convulsions and paroxysms in many family relationships around the world. These behavioural disorders take place regardless of culture, race, colour, ethnicity creed or any other grouping of humanity. What is it that could make some husbands, wives, children or other family members become loose emotional cannons in their homes and communities and in the media? (See p. 64)

## Reactive Emotional Acceleration Rate and Speed (*REARS*)

Dr. Hermon Douce, late president of West Indies College (now Northern Caribbean University, Jamaica) upon arriving at a traffic light, while we were travelling together, shared what he remembered hearing as the explanation of a 'split second'. "It is the time between which the light changes from red to green, and the guy (driver) behind you honks his horn in order to get/keep going!" Other expressions that convey the same meaning, more or less are: 'in a split moment', 'in a heartbeat' or 'in a flash'.

In the continuously-changing high-powered car manufacturing industry, the 2022 listing among those with the fastest acceleration rate is the Lamborghini Aventador SVJ with its speed thrill of 0-62 mph in 2.8 seconds. Others include the Koenigsegg Regera: 0-62 in 2.8; Ferrari SR8: 0-60mph in 2.8. And we could go on to name more super-turbo and other charges of human speed machines on the race tracks and highways, in the air and under water. Unfortunately, we cannot accurately measure the mysterious rate and speed of change, response or worst of all, the reaction time of our very own human mind – the engine of our being (See pp.118, 237, 327, 332).

One fact that we know is that we can be positioned at the North Pole and faster than the speed of light, move with our minds to the South Pole which is over 12, 000 miles away. Supporting this position that the speed of the thought of the mind exceeds that of light, contributing writer in the Economic Times, Swami Sivananda, wrote on June 14, 2021: "While light travels at the rate of 186,000 miles per second, thoughts virtually travel in no time. Thought is finer than ether, the medium of electricity." Thoughts excel light in speed.

Sivananda went on to refer to the mind as a "wireless machine," a parallel description to what we used earlier, the engine of our being. He cited the speed of a person sending out thoughts of peace over the airwaves, and how speedily and instantaneously such thoughts can impact the listener: "A saint with peace, poise, harmony and spiritual waves sends out into the world thoughts of harmony and peace. They travel with lightning speed in all directions and enter the minds of persons and produce in them also similar thoughts of harmony and peace." Incomprehensible, inexplicable and unfathomable! Equally so, is how our emotions can change in even less than the twinkling of our eyes.

Note carefully: There are scholarly, scientific articles that offer indepth, technical treatise on the general subject of human thought process. As with all subjects in this book, *REARS* is developed and presented from the perspective of family relational health, with the understanding that there are more diverse treatment of the issue available elsewhere.

Our reactive emotional acceleration rate and speed (*REARS*) can be determined and influenced by various factors. (Review the definition of Reaction in Glossary p. 411). A simple clinical definition for *REARS* is the inexplicable, immeasurable period/time between which our senses are stimulated, which stimulation is electrically, chemically/hormonally processed in the brain, resulting in a protective or defensive thought for action, depending on the interpretation of the imminence, magnitude and severity of a perceived danger.

The diametric opposite can also be true in the case of a 'good reaction' – a kind of pseudo response, (since a response is the opposite of reaction. Review the definition of Response in Glossary p. 414). In this case, the perception is inviting, alluring or even tantalizing, and one is convinced at the same rate and speed as the sense for defence, that that which is desirable must be had, even sometimes, at all costs, including at the treacherous or perilous risk of life. The story of Samson in Judges 14:1-3 could be cited in part as an illustration for this explanation.

In the multiplicity of human experiences, the *REARS* can make the acceleration rate of man's toys, the Lamborghini or the Ferrari and other state-of-the art inventions, fade into the distance. Unfortunately, in too many instances like that of Will Smith's, the incomprehensible rapidity of the emotional rate of acceleration results in mayhem, demise, destruction and even death. Testimonies coming from penal institutions, including from death row, bear overwhelming evidence of this fact. Like the proverbial sped arrow (now fired gun and in Smith's case, the fired slap!), when the thoughts are expressed into words and actions, they come not back again.

No one can truly claim to know, not to mention having the ability to measure and manage the *REARS*. From a Christian perspective, the only hope is to surrender the will (a major propeller of the *REARS*) to the constraining power of the indwelling Holy Spirit. (2 Cor. 5:14) The Holy Spirit will not only restrain us from impulsive and reactive behaviours, but will motivate and positively drive us to think and act appropriately, correctly and timely. This is our only safe haven from the potential catastrophe of our mysterious reactive emotional acceleration rate and speed. (*REARS*)

## Two Therapy Techniques for *REARS* Management

Enhancing the spiritual counsel above, (more of which can be cited from the Bible), the Holy Spirit also illuminates the scientific and technical aspects of the human mind to come up with answers for further educational and therapeutic practices. Let us consider the following two: (1) "Count to 10" and (2) "Close Your Mouth/Swallow Your Spit/Spittle"

## *REARS* Management Technique No. 1: "Count to 10"

This somewhat folklorish counsel to 'count to 10' before you act is quite germane and therefore worth trying. Counting 1-2-3-4-5-6-7-8-9-10 is an imperative and intended to be literally done. The mental pace guide for this counting process is that which we see or hear or see on the second (or the sweeping) hand of the clock or watch designed by the horologist (clockmaker) to move at intervals of one second.

# Why Count to 10?

Counting 1-10 is a reaction delay technique. By counting 1-2-3-4-5-6-7-8-9-10, the mental energy is distracted from the stimulation to react. It is a quick healthy and positive 'cooling-off' strategy. It is a self-talk therapy so that upon hearing yourself literally counting 1-2-3-4-5-6-7-8-9-10, you are exercising management (which could be a restraint and constraint combo) over your impulse and possible adrenalin rush, which will result in self-control.

A scientific perspective could help to bring this lesson clearer by attempting to answer the question of how long it takes us to become consciously aware of sensory information sent to the brain by the senses. Dr Christian Jarrett, cognitive neuroscientist, writing in the BBC's Science Focus Magazine, March 2014, in response to the enquiry on the speed of thought stated: "By some estimates, we can experience sensory stimuli that's presented for as little as 50 milliseconds (about one-twentieth of a second). It is thought that our brains can, in fact, respond to information that's much briefer than this, lasting less than a quarter of a millisecond."

In a further statement quite comparative to Dr. Douce's explanation of a split second, Jarrett employed the imagery of the time between which the track and field starter's gun goes off and the sprinters take off. He suggested that the action could be done in about 150 milliseconds. He went on to observe: "One limiting factor is how long it takes information to travel down our nerve pathways. In the 19th Century, Hermann von Helmholtz estimated this to be 35 metres per second, but we now know that some well-insulated nerves are faster, at up to120 metres per second."

Against this scientific postulation which is already loaded with measurement and calculation complexity way beyond the average family member's ability to comprehend and manage, consider the task of measuring and apportioning the 'block' of time that each major segment of a sensory stimulation, say from the ears or the eyes, could take in the brain to result in an action by the hands, feet and mouth. Here we see the ears picking up a sound which is enhanced by the eyes capturing the scene, and both senses as a team sending on the message via the auditory and optic nerves respectively to the brain.

We suggest that there are at least six major segments of a sensory stimulation to take place in the brain, for an action to be taken in response to what the ears and the eyes sent in. Those segments could be: 1. Reception of the stimulus; 2. Registration or recording of the stimulus; 3. Processing of the stimulus - maybe in terms of its categorization or type; 4. Impact-assessment of the stimulus in terms of what could likely happen; 5. Summoning the production of chemicals for the agitation of action in response to the stimulus; 6. Defence reaction by the agents of actions in this case: the speech mechanism – pharynx, tongue and lips; the hands and the feet.

The above simple illustration which we will call the 'sensory stimulation-to-action probability' resonates with what was stated in chapter 7, pp. 145-146, about the complex working of our emotions. We noted that psychiatric, neurological and behavioural researchers give the comprehensive study about the calibration of the four lobes of the brain, and names of the chemicals and the functional relationships between areas such as the spinal cord, synapses, receptors, neurons, axons, dendrites, impulses, and neurotransmitters, among others, all being a part of the study of emotions in the human experience.

It is safe to assume that the various 'blocks' of time for each of the six segments and their probable sub-segments named above would have to be measured not only in milliseconds but also in nanoseconds which is 1-billionth of a second – an aspect of random access memory (RAM). At this level we would need assistance from experts, the likes of former Admiral Grace Brewster Murphy Hopper (1906 - 1992), renowned programmer for the Harvard Mark 1 Computer and the calculation of time in minute fractions of a second.

At the family relational health level, we do not need all this mind-blowing statistical measurement and understanding of time in order to manage our thought processes, reaction and response principles and skills. While the Christian will make use of the scientific information to enhance the understanding, his faith will be anchored in the eternal God, the Creator Who has infinitesimal knowledge about time which He, Himself created. David stated that unequivocally in Psalm 90: 2-4 "Before the mountains were brought forth, or ever thou hadst formed the earth and the world, even from everlasting to everlasting, thou art God ... For a thousand years in thy sight are but as yesterday when it is past, and as a watch in the night."

## *REARS* Management Technique No. 2:

**"Keep-the-mouth-closed" and 'Swallow-the-'Spittle'/Saliva' Technique.** Going back into the archives of old custom wisdom, we not only hear: 'Count to 10' which is intended to be a thought process instead of being audibly expressed, we also hear "Keep your mouth closed" and "Swallow your spittle." Doesn't sound too socially welcomed, especially the latter, but they can be strategically and therapeutically helpful.

1. <u>Strategically</u> - By keeping your mouth closed, you avoid or retard making a hasty utterance that you probably would be better off not making. You are thereby taking control of yourself and of the situation in which you are involved.

2. <u>Therapeutic</u> - By swallowing you spittle/saliva, you calm yourself down. The Reverso Dictionary gave two interesting interpretations of this advice: (a) "to refrain from uttering or manifesting;" and (b) "to endure without retaliation." Applied: It is better to consciously swallow it than to eject it, and worse yet, sometimes to be seen frothing and foaming as a result of the chemical interactions taking place due to your

rising anger level. It is uncouth, anti-social to have spit/saliva flying from your mouth. Swallow it! It is yours!! It is Good!!! It is Therapy!!!! Reduce its viscosity by sipping water!

These simple techniques and other appropriate ones have to be acquired, learned and practiced before they are needed, just like any other technique or skill that is needed in life. It takes discipline and effort to master those *REARS* control techniques and skills.

## Machine and Mind Compared

One turbo-charged car changes at a rate of 2.8 seconds: 0-62 mph. By training the mind that designed that machine to control its reactive rate of acceleration towards the display of anger and rage should not be too difficult. Alas! It is not only difficult; it appears to be well-nigh impossible (Review Change Needed in All Relationships, pp. 143-144).

Using the car speed principle or timeline, we see that 2.8 seconds goes into 10 seconds at least three times. (3.75) So that the "Count to 10" principle actually gives the human three times more potential control or slower acceleration than the machine that he makes. This suggests that he is indeed fearfully and wonderfully made (Psalm 139: 14) and does have better, ingrained management options and skills than the machine that he used the same mind to conceive and make.

Among the qualities of life that God has given us, according to 2 Timothy 1:7 is a sound mind with which we are to be able to analyse, appraise, calculate, critique, evaluate, exercise, judge, and rationalize all other such means of gauging, measuring, and reaching a conclusion. The spiritual fact is as Christ our Saviour, Himself said it: "Without me ye can do nothing." (John 15:5). But the healthy counter reassurance that Christ, Himself also inspired through His servant is that: "I can do all things through Christ which strengtheneth me." (Phil. 4:13)

The epitome of the speed of thought, beyond any human conception or imagination for measurement, is in the connection of relationship which God has established between Himself and His people. That direct connecting line that the Divine Thought Maker has created for His children to be instantaneously in touch with Him is called Prayer. In Isaiah 65 verse 24 He said: And it shall come to pass, that before they call, I will answer; and while they are yet speaking, I will hear."

No human scholar of the highest science and intellectual ingenuity can explain the velocity between when a child of God prays and the Holy Spirit illuminates the mind with and or preforms an act in response. And there are thousand times ten thousand throughout history up to the present, who bear testimony to that rich, and inspiring spiritual experience. Against this mysterious and miraculous but certain assurance, we could agree that the thought is the super connectivity that God has created to be the link between our relational minds through Him.

## Prayer for Spiritual Thought Canal Surgery

For any relationship to grow as God intended it to be, we need to have healthy thoughts one towards the other, but of our own efforts and strength it is simply not possible. We therefore need to heed the invitation from the Divine Thought Maker: "Casting down imaginations, and every high thing that exalteth itself against the knowledge of God, and bringing into captivity every thought to the obedience of Christ." (2 Cor. 10:5) Our most earnest prayer then, to the Divine Thought Surgeon or Endodontist would be for Him to perform a 'thought canal' through spiritual surgery, cleaning out all infected thoughts, and filling the space with His/thoughts of righteousness, and cover us with His crown of glory. (1 Peter 5: 4) (See Mind Transplant Needed, p. 139)

# Addendum to Glossary - 3

# Family Relational Health and Physiological Vital Signs Paralleled

To the same extent that there are four basic vital signs of life - heart rate, respiratory rate, blood pressure, and pulse rate - that are checked at triage and give the attending physician a basic indicator of the state of one's physiological health, so are there four basic vital signs that can be checked upon entering into family relational health therapy. The indications from these will give the therapist a clue of the state of the quality of family relational health in the mind of the individual who comes for treatment. They are relational connection, relational rapport, relational bond, and relational support (CPH²).

There are in medical practice other vital signs which, when factored in with the previous basic four, will give the physician further clinical insight into the immediate state of the physiological health of the patient. Among these are *oxygen saturation, respiratory effort, capillary refill time, body height,* and *body weight.* Deeper medical studies will reveal more indicative VS's, depending on the patient's condition and the clinical assessment being made.

To the same extent, also, of the various combinations of family relationships (See p. 466), there are vital signs that can indicate the state of the relationship between any two members, such as husband and wife, father and mother, parent and child, and sibling. For example, in addition to the basic general four mentioned above, there are seven other vital signs that can give the marriage therapist an initial indication of the quality of the marital health in the mind of a husband and wife. These are the status of *mutual matrimonial home, mutual matrimonial bedroom, mutual matrimonial bed, mutual matrimonial intimacy, family meal time, family social time,* and *family spiritual values.* (See Sample Instruments # 4, p. 484).

Inasmuch as there are vital signs that can be assessed for just about any family group combination, the reliability and similar criteria for such an exercise cannot be *conclusive*, the can only be seen as *indicative*. Where there are basic standardized international medical and clinical laboratory test ranges for diabetes, temperature, HDL, LDL, bilirubin, and the plethora of lab tests on the different panels on the lab form, there are no such equivalents for psychological health, and definitely not for the lesser-known family relational health.

This is not suggesting that such is not needed, but there is an underlying basic difference between assessing physiological and psychological health care, and more specifically, family relational health care.

## Physiological and Psychological Vital Signs Differ

As mentioned in Chapter 9, "Demons of the Past Meet the God of the Present," the body generally responds to treatment *involuntarily*, whereas the mind does so *voluntarily (See p. 251)*. No organ, gland, or tissue of the body, upon 'becoming knowledgeable' that a certain medication or drug has been administered and will be heading toward treating it, can protest and refuse to admit it by setting up a roadblock in the bloodstream close to where the medication will enter its cells. That simply does not happen! This is not negating the case of negative effects of chemical reaction in different drugs. Rather, the statement is alluding to an imaginary decision of an organ not to accept a medication that is intravenously or otherwise sent to effect some function in it. Such calculated resistance just does not happen in the body.

The simple physiological fact is that once the drug is administered, the blood carries it to the desired destination, and the affected tissue is thereby treated. As to the result, that is a matter for clinical assessment and monitoring, based on the diagnosis, administering protocol, and prognosis. (Review the drug administering Protocol in Chapter 12, p. 380–382). On the other hand, a family member in his or her active, sound mind, upon hearing that he or she will be asked to do a family relational health vital signs assessment, with a view to treating an existing relational illness, could produce a wide variety of reactions (or responses) influencing the result of the exercise:

- "I am not going to answer any of his questions!"
- "I will tell the counselor/therapist what I know he will want to hear!"
- "I will write down anything I feel like writing down."
- "OK, since I must do it, I will just finish with it quickly. They can't say I didn't cooperate!"

These and various other states of mind will render family relational health care many times more challenging and difficult than physiological health care. But do such assessments need to be done? They sure do! (Review scan/X-ray (relational) p. 414)

One of the underlying purposes of subjecting the body to the array or battery of tests that can at times be so invasively daunting (among them are some biopsies) is for the medical doctor to be aware of the clinical issues within the tissues of the body. It is only by ascertaining the best detail possible that an effective treatment regimen can be designed and an informed a prognosis made.

The same is true in the context of family relational health care. Every undesirable and unacceptable relational reaction or behavior that is inimical to good, quality relationships in the home, church, school, workplace, and society at large has its base in some impaired relational issue within the 'tissue' of the mind. As a society, we bewail, we bemoan, we speak up against, we detest, and we protest against the family relational illnesses that are stalking the land: unkindness, harshness, coarseness, insensitivity, disrespect, insolence, arrogance, selfishness, meanness, callousness, defiance, conceit—the list just seems to expand and spiral out of control.

Racial and ethnic tensions have risen to unprecedented levels, as experienced in the United States of America, Myanmar, and other countries in 2020, and there seems to be no abatement. Called by different names and terminologies, these all end up as impaired relational health of different types among the peoples of the world.

## Family Relational Health: A Laissez-Faire Issue

Each of these unhealthy behaviours (seen firstly in individuals then in groups) is subjected to an array of academic, philosophical, sociological and legal interpretations, perspectives, and they in turn, produce a number of variables, situational ethics, pros, and cons as to how such behaviours and relationships are to be perceived and related with. At the end of the day, through legal and other technicalities, the issue boils down, in many cases, to the individual's choice over what might be considered the common good of the family or group. This is the epitome and summary of the controversy in our very pluralistic, boundary-less and liberal society.

Society, understandably, has a laissez-faire approach to family relational health. Generally, it mandates the education of its citizens from preschool up to the tertiary level, inclusive of private home schooling, so as to ensure that all its citizens will have a basically standardized level of education when they come out to make their contributions to, and impact on, the society at large.

As for general healthcare, there is virtually no stone left unturned, although it often becomes a political football as different political parties have their own platform and proposals for providing universal health care for the citizens. However, there are established guidelines and directives as to how citizens are expected to address this all-important matter of physiological health, from obstetrics to pediatrics on to geriatrics, seeing that in a general sense, what affects one can eventually affect society as a whole.

Since 2020 onward, the experience of the various local or state and national or federal mandates on how the citizenry is to manage the pandemic of COVID-19 is a perfect example. Even if it required the deployment of the law-enforcement officers to ensure that each one abides by the protocols/directives—such as social distancing, the wearing of face coverings, home or state quarantine and all the other instructions—the government in some countries would be prepared to go as far as it considers necessary to ensure that everyone obeys the directives in the interest of all.

For the economic and development businesses of society, there are state regulations and parameters within which practitioners are to operate. A brief example shows that in addition to medicine and education, other fields such as law and order, architecture and construction, business and commerce, manufacturing industry, science and technology, entertainment of every kind, and just about every significant venture of engagement come under government surveillance and management one way or another. There are ministries, departments, and agencies of government, with ministers, secretaries, directors, oversight, and professional bodies to ensure that the practitioners stay within the ambit of the codes and regulations that are acceptable for their operations.

## No Mandate for Family Relational Health

But for family relational health generally, such regulations and parameters are off-limits. Life behind closed doors is totally private and left up to those who live there. While the same behind-closed-door residents have to operate within state guidelines in the various areas listed above, how they practice their lifestyle is entirely a matter of choice. Who can justifiably take exception to that posture of the state? Who wants to have their private life prescribed or circumscribed by the state? No one does.

At the same time, the state (community, county or country) continues to reel and writhe at the disorderly conduct, hooliganism, and breaches of the peace, among other undesirable behaviors that come from behind those same sacred, closed doors and leak out into the school system, on the street, in the general public, and into the workplace. Relational health regulations? Definitely not! A relational value system? Who will determine that? The first caution here will be the probability of imposition of expectations and morals and practices that are not in harmony with a free society.

Any effort to address, not to mention harmonize (not legislate) the issue of the quality of family relational health in the society at large, will be a thorny one, given the potential and controversial fluidity in our present open and liberal society. We have no choice but to continue as in the days of Israel when "… the children of Israel departed …own eyes." (Judg. 21: 24-25; see also 17:5).

Let us be clear with the statement that "there was no king in Israel." The reference to "no king" is actually alluding to the absence of a leader who would give basic, coordinated guidelines and instructions for the behaviour (DSM-5 Conduct Disorder, return to p. 233) and relational practices of the citizenry in the interest of the common good of the society at large—while, at the same time, protecting the inalienable rights of the individual.

In our modern, free, twenty-first-century society, *king* in the context explained would be negatively and conveniently misconstrued to mean a dictator and one who imposes his moral standards upon the society. The fact is that if and where such leadership exists, it would not be in harmony with God's will for His people, whom He has blessed with the power of choice. This does not mean that leadership should not express guidelines for healthy relationships in the homes in more direct ways than now exist. (Revisit Home and Family Leadership, p.311).

## Nineveh's King: Exemplary State Leadership in Family Relational Health

There is a potentially thin line between quality, good state and community leadership that can offer healthy, good model citizenship to which all can aspire for the common good. A case in point is what happened in Nineveh after the wayward prophet, Jonah, was forced by divine providence to go and deliver God's warning to the leadership there. The record is that after the king heard the warning message from the Lord,

> "... he arose from his throne, and he laid his robe from him, and covered him with sackcloth, and sat in ashes. And he caused it to be proclaimed and published through Nineveh by the decree of the king and his nobles, saying, Let neither man nor beast, herd nor flock, taste any thing: let them not feed, nor drink water: But let man and beast be covered with sackcloth, and cry mightily unto God: yea, let them turn everyone from his evil way, and from the violence that is in their hands. Who can tell if God will turn and repent, and turn away from his fierce anger that we perish not?" (Jonah 3:1–9)

The king announced and decreed a spiritual quarantine in the form of a fast in contrition before God. As leader, he acknowledged that the pandemic of moral decadence and poor relational health was spread not only at the community, but at the country level. Contact tracing was not possible and it was about to destroy the whole society. He exemplarily led his people into an act of repentance aimed at achieving spiritual and moral herd immunity against destruction. It is clear that God responded mercifully to the city's response to the warning against its wickedness. Interestingly, He had to challenge the belligerent prophet, Jonah, who sorely disagreed with the fact that God spared the inhabitants based on their nationwide penitential attitude and changed behavior. (Jonah 4: 1-11)

This attitude probably stemmed from Jonah's impression that he would be seen as a false prophet, or maybe he thought that to the same extent that the Lord punished his wayward behavior, the Ninevites should also experience some punishment for theirs. While his was calculated disobedience to God, that of the people of Nineveh was, according to God, out of ignorance. (Review Chapter 4).

God was characteristically the good and merciful God—Who He has always been: "And should not I spare Nineveh, that great city, wherein are more than six score thousand persons that cannot discern between their right hand and their left hand; and also much cattle?" (Jonah 4:11)

The king of Nineveh demonstrated quality personal, home, and state exemplary leadership that would be very difficult for the citizens to question, criticize, and refuse to follow. It is not unlikely that there could have been some skeptics who would probably question the swift moral and spiritual move of the king. But due to his unquestionable personal involvement and sacrifice, no one could accuse him of imposing moral standards of behavior upon them that he himself was not going to follow. They evidently did not question the fast for long but genuinely participated in it, and it redounded to the well-being of all in the city.

Maybe one of the most current case of diametrically opposite experience is that of the politically challenged British Prime Minister, Boris Johnson. A national outcry against him, demanding his resignation (2022) came against his failure as leader to abide by the Covid19 protocols and lockdown directives imposed under his leadership on the citizens (2020). This happened when he joined in a garden party at 10 Downing Street, the state residence from which the highest example should be sent to the nation.

There was such a time also in Joshua's leadership experience of Israel when he felt that he was confronting a free and laissez-faire society, even among the people of God. Then he threw down the gauntlet and spoke as every man who is in charge of his household ought to do, even today: "And if it seem evil unto you to serve the LORD, choose you this day whom ye will serve; whether the gods which your fathers served that were on the other side of the flood, or the gods of the Amorites, in whose land ye dwell: but as for me and my house, we will serve the LORD" (Josh. 24:15).

Quality family relational health for society will continue to be a controversial and potentially divisive issue. What will be acceptable to determine how relationally healthy families are or need to be? It seems to come down to the very opposite of what happened in Nineveh: Each one, each family or household leader along with the members thereof, will determine what their standards of acceptable behavior and operations will be. A complete and totally free and open society.

It is unlikely that there will be any mutually acceptable standards of living and lifestyle, behavior, and relationship in the general society. Instead, we will all operate by our homespun versions of what is right, good, and acceptable, and determine what the vital signs and measurements of them will be for ourselves. This will be totally opposite to the state-regulated, physiological health care and education systems as discussed earlier. Inasmuch as there is not absolute and total consensus on any of the codes and principles and parameters of the operations of the enterprises and practices of the society listed above, by and large, the majority of the society abides by them, inclusive of the practices and expectations of the health protocols.

And, where any major aspects of those principles and regulations are violated or made to become ineffective, there will be a national outcry, even to the point where the political directorate could be punished at the polls for reneging on their responsibilities.

However, for the Christian family, it must be according to Joshua's position: We will order our lives in accordance with that which pleases the Lord, our God of Families. Our family relational health vital signs will be directed by the inspiration of the Lord and will be devised, constructed, taught, and administered by His appointed leaders in harmony with His instructions.

## Addendum to Women's Ordination
## to the Pastorate (from p. 338)

### Female Military and Leadership Gallantry

The Bible gives credit to a long list of women of exemplary gallantry and leadership. Outstanding among them was the record of Deborah, the prophetess, judge and wife of Lapidoth. (Judges 4 and 5) (and another woman named Jael) both of whose courage, bravery and faith in God took the leadership of the army of Israel from a fearful and evidently incompetent male leader, Barak, and secured their victory over the enemies of God.

Further biblical and historical studies show a galaxy of outstanding women who were at the forefront at times of crisis and gained success which would not have been accomplished under the existing male leadership. We see that in many homes and institutions today, mirroring the likes of Abigail's quick thinking and intervention to prevent mayhem and bloodshed between David and Nabal's camps (1 Sam. 25: 2-38). Certainly God's hands were on these women as they fearlessly executed what they had to do. French heroine, Joan of Arc (1412-1431) and others like her can be cited here from a non-Christian perspective. The probable confusion with Deborah in the context of the issue under debate is any suggestion that she assumed a priestly role, and was ordained to the pastorate in order to accomplish what she did. It does not appear that the roles were the same.

In contemplating the rite of ordination, here's another question: Was the laying on of hands by the presbytery (1 Tim. 4:14) a Holy Spirit-inspired act as in the case of Barnabas and Saul (Acts 13: 1-3), or was it religious conception of the male apostles, which tradition has continued to this day? At those times of "laying-on of hands," were women involved in the life of the Church, and was such involvement in the apostleship core? If not, Why not?

Is the "laying-on of hands" a New Testament phenomenon? In observing the Jewish pattern of leadership appointment, is there evidence of the practice? Is there any comparison with the pouring of oil on the head and the subsequent pronouncement of sanctification, meaning being 'set apart'? And, was the "laying on of the hands" and passing on the blessing and the investment of authority, a sacred rite? Is there any difference in the generalized use of 'ordained' (Num. 28:6; John 15: 16; Acts 13:48; Gal. 3:19) as against what appears as a special ceremonial rite of specific appointment (Jer. 1:5; Mark 3:14; Acts 10: 42; 14:23)?

# Appendix 1

# Recommended Family Relational Health Seminar Topics

## Introduction

A family relational health seminar is conducted primarily to impart relational knowledge and skills to the participants. Reflecting on the Anchor Text for Chapter 4, Hosea 4:6, we repeat that it captures the Creator-Redeemer's parental sadness and pain: "My people are destroyed for lack of knowledge." There is one single word that portrays the intensity of the phrase "lack of knowledge." That word is *ignorance.*

On the basis of previous and future comments on the subject, it is safe to declare that the greatest threat to quality family relational health around the world is *ignorance,* as now brought out in the paraphrase for families: Many family relationships have been, are being, and will be destroyed  due to the lack of knowledge about the vital signs of their God-given family relational health and the necessary skills to improve it. This harsh fact brings back to mind the adage, "If you think education is expensive, try ignorance!"

All seminars conducted under the auspices of the Church ought to aim at dispelling the relational ignorance that has beleaguered families down through the centuries, and more so in these days that the prophecy spoke about: "For, behold, the darkness shall cover the earth, and gross darkness the people: but the LORD shall arise upon thee, and his glory shall be seen upon thee" (Isa. 60:2).

In order for the seminars to accomplish the pointed and specific goal of dispelling the darkness in family life, which darkness is anchored in the mind, the Christian family relational health practitioner will seek to follow the didactic method of teaching demonstrated by the Master Teacher, Jesus Himself. He taught, not lectured! His method alone reached the inner man, that is, the mind in which all human relationships begin and continue to exist.

Four of Jesus's methods to be used in family relational health seminars are:

1. **Teach by object lesson.** Jesus utilized imagery and scenes with which His audience was familiar, in order to arrest and engage their minds and get the lessons to them. His parables are examples: "And he spake many things unto them in parables, saying, Behold, a sower went forth to sow …Who hath ears to hear, let him hear" (Matt. 13:3–9). Jesus spoke to people in a farming community, so they could identify with the concept of sowing seeds. For a modern example of this principle, see *FRH Songs of Praise and Bible Verses Paraphrase*, Appendix 4 – The FRH Family Seminar Sandwich Series.

2. **Speak with currency and relevance.** His lessons were always immediately applicable and can make connection with the audience on matters that speak to their experience. "Say not ye, There are yet four months, and then cometh harvest? behold, I say unto you, Lift up your eyes, and look on the fields; for they are white already to harvest" (John 4:35). Again, the reference to harvest resonated with His listeners farming experience, so He could reach them.

3. **Teach simple and easy lessons.** Jesus's lessons were not complex and loaded with scholarly erudition that only served to mesmerize the minds of the people. His method was what could be called down-to-earth in modern vernacular. "And it came to pass, when Jesus had ended these sayings, the people were astonished at his doctrine: for he taught them as one

having authority, and not as the scribes" (Matt. 7:28–29). One of the greatest evidences of a teacher's authority on a subject is his or her ability to present it in such a simple but profound way that just about everyone who desires to understand can do so. This does not mean that the Presenter will not make use of and reference to scholarly material, but he would firstly understand it thoroughly so as to impart it simply enough for his audience to understand.

Again, of Jesus it was said, "The common people heard Him gladly" (Mark 12:37). "Heard" means that the ordinary citizen, the man on the street, the unlearned received, understood, and accepted His teaching because He spoke so that they could connect with and understand Him. At the end of each seminar, each participant should leave better than when he or she came in, and with a desire for more.

4.  **Provide a salvific ending.** That is to say, after addressing the issue with which the people were concerned, He would make the immediate application to their soul salvation. "Again, the kingdom of heaven is like unto a merchant man, seeking goodly pearl..." (Matt. 13:45). He made it arrest their minds in order to create a response to the application appeal that He would come up with afterward. That appeal must address their soul salvation and challenge them to make a decision to accept and serve the Lord. The Christian Psychologist, will be careful not to come across as imposing his or her religious conviction. It is therefore important to do audience analysis so as to know how to say what and where, depending on the demographics.

## The Open-Minded Listener's Listening Litany

In order to help participants get into the right frame of mind for the seminar and to set the pace for an ending as desirable as number 4 above, the presenter could invite them to begin the session by saying this Litany of the Open-minded, Active Listener:

"By the grace of God, I participate in this seminar with an open mind to:

- reaffirm something that I already know;
- learn something new that I need to know;
- unlearn something that I *thought* was right;
- relearn and accept something I might have been unwilling to accept and do." Other versions with similar message and impact can be composed.

The following twenty-five seminar topics are selected from a repertoire of some two hundred such topics developed over the thirty-plus-year period of the development of the family relational health laboratory referred to in Chapter 1. The description of each topic gives an indication as to the particular family group or category for whom it is designed.

Inasmuch as this book is not written to address the principles, techniques, rudiments, and methods of seminar presentation, it is important to mention *audience analysis.* An important aspect of preparation for a seminar is knowing the possible family demographics of the audience: age ranges, marital status, occupational background, possible gender ratio, nationality/ethnicity, culture, among others. From an international presenter's perspective, it is most important to be sensitive of the various dynamics of the audience.

## International Audience Potential Sensitivity

This statement of "Respect for Sensitivity" of Family Relational Health Services International (or a modified version) can serve as a public safeguard against the likelihood of causing unnecessary discomfort to individuals or groups who could be negatively affected by some aspect of the seminar, albeit at the ignorance of the presenter:

> The seminars, teachings, and counsels (of FRHSI) are designed to teach and uphold the Christian, biblical ideals of good family life. At the same time, we are aware that there might be some personal, social, tribal, clannish, cultural, or national practices that could make it challenging for some persons and families here to accept *all* of these ideals. We respect these challenges without compromising the Christian, biblical ideals upon which the teachings are based.

This is a kind of disclaimer and should be positively and painstakingly put forward at the beginning of each seminar.

## Potential Overlapping of Topics

It is not unlikely that as one reads through the various topics and their descriptions, one could sense evidence of overlapping and apparent repetition. Repertoires are dynamic, and topics do flow from an existing one, but with the new one addressing a new focus while maintaining some common elements of its predecessor. During preparation for presentation, the presenter will be careful to bring out the elements of commonality, with emphasis on those of uniqueness and difference.

## The Twenty-Five Topics

### Topic 1: The Family System

A seminar designed to address the internal dynamics of the subgroups comprising the family; to consider the interrelatedness and interdependence of each unit upon the other; and to understand and appreciate the natural element of system complexity, helping each family member to cooperate and avoid system complications in family relationships.

**Topic 2: The Psycho-Chemical Order of Deteriorating Relationships**

A seminar designed to make a chemical analogical explanation of relationships that go through the acidic, corrosive, and toxic states of affairs; to present some biblio-psycho-social symptoms of each stage of deterioration; and offer counsels that can heal and restore such relationships.

**Topic 3: Understanding Physical and Psycho-Spiritual Health**

A seminar designed to educate family members on the relationship between physical, mental, and spiritual health, and to offer counsels and guidelines on how to balance and improve these critical aspects of their being to the glory of God and the blessings of those in their sphere of influence.

**Topic 4: Effective Communication in the Family**

A seminar designed to highlight the importance of effective communication to quality family relational health, and to offer counsel and guidelines for strengthening the communication bond in the family.

**Topic 5: Step-parenting in the Blended Family**

A seminar designed to focus on strategies of effective step-parenting and parenting in a blended family, supported by some statistical evidences. The discussion will include the establishment of boundaries, roles, expectations, unison of parental voice, and strength as one family, and is designed to enhance the success toward a blended family.

**Topic 6: Family Relational Health—A Biblical Psycho-social Priority**

A seminar designed to emphasize the importance of family members placing priority on their understanding and practicing the principles of family relational health, and to show its impact and influence on the quality of our physical, spiritual, mental, emotional, and social health, as well as to offer professional and biblical counsels towards improvement.

**Topic 7: From Obstetrics to Pediatrics to Geriatrics**

A seminar designed to look at the basics of the natural and developmental life cycle from birth to the aged, focusing on the psychosocial impact of the transitions and to help participants make the necessary healthy adjustments toward the desired state of mind: "growing older gracefully."

**Topic 8: Managing Marital Conflicts**

A seminar designed to address four major sources of conflict between husbands and wives—inhibitions, unresolved issues, gender perspectives, and occupation—and to educate them with spousal relational techniques and practical guidelines on solving such conflicts, thereby enriching their lives in the interest of personal and family well-being.

**Topic 9: Intimacy Between the Pauses**

A seminar designed to educate married couples (husbands and wives) on the major issues surrounding the impact of *menopause* and *andropause* on their lives, and to provide counsels and guidelines on how they can maintain a healthy intimate relationship and mature gracefully together.

**Topic 10: The Four Stages of Parenting**

A seminar designed to address the unique and overlapping nature of the four stages of *pre-parenting, expectant parenting, actual parenting and 'post'-parenting,* and to consider the dynamics of each stage and the ultimate effects that each has on the parent–parent, parent–child relationship.

**Topic 11: Men and Personal Development**

A seminar designed to address some current social concerns about the apparent lack of interest of many men in general toward personal, academic and vocational development—a kind of general educational developmental malaise (GEDM); to consider some anecdotal and statistical support for the concerns; and to offer some corrective psychosocial guidelines in stemming the tide of GEDM.

**Topic 12: The Dynamics of Trust in Human Relationships**

A seminar designed to focus on probably the most desirable and at the same time most elusive characteristics of human relationships – *Trust* looking at the various definitions and types of trust—such as *blind trust, invested trust, earned trust, and childlike trust*—and consider ways and means to build and maintain *trust* in the individual, family, and corporate levels of society.

**Topic 13: Conflicts Management and Resolution in the Family System**

A seminar designed to educate family members on the concept of the family system; to explore the nature and different types of family conflicts; and to give counsel and guidelines on how they can be managed to the well-being of the family and the glory of God.

## Topic 14: The Psychosocial Health of Singlehood

A seminar designed to give some positive biblical and psychosocial counsel for the affirmation of a healthy life experience of the various categories of single persons in the Church and community (See p. 358).

## Topic 15: Father, You Are Needed

A seminar designed to challenge and encourage fathers into a fuller understanding of their roles and responsibilities in the lives of their children in particular, and the society at large, and for their personal sense of parental satisfaction.

## Topic 16: The Four Pressure Points in Youth Relationships

A seminar designed to use the comparison of physical and psychological pressure in addressing four major challenges in youth relationships: *negative peer pressure, gang involvement, illicit sexual relationships, and drug/substance abuse*—and to arm them with decision-making skills toward the right choices in preserving personal identity and integrity.

## Topic 17: Teaching Sexuality to Children

A seminar designed to address some of the present-day challenges and issues affecting parents and their children regarding the matter of human sexuality, child growth and development and to impart relational skills toward rounded and healthy growth and development resulting in better homes, schools, and society at large.

## Topic 18: The Six Types of Parents

A seminar designed to clinically group parents into the *ignorant, idolizing, scapegoating, vilifying, image-preserving, and rational/objective* parent based on their awareness of their children's behavior and how they react or respond to the challenges they face as a result of those behaviors that the children display at home and school.

**Topic 19: Family Relational Health and Forgiveness**

A seminar designed to address the spiritual and psychosocial importance of forgiveness in family life, and to teach some necessary relational skills in the interest of the quality of life here on earth and our preparation for the coming Kingdom of God, when Jesus returns.

**Topic 20: Family Relational Health—A Prerequisite for Marital Happiness**

A seminar designed to challenge married couples (husbands and wives) to raise the bar of the quality of their relationship, with the awareness of their God-given responsibilities, to influence others, and to positively represent the mystery of the Christ–church relationship (pp. 303–304), in preparation for the Lord's return.

**Topic 21: Sexuality and the Family**

A seminar designed to raise the bar and deepen the understanding of the highest gift that God has given human beings—our sacred sexuality—and to reaffirm our personal commitment to God's original ideal for sexuality here on earth, amidst the distortions and drudgery of the present time, and to be prepared for the imminent return of Christ.

**Topic 22: The Stewardship of Family Life**

A seminar designed to educate family members on the fundamental biblical teachings of Christian stewardship and to encourage them to practice the principles of *accountability, responsibility,* and *faithfulness* to and for each other, and ultimately to God, the Giver and Owner of all good gifts.

## Topic 23: Strengthening Family Ties

A seminar designed to give reaffirmation of the four vital signs of family relationships (connection, rapport, bond and support) and to give each member the opportunity to measure the intensity of the strength of five main areas of their family bond and togetherness, anchoring these on the biblical principles of family respect.

## Topic 24: Family Relational and Health Spiritual Neuropathy

A seminar designed to address the biblical and psychosocial analogy of neuropathy of the body and the relational and spiritual estrangement that some family members experience, and to offer the psychotherapy for healing and restoration from God's words.

## Topic 25: Understanding DNRA and Family Relational Health

A seminar designed to show that successful relationships do not just happen; they are influenced by the quality of family relational health of each individual which health is anchored in each person's DNRA (developmental notifier of relational aptitude, Chapter 8, p. 173), and to give professional guidelines based on God's words, on how individuals can arm themselves with knowledge and skills in improving their prospects of experiencing successful relationships to the honor and glory of God and the benefit of those around them.

# Appendix 2

# Family Relational Health Assessment and Evaluative Instruments

## Medical and Psychological Testing: A Comparative Brief Overview

When we go to the medical facility for a physiological checkup—that is, for an assessment or evaluation of the state and function of the body—there are several basic devices, beginning at the triage room, that are used to measure certain body functions and features. Among these basic hardware devices and machines are the thermometer, the stethoscope, the scale, the ruler, the blood pressure, the pulse machine, and the ECG/ECC machine.

The list advances and becomes more sophisticated as the testing and diagnosing gets more detailed. Here we will find X-ray Machines, C-T Scanners, MRI Machines, Ultrasound Machines up to the more advanced and sophisticated Linear Accelerator with its daunting size and weight of approximately 1.3 Million lbs. or 589670.081 kilograms.

In the area of psychological care (not the same as *psychiatric* care), where the focus is primarily on the assessment and evaluation of the state and function of the mind from a behavioral and related perspectives, and not physiologically on the brain (which test would be more neurological and performed by a neurologist or neurosurgeon), the devices used to ascertain the indications are not as much hardware as those listed for the medical assessment.

Except in the sophisticatedly advanced setting for different types of brain-imaging techniques, specific hands-on manipulatory equipment and props—such as blocks, balls, mirrors, doughs, chords, and others of the kind—are used, depending on the assessment being made. There are also psychological tests, surveys, or scales, technically called *instruments,* all of which take different designs, layouts, and arrangements and administering protocols.

In the broad, general field of psychological care, there are several categories and subcategories of such tests, surveys, and scales that are administered in the assessment and care of clients. Among the major psychological tests are those that measure intelligence, personality, temperament, aptitude, attitude, achievements. There are also neuropsychological tests, vocational tests, and direct observation tests. One of the largest most comprehensive self-report inventory instruments is the Minnesota Multiphasic Personality Inventory (MMPI) with its 567 True or False Questions.

These tests are administered by licensed clinicians—such as counselors, psychiatrists, psychologists, social workers, psychotherapists—using a combination of techniques through which some hypotheses about the clients behavior, capabilities, personality, temperament, and other psychological attributes can be arrived at. In addition to these psychological tests, there is another large number used in the psychiatric and related disciplines.

Given the intricate working between the mind and the body (psychosomatic), as a standard international practice, detailed psychological assessments are better done after a routine medical exam is performed, seeing that underlying undiagnosed physiological malfunctions of the body can be registered in the mind, through chemical and hormonal imbalances among others in the brain, and therefore could render a psychological assessment less than its true reading and outcome.

*Disclaimer: The material contained herein is not in any way, shape, or form intended to be perceived, read, or understood to be of a medical, psychiatric, or mainstream psychological nature. It is exclusively prepared and presented in the context of family relational health, as discussed in this publication, and from the laboratory experiences detailed in Chapter 1. Any reference to the comments, suggestions, or instruments outside of the aforementioned context, is done at the reader's discretion.*

## Limitation

The instruments presented in this family relational health treatment program are best seen as basic psychometric activities designed primarily to produce an indication on various aspects of family relationships. No results are considered clinically and diagnostically conclusive but indicative. The same is true in some medical tests. When for example, a patient is being assessed to see if he or she is hypertensive or diabetic, the first reading is not usually considered conclusive. Other tests are conducted, noting trends and patterns on various criteria before a conclusive diagnosis is called.

In the case of family relational health, these assessments are intended to raise the awareness in the participant's relational mind about possible relationship factors, attitudes, perspectives, behaviours, among other attributes that need to be cherished and kept. (*CPH2*) Equally, they will be assisted to see any attributes or characteristics that might need to be managed and abhorred, in the interest of the wellbeing of the relationship they are in or is been contemplated.

The instruments at the end of this Appendix are samples of original assessment and evaluative ones that have evolved and modified/up-dated over the three decades of the development of the family relational health laboratory for treating family relational challenges and issues. As in all professional and clinical practices, the instruments presented here are peer- reviewed and needs-based driven—that is to say, they were developed in response to the perceived and evolving concerns and needs of the various family relational health cases that are continuously developing and mutating. They have been assessed, reviewed and validated at various professional conferences, seminars and training workshops in over 30 countries.

In the field of physiological health care, medical and clinical researchers and practitioners have to respond to the ever-growing and complex needs of patients by devising and providing drug and treatment regimens to address the current conditions and disorders as maladies and ailments develop and multiply. So it is in the field of family relational health practice, where the dynamics in individuals and family relationships undergo continuous strain and changes in an even-more-complex society.

Providing care for such relationships cannot be dependent only on the old treatment plans and courses of therapy ten, fifteen, twenty years ago, or even earlier. This is even more so, given the fact that focus has been mostly generalized on family and sometimes directly on husbands and wives, parents and children and patronizingly on singles. The focused-group and specializing approach was virtually unheard of (See p. 472).

To the same extent that some medications and treatment protocols have become outdated as diseases mutate, and even develop resistance to certain drugs, (Review p. 271) so it is that no one theory, concept, hypothesis, or method, nor the accompanying instrument(s) for the treatment procedures of assessing, measuring, and diagnosing every family relational challenge, remain the same ($CPH^2$). Family relational health is dynamic, always growing and changing; therefore, the professional caregivers (psychologists, counselors, therapists, social workers among others) have to remain on the cutting edge just like their counterparts in other areas of health care.

If family relationship issues are not equally cared for as medical issues, the imbalance could render the latter less than totally effective, notwithstanding the billions of dollars being invested into the various researches and technologies to find answers for a physiologically healthier society. Physiological health care will not reach its full potential if family relational health care is not given equal attention in development, given the intricate coordination between the relational mind and the body—psychosomatic health (See pp. 391–394).

This means that family relational health care practitioners have to develop proficiency, expertise, and skills commensurate to the changing society. Such competences and skills need to be enough for them to be able to devise, construct, and formulate treatment programs, procedures, and instruments to address the changing dynamics of the diversity of relationships in tandem with the categories identified (pp. 466–468), that they will encounter in their practice.

## Restriction on Usage

One of the challenges met at the end of many family relational health seminars is the request from laypersons and professionals in the related fields of counseling and social work to be given copies of some assessment instruments and exercises used or mentioned in the presentation.

The exuberant and earnest requests are stated in ways such as:

- "I like that instrument that you used. May I have a copy please?"

- "I have never seen that type of instrument. I would like to use it in my next counseling session."

- "My husband is not here, but I would like him to get that form (or instrument) so that we can do it at home. He needs to get it."

- "Please give me a copy of that seminar. I would like to share it with my group!"

Medication prescribed for a patient with a specific condition ought not to be used for another patient, even with evidently similar condition, without a medical doctor clinically making the diagnosis and advising on the use of the prescription. Patients' clinical data differ, and so will be their needed treatment protocol or regimen. Psychological and family relational health care is no less individual and personal. Any generalization of "one size fits all" does not carry.

It is also to be noted that medical practitioners can, and do at times, differ in their analysis and interpretation of clinical data, and this is reflected in the different treatment approach that some employ. It is professionally and ethically understood, therefore, that in many instances a medical doctor cannot always simply take up his or her counterpart's treatment plan and implement it without the necessary consultation, primarily in order to ensure the patient's best care and for him or her to remain professionally accountable.

Family relational health care practitioners have no less a responsibility and accountability for the treatment they measure out to clients in their care. In order to use a particular instrument, for example, a therapist or counsellor needs to be professionally familiar with the necessary clinical data of the instrument.

## Standard Laboratory Instruments Notes

Each instrument to be used in family relational health care should have the following twelve *standard laboratory instruments notes* (SLIN) so that there will be a unified knowledge base whenever any one of them is referred to in practice. The SLIN consist of the following information points:

1. Name of instrument
2. Year of instrument design (indicating its currency)
3. Name of designer
4. Instrument description
5. Purpose of instrument
6. Client case for which instrument is recommended
7. Administering procedure and protocol
8. Interpretation of the score ranges or other forms of responses
9. Evaluation procedure and case diagnosis
10. Any potential or possible limitation of its usage
11. Expected outcome—prognosis
12. Possible reaction by different clients from its usage

Considering the above parameters and conditions for usage of family relational health care instruments, it is best that before one is taken and applied, the professional checks the source and becomes acquainted with all necessary information on its SLIN.

Only numbers one through five of the SLIN will be provided for the sample of ten instruments that follow at the end of this Appendix. The full clinical data will be available in the *Family Relational Health Practitioner's Training Manual*, which will be used in the training program for family relational health care.

## Family Types and Structures - A Brief General Overview

Any attempt in this 21st Century society to define, discuss, describe and delineate the family structure and composition is a daunting, formidable and potentially controversial undertaking. US Former Secretary of Housing and Urban Development (2017–2021) and world-renowned paediatric surgeon, Dr. Benjamin Carson captured it fully: "Our society is breaking down in terms of family values that you pass on. It is almost politically incorrect to talk about family values and about doing the right thing because when someone comes along and say which family are you talking about? That's not right." (Fox News Interview, July 15, 2020).

The key question is "Which family are you talking about?" Between history, anthropology, sociology, religion, psychology, biology and maybe others, the number of discussions on the various types of family could be mind-blowing and befuddling! There are nuclear, elementary, conjugal, or consanguine families, adoptive families, step-families, single-parent families, foster families, unmarried partners families, and the many other versions in-between, depending on who is speaking and from what perspective.

The suggested outline of family categories below is not considered comprehensive or complete. It is intended to be a guide to help family relational health professionals in preparing to treat the multifaceted issues and challenges that assail the family in general. However, those issues and challenges get hidden and covered over in the relational crevices between the regularly known family categories in mainstream family life programmes, hence the need for the suggested delineation.

## Categories of Family Members – 3 – 36 – 68 TSIFR

The following breakdown, preferably and delineation of the composition of the family system could be described as the compound *three-tier-thirty-six sub-grouping of the sixty-eight inter-dynamic categories of family relationship (TSIFR)* abbreviated as The 3-36-68 TSIFR. This breakdown could also be referred to as the intra-family demographic delineation system (IDDS) of the family relational health laboratory, helping to highlight the intricate complexity of the family system.

Complexity is not the same as complication. The former alludes to the potential high number of components or parts and their varying and various interplays among themselves for the functionality of the system. The latter alludes to the potential difficulties and resultant challenges or problems that such interplay could have within the system, depending on how its functioning is managed.

The human mind, in which all relationships begin and continue to exist, is the most complex of our existence. It cannot be fathomed because it is a minuscule representation of the mind of the omnipotent, omniscient, omnipresent and eternal God Who made it. Had sin not impacted it, the complexity of our various relationships would not have become complicated as unfortunately it has become today.

To the same extent to which God manages the vast, limitless universe, having it in His hand, so would we be able to manage the multiple and ever-expanding family relationships and dynamics on our loving, relational minds. All the complexities of the various family categories would be unified with focus on the well-being of each member of the family system. Unfortunately, such correctly desired unity in the system can only be imagined, but is not likely to be experienced in this society, fraught with its present complexity of the growing human relational complications.

Despite this harsh reality, and even more so, in light of it, we need to study and be aware of the following suggested three-tiers, thirty-six sub-groupings of the sixty-eight inter-dynamic categories of family relationships. A fitting biblical imagery for this family inter-dynamic relationship is Ezekiel's 'wheel within a wheel' (Ezekiel 10: 10-13). Note that the wheels moved in concert and in harmony as they set out to accomplish the purpose for their design. So can the members in the family system accomplish their work together by the grace of God who designed them.

It is important to note that when taken to the finest possible analysis, this delineation can be expanded, given that any inter-family demographics incorporate members down to the third and fourth inter-and multiple generations, with extensions such as parental and even sibling great grands; 2nd, 3rd, and more cousins. Further researches will reveal more in this discipline. - (Review the Anchor Texts of the DNRA – Chapter 173).

The three tiers are indicative of the developmental order in which the family, more or less, develops and expands. It is not absolute as there are variations in how some families develop. Ideally, sequencing here in the family system in primary, secondary and tertiary does not indicate value or esteem of one category over another. The same sacred bond of love holds all family members together. Outlining them in order of primary, secondary and tertiary is done for demographic purpose and not an indication of preferred love over the other. In this context, we should heed the counsel on healthy relationship found in Philippians 2:1-4 and indeed "Let nothing be done through strife and vainglory."

Note well, Primary 11 p. 471, Col. 1 could also fit under Primary 3 p. 470, Col. 1 especially where Primary 1 did not produce Primary 3 biologically. There are the cases when Primary 11 comes after, and in addition to Primary 3 with no distinction/differentiation whatsoever, in terms of the quality of the parental-child love.

## Explanations of Family Categories Terms

**Primary** - This is the same as elementary, conjugal or consanguine, suggesting that after the marriage of the unrelated, non-consanguine man and woman, their combined off-spring and those after them are related by blood with genetic and hereditary connection. This was established at conception when the husband's sperm fertilized the wife's ovum and their two bloods united and began the flow down the generational lines.

It is important to note that when the husband and wife adopt a non-biologically/non-consanguine-related child, he or she is accorded the identical son-ship or daughter-ship status as a child born of them. This includes the sharing of the family name. The connection is considered permanent such that the description of 'adoptive' fades with time and he or she is simply, straightforwardly referred to as son or daughter with no reference to blood lineage. In this case the child is listed under the primary category as defined above.

**Secondary** - Family members in this category share a legal tie as against a biological/consanguine one. In-law status is established at the marriage when the biological/consanguine family of the husband and wife cross the proverbial floor, make a mental/emotional connection and thereby close the non-biological/non-consanguine gap and see themselves as one family. This was made clear earlier that in a healthy family, the tiers are no indication of the quality of the family bond, but only serve for demographic reckoning.

From a Christian perspective, members of the body of Christ, represented by membership in the Church, can even experience this new family relationship, brought on by the connecting blood of Christ, by faith and through baptism. (Matt. 12: 46-50 & 28: 18-20) There are times when such ecclesiastical ties are even felt potentially stronger than the biological blood ties (Ephesians 1:5-14). (See: Family in the Glossary, See p. 402).

**Tertiary** - Unlike the previous two tiers, family membership here does not necessarily share the same affinity, perspective and connection of familiness. Foster relationships are initiated with an understood tentativeness and no permanence intended—at least at the beginning. Togetherness has a time-line as well as relational parameters of a virtual 'thus-far' and no further operation. This simply means that there are limits to which they can go, including not sharing of family name.

Relational arrangements are supervised by the state, hence the term 'ward of the state'. This does not mean that relational connection and bond cannot be experienced among foster family members, given that all human relationships begin and continue to exist in the mind. When such minds are healthily bonded, the bonding can supersede state regulations, and the parties can, on their mutual volition, establish and maintain ties just as strong and even permanent as the primary and secondary ties.

It is understood however, that for any legal continuation and transaction to be entered into, reflecting the nature of the previous two tiers, the parties in the foster family would need to abide by the guidelines and principles of the state governing such arrangements.

## The Three-tier-thirty-six sub-grouping of the sixty-eight Inter-dynamic Categories of Family Relationship -3-36-68 TSIFR

### Tier One - Primary

1. Primary 1: Spousal
   - Husband
   - Wife

2. Primary 2: Parental
   - Father
   - Mother

3. Primary 3: Parental/Child
   - Son
   - Daughter

4. Primary 4: Sibling
   - Brother
   - Sister

5. Primary 5: Parental/Child
   - Grandfather
   - Grandmother

6. Primary 6: Parental/Child
   - Grandson
   - Granddaughter

7. Primary 7: Parental/Child
   - Uncle
   - Aunt

8. Primary 8: Parental/child
   - Nephew
   - Niece

9. Primary 9: Sibling
   - Cousins

10. Primary 10: Parental/Child
    - Adoptive Father
    - Adoptive Mother

11. Primary 11: Parental/Child
    - Adoptive Son
    - Adoptive Daughter

12. Primary 12: Sibling
    - Adoptive Brother
    - Adoptive Sister

13. Primary 13: Parental/Child
    - Adoptive Grandfather
    - Adoptive Grandmother

14. Primary 14: Parental/Child
    - Adoptive Grandson
    - Adoptive Granddaughter

15. Primary 15: Parental/Child
    - Adoptive Uncle
    - Adoptive Aunt

16. Primary 16: Parental/Child
    - Adoptive Nephew
    - Adoptive Niece

17. Primary 17: Sibling
    - Adoptive Cousins

## Tier Two - Secondary

18. Secondary 1: Parental/in-law
    - Father-in-Law
    - Mother-in-Law

19. Secondary 2: Parental/ Child-in-law
    - Son-in-law
    - Daughter- in-law

20. Secondary 3: Sibling-in-law
    - Brother-in-law
    - Sister-in-law

21. Secondary 4: Parental/ Child-in-law
    - Grandfather-in-law
    - Grandmother-in-law

22. Secondary 5: Parental/ Child-in-law
    - Grandson-in-law
    - Granddaughter-in-law

23. Secondary 6: Parental/ Child-in-law
    - Uncle-in-law
    - Aunt-in-law

24. Secondary 7: Parental/ Child-n-law
    - Nephew-in-law
    - Niece-in-law

25. Secondary 8: Sibling-in-law
   - Cousins-in-law

26. Secondary 9: Parental/ Child - Step
   - Step-father
   - Step-mother

27. Secondary 10: Parental/ Child - Step
   - Step-son
   - Step-daughter

28. Secondary 11: Sibling - Step
   - Step-brother
   - Step-sister

29. Secondary 12: Parental/ Child - Step
   - Step-grand-father
   - Step-grand-mother

30. Secondary 13: Parental/ Child - Step
   - Step-grand-son
   - Step-grand-daughter

31. Secondary 14: Parental/ Child - Step
   - Step-uncle
   - Step-aunt

32. Secondary 15: Parental/ Child - Step
   - Step-nephew
   - Step-niece

33. Secondary 16: Sibling - Step
   - Step Cousins

## Tier Three - Tertiary

34. Tertiary 1: Parental: Foster
   - Foster-father
   - Foster-mother

35. Tertiary 2: Parental/ Child - Foster
   - Foster-son
   - Foster-daughter

36. Tertiary 3: Sibling - Foster
   - Foster-brother
   - Foster-sister

## Specialization in Family Relational Healthcare

In analysing the inherent inter-dynamic categorization of family relationships and the potential complexities of their interplay, alongside the structure of the family relational health laboratory, (review Chapter 1, pp. 5 & 6) it is clear that no one practising therapist will be able to adequately provide the necessary care for all the categories of the family.

For family relational health to be at the optimum, each member should ideally be equipped with the best possible intra- and inter-personal skills to be gained through knowledge, treatment and developmental experience. This ideal cannot be accomplished fully through general presentations and counsels on family life as obtained in most present-day practices.

Look for example at the very establishment of the family beginning with the husband and the wife. In order for them to be the best possible spouse to each other, they individually need to be guided and where necessary, treated to be the best person he or she can be. His or her sense of healthy intra-personal quality relationship as a man or woman needs to be ascertained, assessed, affirmed and anchored and where necessary treated for improvement. This is best done through a program of professional counselling/therapy which will include a combination of individual and couples sessions. Such treatment procedure will increase incrementally as he or she assumes the various roles in life while moving through the different categories in the identified demographic three tiers.

Given that each category in each tier experiences overlapping and at the same time unique dynamics, there is the need for specializing family relational health practitioners to study and treat the possible issues and challenges that could be encountered in the growing complexity of the family. This is a basic explanation of how specialization evolved in the medical profession from about the mid to late 19th century. It was the growing and evolving needs of patients that led medical doctors to sharpen their focus on special and different aspects of healthcare, resulting in today's vast diversification in medical practice (Revisit pp. 88, 474).

This suggests that there will be the need for family relational health specialists for pre-marriage, marriage, parenting, siblings, in-laws, step families, blended families, grand parenting, adoptive parenting etc. Specialists also need to focus on families with special needs such as those members with certain disabilities, autism, down syndrome, degenerative mental disorders among others. It cannot be assumed that each sub-category will be naturally benefited from the care and treatment of the main category heading under which it falls. It is such generalization and over-simplification of the dynamics in family relationships that account in part, for the unhealthy state of many relationships today.

In the same vein, provision must be made for family posterity by ensuring that children and youth are properly and healthily educated in quality family relationships so that they can continue, with improvement, where their parents stopped. (See Song Number 1 *Batons of Faith*, FRH Songs of Praise and Bible Verses Paraphrased)

To the same extent that the medical care of the body has been undergoing continuous research, study and specialization, so it ought to be that the relational health of families be delineated, categorised, researched and studied, so that the relational mind can be adequately provided with the necessary knowledge and skills for healthier homes and hopefully, a healthier society. (CPH2) (Revisit pp. 13, 392)

The specialization study and treatment program called for here could be delivered at three levels of professional competence:

*Practitioner Level 1*- Family Relational Health General Practitioner (FRHGP) who focuses on education and guidance and counselling.

*Practitioner Level 2* – Family Relational Health Specialist/ Therapist (FRHST) who focuses on Therapy for different categories of the family, having developed competence and proficiency at Level 1. Sub-designations indicating category of specialization would need to be addressed, eg: *FRHST/P1* could designate a Therapist specializing in Spousal/Marital (Husband–Wife) Therapy

*Practitioner Level 3* – Family Relational Health Consultant (FRHC) who experientially and competently covers Levels 1 & 2 inclusive of research, writing and publishing in areas of professorship. Again, sub-designations could be done developmentally.

The details of these competencies will be fully outlined and addressed in the *Family Relational Health Practitioners Training Manual*, and ideally implemented as a part of The Family Relational Health Respital program.

## Five Points of Desired Unity in the Family System

In light of this structural grouping of the family system, some glaring realities and potential challenges stand out regarding the desired unity in the family. Family relational health care practitioners need to take note of the following five pointers and factor them into the treatment regimen as the various issues and needs arise:

1. Seamless Unity The ideal of a seamless unity among family members in the complexities of our relational minds does not exist in full. This is the result of sin in the mind. (Read p. 469, para 3).

2. All Is Not Lost Thank God, all is not lost! We did not say in number 1 above that the unity does not exist at all; we say it does not exist in *full* as was originally intended at Creation. There is hope and Christian practitioners are to be prepared to work with that which is possible. This hope is made possible by God's grace!

3. Gather Remaining Hope We need to focus on, gather and amplify the hope which remains. Then we are to give it to 'The-Jesus-of-the-feeding-of-the-five-thousands' fame (Matt. 14:14–21) and let Him multiply it for His glory and honor

and the blessing of the family members who are hungry for relational unity among themselves (Review No. 2, p. 449).

Despite the presence of sin and its challenges, if we look carefully and intently enough, we can almost always see even small signs or rays of hope that all is not lost in many unhealthy relationships. We are to acknowledge such signs, affirm them, and give them to Jesus, Who can breathe life and growth in them. When the Spirit then builds up love (charity) in our heart, we will experience the family relational health counsel found in 1 Peter 4:8: "And above all things have fervent charity among yourselves: for charity shall cover the multitude of sins."

Jesus can inspire that unity amidst our complexity. That was part of His supplication prayer request to the Father for His followers when He was about to leave the earth (John 17:11–23). And it is the work of His Representative, the Holy Spirit, to bring about that unity in the complex family system with our cooperation.

## Study Family Systems

4.  Do the correct study and analysis of the interdynamics of the various categories of the human relationship system. To the same extent that continuous research and study on the complex physiological working of the body make medical care and treatment more definitive for the specific needs of patients (Review pp. 88, 368), so it is that continuous study and analysis of the family dynamics will make family relational health care better for the complex family system (CPR$^2$).

## Spread the Knowledge

5.  Disseminate to the families the knowledge and relational skills garnered from such a study under the inspiration of

the Holy Spirit. This will empower and inspire them with the prospects of living good, quality lives here on earth in preparation for the life to come when Jesus returns.

## Basics of Family Dynamics: 10 Factors Determining the Interdynamics of Family Relationships

The following are ten basic factors that, perceptively, or imperceptively, knowingly or unknowingly, influence the power play or power struggle (relational dynamics) in the relational mind of each person in the process of forging and keeping a relationship. Inasmuch as there are potential overlaps in the characteristics of the dynamics of each factor when analysed and delineated, such overlapping element will remain unique to that factor and should be studied by itself.

1. Family-of-origin impact: one's DNRA (Chapter 8)
2. Socialization: exposure and experience
3. One's worldview: personal, societal, and cultural
4. Nonspecific, general relationship with people
5. Private internalized/subconscious relationship perspective
6. Sexual/gender perspective and orientation
7. Knowledge base and intelligence quotient
8. Value system: religious and spiritual
9. Intra/interpersonal relationship perspective (specific)
10. Physiological health status

Over the decades of the development of the family relational health laboratory mentioned in Chapter 1, there has been a continuous and never-ending need to ascertain and understand the dynamics in each client relational mind (Review pp. 17, 18), and more so for him or her to give evidence of his or her own knowledge on the following eight states of mind

1.  What does he/she know about relationships in general and particularly the one in which he or she is engaged.

2.  Does he or she know what he or she wants and what the other party wants in the relationship and how complementary and complimentary they can be in such pursuits?

3.  Does he/she know what is good and acceptable to make a healthy relationship?

4.  What, if any, relational skills does he or she have or is lacking, that is to say, does not possess any at all.

5.  In addition to #2, what is his or her secret/private desire for the relationship?

6.  Does he or she know the factors to be avoided in order to develop and keep a healthy relationship?

7.  What adjustment(s) is he or she willing to make in order for the relationship to work?

8.  Is there any comparative relationship experience that he or she has?

In most cases, this litany of relational introspection is not done by the average person forging a relationship. Their minds have not been arrested to address the dynamics of the relationship in such a structured way. Many times, family members who might be asked some or any of the above introspective questions are not afraid to expose their ignorance:

- "I did not know that all these questions have to do with me and him/her!"

- "I just know that we love each other and we are trying to make things work out. Hopefully, they will!" This is the new trend called "Situationship" instead of relationship.

- "Now that I see the questions on the form [making reference to the assessment instrument], it makes me realize that this thing called *relationship* is more than I was thinking."

It is the responsibility of the family relational health practitioner to find professional ways to raise the bar in the client's mind and help him or her to be in touch with the issues, concerns, desires, goals, and challenges that are in the relationship. In addition, they need to know the necessary relational skills to be practiced in order to get the possible best outcome of the relationship for all the members concerned.

## International Standards of Assessment and Scoring – A Synopsis

For the above ten factors and eight points to be achieved, the practitioner needs to be aufait with the international standards of assessment instruments and their construction and administering procedures. With such knowledge, he will not only know how to use such instruments, but he can go on to construct and administer others which speak directly and specifically to the family relational issues that come up in his practice. Many of such issues are not addressed in the regular instruments supplied in mainstream psychological practice.

In those practices focus is generally on a group or population, be that a classroom, a school, a community, or any circumscribed body of participants. This does not mean that assessment instruments are not devised in mainstream practice for the families and the individuals who make them up, but there is a difference with the definitiveness and sharp focus with which they are presented through a family relational health practice perspective.

The fluidity and generalization of family and family-ness that is characteristic of present mainstream psychological practice does not always go in sync with the Bible-based perspective of family relational health care as developed over the decades of research, study, work, and practice, and presented in this volume. Therefore, only those principles, methods, and practices that are compatible will be engaged and utilized in our delivery of family relational health care.

## Norm and Criterion Reference Measurement

In most cases, score results on assessments are referred to as norm reference scores. This means that such scores represent the average performance of a representative sample from any of the group population sample mentioned above. That acceptable sample now becomes, as it were, the point of reference against which all in that selected population are measured. A norm score does not necessarily focus on the individual per se; it is mostly group-oriented.

In family relational health care, assessment always focuses on the individual, personally, first. This is done to ascertain his or her perspective on the relational issue being addressed. Look again at the 8 relational knowledge questions on page p. 478. Ideally, this individualistic approach should begin from the premarital counseling stage of family relationship-building. Such counseling would be patently flawed if there is no individual session for the fiancé and fiancée with the counselor/therapist.

From the norm reference measurement principle, the group is the couple, but the quality of life among them is going to be influenced firstly by each one's viewpoint and outlook on the ideal to be accomplished in the merger of their lives together, hopefully until death do them part. Therefore criterion reference scoring is the technique employed for the instruments developed and used in this practice.

Criterion reference measurement scoring is that which specifically indicates what an individual family member is capable of; what is expected of him or her; and what his or her knowledge base is on any given aspect of family relationship. The instrument can be constructed based on established, acceptable ideals (norms) against which the participating family member will respond a variety of responses, such as □*yes*, □*no*, and □*not sure*, among others.

Another method is the line scale graduated from 1 to 10 or 1 to 5 in most cases, with *1* being the lowest or least desirable based on the established criterion(a) and *10* or *5* being the highest or most desirable. Again, we will bear in mind that the produced result of this 'relational mind scan' (Review p. 413) will be indicative and the professional family relational health 'Radiologist' will factor that into the reading, interpretation, diagnosis and treatment also with the SLIN (p. 460).

It is not unlikely that the criterion(a) used could itself be arrived at from norm referencing score done at other times and elsewhere among persons of like-minded perspective. Elements from that source or finding are then adopted and built into the standard criteria for a smaller group, such as a married couple, parents, and other individuals and subgroups of the family system.

The simplified adopted version of criterion reference scoring that is used in this practice is understandably not as complex in its analysis and detailing. This is primarily so because the sample population is uniquely small, in most cases it is between two and seven persons comprising the average family or household. Rarely does the assessment involve all family members at one time, but generally subgroups of two or three: husband and wife; father and mother; parent and child; sibling and sibling; father, mother, and child; or any other duo or threesome within the family unit.

For professional integrity, and in order to measure up to international standards, assessment instruments and supportive material in family relational health care have been constructed and put into use, ensuring that the following elements are incorporated in the entire system:

- ✓ objectivity
- ✓ validity
- ✓ reliability
- ✓ deductive reasoning
- ✓ inductive reasoning
- ✓ empirical reasoning
- ✓ the cognitive domain
- ✓ the affective domain
- ✓ the psychomotor/behavioral domain

Details of these aspects of laboratory work comprise some of the contents in book 2, *Family Relational Health: A Missing Dimension in Comprehensive Health Care*, and in the training manual, *Family Relational Health Practitioner's Training Manual*.

**Samples of Family Relational Health Assessment Instruments**

As stated earlier, only numbers one through five of the SLIN will be shared in this Appendix. The full clinical data will be available in the *Family Relational Health Practitioner's Training Manual*, which will be used in the training program for family relational health care.

NB: All sample instruments are considered to be at the basic level, which means that there are upper-level instruments designed for deeper, more intensive assessment depending on the nature of the case being treated.

## Sample Instrument #1 – Single Client's Pre-therapy Goals

**Family Relational Health Services International**
◄—BTHFHFS/FRHS:Raising The Bar in Family Services—►

*Assessing *Evaluating* Analyzing *Training *Educating *Counselling...

### Single Client's Pre-Therapy Goals
(Why I Came to this Session; What I Want to Happen)
©2020 Anthony L. Gordon, Ph.D. Counselling Psychologist & Family Relational Health Specialist. All Right Reserved

Name_____ Age_____
Relational Status: ☐Single ☐Committed(Courting) ☐Engaged ☐Living Together
☐Married ☐Widowed ☐Separated ☐Divorced ☐Remarried
Address_____
_____
Telephone_____ Email_____

**Introduction/Instruction:** In order for the treatment/therapy Session to be properly focused on Your Needs, and for You to benefit from them, it is important that Specific Goals be set from the very beginning. Below is a sampling of Goals that different persons have set when they seek therapy. Read them carefully and if any expresses what You would like to be accomplished, please place a tick (✓) beside it/them. Write any other Personal Specific Goals that You have on the space provided below. Thank You!

**Some General Goals**
☐ I want to understanding and effectively manage the issues affecting my life.
☐ I want to correct some faulty behaviours; replace them with acceptable ones.
☐ I want to find more meaning in life.
☐ I want to achieve a better relationship with_____
☐ I want to love myself more.
☐ I want to become more self-actualizing and accomplished.
☐ I want to build my self-esteem.
☐ I want to stop depending on_____
☐ I want to become more responsible.
☐ I want to release myself of guilt.
☐ I want to learn to communicate more effectively with_____
☐ I want to develop better human relationship skills in general.
☐ I want to learn to handle family conflicts better.
☐ I want to resolve some_____conflicts that I have with _____
☐ I want to improve my social life.

**Personal Specific Goals**
_____
_____
_____
_____

### Standard Laboratory Instrument Notes (SLIN)

1. Name of Instrument : *Client's Pre-therapy Goals*

2. Year of Design : *2016; Revised 2020*

3. Designer : *Anthony L. Gordon, Ph.D.*

4. Description/Purpose:
This exercise is designed to assist the Client to determine what he or she wants to happen as a result of seeking professional therapy.

It also will give the *Relational Health Practitioner* (*RHP*) an idea of how well the prospective client is in charge of his or her mind as indicated by how thoroughly the Form is completed. Take note if the *Personal Specific Goals* is completed that is a further indication of how much the person is thorough and earnest. It also suggests the level of participation and rapport to be expected during the session. The more completed and thorough the Form, the more likely that the Client is intelligent and will be engaging with the prospect of a successful outcome.

5. Administering Procedure:
To be completed by the client ideally *before* the Session begins.

Upon receiving the Form The *RHP* is to go through it thoroughly, noting how many of the 15 *General Goals* are selected. Co-relate these with any *Personal Specific Goals* that are written.

During the Consultation (1ˢᵗ.) Session, a thorough review of the Form including an interpretation of each checked goal, is to be done with the Client. It is to be placed in the right perspective as the 'road map' as it indicates where the session is intended to go, based on his or her expressed needs or goals. Understandably, it can be modified along the way, but at least at the beginning, there is a common understanding between Client and Therapist where they are aiming to go and what is to be achieved.

---

## Sample Instruments #2 & 3
## Single Client's Post-therapy and Married Couple's Post-therapy Exercises

**Family Relational Health Services International**
◄—BTHFHFS/FRHS:Raising The Bar in Family Services—►

*Assessing *Evaluating* Analyzing *Training *Educating *Counselling...

### Client's Post-therapy Review Exercise
(What has Happened for Me as a Result of the Session)
©2020 Anthony L. Gordon, Ph.D. Counselling Psychologist & Family Relational Health Specialist. All Right Reserved

Name_____ Age_____
Relational Status: ☐Single ☐Committed(Courting) ☐Engaged ☐Living Together
☐Married ☐Widowed ☐Separated ☐Divorced ☐Remarried
Address_____
_____
Telephone_____ Email_____

**Introduction:** It is most important that at the end of each Therapy Session You do a *Review* of what took place during the session. A *Session Review* means that You consciously set aside a special time, within **24 hours** after the Therapy Session and playback or recall all that took place in the Session. This review will help You to evaluate the benefits that You ought to get from the Session, and to decide on the action(s) that the Therapist suggested, and some that You will take to help Yourself. Please be prepared to share Your *Review* with your therapist at the next follow-up Session. This will help You and Your Therapist to see how well You are progressing and improving.

**Some Evaluation Questions:** (Answer honestly and NOT to please the Therapist)
☐ Was it a wise decision to go to the Therapist?   ☐ Yes ☐ No ☐ Not Sure
☐ Did the Therapist understand my issue(s)?   ☐ Yes ☐ No ☐ Not Sure
☐ Did I understand the Therapist' Comments?   ☐ Yes ☐ No ☐ Not Sure
☐ Did I feel Safe and Confident with the Therapist   ☐ Yes ☐ No ☐ Not Sure
☐ Did I benefit from going to the session?   ☐ Yes ☐ No ☐ Not Sure

**My Action Plan**
☐ I will_____
☐ I will NOT_____
☐ I want to get a clearer understanding of_____
☐ I will ask the Therapist about_____
☐ I want to_____
☐ I Do NOT want to_____

**Any Other Decision/Action that I Made as a Result of this *Session Review***
_____
_____
_____

**Family Relational Health Services International**
◄—BTHFHFS/FRHS:Raising The Bar in Family Services—►

*Assessing *Evaluating* Analyzing *Training *Educating *Counselling...

### Married Couple's Post-therapy Review Exercise
(What has Happened for Me/Us as a Result of the Session)
©2020 Anthony L. Gordon, Ph.D. Counselling Psychologist & Family Relational Health Specialist. All Right Reserved

Name_____ Age_____
Relational Status: ☐Married ☐Widowed ☐Divorced ☐Remarried
Address_____
_____
Telephone_____ Email_____

**Introduction:** It is most important that at the end of each Therapy Session You, as a Couple, do a *Review* of what took place during the session. A *Session Review* means that You both consciously set aside a special time *within 24 hours* after the Therapy Session and playback or recall all that took place in the Session. This *Review* will help You both to evaluate the benefits that You ought to get from the Session, and to decide on the action(s) that the Therapist suggested, and some that You, individually and together, will take to help Yourselves. Please be prepared to share Your *Review* with Your Therapist at the next follow-up Session in order to see how well Your *marital relationship* is progressing and improving.

**Some Evaluation Questions:** (Answer honestly and NOT to please the Therapist)
☐ Was it a wise decision to go to the Therapist?   ☐ Yes ☐ No ☐ Not Sure
☐ Did the Therapist understand my/our issue(s)?   ☐ Yes ☐ No ☐ Not Sure
☐ Did I/We benefit from going to the Session?   ☐ Yes ☐ No ☐ Not Sure
☐ Did I/We understand the Therapist's Comments?   ☐ Yes ☐ No ☐ Not Sure
☐ Did I/We feel Safe and Confident with the Therapist?   ☐ Yes ☐ No ☐ Not Sure

**My/Our Action Plan**
☐ I/We will_____
☐ I/We will NOT_____
☐ I/We want to get a clearer understanding of_____
☐ I/We will ask the Therapist about_____
☐ I/We want to_____
☐ I/We Do NOT want to_____

**Any Other Decision/Action that I/We Made as a Result of this *Session Review***
_____
_____
_____

483

## Sample Instrument # 4 – Married Couple's Vital Signs Assessment

**Family Relational Health Services International**
BTHFHFS/FRHS:Raising The Bar in Family Services

*Assessing *Evaluating* Analyzing *Training *Educating *Counselling...

### Married Couple's Basic (Pre-Therapy) Relational Vital Signs Assessment

©2020 Anthony L. Gordon, Ph.D. Counselling Psychologist & Family Relational Health Specialist. All Right Reserved

**Introduction & Instruction**

This exercise is designed to help YOU as a Couple to have an indication of the strength of the *Vital Signs* of YOUR Matrimonial Health with which YOU are entering Therapy. Other similar assessments will be done during and after YOUR therapy sessions to see how stable and improved the quality of YOUR relationship will become.

Draw a circle around the number on the line scale that best represents YOUR rating of each *Vital Sign*. 1 is the lowest rating, and 10 is the highest rating.
NB. *This exercise is NOT Diagnostic or Conclusive, it is only Indicative.*

Your Name_____

Spouse's Name_____

Date_____

1. We share ONE Matrimonial Home. ☐Yes ☐No. Rate How YOU Feel about it.
   1  2  3  4  5  6  7  8  9  10

2. We share ONE Matrimonial Bedroom ☐Yes ☐No. Rate How YOU Feel about it.
   1  2  3  4  5  6  7  8  9  10

3. We share ONE Matrimonial Bed: ☐Yes ☐No. Rate How YOU Feel about it.
   1  2  3  4  5  6  7  8  9  10

4. We share MUTUAL Matrimonial Intimacy: Feelings, Emotion, Sexual ...
   1  2  3  4  5  6  7  8  9  10

5. We share Family Meals (eat many or most times) together.
   1  2  3  4  5  6  7  8  9  10

6. We share Family Social Times, (at home or going out)together
   1  2  3  4  5  6  7  8  9  10

7. We share Family Spiritual Values (study, worship, praying) together.
   1  2  3  4  5  6  7  8  9  10

**Complete Calculation Overleaf.** Counsellor will guide You with Score Interpretation

---

### Married Couple's Basic (Pre-Therapy) Relational Relational Vital Signs Assessment Score Sheet

1. For Items 1 – 3, Add the Rating(s) for any 'Yeses' that you have_____

2. Add the Rating(s) for any 'No's that You have_____

3. *Subtract* the Score for the *No's* from the Score for the *'Yeses'*_____

2. For Items 4 – 7 Add All the Ratings_____

3. *Add* this to the Score for **Items 1 - 3**
   _____

4. This New Number is **Your Grand Rating Score**_____

5. This *Grand Rating Score (The Highest possible being 70)* is the *Indicator* of the *Strength* of the *Vital Signs* of Marital Relationship.

   The Counsellor will now give You the Possible Interpretation of Your Score.

---

## Sample Instruments # 5 & 6
## Married Couple's Spiritual and Emotional Passion Assessments

**Family Relational Health Services International**
BTHFHFS/FRHS:Raising The Bar in Family Services

*Assessing *Evaluating* Analyzing *Training *Educating *Counselling...

### Couples Spiritual Passion Assessment

©2020 Anthony L. Gordon, Ph.D. Counselling Psychologist & Family Relational Health Specialist. All Right Reserved

Name_____Age____
Relational Status: ☐Married ☐Widowed ☐Divorced ☐Remarried
Address_____

Telephone_____ Email_____

**Introduction/Instruction:** Here are 10 Simple *'Behind-closed-door'* Spiritual Indicators of a Couple "experiencing Christ" in their marriage. Each Spouse is to do the assessment independently by checking the response as You honestly know it, then share the results with Your husband or wife. Affirm where You agree and make a commitment to improve where necessary.

| | Do | Did | Don't |
|---|---|---|---|
| 1. Hold hands and pray together | | | |
| 2. Kneel and pray together at our bedside | | | |
| 3. Encourage each other to study and be faithful | | | |
| 4. Prayed for him/her by myself and told him/her that I did | | | |
| 5. Commend and affirm each other for a spiritually inspiring word/act | | | |
| 6. Witness to each other regarding some goodness of the Lord | | | |
| 7. Occasionally text/email spiritual commendations or reminders to each other | | | |
| 8. Sit and listen to a Sermon together | | | |
| 9. Watch a religious movie together | | | |
| 10. Discuss and/or do Witnessing Plan or Program together | | | |
| Score: | | | |

Your Counsellor/Therapist will assist You in interpreting Your Responses.

---

**Family Relational Health Services International**
BTHFHFS/FRHS:Raising The Bar in Family Services

*Assessing *Evaluating* Analyzing *Training *Educating *Counselling...

### Couple's Emotional Passion Assessment

©2020 Anthony L. Gordon, Ph.D. Counselling Psychologist & Family Relational Health Specialist. All Right Reserved

Name_____Age____
Relational Status: ☐Married ☐Widowed ☐Divorced ☐Remarried
Address_____

Telephone_____ Email_____

**Introduction/Instruction:** *"...the little foxes, that spoil the vines..."* (Song of Solomon 2:15) Consider the apparent simplicity, but the deep, profound impact that the items listed below can have on the emotional quality of a couple's marital relationship. As you read and respond to each, let your mind think and reason how well your marriage is or could be, as a result of you both sharing in these simple, but very important practices together. Discuss your individual responses and make a commitment to cherish the positives and work on the areas needing improvement.

| | Do | Did | Don't |
|---|---|---|---|
| 1. Hold hands in church, in the car, sitting on the bed, when walking on the street | | | |
| 2. Give a Surprise Hug from the back. | | | |
| 3. Enjoy going out together, wherever, whenever | | | |
| 4. Give a Full Body Hug when you are alone. | | | |
| 5. Bite something and give him/her a piece. | | | |
| 6. Share in a Pillow Talk. | | | |
| 7. Tell a simple, 'foolish' story. | | | |
| 8. Laugh about something rather nonsensical | | | |
| 9. Have an open-heart, down-to-earth talk | | | |
| 10. Rub down his /her feet, hand or full body. | | | |
| Score | | | |

Your Counsellor/Therapist will assist You in interpreting Your Responses.

# Sample Instruments # 7 & 8
## Toxic Relationship Recovery Exercise and Basic Improvement Relationship Exercise

### Family Relational Health Services International
**BTHFHFS/FRHS:Raising The Bar in Family Services**

*Assessing *Evaluating* Analyzing *Training *Educating *Counselling...

**Client's Post-therapy Review Exercise**
**Toxic Relationship Recovery Exercise**
©2020 Anthony L. Gordon, Ph.D. Counselling Psychologist & Family Relational Health Specialist. All Right Reserved

Name_____ Age_____
Relational Status: ☐Single ☐Committed(Courting) ☐Engaged ☐Living Together
☐Married ☐Widowed ☐Separated ☐Divorced ☐Remarried
Address_____
_____
Telephone_____ Email_____

**Introduction/Instruction:** This exercise is designed to help you to grapple with and be decisive about the challenge(s) of a relationship that you are convinced is toxic and which is having an unhealthy impact upon you. In order to do it well, you need to be *calm* and *composed*. Keep your mind focused on what you are convinced is *best* for you at this time. Read each Statement; Think it through carefully; Check the Response Box that reflects the state of your mind NOW. Move to the Next Statement and complete the exercise in ONE sitting – Do Not Stop to do anything else that could shift your thought process.

1. I Know and Understand what the Real Issue(s) is/are about this relationship.
   ☐Yes ☐No ☐Not Sure
2. I Know what I really Want to Happen as a result of the issue(s).
   ☐Yes ☐No ☐Not Sure
3. I will remove All *Ambivalence* about the issue(s) from My Mind.
   ☐Yes ☐No ☐Not Sure
4. I will be Decisive about what needs to be done; and be Prepared to Do it.
   ☐Yes ☐No ☐Not Sure
5. I will resist practising *Reactions* and insist on exercising *Responses* instead.
   ☐Yes ☐No ☐Not Sure
6. I will positively Process and Take Charge of any situation as it impacts me.
   ☐Yes ☐No ☐Not Sure
7. I will Think carefully and decisively and be accountable for what I Say or Do.
   ☐Yes ☐No ☐Not Sure

Your Counsellor/Therapist will assist You in interpreting Your Responses.

---

### Family Relational Health Services International
**BTHFHFS/FRHS:Raising The Bar in Family Services**

*Assessing *Evaluating* Analyzing *Training *Educating *Counselling...

**The Basic 7-Step Plan for Relationship Improvement**
©2020 Anthony L. Gordon, Ph.D. Counselling Psychologist & Family Relational Health Specialist. All Right Reserve

Name_____ Age_____
Relational Status: ☐Single ☐Committed(Courting) ☐Engaged ☐Living Together
☐Married ☐Widowed ☐Separated ☐Divorced ☐Remarried
Address_____
_____
Telephone_____ Email_____

**Introduction/Instruction:** This Exercise is designed to help YOU, Personally to check the Earnestness of YOUR Mind to work towards improving YOUR Relationship with_____.
Carefully Read each Statement; Ask YOURSELF: How True Is This About ME? (NOT about Him or Her). Check the Response beside each Statement that best represents YOUR State of Mind Now about the Relationship.

1. I acknowledge that I Do Not have All of the Needed Relational Skills
   ☐Yes ☐No ☐Not Sure
2. I am willing to admit and expose My *Ignorance* in order to improve.
   ☐Yes ☐No ☐Not Sure
3. I will be specific about the *How's, When's, Why's* and *What's* of Relational Skills that I know that I Do Not Master at this time.
   ☐Yes ☐No ☐Not Sure
4. I have a *Genuine* Desire to acquire those Necessary Relational Skills.
   ☐Yes ☐No ☐Not Sure
5. I am prepared to make the Necessary Adjustments and Practise the Necessary New Relational Skills in order to improve the relationship.
   ☐Yes ☐No ☐Not Sure
6. I will be a *dear* with Myself and _____
   in practising the Needed and Necessary Relational Skills.
   ☐Yes ☐No ☐Not Sure
7. I will learn and use *Affirmation, Encouragement* and *Challenge* as *Motivation* for *Continuation* and *Improvement* of the relationship.
   ☐Yes ☐No ☐Not Sure

Date of Completion_____

---

# Sample Instruments # 9 & 10
## Self-test on Anger Management and Basic Self-esteem Assessment Exercise

### The Family Relational Health Services
**BTHFHFS/FRHS:Raising The Bar in Family Services**

*Assessing *Evaluating* Analyzing *Training *Educating *Counselling...

**My Self-test on Anger Management**
©2020 Anthony L. Gordon, Ph.D. Counselling Psychologist & Family Relational Health Specialist. All Right Reserved

Name_____ Age_____
Relational Status: ☐Single ☐Committed(Courting) ☐Engaged ☐Living Together
☐Married ☐Widowed ☐Separated ☐Divorced ☐Remarried
Address_____

**Introduction & Instruction**
This exercise is designed to help you to become aware of your Anger Management Skills, and to offer professional help where needed, so that you can learn how best to manage such situations and avoid getting into trouble. Be Honest with Yourself and respond to ALL Ten Statements below by ticking "Yes" or "No" If your are in doubt, then select the response that you think is closest to the fact.

1. Do you often or sometimes have to explain to others that: "I'm **not** angry!"
   Yes ☐ No ☐
2. Do you often lose your patience and temper with others or over situations?
   Yes ☐ No ☐
3. Do you sometimes yell or raise your voice to get your point across to others?
   Yes ☐ No ☐
4. Have you ever thought about getting even with, or taking revenge on others?
   Yes ☐ No ☐
5. Do you find yourself frequently in a long, negative arguments with others?
   Yes ☐ No ☐
6. Have you ever been in a physical altercation by attacking another student?
   Yes ☐ No ☐
7. Were you ever warned by the Police because of your behaviour?
   Yes ☐ No ☐
8. Do you find yourself unable to let go of grievances and resentments?
   Yes ☐ No ☐
9. Do you keep replay negative experiences over and over in your mind?
   Yes ☐ No ☐
10. Do you feel that yourself that you have an Uncontrolled Anger Problem?
    Yes ☐ No ☐

**Check Your Score and write the number beside each Response:**

Yes [_____] No [_____]

Now Listen to the Therapist for the Interpretation of Your Score and for further Recommendations.
Date of Completion_____

---

### The Family Relational Health Services
**BTHFHFS/FRHS:Raising The Bar in Family Services**

*Assessing *Evaluating* Analyzing *Training *Educating *Counselling...

**Self-esteem Assessment Exercise**
©2020 Anthony L. Gordon, Ph.D. Counselling Psychologist & Family Relational Health Specialist. All Right Reserved

Name_____ Age_____
Relational Status: ☐Single ☐Committed(Courting) ☐Engaged ☐Living Together
☐Married ☐Widowed ☐Separated ☐Divorced ☐Remarried
Address_____

**Introduction & Instruction**
This is a very special exercise designed to assist you and your Therapist to design a therapy program especially for your need. The findings of this exercise are NOT conclusive, they are only indicative. Please read each statement *carefully*, and then respond to it by placing a tick (✓) in the box that is beside the response that best fits you.

1. I know when I do things correctly, and I enjoy the feeling that I get
   ☐ Yes, Many Times ☐ Sometimes ☐ Not Sure ☐ Not At All
2. I know that I spend time doing the best at whatever work I do.
   ☐ Yes, Many Times ☐ Sometimes ☐ Not Sure ☐ Not At All
3. The important persons in my life encourage me about the good things that I do.
   ☐ Yes, Many Times ☐ Sometimes ☐ Not Sure ☐ Not At All
4. If my friends don't let me feel good with them, I can still be happy with myself.
   ☐ Yes, Many Times ☐ Sometimes ☐ Not Sure ☐ Not At All
5. I can remember hearing teachers or others talking good things about me.
   ☐ Yes, Many Times ☐ Sometimes ☐ Not Sure ☐ Not At All
6. I observe good women/men and know who are good role models for me.
   ☐ Yes, Many Times ☐ Sometimes ☐ Not Sure ☐ Not At All
7. I spend time alone with myself and do the positive things that I enjoy doing.
   ☐ Yes, Many Times ☐ Sometimes ☐ Not Sure ☐ Not At All
8. I know the positive friends who I love to keep, and others who I do not want.
   ☐ Yes, Many Times ☐ Sometimes ☐ Not Sure ☐ Not At All
9. I know the kind of situations or experiences that make me happy.
   ☐ Yes, Many Times ☐ Sometimes ☐ Not Sure ☐ Not At All
10. When I look at the mirror, I love the person who looks back at me.
    ☐ Yes, Many Times ☐ Sometimes ☐ Not Sure ☐ Not At All

**Scoring:** Add and Fill the Boxes: No. of MT [___] ST [___] NS [___] NA [___]
You are now finished; Your Therapist will discuss the interpretations of your responses and the possible indication for future assessment and therapy.

# References

American Psychiatric Association (2013). *Diagnostic and Statistical Manual of Mental Disorders* (DSM-5™), 5th edn. Washington, DC: American Psychiatric Publishing.

*A place to share knowledge and better understand the world.* Quora. (n.d.). https://www.quora.com/.

Baak, G. A. (2017). *The Inheritors: Moving Forward from Generational Trauma.* Berkeley, CA: SWP She Writes Press.

Barthel, T. (n.d.). *Animal Gender and the Taste of Meat.* Sustainable Farming Association of Minnesota. https://www.sfa-mn.org/animal-gender-and-the-taste-of-meat/.

BBC. (2018, March 2). *Kenya doctors 'perform brain surgery on Wrong patient'.* BBC News. https://www.bbc.com/news/world-africa-43255648.

BBC (2019). "Nigeria police free captives 'held in prayer house,'" *New Zimbabwe*, 1 November. Retrieved from https://www.newzimbabwe.com/nigeria-police-free-captives-held-in-prayer-house/.

Bohn, H. G. (1855). *A Hand-book of Proverbs.* London: H.G. Bohn.

Brooks, Charles D. (1980). Sermon: "Sodom-Bound," Breath of Life Ministries.

*CA schools to teach kindergartners about 15 Genders under new guidelines.* EAGnews.org. (2020, June 2). https://www.eagnews.org/2019/01/ca-schools-to-teach-kindergartners-about-15-genders-under-new-guidelines/.

Donne, J. (n.d.). "'No Man Is an Island'—the Meaning and Origin of This Phrase." Retrieved August 2018 from https://www.phrases.org.uk/meanings/no-man-is-an-island.html.

Fletcher, J., and Childress, J. F. (1997). *Situation Ethics: The New Morality*, 2nd edn. Louisville: Westminster John Knox Press.

Freed, P. E. (1918 - 1996). *Transworld Radio: Bonaire.* https://worldradiohistory.com/Archive-Station...

Gutzman, Joseph (2022). *The Hill | Changing America:* Retrieved August 4, 2022 from: https://thehill.cm/changing-america/well-being/mental- health/3569506-depression-is-likely-not-caused-by-a-chemical-imbalance-in-the-brain-study-says/-.

Horobin, W., Szudek, A., & Zyl, V. M. (2016). *How the body works.* Darling Kindersley Limited. DK, a Division of Penguin Random House LLC

Jack, R. (2014, February 3). *Written all over your face: Humans express four basic emotions rather than six, says new study.* University of Glasgow. https://www.gla.ac.uk/news/archiveofnews/2014/february/headline_306019_en.html.

Johnson, J. W. (n.d.). "The Creation." Retrieved January 2017, from https://www.bartleby.com/269/41.html.

Keble, J. (1792 - 1866.). *New Every Morning is Thy Love.* https://hymnary.org/text/new_every_morning_is_the_love.

Lyn, K. (2019, October 13). *What percentage of people are intersex?* Quora. https://www.quora.com/What-percentage-of-people-are-intersex.

Madaus, S. (2019, August 15). 6 *Matriarchal Societies That Have Been Thriving With Women at the Helm for Centuries.* Town

& Country Magazine. Retrieved Aug. 2021 https://www.townandcountrymag.com.

Marks, Emmet (2019). "Spiritism: Wikipedia Audio Article," *Spiritualism World*, 19 July, spiritualismworld.com/spiritism-wikipedia-audio-article-3/.

Merriam–Webster Collegiate Dictionary (1993), 10th edn. Springfield, MA: Merriam-Webster.

Noory, G., and Guiley, R. (2012). *Talking to the Dead*. New York: Forge.

Notifier. (n.d.). https://buildings.honeywell.com/us/en/brands/our-brands/notifier.

Obama, Michelle (2018). *Becoming Michelle Obama*. New York: Crown Publishing.

*Online etymology dictionary: ORIGIN, history and meaning of English words*. Online Etymology Dictionary | Origin, history and meaning of English words. (n.d.). https://www.etymonline.com/.

Osaka, N. (2021, July 8). *Naomi Osaka: 'IT'S O.K. not to Be o.k.'.* Time. https://time.com/6077128/naomi-osaka-essay-tokyo-olympics/?utm_source=roundup&campaign=olympics.

Oxford Dictionary. (n.d.). "Demon: Definition of Demon." Retrieved August 2018, from https/www.lexico.com/en/definition/demon.

Phillips, C. (2001, February 1). *Socrates café: A Fresh Taste of Philosophy* (1st ed.). W.W. Norton Company.

Sinatra, F. (n.d.). "I Did It My Way." Retrieved 11 April 2017, from https://www.youtube.com/watch?v=9SXWX6qg0y4

Skinner, V. (2019). "CA schools to teach kindergartners about 15 genders under new guidelines," *EAGNews*, January 18. Retrieved 14 October 2019, from https://eagnews.org/ca-schools-to-teach-kindergartners-about-15-genders-under-new-guidelines/.

Study.com. (n.d.). Retrieved 6 September 2019, from https://study.com/academy/lesson/reflection-rotation-translation.html

Tarrant, J. (2020, February 17). *'United by Emotion' chosen as Tokyo 2020 Olympics motto.* Reuters. https://www.reuters.com/article/olympics-2020-motto-idINKBN20B0NG.

*The convention on the rights of the child: The children's version.* UNICEF. (n.d.). https://www.unicef.org/child-rights-convention/convention-text-childrens-version.

Traister, R. (2018). *Good and Mad: the Revolutionary Power of Women's Anger.* Waterville, ME: Thorndike Press.

Uwa (2019). "Our Basic Emotions Infographic: List of Human Emotions." Retrieved 8 October 2019, from https://online.uwa.edu/infographics/basic-emotions/.

Vallotton, K. (n.d.). *Kris Vallotton - Chaplain Ronnie Melancon said, "Show me ...* Facebook. https://www.facebook.com/kvministries/posts/10155278342943741.

Wesley, C. (n.d.). "Never Dying Soul to Save." Retrieved 17 October 2019, from https://archive.org/stream/hymnal00pres_1/hymnal00pres_1_djvu.txt.

Wikipedia (2019). "Humanistic Psychology." Retrieved December 2019 from https://en.wikipedia.org/wiki/Humanistic_ psychology.

White, E. G. H., and White, E. G. H. (2000). *True Education: Adaptation of Education by Ellen G. White*. Nampa, ID: Pacific Press Pub. Association.

Winch, G., and Kim, H. (2018). *How to Fix a Broken Heart*. London: Simon and Schuster UK Ltd.

World Health Organization. (n.d.). "Constitution." Retrieved 2017 from https://www.who.int/about/who-we-are/constitution.

Zidwick, V. (2014). "Stress Cardiomyopathy Symptoms," Heart and Vascular Institute. Retrieved September 2019 from https://www.hopkinsmedicine.org/heart_vascular_institute/conditions_ /conditions treatments /stress cardiomyopathy/symptoms_diagnosis.html.

# Topical Index

This index is designed to help the Reader to fast-track and find some of the major topics or issues covered in the book. Hopefully it will answer the enquiring mind as to whether a topic or issue in which he or she is interested was addressed in anyway. The outline does not cover the multiplicity of subtopics of the twelve chapters, three addenda and two appendices, but as the Reader peruses through in search of his or her topic, it will point to possible others that either complement or expand it, thereby leading to the discovery of more than that for which the search is being made.

## G

## H

# I

# J

# L

# M

# N

## O

## P

## Q

## R

## S

# T

# U

# Index of FRHS Original Acronyms, Syndromes and Behavioural Conditions

This index lists some of the major acronyms, terminologies, syndromes and descriptions of behavioural conditions relative to family relational health, developed over the decades of the service. In addition to their usage in the pages indicated, there might be more details in the Glossary. The Reader is here reminded that any reference to these are subjected to the Disclaimer expressed at the beginning of the Glossary.

# I

ICD — impulsive corrective disorder   80-1, 211, 406, 417
IFADD — internal family attention deficit disorder   404, 425, 427-8
II — idiosyncratic inhibition   404

# L

Letusism — a family relational health philosophy   284, 407

# M

M+M=M — the mystery of marriage mastery   264
M–M=M — the mystery of marriage mastery   306
MPS — mind positioning system   293, 408

# N

NERFS — negative emotional reflective fixation Syndrome   258, 409

# P

PSS=PMM — progressive mastery of the marriage mystery   304

# R

REARS — reactive emotional acceleration rate and speed   411-12,
       428, 430-1, 434-5

# S

SLIN — standard laboratory instruments notes   417, 464-5

# T

TRI — terminal relational incorrigibility   81, 406, 417

# Index to Important Names

This index lists a number of persons whose utterances or event, small or great, which they made or in which they were involved, have added to the inspiration, lesson and therapy in the writing of this book. They are not mentioned in the References or in the "Special Thanks" but could not be allowed to go by lost in the pages. Their contributions, directly or indirectly, are counted invaluable to the work.

# Index of Bible Personalities, Events, Places and Teachings

This index lists a sample of some of the major personalities, events, places and teachings of the Bible mentioned in this book. Their references here help to find the lessons, analogies, comparisons or parallels that might be made of them in presenting the message of family relational health. In the interest of space, the listing is not comprehensive and makes a maximum of five mentions of any entry that was cited multiple of times.

For Example, Adam was mentioned 75 times; Jesus(') 133; Christ('s) 99; Solomon('s) 30; Eve 56; Eden(ic) 32; Heaven('s, ly) 50; God('s, ly, liness, head) 1060; Sin(s, ful) 196; Satan('s, ic) 100; Demon(s, ic) 88; Angel(s, ic) 45; Creation(al, ism) 109; Creator('s, ship) 49; Holy Spirit 85; however, between 3–5 mentions will be made, with no selection preference or order.

The Reader who might be interested to do an accumulation research of the biblical references of the personalities, event, places and teachings mentioned herein, could consider doing a tally per chapter and multiply accordingly. In the process, there could even be found some that were not mentioned in this index. This could be one sure exercise to read the entire book through!

## A

restoration of the, part of Jesus' mission   84

trust in family relationship   455

# C

sense of helplessness (Psalm 42:5) 259

## E

## F

# J

# M

## P

## R

## S

# About the Author

# Anthony L. Gordon, Ph.D.

Only those in Dr Gordon's immediate biological family lab know that his career as a counseling psychologist and family relational health therapist did not begin thirty-five years ago, as he has been sharing publicly, but that it really dates back twenty years earlier with his epic story "John Jaganaano Nanco, The Great!" It was then that, while literally reading that old copy of *Chambers Etymological Dictionary* his mom had found in the attic at Ardsheal, St Thomas, where she was working, that he was absolutely fascinated with two of the new words that he met: *psychology* and *schizophrenia*. He had finished Wilmington All-Age School three years earlier, but with his mom not being able to afford to send him on to further studies, he never saw a book again. He spent those years working on the sugar cane, coconut, and pimento plantations. When Mom showed him the dictionary, he was voracious for anything readable. Knowledge for him was a premium!

It took teacher W. R. Veitch (see Dedication) at the Port Morant Trade Training Centre, St Thomas, where Anthony was now studying masonry for building construction, to drive Anthony's quest for knowledge to the zenith. In one English Composition class, the master-teacher created the fictitious and erudite character, John Jaganaano Nanco. He was enthralled with Mr. Veitch's persona and teaching style and everything taught in those English classes, especially the Latin origin of words. Having already drunk in that treasure house of knowledge, the dictionary, and being hooked by the concept of psychology and schizophrenia, Anthony brought them all together in a story that he wrote titled "John Jaganaano Nanco, The Great!" Of course, he was only following Mr. Veitch's writing example.

To summarize the story: Nanco was a student of psychology at his university. A schoolmate started acting very strangely, and no one could account for his disturbing and unsettling behavior. John went into very earnest study and research and discovered the symptoms of schizophrenia, brought it to his professors, and what an excitement it turned out to be! Nanco was extolled and commended for his work which brought help and treatment for his fellow student and new knowledge to light.

Mr. Veitch read the story, made some very interesting corrections of overused words and expressions (Anthony was by then nicknamed *Dr. Wiseacre*), but praised the effort, especially Anthony's use of his character as the main hero of the story. And the rest is history! This is no cliché!

Some fifty years later, Anthony L. Gordon, prefigured by John Jaganaano Nanco, the great psychologist, of his own imagination and literary creation, has the following accomplishments to his name:

- taught for twenty-six years: nineteen as principal for three schools and a college departmental director

- human resource manager and family ministries and counseling services director

- radio and television family counselor

- associate chaplain for the constabulary (police) force

- featured writer on family life issues in newspapers and magazines

- earned bachelor's, master's, and doctorate degrees and certifications in education, counselling, psychology, and human resource management

- author of seven books on education, family life education, and counseling

- happily married for forty-six years to Deloris (also a counseling psychologist and special educator)

- proud father of Delthony and Delthonette, who further expanded his family relational health laboratory to include those mentioned in the Dedication

- founded and established Family Relational Health Services International, a family relational health seminar and clinic program reaching over thirty countries

# The Family Relational Health
# Series Publications

Family Relational Healthcare (FRH) is a new approach to providing professional treatment and care for the issues and challenges that assail the biological and foundational Bible-based family structure and operations in today' society. One of the major motivations behind this concept and practice is the interpretation and applied definition of health by the World Health Organization: "Health is a state of complete physical, mental and social well-being and not merely the absence of disease or infirmity."

Interpreted, this definition suggests that our total health is a combination of the physiological (state and function of the *body*) and the psychological (state and function of the *mind*) factors. This interpretation harmonizes perfectly with David's account of his existence, mentioning the composite working of his body and mind as his being "fearfully and wonderfully made." (Psalm 139: 14) It resonates also with John's inspired admonition to the "Beloved" (Christians) that they should be in health even as their souls prosper (3 John 2).

Given that all human relationships begin and continue to exist in the active, sound mind; and that the mind is the out-working of our psychological health, (combined working of the brain and the senses), then all aspects of our family relationship is unquestionably a health matter, hence *family relational health*. However, correctly analysed, defined, described and delineated, *family relational health* is distinct from mental health, the main focus in most of mainstream psychological practice, but it is a complementary functionality of the said active, sound mind.

The FRH tagline "Treating Relationships The Healthy Way" is strategically worded to bring sustained parallel, analogy and balance between the medical treatment and care of the body (physiological health) and the psychological/psychotherapeutic treatment and care of family relationships (psychological health), thereby raising the bar from the stigma and taboos of the old terminology of 'family counselling', the effects of which stigmas and taboos are family relational illnesses affecting the society at unprecedented and exponential proportions.

Against that background, continuous research, study, practice and writing have been embarked upon over nearly forty years, across some thirty countries on different continents, and is now being documented from the Christian and non-Christian academic/professional perspectives separately, in the following eight publications.

# The Family Relational Health Series Publications

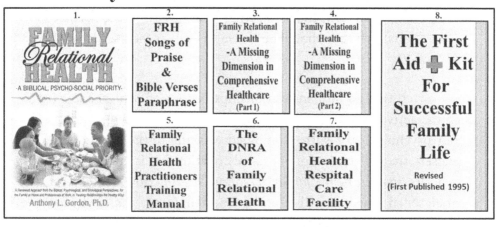

| 1. | 2. | 3. | 4. | 8. |
|---|---|---|---|---|
| FAMILY Relational HEALTH -A BIBLICAL, PSYCHO-SOCIAL PRIORITY- Anthony L. Gordon, Ph.D. | FRH Songs of Praise & Bible Verses Paraphrase | Family Relational Health -A Missing Dimension in Comprehensive Healthcare (Part 1) | Family Relational Health -A Missing Dimension in Comprehensive Healthcare (Part 2) | The First Aid ✚ Kit For Successful Family Life Revised (First Published 1995) |
| | 5. | 6. | 7. | |
| | Family Relational Health Practitioners Training Manual | The DNRA of Family Relational Health | Family Relational Health Respital Care Facility | |

Lightning Source UK Ltd.
Milton Keynes UK
UKHW020238301122
413094UK00005B/51